Humour and Laughter:
Theory, Research
and Applications

Humour and Laughter: Theory, Research and Applications

Edited by

Antony J. Chapman

and

Hugh C. Foot

Department of Applied Psychology,
University of Wales Institute of
Science and Technology

JOHN WILEY & SONS

London · New York · Sydney · Toronto

19451

Library of Congress Cataloging in Publication Data:
Main entry under title:

Humour and laughter.

  Includes index.
  1. Laughter. 2. Wit and humour—Psychology.
I. Chapman, Antony J. II. Foot, Hugh C.
BF575.L3H87   152.4   75-37870

ISBN 0 471 14612 9

Photosetting by Thomson Press (India) Limited, New Delhi and printed in Great Britain by The Pitman Press, Bath

List of Contributors

MELANIE ALLEN
Department of Psychology, California State University, Northridge, California, U.S.A.

RICHARD Y. BOURHIS
Department of Psychology, University of Bristol, 8–10, Berkeley Square, Bristol, U.K.

JOANNE R. CANTOR
Department of Communication Arts, University of Wisconsin, Madison, Wisconsin 53706, U.S.A.

ANTONY J. CHAPMAN
Department of Applied Psychology, University of Wales Institute of Science and Technology, Cardiff, U.K.

ANN P. DAVIES
Department of Psychology, University College, Cardiff, U.K.

GRAHAM J. DAVIES
Department of Psychology, University College, Cardiff, U.K.

JOHN W. EDGERLY
Student Counseling Center, University of Tennessee, Knoxville 37916, Tennessee, U.S.A.

HUGH C. FOOT
Department of Applied Psychology, University of Wales Institute of Science and Technology, Cardiff, U.K.

WILLIAM F. FRY, JR.
888, Oak Grove Avenue, Menlo Park, California 94025, U.S.A.

NICHOLAS J. GADFIELD
Department of Applied Psychology, University of Wales Institute of Science and Technology, Cardiff, U.K.

HOWARD GILES
Department of Psychology, University of Bristol, 8–10, Berkeley Square, Bristol, U.K.

MICHAEL GODKEWITSCH
Department of Psychology, University of Toronto, Toronto 181, Ontario, Canada.

CHARLES R. GRUNER
Department of Speech Communication, University of Georgia, Athens, Georgia 30602, U.S.A.

JAY HADDAD

Bayview Glen Junior Schools Ltd., Toronto, Canada.

JAMES M. JONES

Department of Psychology and Social Relations, Harvard University, William James Hall, 33, Kirkland Street, Cambridge, Massachusetts 02138, U.S.A.

LAWRENCE LA FAVE

Department of Psychology, University of Windsor, Windsor 11, Ontario, Canada.

HOLLIS V. LIVERPOOL

University of the West Indies, Trinidad.

WILLIAM A. MAESEN

Department of Sociology, University of Illinois, Chigaco Circle, U.S.A.

HARVEY MINDESS

Psychology Clinic, 337, S. Beverly Drive, Suite 106, Beverly Hills, California 90212, U.S.A.

GÖRAN NERHARDT

Psychological Laboratories, University of Stockholm, Stockholm, Sweden.

WALTER E. O'CONNELL

Veterans Administration Hospital, 2002 Holcombe Boulevard, Houston, Texas 77031, U.S.A.

HOWARD R. POLLIO

Department of Psychology, University of Tennessee, College of Liberal Arts, Knoxville 37916, Tennessee, U.S.A.

MARY K. ROTHBART

Department of Psychology, College of Liberal Arts, University of Oregon, Eugene, Oregon 97403, U.S.A.

THOMAS R. SHULTZ

Department of Psychology, McGill University, P.O. Box 6070, Montreal 101, Quebec, Canada.

DOLF ZILLMANN

Mass Communication Program, Radio–TV Building, Room 216, Indiana University, Bloomington, Indiana 47401, U.S.A.

Preface

This book is concerned with the psychology of humour and laughter and is designed to bring together in a single volume some of the most important current thinking and research in these subjects. Most of the fifteen chapters are written by psychologists with long-standing academic interests in humour and laughter. Many of our authors are engaged in on-going projects and have been working in the area for some years. It is *their* published works which have largely provided the impetus for the recent upsurge of interest in empirical studies. The chapters they have written for the book map out, therefore, the main areas in which research is currently being conducted. Also well represented in the book is the wide variety of techniques employed in examining the key issues relating to humour and laughter. The reader will find approaches ranging from rigorous controlled scientific study, through in-depth, personalized analyses, to the purely anecdotal. The elusive and ephemeral nature of humour and laughter demands that we retain a broad-based methodology if research as a whole is to progress fruitfully.

The book is divided into two sections, the first focusing upon theoretical developments and the second dealing with the uses of humour in society and professional relationships. Chapters in Section I concentrate particularly upon incongruity, superiority and arousal theories, and upon humour and laughter in social settings. Chapters in Section II are concerned with humour in relation to creativity, West Indian calypso, and mass communication, and the final chapters in the Section speculate about the potential value of humour in psychotherapy. The format generally adopted by authors in both Sections is to review their own research in the context of empirical and theoretical literatures and to present in addition some fresh ideas and new data.

We envisage that our book will appeal to many research-oriented behavioural scientists and that the main readership will be drawn from those with academic or professional interests in social, child and clinical psychology, sociology, education, and other related disciplines. In general it will be of interest to all those who are concerned with human attributes, human emotions and social interaction. This will include many embarking on studies of behaviours which, like laughter, are difficult to subject to systematic investigation. The book addresses many crucial questions about humour and laughter and aims to direct future research in ways which appear most likely to produce a coherent body of knowledge. We hope that those taking up new research find the book a stimulating and enlightening source of ideas. We hope also that they find it provides some insights into ways of tackling investigations into these fascinating topics.

UWIST   TONY CHAPMAN
Cardiff   HUGH C. FOOT

Contents

x

Introduction

Antony J. Chapman and Hugh C. Foot

To possess a good sense of humour or at least to laugh freely and frequently at humorous and pleasurable events is regarded as thoroughly healthy and desirable by virtually all those who have concerned themselves with the subject of humour. The average man is also firmly committed to the belief that having a reputation for a keen sense of humour is something to be treasured and protected. Amongst samples of college students Allport (1961) and Omwake (1937) found that only 6% and 1·4% respectively were prepared to admit to a lower-than-average sense of humour. In the words of Frank Moore Colby [quoted by Bergler (1956)]: 'Men will confess to treason, murder, arson, false teeth or a wig. How many will own up to a lack of humour?'

But man has not always held humour and laughter on such a pedestal of desirability. From an historical perspective, humour has often been characterized as base and degenerate, fit only for the ignorant and foolish. In *Philebus*, Plato claimed that the ridiculous was based on an unfortunate lack of self-knowledge. Laughter, although pleasurable enough, was seen as malevolent behaviour stemming from hurtful aggression, envy, or spite at seeing the enemy vanquished. Ancient Roman nihilistic theories were put forward by Cicero and Quintilian, both of whom were sceptical that anyone could adequately explain laughter. They agreed with Aristotle that laughter has its basis in some kind of shabbiness or deformity, and described it as degrading to morals, art and religion, a form of behaviour from which civilized man should shrink. The view that laughter was closely allied to derision and was a socially disruptive force persisted for some time and Ben Jonson (1599) was one of the first notable littérateurs to suggest that comedy inevitably functioned as a social corrective in its use as criticism of the follies of mankind. Later, Moliere and Swift likewise used humour in the form of satire mirroring the social foibles and hypocrisy of seventeenth and eighteenth century Western society.

Returning to more modern times, the values placed upon humour and the humour 'industry' are clearly reflected in the popularity (sometimes bordering on reverence) accorded comedy artists and comedy routines in the world of show-business. Such popularity is itself evidence enough of the emotional needs which comedy fulfils in our everyday humdrum lives. Yet, despite all this, it is striking how comparatively little research has been done in the area of humour and laughter.

Only a few years ago the editor of one social science magazine, after announcing that one whole issue would be devoted to humour research, reported receiving a number of antagonistic reactions to this announcement from his readers—even though he had alluded to articles by several eminent academics (cf. Friedman, 1969). The lack of research interest in humour and laughter coupled with an apparent unwillingness to take the subject seriously is very strange, particularly in view of Keith-Spiegel's (1969) assessment that 'humor related behavior exceeds all other types of emotional behaviors combined ... by ten or more times'. Perhaps the lack of interest is at least partially a product of what Allport (1960) has termed the 'tenderness tabu' amongst psychological investigators. He complained that the majority of research workers have been preoccupied with decidedly unpleasant emotions at the expense of pleasant emotions such as love, joy and happiness.

To check that this was not just a 'tenderminded illusion' Carlson (1966) analysed the content of 172 introductory psychology texts published between 1877 and 1961. He reported that more terms were available to identify unpleasant emotional states than pleasant emotional states and that there was a disproportionate emphasis upon the unpleasant emotions. They received about twice as much space as pleasant emotions in the books of the late 1940s and over three times as much space (with six times as many references) in the early 1960s. The trend, from 1900 onwards, was towards an ever-increasing emphasis upon the unpleasant emotions. Lindauer (1968) cautiously concluded that 'psychology is idiosyncratically preoccupied with the negative aspects of emotion' after a frequency count in *non*-psychological literature had revealed that pleasant emotions were more frequently referred to than unpleasant emotions, with little change in the balance in recent years.

Let us now examine the nature of humour and laughter. In general theorists are divided over the causes, mechanisms and functions of laughter and there has been little consensus of terminology in the literature as a whole, although in psychoanalytic writings terms like 'humour', 'wit' and 'comic' have clearly defined meanings and are never interchanged. The word laughter is used by most to refer to an exclusively human attribute but by others, notably Darwin (1890) and van Hooff (1972), as a response common to the apes. In fact, amongst psychological humour theorists, there appears to have been a distinct reluctance to define humour and laughter, although many have emphasized particular ingredients (such as incongruity or surprise) as necessary prerequisites for a stimulus to appear humorous. In Drever's (1952) *A Dictionary of Psychology* (published by Penguin Books Ltd.) humour is defined as the 'character of a complex situation exciting joyful, and in the main quiet, laughter, either directly, through *sympathy*, or through *empathy*'. Laughter is defined as an emotional response, normally expressing joy, 'in the child and the unsophisticated adult'. (*Could this be evidence for a tenderness taboo?*). *Webster's New International*

Dictionary (2nd edition) makes more insightful and convincing reading: laughter is defined as 'a movement (usually involuntary) of the muscles of the face, especially of the lips, usually with a peculiar expression of the eyes, indicating merriment, satisfaction or derision and attended by an interrupted expulsion of air from the lungs'.

Outside the psychological literature there is no such reticence to define what humour and laughter are: everyone thinks he knows. It is difficult to refrain from passing judgement upon those who have asserted their opinions in an area where 'angles fear to tread' (although so far no humour theorist has sprouted wings!). Drever would no doubt have found support for his 'inciteful' definition of laughter in the person of Lord Chesterfield, who wrote that 'there is nothing so illiberal, and so ill-bred as audible laughter', but would have been subjected to severe criticism by Erskine (1928), for example, who promoted the view that a sense of humour was something 'to cultivate and achieve'. Elsewhere, laughter has been variously defined as 'the hiccup of a fool' (John Ray) and 'the mind sneezing' (Wyndham Lewis), while, according to Wasson (1926), 'humour is something which causes a tickling of the brain' and 'laughter was invented to scratch it'. Escarpit (1969) has hypothesized that the role of laughter is to 'change the angle of view on reality' and Shaw (1960) has offered laughter as a paradigm of growth.

One obvious problem that bedevils definitions of humour is whether it is to be viewed as a stimulus, a response or a disposition. *The Penguin English Dictionary* allows all three possibilities: humour may refer to that which causes 'good-tempered laughter' (stimulus); or 'cheerful and good-tempered amusement' (response); or 'the capacity for seeing the funny side of things' (disposition). While no one would dispute that laughter is generally a response, it is just as much a response to non-humorous stimuli as it is to humour stimuli. In fact, though not a humour stimulus itself, laughter can act as a stimulus in inducing or augmenting laughter in other persons.

Although the words 'humour' and 'laughter' have sometimes been used synonymously in discussions of theory, Dewey (1894), Potter (1954) and others have argued that laughter can be irrelevant to the study of humour, and vice versa, because each can be experienced independently of the other. Stephen Potter spelt out the obvious when he wrote:

> There are in fact very few situations to which laughter is not appropriate. We laugh when the sea touches our navel ... But we only laugh in company ... We laugh at something because it is familiar and something else because it is unfamiliar. We laugh at misfortunes if they do not incur danger, though what constitutes 'danger' varies enormously between nations and centuries. The day before yesterday, in ethnological time, we laughed to see a lunatic on the end of a chain, or a bear tied to a post and bitten to death by dogs ... We laugh because other people are laughing uncontrollably; but controlled or calculated laughter, on the other hand, can drive our own smiles underground for hours. We laugh if and because we are supposed not to laugh ...
>
> Then there is the laugh which fills up the blank in the conversation ... The laugh to attract attention ... The laugh of the lone man at the theatre, who wishes to show

he understands ... The laugh of creative pleasure ... The laugh of relief from physical danger ... [and so on].

(Reprinted by permission of A. D. Peters and Company).

Strictly speaking, therefore, a distinction can (and indeed should) be drawn between theories of humour and theories of laughter, and clearly theories of laughter need to take into account the numerous types of non-humorous as well as humorous situations which can cause laughter. Undoubtedly, in this context, one of the most difficult problems, for empiricists and theorists alike is to determine precisely what causes laughter in any given situation. Brief taxonomies of laughter and humour have been put forward in a number of articles (e.g. Flugel, 1954; Ghosh, 1939; Hall and Allin, 1897; Monro, 1951) but no classification has yet done justice to the tremendous diversity of situations which can provoke laughter. Presumably each category of humour or laughter-evoking situation has its own antecedents. In recent times, Berlyne (1969) has attributed laughter to triumph, relief from anxiety, agreement, sudden comprehension, embarrassment and scorn. Giles and Oxford (1970) have described seven 'mutually exclusive' categories of laughter situations which produce seven different types of laughter: namely, humorous, social, ignorance, anxiety, derision, apologetic and laughter in response to tickling.

No all embracing theory of humour and/or laughter has yet gained widespread acceptance and possibly no general theory will ever be successfully applied to the human race as a whole when its members exhibit such vast individual differences with respect to their humour responsiveness. The paradox associated with humour is almost certainly a function of its being incorrectly viewed as a unitary process. Humour plays a myriad of roles and serves a number of quite different functions. As Zigler, Levine and Gould (1966) have pointed out, the understanding of humour is far more complex than has generally been acknowledged. Most theories of humour and laughter are concerned with the situations under which laughter is regularly elicited rather than with an *analysis* of its nature or functions. The theories are, in the main, explanations of laughter which occurs fairly reliably under specific sets of circumstances but 'theories of humour' may be something of a misnomer in the sense that not all those situations would always be described as humorous by those who laugh.

Much has been said about the problems of definition and the difficulties encountered in developing theory. There is no doubt that researchers are still a long way from formulating any general theoretical framework which will account for all aspects of humour and laughter, assuming this is even feasible. A substantial part of this book (Section I) is devoted to representing some of the research currently being conducted which is seeking to extend man's knowledge of the processes involved in appreciation of, and responsiveness to, humour. We have made every effort to ensure that most of the active research areas are represented in the book and if any particular formulations appear to be receiving more than their fair share of space then it is because they are currently attracting a large proportion of the research interest. The first section then is concerned with theoretical developments and empirical research in the perception of, and response to, humour. Our first inclination was to separate those chapters which laid more emphasis upon the perception of humour stimuli from those which paid attention to response conditions and measures of humour appreciation. However, it became clear that such a distinction would be rather arbitrary in view of the close interrelationship and dependency between input and output.

The first major theoretical theme which is taken up in the book is represented in the first three chapters by Shultz, by Rothbart and by Nerhardt. These authors take up the notion of incongruity as a basis for perceiving a stimulus as humorous, although they differ on the question of whether the discovery of incongruity alone is a sufficient condition for humour. The developmental studies of Shultz and Rothbart which draw upon Piagetian ideas about cognitive development have much in common. The second main theoretical research area is represented in the chapters by La Fave, Haddad and Maesen, and by Zillmann and Cantor, who discuss their research findings in the context of superiority theory. Specifically they are concerned with humour as a form of disparagement or deprecation and they examine humour responsiveness as a function of the respondent's attitude towards, and relationship with, those being disparaged. La Fave and his colleagues seek also to show the connecting links between superiority and incongruity theories. The third main area of research, pursued by Godkewitsch, is aimed at exploring the relationship between psychophysiological measures of arousal and judgements of funniness; it is based upon Berlyne's theory of collative motivation which regards jokes (pleasurable stimuli) as having arousal inducing properties (cf. Berlyne, 1969). A similar orientation is also expressed by Rothbart in her arousal–safety model of laughter which is characterized by a state of pleasurable 'safety' in a child after a period of tense uncertainty due to a sudden, surprising or incongruous stimulus.

A fourth research area represented by our own work emphasizes the social situation as a determinant of humour responsiveness. Our studies attempt to show how even subtle modifications in the social situation can affect overt behaviour in humour situations, through processes such as social facilitation and social intimacy. Added to this, Giles, Bourhis, Gadfield, Davies and Davies sketch out a model to define, in any given social context, the processes which are brought to bear upon the encoder and decoder of the humour. Pollio and Edgerly also examine the social settings in which humour and laughter occur and relate this to the comic style of some well-known professional comedians. This leads into Section II which brings together some of the main research that has focused upon the purposes for which humour is, or could be, used in society and in professional relationships.

The ten to five chapter split between the two sections does reflect the greater emphasis placed upon the problems and processes concerned with perceiving and responding to humour than upon attempts to explore the impact of humour in society. But this is not intended to suggest that the chapters in Section II are non-theoretical. On the contrary they draw heavily upon dynamic theoretical constructs as a springboard for explaining and speculating upon the creation of humour and the purposes which it serves. Following on from Pollio and Edgerly's consideration of comic style, Fry and Allen, rather appropriately, consider in some detail the creative process involved in producing humour and illustrate this process by reference to the life-style and habits of a well-known (but unidentified) comedy scriptwriter. Jones and Liverpool's chapter introduces an altogether novel perspective by analysing the social functions of humour and satire in the calypsos of the Trinidadian Carnival. Gruner examines the role of humour in relation to mass communication where it is often used for the express purpose of enhancing the communicative effect of the message. Finally, two related chapters by O'Connell and by Mindess speculate about the potential use of humour in psychotherapy, emphasizing its importance to the development of a healthy relationship between therapist and patient.

REFERENCES

Allport, G. W. (1960). *The Individual and His Religion*. New York: Macmillan.
Allport, G. W. (1961). *Pattern and Growth in Personality*. New York: Holt, Rinehart and Winston.
Bergler, E. (1956). *Laughter and the Sense of Humor*. New York: Grune and Stratton.
Berlyne, D. E. (1969). Laughter, humor and play. In G. Lindzey and E. Aronson (Eds.), *Handbook of Social Psychology*, Vol. 3. (2nd Ed.). Reading, Massachusetts: Addison–Wesley.
Carlson, E. R. (1966). The affective tone of psychology. *Journal of General Psychology*, **75**, 65–78.
Darwin, C. (1890). *The Expression of the Emotions in Man and Animals*. London: John Murray.
Dewey, J. (1894). The theory of emotion. *Psychological Review*, **1**, 553–569.
Erskine, J. (1928). Humor. *Century*, **115**, 421–426.
Escarpit, R. (1969). Humorous attitude and scientific inventivity. *Impact*, **19**, 253–258.
Flugel, J. C. (1954). Humor and laughter. In G. Lindzey (Ed.), *Handbook of Social Psychology*, Vol. 2. Reading, Massachusetts: Addison–Wesley.
Friedman, B. (1969). The editor comments. *Impact*, **19**, 223–224.
Ghosh, R. (1939). An experimental study of humour. *British Journal of Educational Psychology*, **9**, 98–99.
Giles, H., and Oxford, G. S. (1970). Towards a multidimensional theory of laughter causation and its social implications. *Bulletin of the British Psychological Society*, **23**, 97–105.
Hall, G. S., and Allin, A. (1897). The psychology of tickling, laughter and the comic. *American Journal of Psychology*, **9**, 1–42.
Hooff, J. A. R. A. M. van. (1972). A comparative approach to the phylogeny of laughter and smiling. In R. A. Hinde (Ed.), *Non-verbal Communication*. Cambridge University Press.
Jonson, B. (1599). *Every Man Out of His Humour*. [Extract in P. Lauter (1964) *Theories of Comedy*. New York: Doubleday].
Keith-Spiegel, K. (1969). Preface to symposium proceedings. *Social Aspects of Humor: Recent Research and Theory*. Western Psychological Association Meeting, Vancouver.
Lindauer, M. S. (1968). Pleasant and unpleasant emotions in the literature: as compared to the affective tone of psychology. *Journal of Psychology*, **70**, 55–67.
Monro, D. H. (1951). *Argument of Laughter*. Melbourne University Press.

Omwake, L. (1937). A study of sense of humor: its relation to sex, age and personal characteristics. *Journal of Applied Psychology*, **21**, 688–704.

Potter, S. (1954). *The Sense of Humour*. Harmondsworth: Penguin.

Shaw, F. J. (1960). Laughter: paradigm of growth. *Journal of Individual Psychology*, **16**, 151–157.

Wasson, M. (1926). What is humor? *Forum*, **76**, 425–429.

Zigler, E., Levine, J. and Gould, L. (1966). Cognitive processes in the development of children's appreciation of humor. *Child Development*, **37**, 507–518.

Section I

Perceiving and Responding
to Humour

Chapter 1

A Cognitive-Developmental Analysis of Humour

Thomas R. Shultz

This chapter is concerned with the ontogenetic development of humour appreciation, particularly with the cognitive aspects of this development. Answers are sought to questions of the following sort: What are the cognitive processes which are engaged during the appreciation of humour? What is the relation between the structural characteristics of the various forms of humour and these cognitive processes? How do these cognitive processes change with psychological development? And how are these developmental changes related to other more general aspects of cognitive growth?

Although the focus of this chapter is developmental, it is of course necessary to examine the cognitive nature of humour appreciation in adults. Any cognitive-developmental analysis must include the terminal stage towards which development progresses. The chapter begins with such an analysis of the cognitive processes used in adult humour and then travels backwards in ontogenetic time in an attempt to delineate the important developmental milestones that bring the child closer to this final stage. As will become apparent, the farther back the analysis goes, the less certain it becomes in terms of both theory and data. The younger the child, the less is known about the cognitive processes that characterize his appreciation of humour. In fact, for the very young child, the nature of humour itself becomes relatively uncertain.

HUMOUR IN ADULTS

In order to study the cognitive processes involved in humour appreciation, many theorists have attempted to identify the structural characteristics of those situations and events which produce humour. It is commonly assumed that, regardless of what the joke happens to be about, it has the same underlying structure as jokes dealing with other content areas. It is further assumed that the person's cognitive processes must correspond to this universal joke structure in order for him to fully appreciate any given joke.

Analyses of humour material

If one decides to follow this strategy the next step is to develop a representative collection of humour which can be analysed for its structural properties. Substantial amounts of time and energy can be invested at this point in determining what constitutes humour and what does not. A number of criteria can be used to make these decisions: (a) Does the event elicit laughter or smiling? (b) Was it produced with the intention of eliciting laughter or smiling? (c) Would other members of the culture agree that it was an instance of humour? Each of these criteria can be applied in either an inclusive, or an exclusive manner and they can be applied singly or in combination. Each criterion can be quantified to enable decisions about the intensity and consensus with which it can be applied to any given event. A great many events can be classified as humorous or not on all three criteria with little or no disagreement. And there are a great many borderline cases which can generate endless discussion and disagreement. The prudent humour researcher avoids these definitional controversies and proceeds with his research on issues of greater theoretical substance. This can best be accomplished by selecting humour stimuli which clearly satisfy all three criteria simultaneously. In this author's experience, a good strategy is to use published collections of humour materials such as jokes, riddles and cartoons. These were clearly produced with the intention of eliciting humour, they do in fact elicit humour on empirical test, and most observers would agree to call them humorous. In addition, they are somewhat easier to analyse than many instances of spontaneous humour. This is because spontaneous, real-life humour may depend very much on the context for interpretation and appreciation. Published materials, while they may have at one time been spontaneous, can most often be adequately analysed without detailed knowledge of the surrounding context.

Once having chosen his sample of humorous materials, the cognitive theorist must then analyse their underlying structure. This is largely an intuitive process whereby the theorist attempts to abstract those structural features which are essential to the humour of large numbers of jokes which differ widely in content. Not all humour theorists have reached the same conclusions. Theorists such as Kant (1790), Schopenhauer (1819), Maier (1932) and Koestler (1964) have proposed that the structure of humour is characterized by incongruity. Incongruity is usually defined as a conflict between what is expected and what actually occurs in the joke. It is a concept which accounts well for the most obvious structural feature of jokes, the surprisingness of the punchline.

A number of other theorists, including Beattie (1776), Freud (1960), Willman (1940), Jones (1970), Shultz (1970) and Suls (1972), have argued that incongruity alone is insufficient to account for the structure of humour. They have proposed in various arguments that there exists a second, more subtle aspect of jokes which renders incongruity meaningful or appropriate by resolving or explaining it. Within this framework, humour appreciation is conceptualized as a biphasic sequence involving first the discovery of incongruity followed by a resolution of the incongruity. The mechanism of resolution is apparently necessary to distinguish humour from nonsense. Whereas nonsense can be characterized as pure or unresolvable incongruity, humour can be characterized as resolvable or meaningful incongruity.

In verbal jokes, the incongruity consists in the relation between the last line, or punchline, and the part that precedes the last line. Consider the old W. C. Fields', joke where someone asked, 'Mr. Fields, do you believe in clubs for young people?' and he replied, 'Only when kindness fails'. At first, his answer does not seem to fit with the question. Whatever expectations were set up by the question are disconfirmed by the answer. This incongruity can be resolved by noticing that part of the material coming before the punchline was ambiguous. The ambiguity in this case resides in the semantic ambiguity of the word 'clubs'. After initially interpreting 'clubs' as social groups, the listener later discovers that 'clubs' could also refer to large sticks. A very similar joke was used by Groucho Marx who maintained, 'I ought to join a club, and beat you over the head with it'. In a one-liner such as this, there is no strict separation between the punchline and the rest of the joke. Nevertheless, the second part of the statement is clearly incongruous in relation to the first part; and the resolution is based on the semantic ambiguity of 'clubs'.

About half the verbal jokes this author has analysed are resolved on the basis of some sort of linguistic ambiguity. In addition to those resolutions based on lexical ambiguity or semantic ambiguity, resolutions based on phonological and syntactic ambiguities are quite common. Phonological ambiguity occurs when a given sound sequence can receive more than one interpretation. This often results from a confusion about the boundaries between words. An example is given in the joke where the teacher asks the student to construct a sentence containing the phrase 'bitter end' and the student replies, 'The dog chased the cat and he bitter end'. This is quite an incongruous use of the phrase 'bitter end' until the listener realizes that it could also be interpreted as 'bit her end'. Recent developments in transformational theory (Chomsky, 1965) have made it possible to distinguish two types of syntactic ambiguity. Surface structure ambiguity occurs when the words of a sentence can be grouped or bracketed (unlabelled) in two different ways with each bracketing expressing a different interpretation. An example of resolution by surface structure ambiguity is provided in the joke where the stranger asks, 'Can you tell me how long cows should be milked?' and the farmer answers, 'They should be milked the same as short ones, of course'. The farmer's answer is incongruous but it can be resolved by re-interpreting the initial bracketing of (how long) (cows) as (how) (long cows). In the case of surface structure ambiguity, two different deep structures are projected onto two different surface structures. In contrast, deep structure ambiguity occurs when two different deep structures are projected onto a single surface structure. An example of resolution by deep structure ambiguity is provided in the following joke: 'Did you know that the natives like potatoes even more than missionaries?' 'Yes, but the missionaries are more nutritious'. The initially incongruous reply is based on the ambiguity involved in the syntactic relations between key words in the question. In the first interpretation 'missionaries' serve as the logical subject of the verb 'like' and in the second interpretation as the logical object of 'like'.

A great many verbal jokes have resolutions which depend on general, non-linguistic knowledge. An example is a joke discussed by Suls (1972) about a man who was tried for armed robbery and acquitted. His reaction was 'Wonderful, does that mean I can keep the money?' This is quite incongruous since it is an admission of guilt when the court has just found him innocent. According to Suls, the resolution is based on the idea that 'courts make mistakes, that legal truth and actual truth do not always correspond, and that legal truth determines public consequences' (1972, p. 91). In other words, he can in fact keep the money since, according to the law, he did not steal it.

The incongruity and resolution theory of humour is not restricted to verbal jokes. It has also been successfully applied to cartoons (Shultz, 1972, 1974c), children's jokes (Shultz and Horibe, 1974), and riddles (Shultz, 1974b). While it may be somewhat extravagant to claim that the incongruity and resolution theory can account for the structure of every instance of humour, this author and others have found it to be of immense heuristic value in accounting for vast samples of humour. It has even been used to explicate the structure underlying jokes, riddles and humorous tales collected from the folklore literatures of a variety of non-Western cultures (Shultz, 1974a). Moreover, there has been no substantive body of humour which has proved intractable to an incongruity and resolution analysis.

Cognitive processing in the appreciation of humour

In addition to being useful in understanding the structure of humour, the incongruity and resolution theory has generated some interesting predictions regarding the cognitive processing of humour. The most general hypothesis is that the incongruity information is processed before the resolution information. Two recent studies were conducted to test the adequacy of this hypothesis in the appreciation of verbal jokes and cartoons by adult subjects (Shultz, 1974c). In the case of verbal jokes, one would expect that the order of information is severely constrained by the temporal nature of linguistic expression. This can be illustrated with W. C. Fields' 'clubs' joke which was discussed above. As long as the recipient hears or reads the joke in its intended order, he should process the first element of the incongruity (Do you believe in clubs for young people?) before the second element of the incongruity (Only when kindness fails). The first or biased meaning of the ambiguity in the resolution ('clubs' as social groups) should likewise be processed before the second element of the incongruity. The only joke element which is not so severely constrained is the second or hidden meaning of the ambiguity ('clubs' as large sticks). Despite the fact that the hidden meaning of the ambiguity is embedded within the first element of the incongruity and potentially expressed at the same moment as the biased meaning, it should theoretically not be detected until after the second element of the incongruity has been processed. The disconfirmed expectations produced by the second element of the incongruity presumably lead the recipient to search for a resolution in the form of the hidden meaning of the ambiguity. This last prediction is consistent with previous research indicating that linguistic ambiguities ordinarily go undetected unless one happens to be looking for them (Foss, Bever, and Silver, 1968). All of these predictions were confirmed using a self-report technique in which the subject read each joke and then ranked its four major elements according to the order in which he had first processed them.

Because cartoons are presented in a visual medium, it was expected that they would constrain the order of processing considerably less than do verbal jokes. This was based on the assumption that visual information processing is not subject to the same temporal constraints as is processing of verbal information. In processing cartoons, the subject can presumably direct his gaze towards any of the various aspects of the cartoon's picture in any conceivable order. Also, he has the option of reading the cartoon's caption before, after, or embedded within his processing of the picture. In some cartoons the resolution is quite explicit while in others it is only implicit. Using a self-report technique similar to that used with the verbal jokes, it was found that cartoons with implicit resolutions place more restrictions on order of processing than do cartoons with explicit resolutions. Resolution information that was only implied, but not actually present in the cartoon, was generally obtained only after the full incongruity had been processed. In contrast, explicit resolutions were obtained before incongruities nearly as often as after them. Some cartoons with implicit resolutions contain an explicit clue to the resolution while others do not. There was a strong tendency for such clues to be processed before the resolution itself.

Cognitive processing in the creation of humour

Cognitive processing in the creation of verbal humour is apparently just the reverse of the processing in the reception of humour. Introspective accounts suggested that the creator of a joke first notices an ambiguity (either linguistic or conceptual) and then creates an incongruity by responding to the hidden rather than the intended meaning of the ambiguity (Shultz and Scott, 1974). As an example, consider how W. C. Fields might have created the 'clubs' joke that was discussed above. The idea for this joke may have begun with his noticing the lexical ambiguity of 'clubs'. Although knowing very well that the questioner intended 'clubs' to mean 'social groups', he created an incongruity by responding to the hidden meaning of 'large sticks'. The response he chose, 'Only when kindness fails', is quite apt as it is decidedly incongruous yet it cleverly suggests only a misinterpretation of the question.

This model of joke creation received empirical support in a recent experiment by Shultz and Scott (1974). In this study, adult subjects were asked to create jokes from partial joke information. They were provided with either incongruity or resolution information from actual jokes and asked to use this information to create as many funny jokes as possible. The resolution form left the first line of the original joke intact and substituted a congruous response for the second line; for example, 'Do you believe in clubs for young people?' 'Yes, I do'. The incongruity form left the second line intact and substituted the intended meaning for the ambiguity in the first line, for example, 'Do you believe in social groups for young people?' 'Only when kindness fails'. It was found that subjects created more good jokes in response to the resolution information than to the incongruity information. This result can be considered as supporting the model since the resolution form closely approximates to the theoretically optimal conditions for joke creation by presenting an ambiguity.

Arousal, pleasure and the humour response

All the research discussed so far has dealt only with the issue of cognitive processing in humour. While the incongruity and resolution theory has been quite successful in generating and interpreting research on cognitive processing, one still might question whether it has any relation to the humour response *per se*. The small amount of available evidence indicates an affirmative answer to this question. Jones (1970) had one group of adult subjects rate each of a number of cartoons for degree of incongruity and a second group of subjects rate the same cartoons for funniness. He found that rated humour was a positive linear function of the degree of incongruity. A series of studies with children (reported in detail in the next section of this chapter) found that removal of resolution or incongruity information from jokes, riddles and cartoons significantly diminished the humour response.

In order to understand the relation of the cognitive structures of incongruity and resolution to the humour response, it is helpful to examine the presumed mediating variables of pleasure and arousal. It may be that the cognitive experience of incongruity and resolution has physiological correlates in terms of momentary fluctuations in arousal. Berlyne (1972) has proposed that there are some features of humorous stimuli that serve to arouse the recipient and other features that serve to decrease this arousal. If both the arousal induction and arousal reduction phases are experienced as pleasurable then one could speak in terms of what Berlyne (1972) has called an 'arousal boost–jag' mechanism in humour. In terms of the theory outlined here, it might be supposed that it is the discovery of the incongruity in a joke which produces the increase in arousal and the construction of a resolution which reduces the arousal. The pleasure-giving potential of arousal induction and reduction in man and animals has been well documented in a review by Berlyne (1969). But the case of humour is somewhat paradoxical in that a relatively mild stimulus is capable of eliciting a rather violent, stereotyped emotional response in the form of laughter. Perhaps the pleasure experienced in humour is greatly intensified by the suddenness with which the sequence of arousal induction and reduction occurs. Perceiving and then resolving the incongruity in a joke probably occurs within a second or less, certainly much more rapidly than the arousal and satisfaction sequence in most other motivational systems. Unfortunately, it has not yet been possible to measure an arousal boost–jag in humour at a physiological level. Widely used techniques such as the galvanic skin response or heart rate may prove to be too gross and too peripheral for these phenomena. Until more precise techniques become available, however, the arousal boost–jag idea may at least provide an intuitively appealing account of the relation between the cognitive and behavioural aspects of humour appreciation.

DEVELOPMENT OF RESOLUTION IN HUMOUR

Any truly comprehensive theory of the structure of humour must take account of cognitive development. Although it seems obvious that the structure of humour for infants and young children is quite different from that for older children and adults, there have been very few theoretical attempts to account for these differences. The most notable exception is Freud's (1960) discussion of the 'psychogenesis' of humour. He proposed that joking develops through three distinct stages. The first stage was termed 'play' and was characterized by absurd and nonsensical combinations of words or ideas. In terms of the theory discussed here, this first stage could be interpreted as the appreciation of pure incongruity without a need for resolution. The second stage is what Freud called 'jesting'. Freud thought it was produced by increased social pressures on the child to be logical and meaningful, even in his joking. Thus, the child finds it increasingly necessary to employ what Freud called the 'joke techniques'. These can be interpreted as resolution techniques which render incongruities meaningful or appropriate by resolving or explaining them. The third and final stage was called 'joking' by Freud. In this stage humour becomes tendentious, that is, capable of serving sexual and aggressive motives. This is more of a change in the content of humour than in the structure of humour.

Until recently, the best evidence for the existence of these stages has been observational studies such as that conducted by Wilson (1931). She studied naturally-occurring laughter in 2,115 subjects ranging from 1 month to 9 years of age. Her primary source of data was written records kept by mothers, teachers and herself. The data indicated that laughter associated with the child's successful use of his own powers was common during infancy and the nursery school period but decreased sharply thereafter. The effectiveness of situations involving pretence or the recognition of oddities increased with age and then decreased, pretence being most effective between 2 years 6 months and 4 years 5 months and recognition of oddities being most effective between 6 years 6 months and 7 years 5 months. The effectiveness of word plays and comparisons with indirect allusion increased steadily with age. Laughter at word plays began as early as 3 years of age and at comparisons with indirect allusions as early as 4 years 6 months.

Careful examination of sample events recorded by Wilson indicated to this author that the categories of pretence and oddities correspond roughly to what has here been termed pure incongruity. Similarly, the categories of word play and comparison with indirect allusion correspond roughly to the resolvable joke forms used by adults. Thus, these observational data offer some support for Freud's developmental theory. They suggest a stage in which pure incongruity is appreciated from about 2 to 6 years and a partly overlapping stage in which resolvable incongruity is appreciated beginning at about 4 to 6 years. The remainder of this section of the chapter deals with more recent experimental studies of the development of resolution in children's humour and the following section deals with the development of appreciation of pure or unresolvable incongruity.

The case of verbal jokes

It is not usually a trivial matter to determine whether or not a given child appreciates the resolvable nature of humour. Consider two hypothetical children, one of whom (child A) appreciates only the incongruous aspects of jokes but has no appreciation of or sensitivity to the resolvable aspects. The other (child B) is able to appreciate joke resolutions and regards pure incongruity as silly nonsense. These differences in cognitive structure may be quite difficult to diagnose on the basis of observational data alone. Both children may show a genuine enjoyment of standard jokes, child A enjoying them for their incongruities and child B enjoying them for their resolutions of incongruity. In addition, both children may be able to relate a whole series of jokes from memory. If they are able to remember the jokes correctly, the differential diagnosis of cognitive structures will have failed again. Observations of both joke appreciation and joke telling may well lead to an overestimation of child A's abilities. This general problem is, of course, not restricted to humour. One of the important lessons of Piaget's monumental contribution to the study of cognitive development is that specially contrived situations must be used to avoid overestimating the child's cognitive structures.

A similar strategy was used in an experiment by Shultz and Horibe (1974) to distinguish appreciation of resolvable incongruity from appreciation of pure incongruity in verbal jokes. The experiment employed standard children's jokes and systematic variations of these which had either the incongruity or the resolution deleted. Incongruity-removed versions were constructed by making the last line congruous or consistent with the preceding lines. For example, 'Yes I do' is a congruent response to 'Do you believe in clubs for young people?' Resolution-removed versions were constructed by leaving the incongruity intact and deleting crucial resolution information. For jokes resolved on the basis of linguistic ambiguity, this manipulation involved the elimination of the second or hidden meaning in favour of the first or biased meaning. For example, the ambiguous term 'clubs' was replaced by the unambiguous term 'social groups'. The incongruity is still present in this altered version, but there is no longer a good resolution for it. A systematic preference for the original over the resolution-removed forms would indicate appreciation of the resolvable aspects of the jokes (an arousal-jag effect). Similarly, a systematic preference for the resolution-removed forms over the incongruity-removed forms would indicate appreciation of the incongruous aspects of the jokes (an arousal-boost effect).

Children of 6, 8, 10 and 12 years of age were presented with a series of original, resolution-removed and incongruity-removed jokes of various resolution types. Measures of the children's appreciation and comprehension of each item were obtained. The results indicated that the 8, 10 and 12-year-olds found the original forms funnier than the resolution-removed forms and the resolution-removed forms funnier than the incongruity-removed forms. In contrast the 6-year-olds showed no difference between the original and the resolution-removed forms but found both of these forms funnier than the incongruity-removed forms. Thus, it appeared that the 6-year-olds appreciated the incongruous aspect, but not the resolvable aspect of the jokes. Children aged 8 and older apparently appreciated both structural components. This conclusion was further supported by an analysis of the comprehension responses to original joke forms where it was found that the 6-year-olds had great difficulty in comprehending joke resolutions, particularly the hidden meaning of the ambiguity in the resolution.

The case of riddles

A similar experiment on the appreciation and comprehension of riddles (Shultz, 1974b) led to very similar conclusions. The riddle is a form of humour which is somewhere between problem solving and the appreciation of jokes; it is a problem whose solution evokes a good deal of pleasure and humour. The riddle can be viewed as a question followed by a surprising or incongruous answer. The answer is usually too difficult for the recipient to obtain on his own so it is provided by the teller after an appropriate length of time. Once he has been given the incongruous answer, the listener then has the task of figuring out how it really does make sense in terms of the original question. This is equivalent to resolving or explaining the incongruity and thus should evoke pleasure and humour. Consider the following example of a riddle resolved on the basis of phonological ambiguity: 'Why did the cookie cry? Because its mother had been a wafer so long'. The answer at first seems incongruous but it can be quickly resolved by noticing the phonological ambiguity of 'a wafer'. After initially interpreting this utterance as 'a type of cookie', the listener suddenly discovers that it could also be interpreted as 'away for'.

Just as in Shultz and Horibe's (1974) verbal joke experiment, cognitive structures were assessed by a comparison of original and altered forms. Incongruity-removed forms were constructed by making the answer a logical or plausible response to the question. For example, in the 'cookie' riddle, the answer was changed to 'Because he was left in the oven too long'. Assuming that one accepts the question's premise that a cookie can cry, this altered response provides a rational explanation. There is no incongruity between question and answer and, consequently, no need for a resolution. Resolution-removed forms were constructed by leaving the incongruity intact and deleting information which was crucial to the resolution. For riddles resolved on the basis of linguistic ambiguity, this manipulation involved eliminating the second or hidden meaning of the ambiguity in the resolution in favour of the first or biased meaning. For example, 'Why did the cookie cry?' was followed by the incongruous but unresolvable 'Because its mother was a wafer'.

The procedure was quite similar to that of the verbal joke experiment. Children of 6, 8, 10 and 12 years of age were presented with a series of original, resolution-removed, and incongruity-removed riddles of various resolution types. The results indicated that children of 8 years and older found the original form funnier than the two altered forms which did not differ in funniness. In contrast, the 6-year-olds rated the three forms as equally funny. Analogous to the verbal joke experiment, it appeared that the 6-year-olds appreciated the incongruous, but not the resolvable, aspects of the riddles, while children of 8 and older appreciated both structural components. This conclusion received additional support from an analysis of the comprehension responses to the original forms of riddles where it was found that the 6-year-olds had particular difficulty in comprehending the hidden meanings of the ambiguities necessary for a successful resolution.

Relevance of the transition to concrete operational thought

The results of the verbal joke and riddle experiments strongly suggest that the transition between an early stage of appreciation of pure incongruity and a later stage of preference for resolvable incongruity occurs between the ages of 6 and 8 years. The particular timing of this transition raises the possibility that it may be related to the onset of concrete operational thought. This would make sense in very general terms since the systematic organization of cognitive schemes that characterizes the period of concrete operations might well serve as a structural base for the propensity to resolve incongruities in order to enjoy them.

A recent study by Shultz and Bloom (1974) examined this relationship in some detail. Seven and 8-year-olds were presented with a series of original and resolution-removed jokes and measures of appreciation and comprehension of each joke were obtained. The child's level of cognitive development was also assessed using Piagetian tests of class inclusion and conservation of length, abilities which are known to develop with the transition to concrete operational thought. Performance on the Piagetian tasks was not strongly related to preference for the original over the resolution-removed joke forms. However, it was related to the ability to detect the hidden meaning of the ambiguity which is necessary for a successful joke resolution. Children who were judged to be concrete operational by their performance on the class inclusion and conservation tests provided significantly more hidden meanings in their comprehension responses to original jokes than did children judged to be pre-operational.

Relevance of the ability to detect linguistic ambiguity

It has been shown that the appreciation of large numbers of verbal jokes and riddles depends on the ability to construct resolutions based on the detection of linguistic ambiguity. This suggests that the transition to an appreciation of resolvable humour may depend on corresponding developments in the ability to detect the various types of linguistic ambiguity. A study of the development of the ability to detect linguistic ambiguity was conducted by Shultz and Pilon (1973). Children of 6, 9, 12 and 15 years of age were presented with a series of sentences, half of which were ambiguous. The child was asked to describe in his own words what each sentence meant. If he gave only one interpretation, he was asked if the sentence could also mean anything else. Then the experimenter presented two pictures illustrating the two possible meanings of the sentence and asked the child to point to the picture which showed the meaning of the sentence. For example, one of the sentences ambiguous at the level of deep structure was 'The duck is ready to eat'. It was accompanied by a picture of a cooked duck on a platter and a picture of a live duck eating from a food dish. If the child chose only one of the two pictures, he was asked to explain why the other picture did not apply. The results indicated that the ability to detect each of four ambiguity types developed at different times. Detection of phonological ambiguity appeared first, with the largest improvement occurring between 6 and 9 years of age. Next to appear was the detection of lexical ambiguity, which showed a nearly linear increase across the age span of 6 to 15 years. Detection of surface and deep structure ambiguities did not appear until age 12.

These results on the detection of sentential ambiguity certainly raised the possibility that the development of the appreciation of verbal jokes and riddles would vary with resolution type. However, the appreciation results in the verbal joke (Shultz and Horibe, 1974) and riddle studies (Shultz, 1974b) did not precisely conform to this expectation. In neither of these studies were there any main or interactive effects of resolution type on humour appreciation. In other words, appreciation of all of the resolution types developed at about the same time (8 years of age). In addition, it appeared that ambiguities were more frequently detected at younger ages in the two humour studies than in the sentential ambiguity study. A possible explanation for this is that certain features of the humour structure, particularly the second element of the incongruity, may have served as a clue to the hidden meaning of the ambiguity. For example, hearing the response 'Only when kindness fails' may facilitate the detection of the hidden meaning of 'clubs'.

There were significant effects of resolution types on the detection of hidden meanings of the ambiguity in the two humour studies. But these effects were only partly consistent with those of the sentential ambiguity study. In the sentential ambiguity study, phonological ambiguities were detected more frequently than lexical ambiguities which were, in turn, more frequently detected than the two syntactic types. In the verbal joke study, phonological ambiguities were again detected more frequently than any of the other three types. However, lexical ambiguities were not detected more frequently than the two syntactic types and surface structure ambiguities were detected more frequently than deep structure ambiguities. In the riddle study, it was the lexical ambiguities that were detected more frequently than the other three types, none of which differed significantly from the others. The only consistent pattern across all three studies was a tendency for phonological and lexical ambiguities to be somewhat easier to detect than the two syntactic types. This is a pattern which is also consistent with the results of some detection time experiments with adults. It has been reported that lexical ambiguities are more quickly detected or completed than surface and deep structure ambiguities (MacKay, 1966; MacKay and Bever, 1967).

DEVELOPMENT OF INCONGRUITY IN HUMOUR

It is somewhat more difficult to specify the beginnings of the appreciation of pure incongruity. This is a form of humour which has not as yet received adequate study. One of the most troublesome problems in this area is the identification of proper humour stimuli. There are no published materials one can draw on as there are in the case of resolvable incongruity. One must rely largely on more spontaneous events, a strategy that entails an examination of contextual variables as discussed above. Another problem is that incongruity sometimes evokes exploratory behaviour instead of humour. The variables which apparently qualify these relationships have not yet been identified. Consequently, the treatment given here can only be regarded as an attempt to outline some of the issues that may prove worthy of further investigation.

Symbolic play as self-constructed incongruity

Piaget's (1951, first edition published 1945) treatment of the phenomenon of symbolic play may be one of the most promising theoretical approaches to the problem of incongruity humour. In addition it is certainly one of the richest sources of relevant observational material. Towards the end of the infancy period, at about 18–24 months of age, an important but poorly understood change occurs in the child's cognitive functioning. In contrast to his earlier 'sensory motor' intelligence, the child rather suddenly becomes capable of symbolic representation. Piaget termed this last stage of the sensory motor period 'mental combinations' and identified it by the presence of two behavioural phenomena—deferred imitation and symbolic play. Deferred imitation refers to the idea that the child can now imitate an action sequence long after it has occurred, presumably because he can now store a symbolic representation of the sequence. Previously he was only able to imitate sequences at the same time he was observing them. For present purposes, the more interesting of the two representational phenomena is symbolic play. In symbolic play, the child reproduces a sensory motor scheme outside its normal context in the absence of its usual objective. In other words, he applies one of his sensory motor schemes to an inappropriate object. In Piaget's view, these developments of symbolic representation can be understood in terms of a progressive differentiation between the 'signifier' and the 'signified'. The signifier is the inappropriate object and the 'make-believe' action applied to it; the signified is the scheme as it would ordinarily be applied and its normal object. It is this differentiation between signifier and signified that generates the possibility of pretence—the child can now pretend to be doing something other than what he is really doing or pretend that an object is something other than it really is.

A classic example of such pretence was first observed in Piaget's daughter Jacqueline at 1 year 3 months of age (Piaget, 1951). At various times, Jacqueline pretended to fall asleep on such objects as a cloth, a coat collar and her toy donkey's tail. It was as if she were applying her 'going to sleep' scheme to objects other than her pillow which was the typical object of the scheme. A similar episode was observed in this author's younger son, also at 1 year 3 months of age. In the few preceding weeks, Kevin had constructed a sensory motor scheme for playing with toy cars. Ordinarily, he would push the car along the floor with his hand, making appropriate motor-like vocalizations. Another of his sensory motor schemes involved drinking from his juice bottle. On one particular day, however, after drinking all the juice from his bottle, Kevin began pushing the bottle along on its side while making the motor-like sounds. He was apparently applying his car-pushing scheme to an inappropriate object, the juice bottle.

In the present context, there are two interesting features of symbolic play—the fact that it is typically accompanied by lots of smiling and laughing and the possibility that it can be interpreted as self-constructed incongruity. The combination of these two features makes it quite likely that early symbolic play or pretence is directly relevant to the development of humour appreciation. The relation between symbolic play and laughter is very striking. Despite the fact that Piaget did not appear to be at all interested in laughter or in humour, every one of the instances of symbolic play he discussed (Piaget, 1951) was reported to be accompanied by laughter. This would be rather unlikely unless the accompanying laughter was quite intense and was regarded as an integral feature of the play itself. This author's observations of early symbolic play strongly corroborate this view. The amount, intensity and regularity of laughter associated with early symbolic play is very striking indeed.

The interpretation of symbolic play as self-constructed incongruity is intuitively appealing. Incongruity in more advanced forms of humour has been defined in terms of a conflict between what is expected and what actually occurs in the joke. Incongruity is never a single object or event but rather a relationship between two objects or events, such that the first sets up expectations which are disconfirmed by the second. In the case of symbolic play, it can readily be seen that there is an incongruous relationship between the object and the scheme applied to it. The object is inappropriate to the scheme and the scheme is inappropriate to the object. Designation of one or the other as 'first' or 'second' is somewhat dubious without detailed knowledge of the context. In the observation of Kevin discussed above, it was quite clear that the context was established by the presence of the juice bottle and its customary scheme of drinking. Within this context, the application of the car-pushing scheme was quite incongruous. This was a case where the object served as first element of the incongruity and the scheme as second element of the incongruity. It could conceivably have occurred the other way round, however, and it would be easy enough to find other observations where the normal operation of the scheme set the context for its application to an incongruous object. An interesting feature of these incongruities, of course, is that they are created by the child himself. Instances where the child is more of a passive recipient of incongruous information are discussed below.

Piaget also reported on further developments in symbolic play. Shortly after using *objects* inappropriately, he begins to project his sensory motor schemes onto novel and somewhat inappropriate *subjects*. After having played for about 2 months at pretending to go to sleep, for example, Jacqueline had her toy bear and toy dog engage in the same pretence. Like the use of inappropriate objects, the use of inappropriate subjects was typically accompanied by a good deal of smiling and laughing. The term incongruity would seem to apply here as well with the scheme serving as one element and the new subject serving as the other.

Piaget's observations indicated that symbolic play continues to develop into forms of greater complexity. It is interesting, however, that none of the instances of these more advanced forms were reported to be accompanied by smiling or laughter. It might be tentatively concluded that this period (about 2 years of age) marks the point at which play and humour begin to differentiate from each other and proceed to follow their own separate lines of development. Play, of course, eventually develops into the formalized 'games with rules' (Piaget, 1932, 1951) while humour apparently develops into the sort of resolvable incongruity structure discussed above.

Reception of incongruity humour

Those developmental studies reviewed in the last section concerning the differential appreciation of original and altered joke forms (Shultz, 1974b; Shultz and Horibe, 1974) provided evidence that young children find pure incongruity to be humorous. This was indicated by the fact that the 6-year-olds in these experiments found the original and the resolution-removed forms to be equally funny but found both to be funnier than the incongruity-removed forms. There are two other studies in the literature which are relevant to this issue.

One is reported by Buehler (1921) who presented children between 2 and 8 years of age with a series of absurd pictures. There was, for example, a tiny horse pulling a huge wagon, a plant with human attributes and a man sawing off the tree branch on which he was sitting. Each picture was incongruous in a nonsensical way that would be difficult to resolve. Buehler found that the percentage of children being amused at these incongruous pictures decreased steadily from 100 % at 2 years of age to 0 % at 8 years of age.

Kreitler and Kreitler (1970) also studied young children's reactions to nonsensical incongruities. They presented 5 and 6-year-olds with a series of incongruous drawings. The incidence of smiling and laughing was highest when the child identified the incongruity and criticized it or wondered about it. The incidence of smiling and laughing was lowest when he merely described the details of the picture. Intermediate levels of smiling and laughing were associated with strategies involving irrelevant criticism, restatement of the theme without identifying the incongruity, and active attempts to resolve the incongruity on the level of fantasy, reality or denial. For present purposes, the most interesting aspect of these data was that children seemed to enjoy the incongruity more when it was appreciated for itself than when they made an attempt to resolve it. This result does not necessarily conflict with the findings of Shultz (1974b) and Shultz and Horibe (1974) since the Kreitlers' subjects were well below the age when resolution becomes an important structural factor. It should also be noted that the Kreitlers used nonsensical incongruities rather than resolvable jokes. Because their pictures were inherently unresolvable, the likelihood of anyone constructing a successful resolution was quite low. Those few children who tried to resolve them were probably frustrated by their lack of success and hence may have enjoyed the incongruities less than if they had merely appreciated them as incongruities.

Some very interesting observations by two of the author's students (Goodz and Cramer, personal communication) suggest the feasibility of using verbal incongruities with young children. Goodz and Cramer were studying the comprehension of time-related words such as 'before' and 'after' in children between 3 years and 3 years 4 months of age. One of the techniques they developed involved semantically anomalous questions describing the sequences of events in routines that the child would be very familar with. Each set of questions was introduced with a brief story. For example, one story described a girl, Wendy, who got so dirty playing in the sandbox that her mother had to give her a bath. For each story, there were four questions: one with 'after' at the head of the first clause (After Wendy takes a bath does she take her clothes off?), one with 'after' at the head of the second clause (Does Wendy take off her clothes after she takes a bath?), one with 'before' at the head of the first clause (Before Wendy takes off her clothes does she take a bath?), and one with 'before' at the head of the second clause (Does Wendy take a bath before she takes off her clothes?). There were four similar anomalous questions dealing with the issues of whether one puts on socks before shoes, eats before cooking, and watches television before turning it on. Twelve of the 15 children tested answered all 16 questions incorrectly, that is affirmatively, indicating that they did not yet comprehend the use of 'before' and 'after'. It was reported that all 12 of these children approached the task with great seriousness, never once even cracking a smile. The 3 remaining children showed quite a different pattern on both comprehension and emotional responses. One of these children answered all 16 questions correctly, that is negatively; and he laughed at hearing each question. Another answered 13 out of 16 correctly and laughed throughout. The third of these children missed the first 4 questions dealing with eating and cooking, then suddenly caught on and answered the remaining 12 correctly. As his responses changed from incorrect to correct, so did his mood change from serious to humorous. While the smallness of the sample precludes any firm interpretation of these results, they do suggest a possibly fruitful technique for the study of incongruity humour in young children. It is a method that offers certain advantages over pictorial methods since the child's answers provide a relatively precise, objective measure of whether or not he perceives the incongruity. The 3 children who correctly answered many questions smiled, laughed and spontaneously commented on the 'silliness' of the questions. Because they understood the usage of 'before' and 'after' these 3 children must have perceived the questions as highly incongruous. And because they perceived the questions as incongruous, they found them humorous as well. The other 12 children presumably failed to laugh because they did not perceive the incongruities.

Other responses to incongruity

Piaget's (1951) observations of symbolic play and the studies by Wilson (1931), Shultz (1974b), Shultz and Horibe (1974), Buehler (1921), Kreitler and Kreitler (1970) and Goodz and Cramer (personal communication) all point to the conclusion that there is a stage during which the child is able to appreciate pure incongruity without having to first resolve it. Taken together, these studies further suggest that this stage begins as early as 18 months of age and lasts until about 7 or 8 years of age, a span roughly equivalent to Piaget's pre-operational period. However, more complete examination of the research literature indicates that humour is not the only response to incongruity. A number of studies (Faw, 1970; Connolly and Harris, 1971; Nunnally, Faw and Bashford, 1969) have confirmed Berlyne's (1960) prediction that incongruity is one of those 'collative' variables that induce perceptual exploration. Both children and adults were found to spend longer periods of time looking at incongruous than at congruous pictures. Since these studies dealt explicitly with visual exploration and not with humour, their reporting of humour indices were sketchy. Yet one gets the impression from the research reports that humour was not the primary response to incongruity for subjects either below or above the crucial 7–8 years of age. Is this merely because indices of humour were not adequately assessed in these studies, or was there perhaps something about the context of these studies which made humour a rather unlikely response? Perhaps the humour response requires a kind of humour set such that the subject is expecting to be exposed to humorous material and knows that it is permissible to express his humour by laughing or smiling. A certain amount of exploration or problem solving is of course necessary for a successful resolution of a joke's incongruity. But when the incongruity is inherently unresolvable, it is quite unlikely that an adequate resolution will be forthcoming. In this case, one would not expect to obtain humour—unless the subject was in the stage where pure incongruities were considered to be humorous. The nature of the young child's responses to incongruity and the qualifying determinants of those responses obviously require a great deal of additional study.

HUMOUR IN INFANCY

There is ample documentation of the fact that human infants engage in a good deal of smiling and laughing. But whether these responses can be interpreted as an early form of humour is uncertain. One problem is an abundance of alternative explanations. The infant's smile has been variously interpreted as an innate response to the stimulus properties of the human face (e.g. Polak, Emde and Spitz, 1964a, 1964b), as an operant under the control of social reinforcement (e.g. Brackbill, 1958) and as the emotional concomitant to understanding a stimulus event (e.g. Piaget, 1951). To the extent that any or all of these alternative explanations of infant smiling are valid, it becomes less tenable to maintain that these smiles represent an early form of humour. This issue is, in part, a definitional one. If the definition of humour is restricted to the appreciation of socially transmitted jokes, then the answer is clearly negative: infants do not evidence any appreciation of such materials. If the definition of humour is extended to include any process which mediates the response of smiling or laughing, then the answer is clearly positive: infants do appreciate humour. Rather than arguing for the appropriateness of various definitions of humour, this section of the paper attempts to follow a more substantive strategy—first, to determine whether the complex data on infant smiling can be interpreted in terms of a coherent cognitive theory and, second, to examine the relevance of the processes specified in this theory for the later forms of humour based on incongruity and its resolution.

Pleasure in mastery: a cognitive interpretation of infant smiling

Piaget's (1951) careful observations of his own 3 infants led to his formulation of the pleasure in mastery hypothesis: after a period of relatively serious accommodation to a stimulus, the infant reveals his success at assimilating it by expressions of pleasurable emotion. Mastery or successful adaptation is said to occur at that point when the child can freely assimilate the stimulus to his newly accommodated scheme. The child's subsequent tendency to engage in such assimilation for its own sake was termed 'practice play' by Piaget. As Piaget's observations reveal, this processs can best be observed during the sensory motor period when adaptation is relatively slow and evident in behaviour.

It is interesting to note that there is some difference between the pleasure in mastery interpretation of infant smiling and Piaget's earlier (1952, first edition published 1936) treatment. In his earlier book, he attributed the infant's smiling not to mastery but to 'recognitory assimilation', which was defined as the identification of a stimulus as familiar. In support of the recognitory hypothesis, Piaget reported several observations where the infant did not smile to a stimulus until he had encountered it several times. Without questioning the accuracy of these latter observations it is still possible to reject the recognitory explanation in favour of Piaget's (1951) later mastery explanation. To apply the mastery explanation to the observation that the infant does not smile to a stimulus on his first encounter with it, one only needs to assume that the first encounter was not long enough for assimilation to occur. In other words, to master a difficult stimulus the infant needs a certain amount of accumulated experience with it. The fact that many of the items mentioned in the recognitory account (e.g. handkerchief, toys, people, infant's own hands) were available to the infant only for limited time-periods is consistent with this interpretation.

Moreover, the recognitory explanation encounters two major difficulties: (a) it cannot account for smiling to a stimulus on its first presentation and (b) it seems to preclude the possibility of a stimulus becoming *too* familiar to elicit pleasurable reactions. Evidence for both of these phenomena, as well as for the basic hypothesis that the timing of pleasurable emotional expression coincides with mastery, was provided in an experiment by Shultz and Zigler (1970). In a repeated measures design, infants between 8 and 18 weeks of age were each presented with a stationary stimulus in one condition and the same stimulus in motion in another condition. An observer recorded the duration of the infant's smiling, non-stressful vocalizing, crying, and absence of fixation of the stimulus with an event-recorder. On the assumption that the moving version of the stimulus would be more difficult to assimilate than the stationary version, Shultz and Zigler predicted that the expression of pleasurable emotion would occur earlier to the stationary stimulus than to the moving stimulus. This hypothesis was strongly confirmed for both smiling and vocalizing. Most of the smiling and vocalizing occurred in the fourth minute in the stationary condition and in the tenth minute in the moving condition. In addition, there was a significant decrement in smiling, vocalizing, and fixation of the stimulus from one session to the next.

Similar decrements in infant smiling to a repeated stimulus have been reported in other contexts (Ambrose, 1961; Wahler, 1967; Zelazo, 1971). These decrements suggest that the assimilation which occurs immediately after mastery is more pleasurable than the continued assimilation which follows. The decreasing pleasure of repeated assimilation has been interpreted in terms of cognitive satiation (Shultz and Zigler, 1970) as well as in terms of a decrease in the amount of effort required for assimilation (Kagan, 1971; McCall, 1972; Zelazo, 1972). Satiation and effort may be two aspects of the same process. With each repetition of assimilation the infant may find it to be both 'easier' and 'less fun' than it was before. The fact that smiling tends to recover during the inter-trial interval

(Ambrose, 1961; Zelazo, 1971) could be interpreted in terms of the stimulus becoming either more difficult to assimilate (as if the infant is 'out of practice') or more 'fun' to assimilate because of its relative novelty. As Zelazo (1972) has pointed out, it is indeed difficult to design research which could separate the effects of effort and satiation. Other recent experiments which support a pleasure in mastery explanation of infant smiling include those by Kagan (1971), Watson (1972), Zelazo (1972) and Zelazo and Komer (1971). In addition, Shultz and Zigler (1970) have suggested that the pleasure in mastery mechanism has considerable adaptive significance for the infant's cognitive growth. If so, it may have acquired a genetic structural base over the course of evolution.

If the pleasure in mastery notion can indeed provide a cognitive account of infant smiling, then the next question to consider is the relevance of pleasure in mastery to more advanced forms of humour. One point to note is that the pleasure in mastery effect is not limited to infancy but rather continues to be an important mediator of smiling throughout later life. Recent studies by Harter, Shultz and Blum (1971), Harter (1974) and Kagan (1971) have demonstrated that the successful solution of problems is accompanied by smiling in older children. Moreover, the amount of pleasure appeared to increase with the difficulty of the problem solved (Harter, 1974; Kagan, 1971). Similar effects have been reported for the appreciation of cartoons (Zigler, Levine and Gould 1966, 1967) and verbal jokes (McGhee, 1973). Thus, pleasure in mastery is not only evident in older children, but it also appears to be involved in their appreciation of humorous materials containing resolvable incongruities.

But it is also of interest to inquire whether the phenomenon of pleasure in mastery bears any fundamental structural similarity to incongruity and resolution. In particular, does it involve a biphasic sequence of arousal and arousal reduction? Kagan (1971) is one author who has suggested that infant smiling does have these characteristics. He has written: 'The smile signifies a cognitive success following some doubt over that success ... a feeling of uncertainty followed by resolution' (1971, p. 157).

However, it could be argued that there are rather important differences between the older child's resolving an incongruity in a joke and the infant's accommodating to a novel stimulus. These differences can in fact be described in terms of Charlesworth's (1969) interesting distinctions between the concepts of 'surprise' and 'novelty'. For the purposes of this analysis, it is assumed that the reaction to the incongruity in a joke corresponds roughly to Charlesworth's concept of surprise. He noted four differences between surprise and novelty. The first concerns the nature of the child's behaviour and internal state before the surprise or novel stimulus impinges on him. In the case of novelty, the child has no particular expectancy about the forthcoming event. In the case of surprise, there are rather precise expectancies about the forthcoming event. In other words, a novel event is *un*expected while a surprising event is *mis*-expected. The second difference concerns the nature of the child's initial reaction to the event. According to Charlesworth, the initial reaction to a surprising event should be more intense and more pronounced than the initial reaction to a novel event. The third difference concerns the child's secondary reactions to the event. In the case of novelty, attention is directed to the novel stimulus alone. The secondary reaction to surprise is cognitively more complex as it involves a search for an explanation of the occurrence of the stimulus event. The final distinction concerns the ontogeny of the two responses. To the newborn infant almost any stimulus event can be considered as novel. Even though more stimulus events become familar as the individual grows older, he can continue to experience novelty often without any particular effort on his part. In contrast, surprise cannot occur until the child has constructed specific expectations that can be clearly disconfirmed. Taking all four of these differences into account, it seems unlikely that the infant's pleasure in cognitive mastery of a novel stimulus event is completely analogous to the older child's humour response to resolving the incongruity in a joke. To draw the distinction even more clearly, one could say that there is no specific novel element in a joke. The entire joke may be novel, but each of its elements must be quite familiar. Otherwise the recipient would be unable to experience the incongruous relation as surprising and unable to resolve it. Thus, it can be very tentatively concluded that pleasure in mastery represents a primitive stage of humour which is qualitatively distinct from the later stages of incongruity and resolvable incongruity.

However, there are a number of infant games which do seem to involve a biphasic sequence of arousal induction and reduction. Because these games elicit a good deal of smiling and laughing, they may be regarded as early forms of humour. Three of them discussed below are peek-a-boo, tickling and chasing.

The peek-a-boo game

The game of peek-a-boo involves an alternating interruption of visual contact with another person and re-establishment of contact. Usually the other person is one with whom the infant shares a close interpersonal attachment such as his mother, father or sibling. The game is very widely played in our culture and may in fact be universally played although there are no data at present to document this. Wherever it is played, it is one of the most effective elicitors of infant laughing and smiling (Kleeman, 1967; Sroufe and Wunsch, 1972; Washburn, 1929). Kleeman has distinguished two forms of peek-a-boo, active and passive. The passive form involves the other person controlling the alternating sequence of the offset and onset of visual contact. This can be done either by covering or hiding his own face or by covering the infant's eyes. In active peek-a-boo, it is the infant himself who controls the alternating sequence, usually by covering his eyes with his hands or some suitable object. Observations discussed by Kleeman suggest that passive peek-a-boo begins in most infants between 5 to 9 months of age with active peek-a-boo beginning between 8 and 11 months of age. Both the passive and active forms may be supplemented by animated verbal comments by the other person such as, 'Where is the baby? There he is!'

Without having empirical documentation, the author would propose the following interpretation of this most interesting phenomenon. The visual disappearance of a loved person may produce a sharp increase in the infant's cognitive arousal. The source of this arousal is a sincere uncertainty about whether or not the loved person will return. It is reasonable to assume that this uncertainty would be at a maximum in the 6 to 12 month old infant. According to Piaget (1952), this is the time when the infant is just beginning to form a stable concept of the permanence of objects. Prior to this period, the disappearance of objects should cause no particular concern since the object as such does not exist apart from the infant's encounters with it. After 12 to 18 months of age, the infant's sense of object permanence is so well-formed that temporary disappearance will also cause him no particular concern. The older infant is quite certain that when objects disappear they do not cease to exist, but rather are likely to reappear in a short time. Thus, it is only the infant who is in the process of constructing the concept of permanent objects who would experience uncertainty at loss of visual contact with a loved person. The close relation between the development of object permanence and emotional attachments to specific individuals has been documented in a study by Bell (1970). However, the loss of visual contact does not produce laughter; it is more likely to produce an anxious, intent visual search of the area where the person was last seen. The laughter occurs at the instant when visual contact is re-established, presumably as a function of a sharp decrease in arousal following the reduction of uncertainty.

Some unpublished data collected by Boswell and Shultz indicate that peek-a-boo is not solely a cognitive phenomenon related to disappearing and re-appearing objects. Boswell created a direct analogue of the peek-a-boo game which involved 10 trials of a disappearing and re-appearing toy. The infants tested included 4 at each of 3 age levels—9, 12 and 18 months. The infants were also exposed to 3 trials of a passive version of the peek-a-boo game with the mother as object. While every infant smiled or laughed during every trial of the peek-a-boo game, not a single one of them smiled or laughed to a single trial of the inanimate analogue game. The clear implication of these pilot data is that the disappearance of a loved person is much more arousing than the disappearance of a toy, albeit a highly attractive toy. Both cases of disappearance might create some uncertainty, but only in the case of the person is this uncertainty arousing enough for the re-appearance to produce smiling and laughter. Peek-a-boo is quite clearly a social phenomenon involving intense interpersonal attachments. The ethological significance of this point is discussed below.

Although the foregoing interpretation of peek-a-boo is extremely tentative, it does appear to account for the particular period when the game is most effective in eliciting infant laughter. Also, it is an interpretation which has a definite structural similarity with the incongruity and resolution theory of humour. As noted above, Berlyne (1960) has identified uncertainty and incongruity as two members of a whole class of so-called 'collative' variables which have the special properties of increasing arousal, focusing attention and eliciting exploration. The question of why such a structural sequence should govern the humour of children so far below the period of concrete operations is dealt with below.

The tickling game

Tickling is another game which appears to mediate laughter with a rather precocious uncertainty and resolution sort of structure. Darwin (1872) correctly pointed out that the primary response to tickling is not laughter at all. It is rather a frantic attempt to avoid being tickled, by squirming, wriggling and withdrawing the part of the body which is being tickled. He interpreted this response as an innate mechanism to defend against attack to various vulnerable areas of the body such as the neck, the abdomen, and the soles of the feet. Koestler (1964) has made the interesting suggestion that tickling will produce laughter only when the person being tickled perceives the attack as harmless and playful, that is, as a 'mock attack'. There are two important implications in Koestler's suggestion. One is that the tickling must come from another person; otherwise it could not be interpreted as an attack. Tickling oneself is not known to produce much of a response of any kind (Weiskrantz, Elliott and Darlington, 1971). The other implication is that the tickling, while initially interpreted as an attack, is quickly reinterpreted as a mock attack. If it were interpreted as a real attack, the emotional response would presumably be quite negative. Koestler mentions some uncited research which found that infants laughed 15 times more often when tickled by their mothers than when they were tickled by strangers. He suggests that in both cases the tickling creates some initial uncertainty but that this uncertainty is quickly reduced when the infant realizes that the tickler is only his mother. With a stranger, it is more difficult to be certain that the attack is not a real one. Thus, like the case of peek-a-boo, laughter at being tickled can be interpreted in terms of a sequence of arousal and arousal reduction. In both cases, the arousal is produced by uncertainty and reduced by a resolution of the uncertainty. And in both cases, there is a suggestion that the arousal is of some considerable ethological and social importance.

The chasing game

Chasing is yet another game which appears to produce humour responses in very young children through a sequence of arousal induction and reduction. While chasing games are extremely common in preschool children, a very early example was noted by Kleeman (1967). The mother would say, 'I am coming after you' and her 47-week-old daughter would creep away '. . . there was no visible evidence of anxiety, but considerable pleasure in being chased. The game reached the point where the baby would begin to laugh and "run" away as soon as she saw a familiar facial expression on the mother which conveyed "I am going to catch you!" '.

Such games involving chase could be interpreted in terms of an initial arousal at the threat of being chased followed by a decrease in arousal as the child realizes the chaser is only playing. The child's initial uncertainty about whether he is in danger is quickly resolved as he notices the playful smile on his mother's face. Rothbart (1973) has suggested that a stranger playing the same game would evoke quite a different reaction: the child would cry and run away, presumably because the arousal remains high. There is no certainty that the stranger is only playing.

The ethological significance of peek-a-boo, tickling and chasing

The three games share some rather peculiar characteristics. Each produces a great deal of laughing and smiling in very young children. Each can be characterized by a biphasic sequence of arousal induction (based on uncertainty) and arousal reduction. And the arousal induction phase in each game appears to involve an ethologically relevant social interaction. The theme of this interaction is abandonment by the primary caretaker in the case of peek-a-boo and predatory attack in the cases of tickling and chasing. This raises the possibility that the arousal created by these games is a genetically-based vestige from the time when most human characteristics evolved—our pre-agricultural, hunting and gathering period. In this sort of existence, abandonment and predatory attack were probably frequent threats to the survival of the young. Any behavioural characteristics which countered these threats would presumably have been naturally selected for over the course of many generations. The possible genetic base of these sources of arousal could account for the fact that games based on them are enjoyed so early in development. In contrast to most other forms of humour which do not evidence an incongruity and resolution structure until the period of concrete operational thought, these games are enjoyed by many infants in the first year of life. Like many other 'precocious' behavioural systems under strong genetic control, they are not easily generalized and abstracted to other content areas. Rather, they are restricted to quite a narrow range of thematically relevant activities.

In contrast to later forms of humour in which the arousal phase itself is enjoyed (the arousal-boost effect), the arousal phase in these primitive games has a definite negative affective tone. The infant exhibits an anxiety-laden response to the arousal which can easily erupt into crying if the arousal is not reduced. In this connection it is interesting to note that Sroufe and Wunsch (1972) have found a close connection between laughing and crying in infants. Those events which were the most effective elicitors of laughing were, in other contexts, also the most effective elicitors of crying. Similarly, Rothbart (1973) has proposed an 'arousal–safety' model of young children's laughter containing the assumption that arousal is experienced as negative as a direct function of its intensity (see Chapter 2). Systematic study of some of these laughter-inducing infant games may prove to be of immense value to the understanding of the development of humour.

SUMMARY AND CONCLUSIONS

In this chapter an attempt has been made to understand the cognitive-developmental features of humour. Humour in older children and adults is accounted for in terms of the biphasic sequence of incongruity and resolution. Appreciation of the resolvable aspects of jokes coincides with the development of concrete operational thought at about 7 years of age. An earlier stage characterized by the appreciation of pure, unresolved incongruity coincides roughly with the period of pre-operational thought, from about 2 to 7 years of age. Humour in infancy is characterized principally in terms of pleasure in cognitive mastery. A few games common to infancy are found to possess a biphasic sequence involving the arousal and reduction of uncertainty. Unlike more advanced forms of humour the emotional tone of the arousal in these games is negative and appears to have a specific evolutionary basis.

ACKNOWLEDGEMENTS

Much of the author's research reported herein was supported in part by grants S71-0044 and S72-0771 from the Canada Council and in part by a grant from the Faculty of Graduate Studies and Research of McGill University.

REFERENCES

Ambrose, J. A. (1961). The development of the smiling response in early infancy. In B. M. Foss (Ed.), *Determinants of Infant Behaviour*, Vol. 2, London: Methuen.

Beattie, J. (1776). On laughter and ludicrous composition. In *Essays*. Edinburgh: Creech.

Bell, S. M. (1970). The development of the concept of object as related to infant–mother attachment. *Child Development*, **41**, 291–311.

Berlyne, D. E. (1960). *Conflict, Arousal and Curiosity*. New York: McGraw-Hill.

Berlyne, D. E. (1969). Laughter, humor and play. In G. Lindzey and E. Aronson (Eds.), *Handbook of Social Psychology*, Vol. 3. Reading, Mass.: Addison–Wesley.

Berlyne, D. E. (1972). Humor and its kin. In J. H. Goldstein and P. E. McGhee (Eds.), *The Psychology of Humor*. New York: Academic Press.

Brackbill, Y. (1958). Extinction of the smiling response in infants as a function of reinforcement schedule. *Child Development*, **29**, 115–124.

Buehler, C. (1921). *Kindheit und Jugend* (3rd edition). Leipzig: Hirzel Verlag.

Charlesworth, W. R. (1969). The role of surprise in cognitive development. In D. Elkind and J. H. Flavell (Eds.), *Studies in Cognitive Development*. New York: Oxford.

Chomsky, N. A. (1965). *Aspects of The Theory of Syntax*. Cambridge, Mass.: MIT Press.

Connolly, M. F., and Harris, L. (1971). Effects of stimulus incongruity on children's curiosity as measured by looking time and expression change. *Psychonomic Science*, **25**, 232–234.

Darwin, C. R. (1872). *The Expression of The Emotions in Man and Animals*. London: Murray.

Faw, T. T. (1970). The effects of stimulus incongruity on the free looking time of adults and children. *Psychonomic Science*, **19**, 355–357.

Foss, D. J., Bever, T., and Silver, M. (1968). The comprehension and verification of ambiguous sentences. *Perception and Psychophysics*, **4**, 304–306.

Freud, S. (1960). *Jokes and Their Relation to The Unconscious*. New York: Norton. (Original German edition, 1905.)

Harter, S. (1974). Pleasure derived by children from cognitive challenge and mastery. *Child Development*, **45**, 661–669.

Harter, S., Shultz, T. R., and Blum, B. (1971). Smiling in children as a function of their sense of mastery. *Journal of Experimental Child Psychology*, **12**, 396–404.

Jones, J. M. (1970). Cognitive factors in the appreciation of humor: a theoretical and experimental analysis. Unpublished doctoral dissertation, Yale University.

Kagan, J. (1971). *Change and Continuity in Infancy*. New York: Wiley.

Kant, I. (1790). *Kritik der Urteilskraft*. Berlin: Lagarde.

Kleeman, J. A. (1967). The peek-a-boo game, Part I: Its origins, meanings, and related phenomena in the first year. *Psychoanalytic Study of the Child*, **22**, 239–273.

Koestler, A. (1964). *The Act of Creation*. New York: Macmillan.

Kreitler, H. S., and Kreitler, S. (1970). Dependence of laughter on cognitive strategies. *Merrill-Palmer Quarterly*, **16**, 163–177.

MacKay, D. G. (1966). To end ambiguous sentences. *Perception and Psychophysics* **1**, 426–436.

MacKay, D. G., and Bever, T. (1967). In search of ambiguity. *Perception and Psychophysics*, **2**, 193–200.

Maier, N. R. F. (1932). A Gestalt theory of humour. *British Journal of Psychology*, **23**, 69–74.

McCall, R. B. (1972). Smiling and vocalization in infants as indices of perceptual-cognitive processes. *Merrill-Palmer Quarterly*, **18**, 341–347.

McGhee, P. E. (1973). Children's appreciation of humor: A test of the cognitive-congruency principle. Paper presented at the meeting of the Society for Research in Child Development, Philadelphia.

Nunnally, J. C., Faw, T. T., and Bashford M. B. (1969). Effect of degrees of incongruity on visual fixations in children and adults. *Journal of Experimental Psychology*, **81**, 360–364.

Piaget, J. (1932). *The Moral Judgment of The child*. London: Kegan Paul.

Piaget, J. (1952). *The Origins of Intelligence in Children*. New York: International Universities Press. (Original French edition, 1936.)

Piaget, J. (1951). *Play, Dreams, and Imitation in Childhood*. New York: Norton. (Original French edition, 1945.)

Polak, P. R., Emde, R. N., and Spitz, R. A. (1964a). The smiling response to the human face I: Methodology, quantification, and natural history. *Journal of Nervous and Mental Disease*, **139**, 103–109.

Polak, P. R., Emde, R. N., and Spitz, R. A. (1964b). The smiling response II: Visual discrimination and the onset of depth perception. *Journal of Nervous and Mental Disease*, **139**, 407–415.

Rothbart, M. K. (1973). Laughter in young children. *Psychological Bulletin*, **80**, 247–256.

Schopenhauer, A. (1819). *Die Welt als Wille und Vorstellung*. Leipzig: Brockhaus.

Shultz, T. R. (1970). Cognitive factors in children's appreciation of cartoons: Incongruity and its resolution. Unpublished doctoral dissertation, Yale University.

Shultz, T. R. (1972). The role of incongruity and resolution in children's appreciation of cartoon humor. *Journal of Experimental Child Psychology*, **13**, 456–477.

Shultz, T. R. (1974a). A cross-cultural study of the structure of humor. In preparation.

Shultz, T. R. (1974b). Development of the appreciation of riddles. *Child Development*, **45**, 100–105.

Shultz, T. R. (1974c) Order of cognitive processing in humour appreciation. *Canadian Journal of Psychology*, **28**, 409–420.

Shultz, T. R., and Bloom, L. (1974). Concrete operational thought and the appreciation of verbal jokes. In preparation.

Shultz, T. R., and Horibe, F. (1974). Development of the appreciation of verbal jokes. *Developmental Psychology*, **10**, 13–20.

Shultz, T. R., and Pilon, R. (1973). Development of the ability to detect linguistic ambiguity. *Child Development*, **44**, 728–733.

Shultz, T. R., and Scott, M. B. (1974). The creation of verbal humor. *Canadian Journal of Psychology*, **28**, 421–425.

Shultz, T. R., and Zigler, E. (1970). Emotional concomitants of visual mastery in infants: the effects of stimulus movement on smiling and vocalizing. *Journal of Experimental Child Psychology*, **10**, 390–402.

Sroufe, L. A., and Wunsch, J. C. (1972). The development of laughter in the first year of life. *Child Development*, **43**, 1326–1344.

Suls, J. M. (1972). A two-stage model for the appreciation of jokes and cartoons: an information processing analysis. In J. H. Goldstein and P. E. McGhee (Eds.), *The Psychology of Humor*. New York: Academic Press.

Wahler, R. (1967). Infant social attachments: a reinforcement theory interpretation and investigation. *Child Development*, **38**, 1074–1088.

Washburn, R. W. (1929). A study of the smiling and laughing of infants in the first year of life. *Genetic Psychology Monographs*, **6**, 397–537.

Watson, J. S. (1972). Smiling, cooing, and the 'game'. *Merrill-Palmer Quarterly*, **18**, 323–339.

Weiskrantz, L., Elliott, J., and Darlington, C. (1971). Preliminary observations on tickling oneself. *Nature*, **230**, 598–599.

Willman, J. M. (1940). An analysis of humor and laughter. *American Journal of Psychology*, **53**, 70–85.

Wilson, C. O. (1931). A study of laughter situations among young children. Unpublished doctoral dissertation, University of Nebraska.

Zelazo, P. (1971). Smiling to social stimuli: eliciting and conditioning effects. *Developmental Psychology*, **4**, 32–42.

Zelazo, P. (1972). Smiling and vocalizing: a cognitive emphasis. *Merrill-Palmer Quarterly*, **18**, 349–365.

Zelazo, P., and Komer, M. (1971). Infant smiling to non-social stimuli and the recognition hypothesis. *Child Development*, **42**, 1327–1339.

Zigler, E., Levine J., and Gould, L. (1966). Cognitive processes in the development of children's humor appreciation. *Child Development*, **37**, 507–518.

Zigler, E., Levine, J., and Gould, L. (1967). Cognitive challenge as a factor in children's humor appreciation. *Journal of Personality and Social Psychology*, **6**, 332–336.

Chapter 2

Incongruity, Problem-Solving and Laughter

Mary K. Rothbart

INTRODUCTION

Principles of incongruity and conflict have been frequently proposed as explanations for laughter and humour. The present paper explores the relation between incongruity appreciation and an individual's attempt to make sense of, or solve, an incongruity.

> Of man, it is observed by Homer, that he is the most wretched, and, by Addison and others, that he is the merriest animal in the whole creation; and both opinions are plausible and both perhaps may be true. If, from the acuteness and delicacy of his perceptive powers, from his remembrance of the past, and his anticipation of what is to come, from his restless and creative fancy, and from the various sensibilities of his moral nature, man be exposed to many evils, both imaginary and real, from which the brutes are exempted, he does also from the same source derive innumerable delights, that are far beyond the reach of every other animal (Beattie, 1776, p. 321)

Although 200 years have passed since James Beattie proposed a link between distress and laughter, we have only just begun to test and incorporate similar ideas in our present-day models of the laughter process. Twentieth-century psychologists of humour may find it both informative and humbling to review some of the dimensions Beattie identified as important to the expression of laughter, a few examples being the following:

Incongruity: 'Laughter arises from the view of two or more inconsistent, unsuitable, or incongruous parts or circumstances, considered as united in one complex object or assemblage, or as acquiring a sort of mutual relation from the peculiar manner in which the mind takes notice of them' (Beattie, 1776, p. 348).

Intensity: '... the greater the number of incongruities that are blended in the same assemblage, the more ludicrous it will probably be' (p. 349).

Sympathy: 'While the moral faculty is inactive or neuter, the ludicrous sentiment may operate; but to have a sense of the enormity of a crime, and at the same time to laugh at it, seems impossible, or at least unnatural' (p. 426).

Fear: 'To conceal one's fear, one may feign a laugh ... but nobody laughs at that which makes him seriously afraid, however incongruous its appearance may be' (p. 432).

Socialization: 'Good breeding lays many restraints upon laughter, and upon all other emotions that display themselves externally' (p. 433).

World politics: 'All the nations of Europe, and perhaps all the nations on earth, are, in some particulars of dress or deportment, mutually ridiculous to one another' (p. 420).

To Beattie's credit, three of the chapters in the present volume contain the word 'incongruity' in the title, and numerous theorists of laughter and humour have used an incongruity principle to define a laughter- and humour-producing situation (cf. Berlyne, 1969; Shultz, 1972). Theories of laughter and humour based on an individual's experience of surprise or incongruity have been especially useful to observers of laughter and humour in children. We expect that an infant or young child will find different stimuli to be more incongruous or surprising than will older children or adults, making possible both (a) developmental predictions about the probable occurrence of laughter and smiling and (b) the use of laughter and smiling as indices of the existence of a child's expectations (McGhee, 1971; Rothbart, 1973).

A MODEL FOR LAUGHTER

As helpful as the concept of incongruity may be to our developing understanding of laughter and humour, however, there remains a major obstacle to the use of incongruity as an explanatory principle: although perception of an incongruous or unexpected event may lead to laughter, perception of an unexpected event may also lead to fear (Hebb, 1946), curiosity (Berlyne, 1960), problem-solving, or concept learning (Hunt, 1963). In a review paper (Rothbart, 1973) this author attempted to identify situational conditions differentiating laughter from distress as responses to the perception of incongruous stimuli. A revised version of this model developed in response to helpful criticisms from Susan Harter of Yale University is illustrated in Figure 2.1.

Briefly, this model proposes that when an individual attends to sudden, intense, or incongruous stimulation, several judgements will be related to whether he or she will laugh: (1) Is the stimulus dangerous?; (2) Is the stimulus evaluated as a serious challenge to the person's knowledge or is it seen as playful or inconsequential?; (3) Can the incongruity be resolved? Extremely sudden, intense, or highly incongruous stimuli, or stimuli judged to be dangerous, are likely to lead to expressive reactions of distress and behavioural reactions of avoidance or aggression. Incongruities experienced in a safe or playful setting are likely to lead to expressive reactions of pleasure and possible behavioural reactions of approach. Resolution of the incongruity, either within the context of a joke (Shultz, 1972) or in an achievement setting (Harter, 1973), may lead to smiling and laughter. Failure to resolve the incongruity in the joking situation leads to perplexity or confusion and no smiling or laughter. This model has been derived from the theoretical positions of Spencer (1860), Berlyne (1960, 1969), Hebb (1955), Sokolov (1963) and Schneirla (1959), among others, and from the

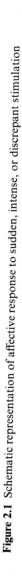

Figure 2.1 Schematic representation of affective response to sudden, intense, or discrepant stimulation

empirical findings of early observers of child laughter. The model has found support in recent findings of Sroufe and Wunsch (1972).

The *arousal-safety model* has its clearest application to instances of laughter in young children. Children under the age of two laugh at *incongruous sights*: the mother shaking her hair or crawling about the room on her hands and knees; *incongruous sounds*: the mother making lip-popping and 'horse sounds'; and *tactile stimulation*: the mother blowing and pecking at the baby's bare stomach (Sroufe and Wunsch, 1972). This author has suggested (Rothbart, 1973) that whether the child will laugh at these antics depends on (a) who is performing them, with a 'safe' and familiar parent being more likely than a stranger to evoke laughter in an older infant, (b) the familiarity or strangeness of the situation, (c) the state of the child—whether ill or fatigued or feeling alert and well—and (d) individual differences in reactivity to the stimulation.

One interesting aspect of the model is that it emphasizes the difficulty of differentiating fear stimuli from laughter stimuli without further information about the situation and state of the individual. A stimulus used for evoking fear in one situation, such as the mask in Scarr and Salapatek's (1970) study of fear development, has been used in another context (Sroufe and Wunsch, 1972) to evoke laughter. The same action performed by a stranger and a familiar person toward a child may in the former case lead to crying and distress, in the latter case to laughter. Lewis and Brookes-Gunn (1973) created a situation in which a strange adult, a strange child, the child's mother, and the child's own reflection in a mirror approached an 8 to 18-month-old child. Each stimulus figure moved, or in the case of the mirror was carried, across a room until it was standing next to and touching the child. The degree of affect expressed by the child was related to the distance of the figure from the child: the closer the figure, the greater the affect. In addition, the direction of affect (positive or negative) appeared to be related to the familiarity and the size of the person or image. Strange adults elicited crying and distress when they reached the child; the strange child elicited a moderately positive reaction of smiling and some laughter, while the child's mother and the image of the child in the mirror elicited distinct expressions of laughter and pleasure.

These findings suggest that rather than labelling a stimulus as a fear stimulus or a laughter stimulus, it may instead be located on a continuum of surprise, suddenness or intensity, and related to the state of the child and the characteristics of the situation before reactions of laughter or fear are predicted. The close relation of fear and laughter may be observed in a young child on a swing. When the swing is pulled back, the child's eyes are open wide in an expression of apprehension or fear. As the trajectory of the swing proceeds forward and then back again, the child may be seen to be laughing heartily. Adult laughter to the shock of a roller-coaster or a carnival house-of-horrors are similar phenomena.

Blurton Jones (1972) has found laughter to be a highly reliable behavioural marker for the cluster of activities identified among nursery school children as rough-and-tumble play: wrestling, running, chasing, and so on. He also reports (Blurton Jones, 1969) that a child laughing while being chased by another child may suddenly develop a fearful expression. The sound of laughter is then replaced by screaming and distress; we may speculate that the child has adjudged the rough-and-tumble play situation to be no longer safe, or that the arousal level of the child has been raised above his or her tolerance in the situation.

The close relation of laughter and distress suggests the hypothesis that stimuli effective in evoking fear may also be effective in evoking laughter. Lewis and Brookes-Gunn's (1972) study shows the effectiveness of size and familiarity as factors. We might also predict that movement of the stimulus, especially unpredictable movement, would be related to the production of laughter or fear.

Applying the model to laughter and humour of older children and adults is more difficult. Numerous theorists, most recently Koestler (1964), Shultz (1972), and Suls (1972), have analysed the appreciation of jokes as a problem-solving process. The clearest example of problem-solving in humour is the riddle. The joke in riddle form is quite simply posed as a problem: Why did the elephant sit on the marshmallow? How do you catch a rabbit? What goes up white and comes down yellow? (Answers: Because he didn't want to fall into the hot chocolate. Hide in the bushes and make noises like a carrot. An egg.) Jokes in anecdote form also pose problems or raise incongruities. We may analyse one anecdote as an example: *Teacher* 'Use the word "fascinate" in a sentence'. *Child* 'There are ten buttons on my coat, but I can only fasten eight'. The teacher's request prepares us for the word 'fascinate', which we hear, but the word is misrepresented in the child's sentence. The incongruity is resolved in the joke when we recognize that 'fasten eight' is a homophone for 'fascinate.' Understanding the joke requires that (a) we recognize the joke as raising a problem for us to solve and (b) we recognize the phonological ambiguity between 'fascinate' and 'fasten eight'.

I have suggested, however, that application of the model to the humour in jokes is a difficult task. Where does the difficulty lie, if jokes may be interpreted as problem solutions? The 'fascinate' anecdote was deliberately chosen to allow a clear-cut resolution of incongruity, but incongruity solutions of jokes seldom represent complete problem solutions of the sort encountered in the real world. Rules of logic and our knowledge of reality are rarely entirely satisfied by a joke 'solution'. Although it is possible to recount jokes corresponding to real-life situations such as the 'fascinate' anecdote, in which understanding the joke completely resolves the challenge to our knowledge posed by the joke, this is often not the case. Consider, for example, the elephant-on-a-marshmallow riddle. The 'solution' given in the correct answer to the riddle combines our knowledge (a) that when drowning threatens we will seek refuge on a floating object and (b) that marshmallows float in cups of hot chocolate into a creative *'Aha'* experience. Of course, the elephant is sitting on the marshmallow to keep from drowning. Nevertheless, even after 'solving' the joke, we are left with an elephant adrift on a marshmallow, a situation that must surely challenge any knowledge of elephants and hot chocolate we may possess.

Thus, although we may resolve one or more incongruities in a joke in order to understand or 'get' the joke, additional incongruities or discrepancies with reality may remain. For laughter to occur, the communication that *this is a joke*, or *this is for fun*, thus becomes extremely important. Solving problems in the context of a joke frequently involves solving an incongruity at one level of the joke while suspending our problem-solving faculties at a second level and enjoying the remaining incongruity.

This discussion has, however, extended substantially beyond the research to be presented here. The present chapter reports research attempting to explore the relation between perception of an incongruity and problem-solving. If a child laughs at an incongruity (i.e. at a mismatch or conflict between what he or she expects and in fact experiences), will that child also be likely to attempt to resolve the incongruity and 'make sense' of it? An exploratory study was initially performed attempting to investigate the relation between laughter and problem-solving. When a child experiences an incongruous but non-dangerous event, do expressions of positive affect reliably precede attempts to make sense of the discrepancy? It was hypothesized that both laughter and problem-solving would occur when a child was most sensitive to an incongruity, and hence that children who laughed more at a discrepant event would also be more likely to attempt to 'solve' the discrepancy than children who laughed less.

A second purpose of the study was to consider McGhee's (1971) proposal than perception of an incongruity in itself leads only to mild amusement, not to vigorous laughter. McGhee proposed that an additional element of sex or aggression is necessary for strong laughter to occur. To test this hypothesis, an attempt was made to create an unexpected event without explicit or implicit aggressive or sexual content and to see whether laughter would occur in children. The study thus attempted to discover whether the perception of a simple discrepancy between a child's expectancy and his or her experience would lead to laughter, and whether laughter would be correlated with the child's attempt to cope with the discrepant information, that is, to engage in problem-solving.

To investigate these questions, it was necessary to identify a concept that undergoes developmental change in children, is readily measurable and is suitable for presentation in a situation where a child might laugh. The concept of conservation of liquid quantity was chosen as satisfying all these requirements. Although non-conserving children might expect liquid quantity to remain constant, they would also be surprised to see that pouring liquid from a container of one size to a container of another size appears to change the amount of liquid presented. For example, Bruner, Olver and Greenfield (1966) reported that young children identified as non-conservers by the usual Piagetian tests predicted correctly that the amount of water transferred from a short, wide glass to a tall, thin glass remains the same, but they could do so *only* when the second glass remained hidden behind a screen. When these children witnessed the actual transfer, their perception of differing water levels in the two glasses appeared to convince them that the amount of water had changed. It was thus predicted that, when non-conserving children are presented with water transfer from a short, wide jar to a tall, thin jar, there would exist a discrepancy between their expectancy that the amount of water *should* remain the same, and their perception that the amount of water appeared to have changed. The incongruity would be made more salient, possibly leading to laughter, if the person performing the transfer reported that she was performing a magic trick, changing a small amount of water into a large amount of water.

STUDY I

It was hypothesized that (a) children who had attained the concept of conservation of liquid quantity would see no discrepancy between observed water levels and their expectations, thus showing less laughter and smiling at a presentation of a water transfer 'trick' than non-conservers, and (b) older non-conservers, presumably expecting more strongly that the quantity should remain the same and hence more sensitive to the discrepancy, would be more likely to smile and laugh at the trick than younger non-conservers.

Subjects

Subjects were fifteen $4\frac{1}{2}$–5-year-old nursery school children (six girls and nine boys; mean age, 56·04 months) and nineteen $5\frac{1}{2}$–6-year-old kindergarten children (eight girls and eleven boys; mean age, 68·50 months). With the exception of one black child in each group, children came from white, predominantly middle-class homes in Eugene, Oregon.

Procedure

Subjects were observed individually in two sessions, held seven days apart. During Session 1, children were exposed to five different laughter presentations concluding with the water transfer 'magic' trick. In Session 2, children were given tests of conservation of liquid quantity, using both clay and water materials. (The study was originally designed with the conservation tests to be presented first, but it was found that making conservation judgements established such a serious set for the children in the study room that it was difficult to induce laughter in the second session.)

Session 1. Four different laughter stimuli preceded the water transfer presentation in the first session in order to establish the situation as a comfortable one for the child (with laughter a permissible response), and in order to determine whether one age-group of children might be laughing more than another age-group to all laughter stimuli, rather than just to the water transfer. Children were approached individually by a female experimenter and asked, 'I have some things to show you and tell you that I think you might like. Would you like to come with me?' The child then accompanied the experimenter to an adjacent room, where five laughter presentations were made for the child. (1) The experimenter applied the child's name to a nonsense formula, asking the child first, 'Would you like to have your name turned into a silly name?' Examples of the silly names given are: 'Billy, Billy, Bofilly, Banana fana momana,' and 'Kristen, Kristen, Bofisten, Banana fana momana'. (2) The experimenter asked 'Now would you like to have me count for you in a silly way? Put both your hands out on the table and I will count your fingers'. The experimenter then counted, 'Onery, twoery, ickery Ann, fillason, follason, Nicholas, John, queavy, quavy, Irish navy'. (3) The experimenter told the child an elaborate story about the biggest man in the whole world chopping down the biggest tree in the world, which fell into the biggest sea in the whole world, concluding with the question, 'Can you imagine what a big splash that would be?' (4) The child was shown a Jack-in-the-box, operated by a button, with a plastic duck on top that bounced off whenever the box opened. The Jack-in-the-box was presented four times, twice with the experimenter pushing the button and twice with the child pushing the button. (5) The water transfer was presented to the child. The experimenter said, 'Now, I'm going to show you a magic trick. Watch closely and I will turn a little water into a lot of water'. The experimenter then poured the water from a short, wide jar into a tall, thin jar. When this was done and the child's reactions recorded, the experimenter asked, 'Now would you like me to turn a lot of water back into a little water?' After this trial the experimenter asked, 'Shall I do it again?' The water transfer was repeated up to five times if the child desired it.

The child's reactions to each of the presentations were recorded by the experimenter and scored according to the following categories: *serious* = 0; *partial smile* (corners of mouth turned up) = 1; *full smile* = 2; *laugh* = 3 (smile with vocalization). Before beginning the study, the experimenter and a second coder observed pre-test subjects responding to the laughter presentations described above. Agreement between the two coders was good, with exact agreement for 80% of the 35 ratings, and agreement within one rating point for 97% of the ratings. An initial attempt to differentiate between a laugh and a prolonged laugh was not reliable and these two categories were combined. *Session* 2. One week after presentation of the laughter stimuli, children were tested for conservation of liquid quantity by a second female experimenter. Both clay and water materials were used. Procedures used by Gelman (1969) were followed: subjects were designated as conservers on the two tasks if they gave both conserving answers and explanations to the experimenter's questions.

Results and discussion

None of the $4\frac{1}{2}$–5-year-olds gave conserving responses on the tests for conservation of liquid quantity; five of the nineteen $5\frac{1}{2}$–6-year-olds gave conserving responses on the water test, and three of the five conserved on both clay and water tests. It was thus possible to test for differences between conservers and non-conservers within a single age-group on their response to the water transfer trick. Although the author recognizes that objections may be raised to using parametric analyses for rating data, investigators (e.g. Zigler, Levine and Gould, 1967; Shultz, 1972) have traditionally used parametric analyses. Further, McNemar's argument (1962) that although interval scales are rarely attained in psychological research, parametric statistics will follow their theoretical sampling distributions when score distributions are not markedly discrepant from normality, is persuasive to the author.

There were no differences between responses of $5\frac{1}{2}$–6-year-old conservers and nonconservers to the first four laughter situations, suggesting that there were no overall differences in tendency to laugh between conservers and non-conservers. For the water transfer, however, the non-conservers laughed more on the first trial ($t = 3\cdot88$, $df = 17$, $p < 0\cdot01$), had a higher mean laughter score over all repetitions of the trick ($t = 6\cdot10$, $df = 17$, $p < 0\cdot001$) and asked to have the trick repeated more times ($t = 4\cdot08$, $df = 17$, $p < 0\cdot001$) than did the conservers (see Table 2.1).

Table 2.1 Means and standard deviations of laughter scores for $5\frac{1}{2}$–6-year-old conservers and non-conservers

	Silly name		Nonsense counting		Story		Jack-in-the-box		Water transfer	
	M	SD	M	SD	M	SD	M	SD	M	SD
Non-conservers ($N = 14$)	2·71	0·49	2·71	0·47	1·86	0·77	9·43	1·60	2·07	0·90
Conservers ($N = 5$)	3·00	0·00	2·60	0·89	2·40	0·55	8·80	2·05	0·40	0·77

Two of the children who were identified later as conservers stated, 'That's not a trick', and a third child who apparently solved the trick after observing it being repeated, said, 'I can see how kids might think that was a trick, but I don't'. The other two conserving children made no comment, but did not wish to see the trick repeated.

The finding that non-conserving children laughed more at the water transfer trick than children giving conserving responses on tests of liquid quantity gives support to the discrepancy hypothesis and calls into question McGhee's proposal that an element of sex or aggression is needed for hearty laughter to occur.[1] The mean affect score for non-conservers fell between a full smile and a laugh. Hearty laughter on the first trial was common, especially for the $4\frac{1}{2}$–5-year-olds, accompanied often by appreciative comments including, 'That's really magic', 'You're really a good magician', 'That's weird', and 'Tell me how you did it'. The difference between conservers and non-conservers in laughter to the water trick was not due to a generally greater tendency for non-conservers to laugh; no differences were found between the groups on the first four laughter measures. McGhee's failure to find strong laughter in children's responses to fairly neutral cartoons may have resulted in part from the highly judgemental task given to children in his studies, a problem addressed later in this chapter.

The other hypothesis tested was that older non-conservers, presumably more sensitive to the discrepancy as a result of more experience with conservation of liquid quantity, would laugh more at the water transfer than younger non-conservers. This hypothesis was not supported: no significant differences were found between older and younger non-conservers on laughter at the water trick. Two-way analyses of variance were performed for non-conservers' responses to all laughter situations in an Age × Sex analysis (see Table 2.2).

Table 2.2 Means and standard deviations of laughter scores for $4\frac{1}{2}$–5-year-old and $5\frac{1}{2}$–6-year-old non-conservers

| | $4\frac{1}{2}$–5 years | | | | $5\frac{1}{2}$–6 years | | | |
| | Girls ($N=9$) | Boys ($N=6$) | | | Girls ($N=8$) | Boys ($N=11$) | | |
	M	SD	M	SD	M	SD	M	SD
Silly name	2·00	1·10	2·11	1·05	2·71	0·49	2·71	0·49
Nonsense counting	2·50	1·23	2·22	0·83	2·57	0·53	2·89	0·38
Story	1·83	0·75	1·22	0·97	2·00	0·82	1·71	0·76
Jack-in-the-box	7·50	1·28	7·55	2·13	9·86	1·11	9·10	2·04
Water transfer	2·33	1·21	2·55	0·73	2·14	1·18	2·00	0·82

If there were a general trend towards laughter for the first four presentations, it was for the older children to laugh more; these age differences were significant for the silly name ($F = 5·17$, $df = 1/25$, $p < 0·05$) and the Jack-in-the-box ($F = 5·30$, $df = 1/25$, $p < 0·05$). The direction of differences was reversed, however, for the water trick, with the younger children showing a numerically higher but not significantly different mean score.

Moreover, there was some evidence to suggest that the younger non-conservers were laughing more to the trick than older non-conservers. In conducting pre-tests for the study, the experimenter in Session 1 had noted differences in the quality of some children's laughter to the water transfer trick. Some children laughed during the water transfer, showing direct appreciation for the trick; others looked at the water transfer, then turned and directed laughter and smiling to the experimenter. A record was therefore made of the direction of each child's laughter in the first session, and an analysis performed relating age of non-conserver to whether the child laughed at the trick or to the experimenter. In this analysis, younger children were more likely to laugh directly at the trick and older children to the experimenter, although the results were not statistically significant ($p = 0·057$, exact test).

Contrary to expectation, laughter directed toward the trick thus appeared to be more likely for younger non-conservers than for older non-conservers, and children seemed more likely to laugh when they accepted the trick as resulting from the 'magic' of the experimenter, rather than viewing the trick as a problem to be solved. Laughter to the experimenter may have been more likely to occur when the child was trying to understand the discrepant event but could not (nervous laughter); this interpretation was not testable within the present study.

Finally, smiling or laughter may have occurred after a child felt he or she had solved the trick: of four older children who announced in the course of Session 1 that they had solved the trick (only one of whom was later designated a conserver), three children laughed or smiled immediately before making this announcement. Harter's research on problem-solving and laughter (1973) indicated clearly that children express positive affect after problem-solving and that more positive affect is shown after the achievement of solutions requiring more effort.

Laughter at the water trick thus may have been likely if the incongruity was recognized but accepted as an inconsequential event, as something 'for fun'. Although the conservers in this study might also have been expected to experience a discrepancy (i.e. the discrepancy between expecting a trick to occur and seeing no trick at all), the lack of a playful or humorous context for their experience of discrepancy in all likelihood prevented laughter and smiling. If the experimenter had been introduced as a clown who always failed in what she did, the failure of the trick might have led to more laughter from the conservers than from the non-conservers.

Intercorrelations of laughter measures give some support to the view that some older non-conservers showed a different kind of laughter to the water trick than younger non-conservers. For younger non-conservers, laughing at the water transfer correlated highly with laughter at the silly name, the nonsense counting and the Jack-in-the-box (see Table 2.3). For older non-conservers, laughter at the water transfer did *not* correlate with laughter at the silly name, with nonsense counting or with the Jack-in-the-box, even though these last three measures correlated with each other. Measures of laughter to the story failed to correlate positively with the other laughter measures. The story was generally received as a question being directed to the child, 'Can you imagine what a big splash that would be?', rather than as a humorous story.

Table 2.3 Intercorrelations among laughter measures for 4½–5-year-old and 5½–6-year-old non-conservers

	Silly name	Nonsense counting	Story	Jack-in-the-box	Water trick
Silly name		0·47	−0·27	0·61*	0·80**
Nonsense counting	0·65*		−0·11	0·77**	0·77**
Story	−0·32	−0·12		−0·18	0·70**
Jack-in-the box	0·58*	0·58*	−0·25		0·06
Water trick	−0·16	0·06	−0·09	0·42	

*$p < 0.05$
**$p < 0.01$

Coefficients for 4½–5-year-olds are above the diagonal.
Coefficients for 5½–6-year-olds are below the diagonal.

Stability measures for the responses of 18 children available for a second testing were obtained for situations involving the silly name, nonsense counting and the Jack-in-the-box. The repeated measures were made three months after the initial session and differed from the first session only in omission of the duck from the Jack-in-the-box. Product moment correlations for subjects on the repeated measures were $r = 0.45$ ($p < 0.05$, $df = 16$) for the silly name, $r = 0.14$ (ns.) for the nonsense counting, and $r = 0.61$ ($p < 0.01$, $df = 16$) for the Jack-in-the-box.

The low stability correlations for the silly name and nonsense counting responses in the study were probably due in part to the narrow range of scores on these measures. The correlations may also reflect individual differences in hearing the same joke for the second time. Some children who did not see the words and counting as silly on the first presentation may have found them amusing on the second presentation, and children who laughed at the first presentation may have become bored when it was repeated a second time. The greater stability of the Jack-in-the-box scores probably resulted from the vigorous and sudden action of the Jack-in-the-box, which was likely to be amusing during the second session even to the children who had laughed at it before. Fairly high intercorrelations of quite different laughter situations suggest that individual differences in smiling and laughter thresholds (humour appreciation) may be a good subject for future research.

Since the results of this exploratory study were contrary to the second hypothesis, the possibility of more than one discrepancy existed; and the size of sample was small, so a second study was designed to test more directly the relation between positive affect to an incongruous stimulus and problem-solving.

STUDY II

In an attempt to study the effects of incongruity-resolution on children's expressions of smiling and laughter and humour judgements, an additional group of 32 $5\frac{1}{2}$–6-year-old children were shown pictures containing visual incongruities. Descriptions of pictures by the experimenter took the form of either (a) indicating the visual incongruity or (b) indicating the incongruity and at the same time explaining how it might really have happened.

Subjects

Subjects were 16 girls and 16 boys from two kindergarten classes in Eugene, Oregon. Since the study was run in the Spring term, most children were 6 years of age or older. All children available from both kindergarten classes were used in the study.

Materials

Twelve pictures involving visual incongruities were drawn by an artist and pre-tested with 20 4–6-year-old children. From the original selection of pictures, eight were chosen for the present experiment. The pictures included a bicycle with square wheels, a boy with an umbrella turned inside-out, a pumpkin with hands and feet and a girl in oversized shoes. Pre-test subjects were also asked for descriptions as to how the event in the pictures 'might really have happened'. Two descriptions were then written by the experimenters for each picture: one describing the incongruity (*Incongruity description*) and one explaining and resolving it (*Explanation description*). For example, the umbrella picture was described in the Incongruity condition as an upside-down umbrella; in the Explanation condition it was described as an umbrella the wind had turned inside-out. The pumpkin picture was described in the Incongruity condition as a pumpkin with arms and legs; in the Explanation condition it was described as a pumpkin so large a child could stand behind it and give it arms and legs.

Since each child could hear only one description of a given picture, children in the study saw half of the pictures with an Incongruity and half with an Explanation description, and two forms of the test were developed to test for effects of a particular set of pictures on children's responses. The first form thus included eight pictures assigned randomly to Incongruity or Explanation condition. The second form included the alternate descriptions of each picture. The order of presentation of pictures for each form was randomly determined, with the constraint that each block of four pictures contain two Incongruity and two Explanation descriptions. Eight boys and eight girls were randomly assigned to hear each of the two forms of the test. A three-way experimental design was thus created, comprising sex, form and instruction conditions, with sex and form of presentation as between-subjects factors and instruction as a within-subjects factor in the study.

Procedure

Each subject was tested by a female experimenter. Children were told the experimenter wished to find out the kinds of pictures children thought were funny. Some of the pictures might be funny and some of them not so funny. The child's reactions were scored according to the categories described earlier. Children were also asked to rate the pictures for funniness. They were first asked whether they thought the picture was funny or not funny. Then they were shown a sheet depicting two red squares, a larger one and a smaller one, and asked, 'Did you think it was a little funny (not funny) or a lot funny (not funny)?' When the experimenter said, 'a little bit (not) funny', she pointed to the smaller square, and when she said, 'a lot (not) funny', pointed to the larger square. This procedure allowed the experimenter to record the child's response on a scale from 1 to 4, with 4 the highest humour rating. Although almost all the children appeared to be comfortable in using this scale, one child attempted to use a neutral category unavailable to him in the scaling procedure. A 5-point scale would thus be a better technique for representing children's humour ratings.

Results

Predicted results of greater positive affect and humour for the Incongruity condition were found for both affect and humour rating measures (Table 2.4). No significant main effects nor interactions were found for sex of child or for form of test, while the Incongruity versus Explanation main effect was significant for expressions of smiling and laughter ($F = 40.27$, $df = 1/28$, $p < 0.001$) and for humour ratings ($F = 32.44$, $df = 1/28$, $p < 0.001$). The third-order interaction effect was also non-significant.

Table 2.4 Means and standard deviations of affect and humour ratings

| | Incongruity instructions | | | | Explanation instructions | | | |
| | Affect | | Humour | | Affect | | Humour | |
	M	SD	M	SD	M	SD	M	SD
Girls	6·38	3·52	11·62	2·19	4·56	3·37	9·19	2·17
Boys	5·56	3·72	11·56	1·67	4·06	3·47	9·62	2·31

DISCUSSION

Results of Study II are in agreement with prediction: children showed greater smiling and laughter and gave higher humour ratings when the incongruities were identified than when they were also explained. In a situation involving pictorial incongruities, problem-solving thus appeared to detract from, rather than enhance, humour appreciation.

It should also be noted that children appeared to show less smiling and laughter overall in Study II than in Study I. The mean affect rating per trial for the more humorous instruction condition, that of identifying the incongruity, was only 1·25, at the level of a slight smile. One factor possibly interfering with appreciation of the pictures may have been sympathy, or identification of the self with the object of humour. For example, children in both Incongruity and Explanation conditions showed very little smiling at the picture of the boy with the upturned umbrella. Children also told the experimenter, 'That's not funny', and frequently recounted their own troubles with umbrellas, saying, 'It's no fun getting wet'. It is quite possible that the wet climate of Oregon was related to the sympathy they felt for the child. Either sympathy or a feeling of threat to themselves may have played a role in inhibiting laughter to other pictures as well; for example, the bicycle with square tyres in the Explanation condition (where children were told the bicycle stood for so long that the tyres went square). The fact that children were depicted in the incongruous pictures may also have contributed to self-identification, inhibiting laughter and pleasure in cases where the incongruity could be identified as harmful to the child. For at least some children, simply making judgements about the funniness of the pictures may have detracted from the humour experience. Some children appeared to take the job very seriously, staring intently at the pictures before making humour judgements, and never showing even a smile. As in other observations of children's laughter (Rothbart, 1973), there were strong individual differences in children's reactions to these humour materials, with some children laughing throughout the session and others maintaining a continuously serious expression.

Apart from these hypotheses for possible future research, it will be helpful to consider the results of these studies in relation to McGhee's concepts of 'fantasy assimilation' and 'reality assimilation'. McGhee suggests that, 'The child perceives expectancy violations as being funny only when he has acquired a stable enough conceptual grasp of the real world that he can assimilate the disconfirmed expectancy as being only a play on reality' (McGhee, 1971)—the condition of 'fantasy assimilation'. 'Prior to the achievement of such conceptual mastery over the environment, an effort will be made to incorporate the new stimulus into relevant schemas the child has developed; that is, "reality assimilation" will occur' (McGhee, 1971).

According to McGhee (1972), a true humour response requires: (1) a concept, (2) awareness that the stimulus violates the concept and (3) 'confidence in the impossibility or improbability of the stimulus elements occurring as depicted' (p. 66). The Explanation condition of Study II appears to impose reality assimilation upon material requiring only fantasy assimilation for appreciation, thereby reducing children's enjoyment of the incongruities.

We might thus consider the use of the term 'fantasy assimilation' for all instances of humour and laughter where problem resolution does not occur. However, children frequently laugh at simple real-life visual incongruities, as when another child sets a pot on his head or makes a funny face. In these situations, fantasy in the sense of unreality is not involved, although there is frequently an attitude of playfulness and the message 'this is for fun' is communicated among participants in the situation. Similarly, there are unresolved incidents involving reality, not fantasy, that we find humorous. In the following anecdote, a jokester has embroidered on what might be a humorous real-life situation: puffing and red-faced, the man sprints down the ramp and makes a flying leap for the rail of the ferry. With a superhuman effort, he pulls himself aboard. 'No need for all that', says the attendant, 'She's just pulling in.' What seems to constitute humour in response to this joke is the condition that there is nothing more that can be done about the deflating outcome: our exaggerated expectation has simply come to nothing.

In the case of visual incongruities or jokes, the humorous or playful context becomes important in communicating that the incongruity is not really a problem but is intended for enjoyment. When humorous material is presented for entertainment, context is extremely important. The identification of a book as fiction, the presentation of action with animated cartoon or puppet characters, or clearly staged plays or films, convinces us at the outset that the problems are not really problems and we should not attempt to solve them in the ordinary way. The man and the ferry boat situation is a real-life counterpart of the entertainment condition: there is nothing more for the man to do who has taken the great leap (or for those who have witnessed it) but to laugh. Any further action would not change the situation in any important way; the event is at this point inconsequential. Fantasy assimilation is thus only one case of humour to unresolved incongruity, but in all cases of incongruity humour the remaining incongruity is for a variety of reasons *not* viewed as a problem to be solved. Viewed in the context of the model presented above, laughter may occur when an arousing stimulus is judged to be safe, when a problem is solved, or when an incongruity or improbable act has occurred and we can do nothing about it. The most frequent occurrence of the latter condition is in a joking or playful situation, when incongruities may not be fully resolved.

Incongruity resolution or problem-solving thus appears to play an equivocal role in a humorous outcome. In the context of a joke, incongruity resolution may be essential to humour: in other cases, such as the perception of visual incongruities in the present study, resolution may interfere with humour appreciation. Even when problem-solving occurs within a joke, the solution is rarely one that would be adequate to solution of a real-life problem.

Freud (1960) has suggested that taking pleasure in nonsense allows an adult to take leave of the rules of logic and constraints of rationality usually influencing his or her thought and to think again as a child. Within the joking or humorous situation, a person can take pleasure in the sound and rhythm of nonsense words, can accept an incongruity without making complete sense of it and can indeed suspend to a greater or lesser extent the rules of logic and rational thought.

SUMMARY AND CONCLUSIONS

Results of the present studies suggest that for laughter to occur following the perception of simple visual incongruities, the incongruities should not be interpreted as problems to be solved. Instead they should be represented as something outside the problem-solving sphere: something for entertainment, play or fun. The joking, playful or humorous context also allows adults to take pleasure in unresolved incongruities, as well as achieving pleasure through the mastery of 'solving' jokes.

NOTE

1. The author may have misinterpreted McGhee on this point. In a personal communication (1974) he has indicated that emotionally salient materials might be expected to result only in higher levels of affect; laughter is not thereby precluded for purely incongruous stimuli.

ACKNOWLEDGEMENTS

This research was supported by National Institutes of Health Special Fellowship No. 1 F03 HD 49722-01 from the Institute of Child Health and Human Development. The author wishes to acknowledge Benson Schaeffer and Ray Hyman for their generous help in designing the exploratory research, Martha Neighbor and Peter Weinrobe for acting as experimenters, Paul McGhee for his helpful criticisms of an early draft of the chapter, and the nursery schools and kindergartens of Eugene, Oregon, for providing subjects for the research.

REFERENCES

Beattie, J. (1776). On laughter and ludicrous composition. In *Essays*. Edinburgh: Creech

Berlyne, D. E. (1960). *Conflict, Arousal and Curiosity*. New York: McGraw–Hill.

Berlyne, D. E. (1969). Laughter, humor and play. In G. Lindzey and E. Aronson (Eds.), *Handbook of Social Psychology*, Vol. 3. Reading, Massachusetts: Addison–Wesley.

Blurton Jones, N. G. (1969). An ethological study of some aspects of social behaviour of children in nursery school. In D. Morris (Ed.), *Primate Ethology*. New York: Doubleday.

Blurton Jones, N. G. (1972). Categories of child–child interaction. In N. G. Blurton Jones (Ed.), *Ethological Studies of Child Behaviour*. Cambridge: Cambridge University Press.

Bruner, J. S., Olver, R., and Greenfield, P. M. (1966). *Studies in Cognitive Growth*. New York: Wiley.

Freud, S. (1960). *Jokes and Their Relation to The Unconscious*. (Translation by J. Strachey). New York: Norton (Original German edition, 1905.)

Gelman, R. (1969). Conservation acquisition: a problem of learning to attend to relevant attributes. *Journal of Experimental Child Psychology*, 7, 167–187.

Harter, S. (1973). Pleasure derived by children from cognitive challenge and mastery. Unpublished manuscript, Yale University.

Hebb, D. O. (1946). On the nature of fear. *Psychological Review*, 53, 259–276.

Hebb, D. O. (1955). Drives and the C. N. S. (Conceptual Nervous System). *Psychological Review*, 62, 243–254.

Hunt, J. McV. (1963). Motivation inherent in information processing and action. In O. J. Harvey (Ed.), *Motivation and Social Interaction*. New York: Ronald.

Koestler, A. (1964). *The Act of Creation*. New York: Macmillan.

Lewis, M., and Brookes-Gunn, J. (1972). Self, other, and fear: the reaction of infants to people. Paper presented at the meeting of the Eastern Psychological Association, Boston.

McGhee, P. E. (1971). Development of the humor response: a review of the literature. *Psychological Bulletin*, 76, 328–348.

McGhee, P. E. (1972). On the cognitive origins of incongruity humor: fantasy assimilation versus reality assimilation. In J. H. Goldstein and P. E. McGhee (Eds.), *The Psychology of Humor*. New York: Academic Press.

McNemar, Q. (1962). *Psychological Statistics*. New York: Wiley.

Rothbart, M. K. (1973). Laughter in young children. *Psychological Bulletin*, 80, 247–256.

Scarr, S., and Salapatek, P. (1970). Patterns of fear development during infancy. *Merrill-Palmer Quarterly*, 16, 53–87.

Schneirla, T. C. (1959). An evolutionary and developmental theory of biphasic processes underlying approach and withdrawal. In M. R. Jones (Ed.), *Nebraska Symposium on Motivation*: 1959. Lincoln: University of Nebraska Press.

Shultz, T. R. (1972). The role of incongruity and resolution in children's appreciation of cartoon humor. *Journal of Experimental Child Psychology*, 13, 456–477.

Sokolov, Y. N. (1963). *Perception and The Conditioned Reflex*. (Translation by S. Waydenfeld). New York: Pergamon. (Original Soviet edition, 1958.) 1, 395–402.

Spencer, H. (1860). Physiology of laughter. *Macmillan's Magazine*, 1,395. (Reprinted: *Essays, Scientific, political and speculative*. Vol. 2. New York: Appleton, 1910).

Sroufe, L. A., and Wunsch, J. C. (1972). The development of laughter in the first year of life. *Child Development*, 43, 1326–1344.

Suls, J. M. (1972). A two-stage model for the appreciation of jokes and cartoons: an information-processing analysis. In J. H. Goldstein and P. E. McGhee (Eds.), *The Psychology of Humor*. New York: Academic Press.

Zigler, E., Levine, J., and Gould, L. (1967). Cognitive challenge as a factor in children's humor appreciation. *Journal of Personality and Social Psychology*, **6**, 332–336.

Chapter 3

Incongruity and Funniness: Towards a New Descriptive Model

Göran Nerhardt

Incongruity humour theory directs attention towards stimulus variables amongst which is similarity–dissimilarity. Historically the concept of incongruity is ancient but its constituents appear not to have been explicitly recognized until the time of Joseph Addison and David Hartley (cf. Piddington, 1963). Addison, in answering John Locke, said that resemblance and opposition are what may call forth laughter in response to wit. Hartley mentions similarities and differences in connection with what is funny.

Incongruity is seen by this author as a necessary ingredient for funniness. Laughter, for example, does not strictly deserve the designation 'laughter at the funny' unless the presence of incongruous elements can be inferred. In addition there are several facilitating and inhibiting variables: emotional, motivational and cognitive states, some stimulus induced, some not. Some variables may facilitate laughter in the absence of a funny stimulus, while others may inhibit completely any kind of laughter.

In addition to 'incongruity', the terms 'laughter', 'smiling', 'funniness' and 'humour' are used in this chapter. Funniness is used to denote the variable which enables the experimenter to discriminate between potentially incongruous stimuli on the basis of subjects' laughter, smiling or verbal labelling in response to them. The term humour is used to denote the funniness of complex stimuli: a single, sudden change in temperature, though experienced as funny, would not be called humorous. As far as laughter and smiling are concerned, most authors agree that they are fundamentally expressions of the same affective states.

This chapter reviews some experimental work representing achievements in the field of incongruity humour; it introduces a theoretical model; and it summarizes some new studies derived from the model.

EARLY RESEARCH

Though there has been much theorizing on the subject of incongruity as a source of funniness, only a few experimental studies have been carried out.

Ideally experiments should contain indicants of incongruity as independent variables, and responses defining funniness as dependent variables. These requirements were met in a study by Mull (1949) where subjects indicated which passages in two pieces of music they experienced as humorous. The passages could be characterized in terms of degree of contrast in timbre, intensity, pitch, rhythm, complexity and so on. Kenny (1955) set out to test incongruity theory by manipulating the degree of expectedness of joke endings. Since subjects were presented with jokes and were therefore expecting incongruity, Kenny was in fact confounding discrepancy from most *predictable* 'divergence from expectations' with 'divergence from expectations'.

Most relevant to the problem area is research on exploration and the orientation reaction. Berlyne (1960) has explained both motivation for specific exploration and laughter in terms of increments and decrements in arousal (i.e. 'arousal–jags'). A jag appears in connection with new stimuli. It is rewarding, it motivates exploration, and it constitutes a neurological concomitant of humour. Lewis and Harwitz (1969) argued that smiling by children satisfies the criteria of an orienting reflex. They presented the same picture of randomly placed straight lines six times to children. On the seventh trial the stimulus picture contained one of four alterations. They found a decrement in duration of smiling with successive presentations of the first stimulus and a recovery at the presentation of the altered stimulus. Of course, exposure to the altered picture is a violation of the expectancies built up during the preceding trials.

In a study not previously published the present author tested the prediction that relatively high frequencies of laughter and/or smiling would be associated with stimuli having unexpected qualities. Male and female adults ($N = 815$) passing through two underground stations in Stockholm were asked to lift a suitcase varying in weight and to judge its heaviness. A range of expectancy was defined as weights of the suitcase eliciting 'heavy' ratings from about half the subjects and 'light' ratings from the other half. It was predicted that laughter and smiling associated with lifting the suitcase would increase as the weight of it diverged from the range of expectancy, but the results did not coincide with this prediction. Even with the suitcase at weights of 5 kg and 25 kg (about whose heaviness there was complete agreement and almost complete agreement respectively) there was neither laughter nor smiling.

Why was this so? The most plausible explanation is that responses were inhibited because subjects did not believe laughter and smiling would be considered appropriate in connection with the task, and at the same time were inhibited through the subjects' motivational set to perform, which might activate competing responses. This is not to say that there was no laughter and smiling, but none occurred in response to the lifting of the suitcases. When there was laughter or smiling it was of a social nature, sometimes occurring after the completion of a trial when subjects might ask a question of the type, 'Is that all?' The occurrence of these types of social response does not, of course, mitigate against the explanation for the non-occurrence of laughter and smiling in the lifting task. It would be too hasty to conclude from this study that incongruity has nothing to do with laughter.

A related study supports the view that inhibiting variables were present (Nerhardt, 1970). In a private laboratory setting, psychology students who were experienced in acting as subjects were tested individually in the presence of the experimenter after a lengthy introductory phase designed to put them at their ease. With their eyes closed they lifted a series of weights having identical handles. Results confirmed the predicted relationship between frequency of laughter and divergence from range of expectancy, defined as before. Laughter and smiling occurred even for weights about whose heaviness there was not complete agreement amongst subjects. Other results were very similar to those of Lewis and Harwitz. Individual weights which did not initially elicit laughter or smiling did so when preceded by a series of dissimilar weights: the greater the contrast between an individual weight and the preceding range of weights, the higher the frequency of laughter.

OUTLINE OF A THEORETICAL MODEL

The following propositions, representing the author's conception of incongruity theory, are spelt out as precisely as possible. Points (1) to (12) lead up to the basic postulate [point (13)] about funniness as a function of divergence from expectations.

(1) For a person there exists a measure which will be called total, class-independent similarity. It is total because it applies to stimulus objects in their entirety. It is class-independent in the sense that it exists prior to any knowledge that the objects belong to the same class and because degrees of this similarity do not change as a consequence of the knowledge that they are classified together. If one thinks of images of stimuli being ordered in a space such that proximity between stimuli reflects this similarity, then there will be clusters, and clusters within clusters, of images in this space. Sometimes the relation between more than two stimuli can be described along a single dimension in this space, but the description may require a number of dimensions.

(2) Clusters aid in defining a person's classes, and stimuli within classes can be ordered in relation to a class type. As similarity to the class-type decreases, so stimuli generally occur less frequently [see Figure 3.1 (a)].

(3) A class is wide if there are members of low similarity to the class-type.

(4) If a person's total experience comprises only one stimulus or a limited number of stimuli which can form the basis for a class, a hypothetical class will form around them having the same general distribution of similarity as would form had more stimuli been experienced. The limited number of stimuli will represent the most frequent degree of similarity with class-type and, if there is only one stimulus, then this will approximate the class-type.

(5) The probability of a perceived stimulus being referred to a psychologically highly available class [see point (6)] normally increases as its degree of similarity

58

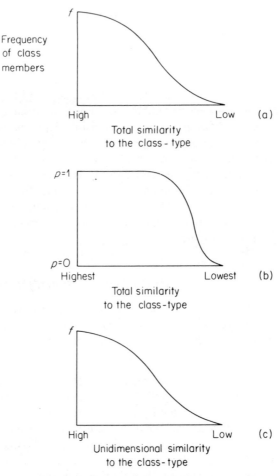

Figure 3.1 Theoretical distributions: (a) frequency of class members having total similarity to the class-type; (b) probability of a stimulus entering a class according to its degree of total similarly with the class-type; (c) frequency of class members having unidimensional similarity to the class-type

to the class-type increases, and it is zero at some low resemblance of the stimulus to the class-type. However, it is assumed that there can be a high probability (1 or almost 1) of a stimulus entering a class even though it has relatively low similarity with the class-type, while another stimulus slightly more removed from the class-type will have very low probability of entering that class [see Figure 3.1 (b)]. It is, of course, possible for a stimulus to enter a number of classes and to vary from the respective class-types by different degrees of similarity.

(6) Whether a stimulus is referred to a specific class depends upon the psychological availability of that class, as well as upon the probability of it being referred to that class when the latter is psychologically available. This availability is a direct function of recency and frequency of class usage. Other things being equal, availability is higher for a narrow class than for a wide class. It is reasonable to assume this: a narrow concept is more readily formed than a more inclusive or abstract concept (cf. Bourne, 1966).[1]

(7) A perceived stimulus has no immediate influence on the similarity distribution of the class it enters. In time, however, the stimulus is (representationally) incorporated into the distribution.

(8) A stimulus established in a person's experience is usually a member of more than one class.

(9) Total similarity is built up from (class-independent) similarities in single dimensions. It is dependent upon: (a) degree of unidimensional similarities (high degree—greater total similarity); (b) number of unidimensional similarities (high number—greater total similarity); (c) number of different dimensions on which each and all of similar stimuli are describable (low number—greater total similarity). Two stimuli are unidimensionally similar when a proportion of stimuli in general does not possess the stimuli's degrees of that quality or intermediate degrees. The smaller the proportion which does possess these degrees of the quality the greater is the degree of unidimensional similarity between those two stimuli. A dimension is 'relevant' to a class when the proportion of members in that class which can be described by certain adjacent degrees in that dimension is greater than the proportion from the nearest 'overriding' class. (By 'overriding' class is meant a subsuming, *general* class). Degrees of continuous qualities may be defined in terms of psychologically discriminable changes.

(10) Distributions of unidimensional similarity in relevant dimensions are generally of the same shape as the distribution of total similarity. As illustrated in Figure 3.1 (c), there is a positive (S-shaped) relationship between frequency of stimuli and degree of similarity to a class-typical degree of a unidimensional quality.

(11) To perceived stimuli are tied expectations of occurrence based upon experiences of other class members. In any one dimension it is expected that a stimulus will display high similarity to the class-type.

(12) The expectation of occurrence associated with a given stimulus is a positive function of the proportion of class members differing to the same extent from the class-type with respect to any particular dimension.

(13) The greater the divergence of a stimulus from expectation in one or many dimensions, the funnier the stimulus.

TESTING THE MODEL

It is implied in the model that a stimulus is referred to a class or successively to many classes. If the stimulus is simultaneous with, or immediately precedes, a second stimulus, then it is likely to determine the availability of classes for the second stimulus, as availability is dependent on recency of class usage *inter alia*. The second stimulus, being referred to one of the available classes, becomes the object of expectations associated with membership of that class. This implies that there is in the individual a generalized expectation as to degrees of uniformity of environmental stimuli.

Three studies have so far been conducted to test these notions. Stimuli in all experiments are non-representational moving figures (six in total) projected by two synchronized super-8 film projectors onto two screens placed side by side.

Study I

A single figure progresses from left to right across the left-hand screen and disappears with the same or different figure continuing the motion in the same trajectory across the right-hand screen. Subjects rate funniness of the right stimulus as it appears and perceived divergence between left-hand and right-hand stimuli. Stimuli in this study are not coloured, they are equal in size and they move at equal speed.

It is reasoned that while a stimulus is visible on the left-hand screen it becomes a part of several classes. Since the figures are non-representational, the classes are highly hypothetical: a stimulus approximates to the class-types. There is of course the possibility that subjects build up classes for the right-hand stimulus experiences accumulating during the experiment, but it is implicitly assumed that these classes are largely extinguished by the left-hand figure. Owing to recency, the classes forming around the left-hand stimulus are high on availability for classification of the right-hand stimulus, and the narrowest class is most available. The probability of the right-hand stimulus entering the classes is zero when the stimulus holds a certain low degree of total similarity to the various class-types, and it increases rapidly with increasing similarity.

If we make the added assumption that a right-hand stimulus enters equally wide classes for different left-hand stimuli, the model predicts that funniness of right-hand stimuli will increase as similarity with left-hand stimuli decreases. The results confirmed this prediction.

Studies II and III

Stimuli in these studies are similar figures to those in Study I but, in Study II, they vary in size, colour, speed and direction of movement, and, in Study III, they vary in size and colour.

Funniness should not increase indefinitely with increasing dissimilarity between stimuli. Divergence of a right-hand stimulus in unidimensional similarity and hence also in total similarity from the left-hand stimulus should ultimately cause the right-hand stimulus to leave a particular common class. It should fall into a class in which considerably less total similarity with the

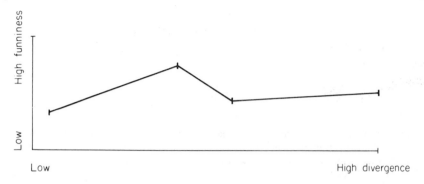

Figure 3.2 Relationship between funniness and divergence from expectancy

class-type (the left-hand stimulus) is tolerated—a distinctly wider common class. Classification makes one reaction valid for many stimuli and enables an individual to manage with fewer reactions than there are stimuli. Two stimuli, when diverging from the similarity necessary for membership of a common class will form a distinctly wider class; the change in tolerated similarity in the two classes is greater than the change in similarity between the stimuli.

The (hypothetical) distributions in single dimensions are wider in a wider class, and more divergence from the class-type is tolerated before an effect of divergence from expectancy emerges. The stimuli in the studies are varied so as to give two different series of common classes, varying in width, for left-hand hand and right-hand stimuli. A relationship like that in Figure 3.2 between rated funniness of a right-hand stimulus and divergence of it from the left-hand stimulus was consequently predicted.

In one series of trials in Study II right-hand and left-hand stimuli both moved from left to right, as in Study I, and in a second series right-hand stimuli again moved as before but left-hand stimuli moved from the bottom to the top of the screen. There was less divergence between stimuli in the first series: they diverged only in colour and shape. Within this series there were increases in funniness with increasing divergence. Funniness ratings were lower in the second series and there were no corresponding increases in funniness with increasing divergence in colour and shape of stimuli within that series.

The results from Study II are supported in Study III, where the right-hand and left-hand stimuli were either of the same or different shape. The greater the divergence in size and colour for stimuli of the same shape, the higher the ratings of funniness, but no such effect emerged for stimuli of different shape.

CONCLUSION

Close inspection of the rating data (Nerhardt, in preparation) indicates that we should exercise caution in attempting to operationalize the similarity proposed in the model in the manner adopted in the studies. It may be necessary, for example, to obtain more direct evidence of the attribution of stimuli to existing classes by having the subjects spontaneously generate their own classes. The model may be tested further by employing stimuli that are similar to those in the above studies but vary along new dimensions such as nearness in space and time.

NOTE

1. The concept 'availability' may be compared with the concept underlying 'tacit' and 'explicit' knowledge in Polanyi's (1967) discussion of creativity. It may be said to denote the distinctness in consciousness of a piece of knowledge at a certain moment in time. The class is thought to remain in the tacit range, that is, it will not in itself come into the focus of attention.

REFERENCES

Berlyne, D. E. (1960). *Conflict, Arousal and Curiosity*. New York: McGraw–Hill.

Bourne, L. E. (1966). *Human Conceptual Behavior*, Boston: Allyn and Bacon.

Kenny, D. T. (1955). The contingency of humor appreciation on the stimulus-confirmation of joke-ending expectations. *Journal of Abnormal and Social Psychology*, 51, 644–648.

Lewis, M., and Harwitz, M. (1969). The meaning of an orienting response: a study in the hierarchical order of attending. Princeton, N. J.: *Educational Testing Service Research Bulletin*, 69–33, April.

Mull, H. K. (1949). A study of humor in music. *American Journal of Psychology*, 62, 560–566.

Nerhardt, G. (1970). Humor and inclination to laugh: Emotional reactions to stimuli of different divergence from a range of expectancy. *Scandinavian Journal of Psychology*, 11, 185–195.

Piddington, R. (1963). *The Psychology of Laughter: A Study in Social Adaptation*. New York: Gamut Press.

Polanyi, M. (1967). *The Tacit Dimension*. London: Routledge and Kegan Paul.

Chapter 4

Superiority, Enhanced Self-Esteem, and Perceived Incongruity Humour Theory

Lawrence La Fave, Jay Haddad
and
William A. Maesen

This chapter reviews humour experiments concerned with superiority and ego enhancement and depreciation, criticizes well-known humour theories, and draws some counter-intuitive conclusions regarding such matters as whether anyone possesses a sense of humour, whether anyone has ever been amused at his own expense, and whether jokes exist. It concludes on a more positive note, suggesting some connecting links between superiority and incongruity humour, with special reference to social psychology.

HOBBES' SUPERIORITY THEORY OF HUMOUR

Beginning with Wolff, Smith and Murray (1934), we find 16 humour experiments which are in substantial part indebted to the superiority humour tradition offered over three centuries ago by the British philosopher, Thomas Hobbes. Some confusion exists regarding what Hobbesian superiority humour theory actually states, though his treatment of the subject apparently limits itself to a few hundred words:

> *Sudden Glory*, is the passion which maketh those *Grimaces* called LAUGHTER: and is caused either by some sudden *act of their own* [italics supplied], that pleaseth them; or by the apprehension of some deformed thing in another, by comparison whereof they suddenly applaud themselves. And it is incident most to them, that are conscious of the fewest abilities in themselves; who are forced to keep themselves in their own favour, by observing the imperfections of other men. And therefore much Laughter at the defects of others, is a signe of Pusillanimity. For of great minds, one of the proper workes is, to help and free others from scorn; and compare themselves onely with the most able. (Hobbes, 1968, p. 125; reproduced by permission of Penguin Books Ltd.)

In addition to his above statement on humour from *Leviathan*, Hobbes also wrote of humour in another book, *Humane Nature*, also published in 1651. In *Humane Nature* Hobbes (1651, p. 101) observes that laughter always involves joy. He adds:

whatsoever it be that moveth laughter, it must be new and unexpected. Men laugh often (especially such as are greedy of applause from every thing they do well) at their own actions performed never so little beyond their own expectations; as also at their own jests: And in this case it is manifest, that the Passion of Laughter proceedeth from a sudden conception of some ability in himself that laugheth ... Also men laugh at Jests, the Wit whereof always consisteth in the elegant discovering and conveying to our mindes some absurdity of another: And in this case also the Passion of Laughter proceedeth from the sudden imagination of our own oddes and eminency: for what is else the recommending of our selves to our own good opinion, by comparison with another mans infirmity or absurdity? For when a jest is broken upon our selves, or friends of whose dishonour we participate, we never laugh thereat ... for men laugh at the follies of themselves past, when they come suddenly to remembrance, except they bring with them any present dishonour. It is no wonder therefore that men take hainously to be laughed at or derided, that is, triumphed over. Laughing without offence, must be at absurdities and infirmities abstracted from persons, and when all the company may laugh together: For, laughing to ones self putteth all the rest into jealousie, and examination of themselves. Besides, it is vainglory, and an argument of little worth, to think the infirmity of another sufficient matter for his Triumph. (Hobbes, 1651, pp. 101–103).

We are moved by the brilliance and profundity of Hobbes' reflections on humour over three centuries ago, finding them more viable than the views of a number of contemporary humour researchers. Nonetheless, Hobbesian formulations do present a few problems:

(1) Hobbes clearly and correctly views laughter as an externally observable behaviour. He does *not*, in other words, treat laughter as *identical* (i.e. co-extensive) with the mental experience of amusement. Nonetheless, he obviously conceives of amusement (i.e. humour) and laughter as *equivalent*, as necessary and sufficient conditions of one another. Later we shall see that such an equivalence assumption is definitely *not* justified.

(2) Hobbesian humour theory not only focuses upon superiority (i.e. glory) but also *suddenness*. Suddenness seems a necessary ingredient in an adequate recipe for humour—a humorous mental experience appears to require that the amused experience a sufficient rate of increment in happiness or joy per unit time. Without suddenness the slope of the happiness increment would conceivably be insufficiently precipitous to generate amusement. However, Hobbes apparently conceives of suddenness in a different sense: that which is new and unexpected or generates *surprise*. Clearly, however, surprise cannot be a necessary component of humour, or jokes heard before could scarcely amuse. Yet often they do. Contrary to Hobbes' opinion Hollingsworth (1911) reported some types of jokes more amusing if already familiar. Apparently surprise is neither a necessary nor sufficient condition of amusement (though such 'novelty' probably does often serve to enhance the magnitude of amusement). In any event Hobbes' view on suddenness seems clearly erroneous.

(3) Even if both glory and some sense of suddenness are necessary conditions of amusement, sudden glory cannot be sufficient. Another necessary ingredient would appear to be *perceived* (i.e. subjective) *incongruity*. Hobbes *does* allude to incongruity (albeit *objective* incongruity) when he speaks of absurdities in others

as prompting laughter. However, he reveals his conception of such absurdities from a superiority (rather than incongruity) point of view by writing only of absurdities in other people, never of absurdities 'in the abstract'.

(4) The main thrust of the Hobbesian notion of glory or superiority appears to be highly individualistic, competitive and egocentric. The soundness of this interpretation of Hobbes seems reinforced by his political philosophy, which finds man forming a social contract with others *not* because of the altruistic gratification he experiences in helping them but, rather, simply to protect himself against external danger. By this egocentric, competitive interpretation of superiority humour theory, the individual is amused only when he feels triumphant and/or another person looks bad in comparison with himself.

Such an individualistic interpretation of Hobbes argues that none of the 16 experiments we find especially relevant to his humour theory actually tested it or, if any did, the result was almost invariably disconfirmatory. For none of these experiments involved the experimental subjects personally (either by name or their action) in either triumph or defeat *vis-a-vis* another person.

The first attempted experimental test of Hobbesian theory (Wolff, Smith and Murray, 1934) found impracticable the attempt to use the personal names of experimental subjects. Wolff and co-workers therefore substituted names of representatives of the subjects' or others' ethnic membership groups (e.g. 'Ikey' in an anti-Jewish joke). Other relevant experiments have also consistently avoided use of the subject's own name in the jokes.

Wolff and co-workers correctly predicted that jokes disparaging Jews would be funnier to Gentiles than to Jews, but jokes disparaging Scots would equally amuse both. Counter to expectation, Jewish subjects found anti-Scottish jokes less funny than did Gentiles, thus apparently contradicting the Wolff and co-workers interpretation of Hobbesian theoretic prediction.

With post-experimental hindsight the Scots, Wolff and co-workers reasoned, had been an unfortunate choice for 'control joke' victims. The Scots were negatively stereotyped as stingy, as the Jews had been; therefore, the authors concluded, the Jews must have sympathized with the Scots, finding in consequence anti-Scot jokes relatively unfunny (cf. La Fave, 1967; La Fave, 1972a, p. 200).

On this adroit reinterpretation of their results, however, Wolff and co-workers appear no longer, even by the most liberal interpretation, to function within an Hobbesian theoretic framework. On the contrary, their reinterpretation contradicts Hobbes; never does he allow that a joke can be reduced in funniness because the subject sympathizes with the victim strangers. One Hobbesian sentence quoted above, though, seems to allow amusement reduction if the victims are friends. However, that one sentence appears to be inconsistent with Hobbes' general position, cannot cover sufficient territory to bring the anti-Scottish joke results in line with Hobbes and cannot account for reduction in amusement due to sympathy with victims other than oneself or friends.

Also, Hobbesian theory does not seem to allow: (a) that the *triumph* of persons other than oneself can facilitate amusement or (b) that a subject could ever be more amused by the victory of a non-membership group over one to which he belongs than by the converse. Nor does Hobbesian theory allow for (c) the effects of *attitude switching* on amusement. This chapter seeks to demonstrate that (a), (b) and (c) above also expose severe limitations in Hobbesian humour theory.

A MORE GENERAL 'SUPERIORITY' OR SELF-ESTEEM HUMOUR THEORY

The discussion above suggests that the 16 humour experiments we find especially influenced by Hobbes require a more comprehensive superiority humour theory than his. The following statement is perhaps sufficiently general and abstract to encompass all the superiority humour hypotheses which these 16 humour experiments test:

Let S believe J is a joke in which A seems to S victorious and/or B appears the butt. Then the more positive S's attitude towards A and/or towards the 'behaviour' of A, and/or the more negative S's attitude towards B and/or towards the 'behaviour' of B, the greater the magnitude of amusement S experiences with respect to J.

In the above general statement A and B can refer to individual persons, or classes of persons, or animals, or classes of animals, or perhaps even to inanimate objects or classes of such objects. In most of these 16 experiments in this area A and B refer to classes of persons (i.e. *identification classes*) while in the remainder they refer to individual persons.

Our general statement above is also insufficient, by itself, to deduce all superiority hypotheses in these 16 experiments; typically additional assumptions are also needed. However, all such superiority hypotheses can be deduced from our general superiority statement in conjunction with other, usually conventional, assumptions which do not themselves require any superiority assumptions.

Our own five experiments in this area always treat A and B as identification classes (or, more loosely, reference groups). The construct of 'identification class' seems to improve upon that of 'reference group' in a number of ways (cf. La Fave, Haddad and Marshall, 1974). The basic design of our five experiments is also quite different from designs employed by other researchers in this area. So it seems more effective to discuss our theory and design separately from those of other research groups. Because our theory and all five of our experiments concern identification classes, let us first explicate that construct.

Identification classes

An identification class (IC) is a special type of *attitude-belief system*. The kind of IC this chapter exclusively concerns itself with always involves a class (or set or category) of persons. If a given IC exists for S: (1) then S either believes himself at a given moment a member of that class, or believes he is a non-member, or his belief with respect to that particular IC lies dormant at that moment in his non-conscious storage system; and (2) S either feels positive, neutral or negative about that class, or else it lies dormant at that moment in his non-conscious.

For instance, suppose Reginald presently believes himself a professor and holds a positive feeling towards the professor class. Then the class *professor* is an IC for Reg. More specifically, it is a *positive membership* IC for him and is active (i.e. in his *awareness*) at the present time.

An attitude holds both an emotive and a cognitive component. The cognitive component of the attitudinal part of the IC is the conception of the class itself, while the emotive component is the feeling towards that class (which may vary on a continuum from positive affect through neutral to negative affect). Nonetheless, the cognitive component of the belief part of the IC is more complex, being a *proposition*, rather than simply a predicate (as in the case of the cognitive component of the attitude). In the above example, then, 'professor' is the cognitive component of Reg's attitude, while 'I am a professor' is the cognitive component of his belief. Thus the belief component of an IC is distinct from, but functionally interdependent with, the attitudinal component.

It is a homeostatic steady state when a positive (+) IC is believed to win or a negative ($-$) IC is believed to lose (regardless of whether one believes himself a member of these ICs or not). However, it is a non-steady state when either a + IC is believed to lose or a $-$ IC to win (regardless again of whether one believes himself a member of these ICs).

Homeostatic steady states are viewed as pleasant and non-steady states as unpleasant. Since amusement is pleasant (Gutman and Priest, 1969), it is assumed that jokes which bring about steady states will be viewed more amusing than those which usher in non-steady states. Jokes which bring about such steady states also increase self-esteem. Hence jokes are believed funnier when self-esteem is enhanced and less humorous when the ego is deflated. Self-esteem increment thus is viewed as at most a necessary (albeit not sufficient) condition of amusement.

The jokes we employ always explicitly mention both ICs A and B discussed above. So the general superiority statement required for our five experiments is as follows:

Let S believe J is a joke in which identification class A is victorious over identification class B. Then the more positive S's attitude towards A and the more negative S's attitude towards B, the greater the magnitude of amusement S experiences with respect to J.

Our general theoretic statements above possibly sound commonplace. However, this chapter hopes to exhibit, later, that such general theoretic statements (conjoined with other conventional assumptions) lead to counter-intuitive derivations. In addition, our general statements of superiority theory do seem to exhibit the advantages of being quantitative and quite comprehensive in the number of jokes they embrace.

Abstract hypotheses

When the hypotheses involved in our five superiority humour experiments are stated abstractly enough to omit specific content of ICs (e.g. Baptists, professors etc.), the number of hypotheses these experiments tested reduce to six or seven:

H1: A joke which esteems a subject's (S's) + IC and disparages S's — IC tends to be judged funnier than a joke which esteems S's — IC and disparages S's + IC.

H2: A joke which esteems S's + IC and disparages S's — IC tends to be judged funnier than a joke which esteems S's — IC and disparages S's — IC. (Since *H2* holds S's attitude towards the disparaged IC roughly constant, it essentially simplifies to the following: a joke which esteems S's + IC tends to be judged funnier than a joke which esteems S's — IC.)

H3: A joke which esteems S's — IC and disparages S's + IC tends to be judged less funny than a joke which esteems S's — IC and disparages S's — IC. (Since *H3* holds S's attitude towards the esteemed IC roughly constant, it essentially simplifies to the following: a joke which disparages S's + IC tends to be judged less funny than a joke which disparages S's — IC.)

H4: Hypothesis 4 is an *attitude switching* hypothesis. Attitude switching, not to be confused with attitude change, is discussed in La Fave and co-workers (1974). *H4* asserts: A joke which prompts enemy groups to identify positively with a more inclusive IC which combines these enemy groups against a common enemy will prompt members of these enemy groups to judge similarly in loyalty to that more inclusive 'supergroup' against the common enemy. *H4* differs from *H1* (since *H1* requires no attitude switching), yet for purposes of superiority humour theory *per se H4* is identical to *H1*. (This is the reason we vacillate as to whether we should state six or seven abstract hypotheses with respect to superiority humour theory.)

H5: If S has a membership + IC and a non-membership + IC such that S prefers his non-membership + IC to his membership + IC, then S tends to judge funnier a joke which esteems S's non-membership + IC and disparages S's membership + IC than a joke which esteems S's membership + IC and disparages S's non-membership + IC.

For abstract hypotheses *H6* and *H7*, consider two experimental groups (G_1 and G_2) and two permutations of jokes (P_1 and P_2):

H6. Suppose G_1 wins on P_1 and loses on P_2, and G_2 wins on P_2 and loses on P_1. Assume for G_1, IC_1 is a membership + IC and IC_2 is a non-membership — IC, while for G_2, IC_1 is a non-membership + IC and IC_2 is a membership + IC such that G_2 also prefers IC_1 to IC_2 (but by a lesser magnitude than does G_1). Then P_1 is funnier relative to P_2 for G_1 than for G_2.

H7: Assume G_1 and G_2 both win on P_1 and lose on P_2. Suppose for G_1, IC_1 is a membership $+ IC$ and IC_2 is a non-membership $- IC$, while for G_2, IC_1 is a membership $+ IC$ and IC_2 is a non-membership $+ IC$ such that G_2, contrary to G_1, prefers IC_2 to IC_1. Then P_1 is funnier relative to P_2 for G_1 than for G_2.

(Note that the above hypotheses consider the *attitudinal* component of the IC system, rather than the *belief* component as defined above, as the important predictor of humour judgements. Thus, if *S* is more ego-involved with his non-membership group than his membership, his non-membership should better predict his humour judgements.)

REVIEW OF OUR VICARIOUS SUPERIORITY HUMOUR EXPERIMENTS

Our independent variable is an *attitude*, and valid measurement requires disguising this fact. The conventional experimental design incorporates these attitudinal differences between samples within different experimental treatments. Attempts at manipulating *S*s' attitudes are too likely invalidated by *S*s' ability to 'see through' the purpose of the experiment. In addition, the attitudinal differences introduced by different treatments are likely to lack sufficient *ego-involvement* to reflect themselves in differential humour judgements.

Apparently the most plausible approach would be to select samples from populations sufficiently *different* on the attitudinal independent variable, treat these different samples the *same*, then predict *differences* between samples in humour judgements.

The present approach is in the tradition of our work with Sherif and Hovland (Sherif and Hovland, 1961; Sherif, Sherif and Nebergall, 1965; La Fave and Sherif, 1968). The Sherif–Hovland procedure permits measurement of ego-involving attitudinal differences and also disguises the experimenter's bias from *S*s. However, such a procedure could represent a mere matching design, rather than a controlled experiment. Therefore, each group (through *counterbalanced permutations*) was used as its own control, *familiar jokes* were eliminated and a series of experiments were performed across a *variety* of social issues.

The experimental designs of the five superiority experiments share much. The first (La Fave, 1961, 1972a) was on the social issue of *religion*; the second (La Fave and co-workers, 1974) concerned a student *Sit-in* in the Theology Department of the University of Windsor; the third (La Fave, McCarthy and Haddad, 1973) involved Canadian–American relations (*Can–Am*); the fourth (La Fave, Billinghurst, and Haddad, in preparation) *Women's Lib*; and the fifth (Haddad and La Fave, in preparation) professors versus students (*Prof–Stud*). Each experiment asked the *S*s to sort 20 jokes under five degrees of amusement. These five label cards for the first four experiments read: 'Very funny'; 'Funny'; 'Indifferent'; 'Unfunny'; 'Very unfunny'. The fifth experiment also employed five such category cards, with the word 'Amusing' substituted for 'Funny'.

Every joke in all five experiments employed dialogue between two opposing groups on the social issue in question. For each set of jokes involving the same two groups, Group A was victorious in exactly half of these jokes with rival Group B the butt (P_1) and Group B was esteemed in the other half with Group A disparaged (P_2). In all but the first or religious experiment only two different groups were mentioned in all 20 jokes, so P_1 consisted of 10 jokes and P_2 also of 10. The religious experiment's design was more complicated: four different groups were mentioned in the jokes plus one 'supergroup'. Thus the 20 jokes were first partitioned into five sets of four jokes each, and any set of four jokes was sub-partitioned into permutations of two jokes. An example of a joke from P_1 on the fifth experiment is:

Prof.: Half of this class appears to have been arrested at Freud's oral stage of psychosexual evolution, and the other half at his anal stage.
Student: You must have been arrested at both stages because your lectures are nothing but verbal diarrhoea.

An example of a joke from P_2 of the same experiment is:

Prof.: Today's student is too wrapped up in himself!
Student: What's wrong with that?
Prof.: Nothing! Except that he makes a very small package!

Each of the 20 jokes for a given experiment was randomly numbered on a different card. Any S's deck of 20 jokes had been shuffled into a different order, randomizing out order effects. Ss sorted the jokes in groups of five or more; so, any differential effect of social interaction (such as social contagion through overhearing another S laugh, social inhibition, and conformity) was randomized out also.

Ss, having finished sorting the 20 jokes under the five label cards, completed a brief questionnaire—requesting such information as age, sex and educational attainment. Ss also were asked (except, unfortunately, on the hastily done Sit-in experiment) which group they preferred relative to the social issue on which the experiment was based. The experimenters had employed espionage prior to the experimental phase to assign Ss correctly to positive identification classes. If 'S' did not also check the predicted category as his preferred identification class on the questionnaire, his results were discarded. Thus this questionnaire item provided a cross-check on the validity of the spy system; and only persons whose data were consistent on the two measures counted as Ss. (Fortunately, very few 'Ss' needed to be disqualified.)

All five experiments, testing more concrete versions of abstract hypothesis $H1$, predicted that a joke would be funnier when the positive identification class (good guys) won and the negative identification class (bad guys) lost than when the bad guys were esteemed and the good guys the butt. The Sit-in, Can–Am, and Women's-Lib experiments tested only this first hypothesis. These three experiments were mainly employed as semi-replications of the religious experiment on *H1*. Each of these semi-replications differed of course from the religious experiment and from each other on the social issue. The primary function of these three semi-replications then was to preclude the possibility that the religious experiment 'substantiated' its main hypothesis as an artifact of the social issue chosen.

The Sit-in and Can–Am experiments share the simplest design of the five, since each employs only two groups of Ss. The former used pro-sit-inners and anti-sit-inners. However, the Women's-Lib experiment employed three groups of Ss: male-rule males, equal-rule males and equal-rule females. The two groups of males were distinguished by how they answered an item on the questionnaire regarding which sex ought to rule (cf. La Fave, 1972a, p. 205). Consistent with abstract *H1*, the pro-male–anti-female permutation of 10 jokes was predicted to be funnier to male-rule males than to equal-rule females relative to the pro-female–anti-male permutation of 10 jokes. A second prediction derived with the help of *H1* was that equal-rule males would score on the female side relative to the male-rule males. Third, also using *H1*, these equal-rule males were predicted to score on the male side relative to the equal-rule females.

Predictions on all hypotheses for all five experiments are by jokes rather than by Ss. The formula used in predicting each joke is: $(M - \bar{M}) > (L - \bar{L})$, where M refers to the percentage of humorous judgements for the group predicted to be *more* frequently amused on the joke in question and L refers to the percentage of humorous judgements for the group predicted to be *less* frequently amused on that same joke. $\bar{M}$ denotes the average percentage of humorous judgements across all 20 jokes for the group predicted more frequently amused on the joke in question, and $\bar{L}$ the average percentage of humorous judgements across all 20 jokes for the group predicted less frequently amused on the joke in question [except in the La Fave (1961) experiment across four jokes at a time]. To predict for each joke, the five humorous judgement categories are collapsed into two (i.e. a 'none–some' scale). *Humorous* thus includes the Very Funny and Funny categories or, on the Prof–Stud experiment, the Very Amusing and Amusing categories. The other three categories (either Indifferent, Unfunny and Very Unfunny; or Indifferent, Unamusing, and Very Unamusing) are lumped together as non-humorous.

The probability of a given joke being predicted correctly is 50% and incorrectly 50%. Thus the probability all 20 jokes on the Can–Am experiment would be predicted correctly by chance is $\frac{1}{2^{(20-1)}} \equiv p < 0.000002$. (The exponent is 19 rather than 20 as use of group means costs one degree of freedom.)

Though both possible permutations of jokes are used, at least two groups varying on the attitude being measured are needed. Suppose only one group were used, for instance, loyal Canadians. Superiority theory would then apparently predict these loyal Canadians to find the pro-Canadian–anti-American set of jokes funnier than the pro-American–anti-Canadian permutation. However, the above discussion discloses that such an experimental design would fail to exclude the alternative interpretation—that (rather than superiority theory having been supported) the pro-Canadian–anti-American permutation was a funnier set of jokes than the other permutation.

Only our fifth (Prof–Stud) experiment tests the last three of the seven abstract hypotheses. This experiment represents part of a thesis completed by JH under the direction of LL (with University of Windsor professors Sally Snyder, John La Gaipa and James Duthie the remaining committee members). One of the four experimental groups employed consists of 27 professors who are pro-professor–anti-student ($+$PP). Another comprises 28 pro-student–anti-professor students ($+$SS). Thus these first two groups are analogous to two groups on each of our previous experiments, except of course the social issue differs. However, the remaining two experimental groups are unique. One consists of 28 pro-professor students (i.e. students who prefer professor to students, $+$PS); and the other is its 'mirror image', composed of 28 pro-student professors, $+$SP.

Six relatively concrete superiority humour hypotheses concern the rank ordering of these four experimental groups. Thus, we would predict that $+$SS: $+$SP. [It is predicted that the experimental group ($+$SS) to the left of the symbol: finds P_1 jokes funnier relative to P_2 than does the group ($+$SP) to the right of:.]

So also we predict $+$SP: $+$PS and $+$PS: $+$PP. Since the mathematical relation group-x-is-to-the-left-of-group-y appears transitive, three theorems would also seem predicted, i.e. $+$SS: $+$PP; $+$SS: $+$PS; and $+$SP: $+$PP. However, a close examination of the aggregate nature of our predictions should make clear that these last three predictions are *not* deducible from the first three but represent separate hypotheses. (For a similar reason three relatively concrete hypotheses test abstract hypothesis *H1* on the Women's-Lib experiment as it employs three experimental groups.)

$+$SS: $+$PP is a relatively concrete hypothesis derived from abstract hypothesis *H1*. Similarly $+$SP: $+$PS is an instance of abstract hypothesis *H5*. However, two relatively concrete hypotheses follow from abstract hypothesis *H6* $- +$SS: $+$SP and $+$PS: $+$PP. Also from abstract hypothesis *H7* are derived two relatively concrete hypotheses $- +$SS: $+$PS and $+$SP: $+$PP. Substantiation of abstract hypotheses *H5* and *H7* would seem to suggest that when the preferred $+$IC differs from the membership class (or, more loosely, the preferred reference group differs from the membership group) the former is a better predictor of humour judgements than is the membership class (or group).

Only the experimental design of our religious experiment was complex enough to test abstract hypotheses *H2*, *H3* and *H4*. These relatively concrete hypotheses testing abstract hypotheses *H2* and *H3* have previously been referred to as mathematically interrelated sub-hypotheses (La Fave, 1961, 1972a). Substantiation of *H2* and *H3* would resolve some conflicting findings in the literature. Support for *H1* and *H3* would appear to contradict the Freud and G. H. Mead theory (as interpreted by Roberts and Johnson, 1957) of a positive correlation between humour and empathic identification. Support for *H1* and *H2* would also seem to contradict the 'playful pain' theory of Max

73

Eastman (1936). Conversely, support for *H2* would seem to contradict the earlier theories presented by Wolff and co-workers (1934) and Middleton (1959). Apparently substantiation of *H2* also would contradict Arthur Koestler's (1964) distinction between amusing and aesthetic experiences by which aesthetic experience requires identification whereas amusing experience demands detachment—since *H2* predicts *S* is more amused, *ceteris paribus*, if he identifies with the victor in a joke than if *S* detaches from the esteemed.

However, our care to test *H2* and *H3* as long ago as 1961 certainly contradicts a recent statement by Cantor and Zillmann (1973) who, after mentioning our 1961 religious experiment, conclude: 'Similarly, all the other experimental investigations mentioned above have, to various degrees, procedurally confounded the disparagement of one protagonist with the success of another ...' In fact, they seemed totally unaware of our two mathematically interrelated sub-hypotheses *H2* and *H3*. [A later experiment by Gutman and Priest (1969) employing a very different design, Latin Square, perhaps avoided such alleged confounding also.] They employed four 'squelch' jokes: (a) good aggressor, bad victim; (b) good aggressor, good victim; (c) bad aggressor, bad victim; and (d) bad aggressor, good victim. In a very different way La Fave's religious experiment had earlier tested amount of amusement with respect to three of the conditions above, excluding (b). By vicarious superiority humour theory: (a) should be most amusing, (b) and (c) roughly tie for next, and (d) be least amusing. The last five of our concrete hypotheses on the Prof–Stud experiment, however, all seem to test (b) above. On the + SP: + PS hypothesis, from both groups' perspectives, all jokes involve a good aggressor and a good victim. On any of the four concrete hypotheses related to abstract hypotheses *H6* and *H7*, one of the two groups judges every joke to involve a good aggressor and a good victim also, while the other group perceives condition (a) above on one permutation and condition (d) on the other.

The fourth relatively concrete hypothesis on the religious experiment tests abstract hypothesis *H4*.

One of the problems with reference group theory has been that the typical *S* holds many reference groups and the theory does not let us know which of these reference groups will be the independent variable(s) on a given occasion as regards *S*'s judgements (cf. Kelley, 1973). Our *attitude switching* construct (La Fave and co-workers, 1974) enables us to distinguish active from inactive ICs in *S*'s humour and other judgements.

Catholic, Baptist and Jehovah's Witness *S*s all reported preferring to consider themselves Christian while our agnostic *S*s did not. Therefore, the former three groups should, at the more general Christian level which includes all three, combine to judge alike against the common agnostic enemy, assuming *H1* to be substantiated.

Results

Between our five experiments a total of 15 relatively concrete hypotheses tested the seven abstract hypotheses. Each experiment tested abstract hypothesis $H1$—and each substantiated it ($p < 0.05$). In three of the experiments (Religious, Sit-in and Prof–Stud) all 20 jokes were predicted in the correct direction. On $H1$ for the Can–Am experiment 16 of 20 jokes were predicted correctly. On Women's Lib for $H1$, male-rule males were predicted on the correct side of equal-rule females on 17 of 20 jokes. Our two other predictions on that experiment also seemed based on $H1$: male-rule males will find pro-male–anti-female jokes funnier than will equal-rule males relative to the other permutation (14 correct predictions, $0.10 > p > 0.05$). Since we suspected our equal-rule male Ss of holding a definition of 'equal-rule' more flattering to themselves than the equal-rule females' definition of 'equal-rule' was to these males, so $H1$ predicted that the former would find pro-male–anti-female jokes funnier than would the equal-rule females relative to the other permutation (16 jokes predicted correctly, $p < 0.005$).

As our three semi-replication experiments only tested $H1$, we need consider them no further here. The remaining eight relatively concrete hypotheses derive from the remaining six more abstract hypotheses.

Our religious experiment tested abstract hypotheses $H2$, $H3$ and $H4$ once each. $H2$ was found to be tentatively substantiated. Of 16 relevant jokes 12 were predicted correctly. However, consistent with superiority humour theory, the four wrong predictions were wrong by smaller magnitudes than any of the 12 correct were correct ($p < 0.001$). For this reason and others discussed elsewhere (La Fave, 1972a, pp. 203–204) $H2$ is considered tentatively substantiated.

$H3$ was also substantiated on the religious experiment; 13 of 16 jokes were predicted correctly. $H4$ predicted for only four jokes. However, the chance probability of each of these four jokes being correctly predicted was $\frac{1}{4}$, since the agnostics were predicted to be on one side of each of the other three groups. $H4$ was also substantiated, as all four jokes were predicted correctly.

The remaining five of the 15 concrete hypotheses were only tested on the Prof–Stud experiment and only concern abstract hypotheses $H5$, $H6$ and $H7$.

Abstract hypothesis $H5$ was tested in the comparison between the pro-student professors' and pro-professor students' experimental groups and its concrete derivation predicted $+ SP : + PS$, as discussed earlier. This concrete hypothesis predicted 14 of 20 jokes correctly ($0.10 > p > 0.05$).

The two concrete hypotheses derived from abstract hypothesis $H6$ are $+ SS : + SP$ (17 jokes correctly predicted, $p < 0.003$) and $+ PS : + PP$ (18 correct, $p < 0.0005$).

The two concrete hypotheses deduced from abstract hypothesis $H7$ are $+ SS : + PS$ (all 20 correct, $p < 0.000002$) and $+ SP : + PP$ (16 correct, $p < 0.005$).

Thus 13 of 15 relatively concrete hypotheses were substantiated, while the remaining two were tentatively substantiated at $p < 0.10$. All inferences discussed earlier, then, concerning what theoretic implications such substantiations would have, seem now applicable.

OTHER VICARIOUS SUPERIORITY HUMOUR EXPERIMENTS

The six vicarious superiority humour experiments other than our own reported prior to 1972 are reviewed in La Fave (1967; 1972a) and require little additional comment here. They are by Wolff and co-workers (1934), Middleton (1959), Priest (1966), Gutman and Priest (1969), Priest and Abrahams (1970), and Priest and Phillips (unpublished). Since then we have found, other than our own, five new experiments in this area [Zillmann and Cantor, 1972; Cantor and Zillmann, 1973; Priest and Wilhelm, 1974; Zillmann, Bryant and Cantor, 1974; and Zillmann and Bryant (in press)]. The four involving Zillmann and colleagues are also summarized elsewhere in this book (see Chapter 5).

Of the 16 experiments in this area, 11 seem to provide results consistent with our vicarious superiority model (the five by our group, five by Priest and co-workers and the 1972 experiment by Zillmann and Cantor). [Also essentially supportive of the ICs construct over that of membership group is a study by Clément (1974)]. Approximately half of the results on each of the remaining five experiments appear to support our model and half do not. However, all these negative results seem readily explicable in terms of inadequate experimental controls not difficult to pinpoint. We also discount somewhat the results supporting our model for the four experiments by Priest and his colleagues other than the excellent Gutman and Priest experiment, because we do not believe these other four experiments were well controlled. The only one of these we have not discussed previously (La Fave, 1972a) is by Priest and Wilhelm (1974). Although these authors offer their results as supporting their conflict theory, with which we have no quarrel, and it seems to tie in nicely with Martineau's (1972) excellent work, their results are also consistent with our position.

We find two basic criticisms common to the Priest and Zillmann groups: (1) The last three experiments by the Zillmann group, like the four mentioned above by the Priest group, lack adequate experimental controls. (2) Both groups are too generous in attributing superiority theory substantiation to experiments which we claim do not substantiate superiority theory.

For instance, Priest (1966) and Zillmann and Cantor (1972) maintain that Wolff and co-workers supported superiority humour theory. Yet Wolff and co-workers acknowledged themselves that they had failed and seemed to show excellent hindsight in working out why—Jewish Ss sympathized with the Scots in anti-Scottish jokes, finding such 'control' jokes less funny than did Gentiles. Later, half of Middleton's (1959) superiority humour predictions failed—it seems for a similar reason which Middleton adroitly acknowledged *ad hoc* (the reference group was not always the membership group).

So the first successful substantiation of any version of superiority humour theory seems to have been by our religious experiment (La Fave, 1961; 1967; 1972a).

However, we have also carelessly stated in previous publications that our own results support Hobbesian superiority theory. Cantor and Zillmann

(1973) also have erroneously attributed support for Hobbes to experimental work in the area. While this research area owes much to Hobbes, the results generally contradict his theory.

Apparently some of us have been guilty of redefining Hobbes, beginning with Wolff and co-workers, rather than returning to his original work. To correct the historical record, the beginning of this chapter quotes Hobbes quite extensively.

Wolff and co-workers improve upon Hobbesian theory by rendering superiority theory more vicarious, writing of amusement as a result of 'an unaffiliated object in a disparaging situation', where the affiliated object need not be restricted, as with Hobbes, to oneself and possibly friends. We (beginning with La Fave, 1961) then attempted to improve the theory further by adding, in effect, an 'affiliated' object in an 'esteemed' situation, and have demonstrated in our Prof–Stud experiment that the 'affiliated object' need be neither oneself, nor friends, nor even a membership group.

Zillmann and Cantor (1972) suggest a further theoretic improvement: 'In contrast to the long duration or permanence of affiliation implied, the present model permits positive and negative affect to fluctuate freely over time—thus accommodating mirth-related motivational dynamics'.

We basically agree. In fact, La Fave (1961) tested abstract hypothesis *H4* because of concern for *attitude switching* phenomena. The individual probably is not merely ambivalent towards others he knows well (i.e. has much information about) but *polyvalent*. He probably holds as many attitudes towards each other person as he has categories (i.e. *identification classes*) to assign that other person to. We shall return to this subject below (see also La Fave and co-workers, 1974).

Cantor and Zillmann (1973), as mentioned earlier, also misinterpret the experimental literature when they state that their experiment was the first to avoid confounding the success of one protagonist with the disparagement of another. Such confounding was avoided both by testing abstract hypotheses *H2* and *H3* in our religious experiment and perhaps later by Gutman and Priest (1969).

The Gutman and Priest experiment in fact can most fruitfully be conceived as a major step forward in rendering vicarious superiority humour theory more comprehensive. All vicarious superiority humour experiments prior to that time treated as the independent variable *Ss*' pre-experimental attitudes towards victims and/or victors in jokes. Gutman and Priest, however, treated as the independent variable attitudes towards the *behaviour* of the protagonists in the jokes.

While that experiment ostensibly relates aggression to humour, it is best conceived as a connecting link between aggression and superiority theory. Before the Gutman and Priest experiment, the experimental literature on hostility and humour was typically poorly controlled (La Fave, 1972a, pp. 207–208) and quite confused. Their experiment can be reconceptualized to render vicarious superiority humour theory sufficiently comprehensive (as in our general statement on p. 66) that the hostility and humour literature becomes in large part, if not entirely a special case of vicarious superiority humour theory.

We are much indebted to the Zillmann group for helping us see more fully the significance of the Gutman and Priest article. However, Zillmann and Bryant (1974) have developed a curvilinear model which predicts that *retaliatory equity* maximizes amusement and that mirth decreases symmetrically as either under- or over-retaliation increases. They argue that the Gutman and Priest model is linear, predicting, like theirs, that amusement increases from extreme over-retaliation to retaliatory equity. However, unlike theirs, they argue that the Gutman and Priest model predicts that amusement continues to rise, reaching its apex at extreme under-retaliation. Zillmann and Bryant's findings are completely consistent with their own curvilinear model—allegedly supporting the Gutman and Priest model for over-retaliation but contradicting it for under-retaliation.

Zillmann and Bryant published two of their six manipulated jokes. Their truckdriver joke is shortest for both degrees of over-retaliation (i.e. over-retaliation and extreme over-retaliation) and then continues to lengthen as it moves towards the under-retaliation end, being easily the longest for extreme under-retaliation. We suspect, other specifiable conditions being controlled, the operation of the epigram 'brevity is the soul of wit'. If so, the authors inadvertently 'stacked the cards' in favour of their model.

Their other published joke involves a maid who squelches her boss, 'Mrs. Foppingham, a Shaker Heights society matron'. Under both under-retaliation degrees, the maid has just been fired. Since the maid's squelch cannot possibly damage Mrs. Foppingham as much as the maid has been damaged, the real victim in these under-retaliation conditions is *not* Mrs. Foppingham (counter to their assumption) but the maid. The Ss in this experiment are college students. The excellent Zillmann and Cantor experiment reports that similar college students identify positively with the subordinate (which in the Zillmann–Bryant experiment would be the maid) and negatively with the superordinate (the society matron). Therefore, the Gutman and Priest model (and our vicarious superiority theory) predict what Zillmann and Bryant apparently found—that the two degrees of under-retaliation in this joke would be less funny than the retaliatory equity condition. However, counter to their findings, our model would then apparently predict for this joke that the over-retaliatory conditions would be most amusing of all. However, no *real* damage is done to the maid in either the extreme over-retaliation, or the over-retaliation or the fair retaliation (i.e. retaliatory equity) conditions; in all three instances she merely is verbally rebuked. Thus the three ought to be roughly equal in funniness. Yet the two over-retaliation conditions are longest and written in a *forced* style so as spuriously to render them, as apparently found, less funny than the retaliatory equity condition.

Hence the two of six jokes published not only apparently offer no findings against vicarious superiority theory, but, when lack of needed experimental controls is allowed for, seem to support it.

Both the Cantor and Zillmann and the Zillmann and co-workers' experiments also provide results (for the more-harm-to-victim condition) which appear to contradict our vicarious superiority model's predictions. However, such results surprised the Zillmann group too—which candidly discussed how faulty designs could have accounted for their results. We found their experimental manipulations entirely unconvincing for additional reasons which space does not allow discussion of here. Apparently Zillmann and Bryant also discount those results, ignoring them though they are obviously relevant to retaliatory equity theory.

Therefore, no real evidence appears to exist that a curvilinear retaliatory equity model is needed. All valid results for the 16 most relevant experiments seem to cuddle quite snugly within a unidimensional vicarious superiority model. On intuitive grounds we cannot imagine an area of psychology where retaliatory equity theory would seem more superfluous than humour, since humour often relies on a *playful, fantasy* mental state, rather than the realistic one which retaliatory equity would at best seem applicable to.

SENSE OF HUMOUR: A MYOPIC ILLUSION?

Definition of sense of humour

Almost everyone seems convinced that a sense of humour exists, and that some people have it while others do not. Yet a closer look at what is meant by *sense of humour suggests some paradoxes.*

Two main senses of sense of humour seem prevalent:

(1) A person possesses a sense of humour if and only if he is readily amused. For instance, if X finds a larger variety of stimulus situations amusing than does Y, then X has a better sense of humour than does Y.

It appears doubtful, however, that an individual who seems to find everything funny would be considered to hold the best possible sense of humour. On the contrary, since he apparently would be amused at situations which his community considers 'no laughing matter,' he would more likely be judged a lunatic.

Yet it is quite inconceivable that even the proverbial lunatic could find everything funny. For one thing, if superiority theory be correct, jokes should tend to loss funniness when one's own ox is getting gored, a 'bad guy' appears victorious, etc. For another, jokes too difficult for one to get the point will probably not be judged funny. Nor will jokes now too easy (i.e. 'kid's stuff', Berlyne, 1972, p. 49).

No one appears to use the phrase *sense of humour* consistently with the above definition. Since *sense of humour* is usually conceived as a virtuous personality trait, the phrase is typically used ethnocentrically (i.e. you have a sense of humour if and only if you find pretty much the same jokes funny as I do). Thus Tibbets (1973) observes that some investigators, finding that children do not appreciate the sort of humour that appeals to adults, have concluded that children possess almost no sense of humour.

(2) It seems more useful to define sense of humour in the other common way—as the ability to be amused at one's own expense. Thus, for any X, X possesses a sense of humour if and only if there exists an occasion on which X is amused at X's expense.

The construct *amused* seems intuitively clear enough to deserve treatment as an undefined (i.e. primitive) term. Amusement is *always* a happiness increment mental experience—though happiness increment mental experiences need not be amusing. But what of the construct *own expense*? We think of a happening at our own expense as unhappy. Yet the set of unhappy mental experiences is (by logical necessity) mutually exclusive with respect to the set of happy experiences. Hence the paradox: to possess a sense of humour entails mental experiences unhappily happy.

Sociologist Charles Horton Cooley (1902) helps resolve this dilemma by denying in effect the very existence of self-sacrifice. For 'self-sacrifice', as with 'amused-at-own-expense', seems a self-contradictory construct. Since to deny anyone has ever been amused at his own expense asserts that no one holds a sense of humour, the paradox resolves.

Sense of humour, thus defined, is something no mortal could possess. Psychologists, like laymen, erroneously assume the existence of such a sense of humour to flatter themselves. The intellectual typically supposes that only a minority of the human species (himself and a few other intellectuals of his persuasion) possess a sense of humour, while the vulgar masses only are amused at others' expense. But he who credits himself with a sense of humour is ethnocentrically myopic—eluding the truth by deluding himself.

Why is sense of humour a myopic illusion? The reasons are not few.

Reasons why sense of humour is a myopic illusion

(1) The best-known humour theorists (*viz.* Freud, Hobbes, Eastman, Bergson, *et al.*) consistent with each other (and with most laymen), confound humour with laughter.

Of course if by sense of humour be meant the ability to *laugh* at one's own expense, there is no denying some men have a sense of humour. Laughter seems to be a desirable scientific construct in that it is so 'operational'. But as *humour* is synonymous with *amusement*, we now must ask: Is laughter synonymous with amusement? Clearly amusement is a mental experience (i.e. organismic variable or O) in a Stimulus–Organism–Response (S–O–R) model—unlike laughter, which is a response (R). Stearns (1972, p. 44) observes: 'Laughing is essentially a parasympathetic efferent reaction'. Obviously then, amusement and laughter are not identical. They would be equivalent if amusement were both a necessary and sufficient condition of laughter. On the contrary, a person apparently may laugh under any of the following conditions of non-amusement: when literally tickled, embarrassed, afraid, releasing tension, or pretending to have grasped the point of a 'joke' which oversailed his head. Children have been found to laugh at 'jokes' which they did not understand (Zigler, Levine, and Gould, 1967). Reynolds (1971) reminds us that human neurological disorders can precipitate laughter unaccompanied by amusement, and Stearns (1972, pp. 25–30) provides numerous examples. Druckman and Chao (1957) summarize the pathological conditions that can accompany inappropriate laughter as follows: (1) generalized cerebral arteriosclerosis, (2) frontal lobotomy and (3) some kinds of seizures. Reynolds notes that gelolepsy (a form of epilepsy) is such a seizure.

But is amusement a sufficient condition of laughter? An amused person may avoid laughing to keep from embarrassing the butt of the joke, to remain unnoticed, or to appear sophisticated. Dott [1938, cited in Reynolds (1971)] also relates that 'at least one case involving damage of the ventral hypothalamus has been reported in which *laughter could not occur even though the appropriate emotion was present*' [italics added].

Stearns (1972, p. 19) adds that weeping can result from extreme hilarity.

In other words, amusement is *neither* a necessary nor sufficient condition of laughter. Two suggestions for future research immediately become apparent:

(a) It would seem useful to investigate distinctions between *types* of laughter [e.g. does 'amused laughter' sound and look different from 'embarrassed laughter'? La Gaipa (1971) and his associates have been investigating such distinctions via video and audio tapes of cohesive groups]. Pollio and co-workers (1972), in a highly imaginative and provocative piece of research, distinguish between different types of aggregate audience laughters in response to different comedians. Stearns (1972, p. 20) writes of a 'voluntary laughter' which apparently is not the consequence of amusement.

(b) We who lack extrasensory perception cannot read other minds directly and, therefore, must infer, from some operational indices (i.e. from responses), whether these others are amused. However, as we have seen, neither laughter nor its absence is necessarily a valid indicator of amusement *per se*. Sometimes smiling operationally defines amusement; sometimes the statement 'That's funny' defines it; sometimes applause etc. It appears then that humour research and theory must move in the direction of what Webb, Campbell, Schwartz and Sechrest (1966) refer to as *multi-operationalism*, and Sherif (personal communication) describes as *validity cross-checks*.

The preceding argument permits some rather strong conclusions. One is that 'humour' theories by Freud (1928, 1960), Hobbes (1651, 1968), Bergson (1911), Eastman (1936) and other well-known humour theorists are really not theories of humour at all but, at best, theories of laughter. Thus, since as was just shown, humour and laughter are *not* synonymous, we have demolished all such 'humour' theories which equate laughter and humour.

For instance, let us single out Freud since, of the preceding theories, his has generated by far the most research. By confounding humour with laughter, the psychoanalyst is able to develop a pseudo-sophisticated, non-nullifiable 'theory' of humour which appears profound to the fuzzy-minded. Psychologists seem to consider Freud the leading contributor to the psychology of humour. In truth, Freud never performed any controlled research on humour—and it would be exceedingly difficult to find a person of at least average intelligence who knows less about humour than did Freud.

Observing that people laugh when literally tickled, Flugel (1954), following Freud's erroneous assumption that laughter necessarily indicates humour, feels duty bound to give a Freudian explanation as to why the person tickled is amused. However, what is needed is a theory of humour, not a humorous theory. And once we cease confounding laughter with amusement, our task as humour researchers and theorists becomes less unreasonable.

Of course the above discussion is not meant to imply that laughter is never a valid 'operational' indicator of amusement. For instance, when a comedian tells a joke and audience laughter follows, it seems reasonable to suppose that amusement got itself involved. Nevertheless, the comedian errs when he assumes, as comedians often do, that the magnitude of laughter is a direct, monotonic function of the magnitude of amusement. Part of the audience laughter in such a situation is probably a consequence of non-amused independent variables—such as embarrassment and conformity. [The role of conformity emerges quite clearly in an experiment by Nosanchuk and Lightstone, 1974. See also Chapman (1973a, 1973b.)]

One of the implications of this non-monotonic relationship is that the research by Pollio and co-workers (1972) on early-, middle- and late-riser comedians with respect to duration, amplitude and latency of audience laughter cannot presently be given an unambiguous interpretation. Other related problems in interpreting a laughometric rating are that some uninhibited souls with large lungs may disproportionately push the needle, and some so-called types of jokes (puns are a good candidate) might receive higher laughter than amusement magnitudes while other types of humour (e.g. satire) may do the converse.

In any event we can concede that an individual may laugh at his own expense without committing ourselves thereby to the assumption that he possesses a sense of humour in the sense of being amused at his own expense.

(2) A second reason for the illusion that men have a sense of humour thus defined is that a joke may be funny for more than one reason, and a person can be amused because of humorous components of the joke other than those which reduce his self-esteem.

Consider the following joke: 'She chased him all around the church till finally she caught him by the organ'.

Suppose the subject is a socialist Women's Libber who believes that the joke demeans females and that religion is the opiate of the masses and the Church a decadent, hypocritical, capitalistic institution. She may find the joke funny, despite her belief that it ridicules women, because she thinks it helps reduce the Church.

(3) The illusion that a person is amused at his own expense may issue from *miscommunication*. For instance, a joke may actually be intended to be at the listener's expense; yet he may *mistakenly believe* the joke renders him victor rather than victim.

(4) The illusion that a person is amused at his own expense could result from his belief (correct or incorrect) that the 'insulting' communication addressed to him is intended *ironically*. In such an instance the 'butt' may actually feel complimented (i.e. superior), believing the 'insulter' considers him such a good sport that he can 'take a joke'.

The successful user of such pseudo-insults apparently must carefully pick for the 'joke's butt' one so chosen that the following properties are satisfied: (i) The dimension selected is not so high in the 'victim's' ego involvement hierarchy as to be 'no laughing matter'. (ii) recipient of the left-handed insult must believe that the communicator really thinks well of him. (iii) The recipient must also think well of the communicator. (iv) Oh! irony of ironies, the pseudo-insult must be not mildly insulting but so way out (i.e. extremely insulting) on the dimension of the communication that the receiver cannot possibly take the remark seriously and, consequently, rather than contrasting it, judges that the communicator is joking. In other words, under such circumstances, an extreme insult is less insulting than a mild insult.

Balance theory seems useful in showing why pseudo-insults, under the above conditions, are likely to amuse. It would be a state of painful imbalance if a friend insulted one. Balance would happily be restored, however, when one suddenly became aware that the insult was too 'unrealistic' to be seriously intended. The sudden happiness increment or enhanced self-esteem resulting from judging the insult incongruous and, consequently, pseudo would then result in amusement.

(5) Another reason for the illusion that some men have a sense of humour is that the membership group may not be the reference group. Thus Middleton (1959), following his interpretation of Hobbes, did not foresee that university Ss of lower-class parentage might identify positively with the middle-class and that Negroes—perhaps Uncle Toms and Aunt Jemimas—would find anti-Negro jokes as funny as Whites would.

(6) Still another reason for the illusion that some men possess a sense of humour is that one part of the self may be amused at the expense of another, conflicting part—but this is *not* the same thing as being amused at one's own expense (the amused part of the self being a *different* part from the butt part). In such an instance S may seem possessed of 'self'-hatred or masochism or altruism. The earlier substantiation of abstract hypothesis H5 provides experimental support for this illusion.

(7) Often someone is genuinely amused, while relating an embarrassing past event (perhaps of his childhood), at his own expense. However, as part of a Hobbes' quotation early in this chapter indicates, Hobbes apparently did not judge such an event contrary to superiority theory, and we do not believe it necessarily contradicts the assumption a sense of humour is illusory. Such amusement, we predict, can only transpire, *ceteris paribus*, if the storyteller differentiates 'past me' from 'present me'. If so, he considers the butt of the joke his *former* (rather than *present*) self. [Our argument, that sense of humour is illusory, may seem to have degenerated into a thinly veiled tautology. However, this seventh reason for the illusion (involving *temporal* attitude switching) also seems experimentally testable: Ss who do not make a 'present me'–'past-me' differentiation would be predicted to remain unamused.]

(8) Lastly, another type of attitude switching can also create the illusion that some men have a sense of humour: the confounding, at a given time, of different *levels of generality*. For instance, an apparently anti-Jewish joke proves hilarious to good Jews. Closer inspection reveals, however, that the joke is anti-Rabbi, and the amused Jews in question are not Rabbis. An observer could ministerpret such amusement as indicating that these Jews hold a sense of humour—because they misjudge the relevant ingroup in this instance to be the class *Jew* when it is rather the properly-included class *non-Rabbi Jew*. Substantiation of abstract hypothesis *H4* adds substance to the possible occurrence of this myopic illusion.

We deny then that a sense of humour, thus defined, exists. To deny that a sense of humour exists is not of course to deny that humour exists. But where does humour exist? *Humour lies neither in laughter nor in jokes but only in the minds of men.* How mindless then be those men who have identified humour with laughter.

In other words humour is a mental experience—an O in the model S–O–R. Laughter is an R; a joke is an S. This chapter concedes humour and laughter exist and has talked, until now, as if jokes also exist. The number of logical possibilities regarding whether each of these three two-valued variables is present in a given event is shown as the eight rows in Table 4.1.

Table 4.1 Logical possibilities on three two-valued variables

	S – Joke	O – Humorous	R Laughter
(1)	Yes	Yes	Yes
(2)	Yes	Yes	No
(3)	Yes	No	Yes
(4)	Yes	No	No
(5)	No	Yes	Yes
(6)	No	Yes	No
(7)	No	No	Yes
(8)	No	No	No

The last row of Table 4.1 is irrelevant to humour theory and the first lacks paradoxical import. And all these eight logical possibilities are empirically (i.e. psychologically) possible.

As discussed earlier, humour is neither a necessary (rows 3 and 7) nor sufficient (rows 2 and 6) condition of laughter. A joke is also neither a necessary (5 and 6) nor sufficient (3 and 4) condition of amusement. And a joke is neither a necessary (5 and 7) nor sufficient (2 and 4) condition of laughter.

ARE THERE ANY JOKES?

Psychologists and laymen probably generally agree that a joke is a humorous stimulus. That is, for any X, X is a joke if and only if X is a humorous stimulus.

Our cultural bias is that jokes actually exist and the ethnocentric defence of this commitment reduces it to a disguised tautology. If we deny a so-called joke funny, we are accused of either lacking a sense of humour and/or being too stupid or ignorant to get the joke's point. If we find amusing that to which our culture denies joke status, we put ourselves in danger of being stigmatized as psychotic. The individual, in any event, who either fails to show amusement at that which his culture categorizes as a joke, or finds amusement at what by his culture's standards is a non-joke, is placed on the defensive. So the cultural ontologic commitment to jokes is retained unimpaired.

In truth, there are no jokes. The presentation of a 'joke' is an insufficient condition to generate amusement: (1) Superiority humour experimental evidence discussed earlier suggests that a 'joke' may fail to amuse because one's own proverbial ox is getting gored. Thus one man's joke may be another man's insult. (2) A 'joke' may not amuse because one fails to get its point (i.e. perceive the incongruity).

In the case of (1) above we probably have what is perceived as a *non-funny joke*—and the reason for non-amusement appears basically *emotional*. However, in (2) what is probably perceived is a *non-joke*—and the basis for non-amusement seems *cognitive*. Yet (1) above could apparently also generate the mental experience of a non-joke, as the S may be too threatened to get the point.

The cultural bias dictates that the 'joke' contains a point (such as an incongruity) and not getting the point is equivalent to failing an intelligence test item. This ethnocentrism insists that 'jokes' are inherently (i.e. objectively) funny and some 'jokes' are better than others. Flugel (1954, p. 726) wisely questions, however, whether such a thing as a good 'joke' exists.

It can be questioned, therefore, that 'jokes' have points or inherent incongruities which transcend cultural boundaries. For instance, a large number of alleged 'jokes' in our culture have as their apparent point a domineering woman attacking a submissive man. The point of that type of 'joke' is the *incongruity* that men, not women, are supposed to be the aggressors. However, Margaret Mead (1950) found a society (Tchambuli) in which the women were the aggressors. This type of 'joke,' we predict, would be found unfunny in such a culture.

Nor does a 'joke' appear to be a necessary condition for amusement. Experiments by Nerhardt (1970; see Chapter 3) and Deckers and Kizer (1974) measured discrepancy of weights from weights previously lifted. The more discrepant weights, these authors concluded, more often generated laughter and humour. However, neither these authors nor anyone else conceives of the weights which generated the amusement as 'jokes'. (Note that these experiments also seem to provide evidence for the cultural relativity of incongruity; one's background of weight-lifting and other experiences are often culturally relative.)

Nothing is funny to everyone and anything seems potentially funny to someone. Hence, not only is the presentation of a 'joke' neither a necessary nor sufficient condition of humour, there is also other evidence that a 'joke', defined as a humorous stimulus (external to the observer), non-exists. The same humour researchers who define a 'joke' as a humorous stimulus or humorous communication would doubtless concede that the same 'joke' may be expressed in different sensory modalities. A 'joke' may be heard, read etc. Evidently, the stimulus (or set of stimuli) changes, however, with a sensory modality transformation. Even within the same sensory modality, the same 'joke' can be recognized though the stimuli differ. The 'joke' may be typed in black, or handwritten in red, in big or small letters, etc. That which we call the same 'joke' also often expresses itself in different languages.

The *incongruity* property which conventional wisdom insists inheres in 'jokes' demands the question: 'Incongruous with respect to what?'—for incongruity connotes a *binary relation*. Nonetheless, such a relation, by any reasonable definition of *stimulus*, can be neither a stimulus nor a set of stimuli. Clearly then, 'jokes', conventionally defined, non-exist. To argue otherwise requires such radical redefinition that the application of the label 'joke' to whatever *relationship* or *Gestalt* it is which amuses would only generate negative transfer of training. A pedagogic norm of science would thus be violated; a term ought not be used in ways contradictory to, or radically divergent from, its originally understood meaning.

(Incidentally, as humour closely relates to aesthetics, and as 'jokes' non-exist, so perhaps, for similar reasons, there are no works of art. Beauty, as with amusement, is in the eye of the beholder.)

SUPERIORITY AND PERCEIVED INCONGRUITY

What relationships between superiority and incongruity humour theories exist? The presence of incongruity alone appears neither a necessary nor sufficient condition of an adequate humour theory. Since beliefs can prove mistaken, incongruity, if not perceived, will fail to be funny; conversely, misperception of an absent incongruity could under some conditions amuse. We have also questioned earlier the assumption that the incongruity is 'out there' within some humorous stimulus; and human perception, it seems clear, is in some degree culturally relative. Hence the proper focus in humour theory appears to be not on incongruity *per se*—rather on incongruity *perceived*.

However, *perceived incongruity* at best is a necessary condition of humour, clearly *not* sufficient. Many alleged jokes seem unwilling to amuse unless the 'docoder' perceive an ambiguity and resolve it (cf. Shultz, 1972; Suls, 1972). We doubt that the second step, *resolution*, must necessarily follow perceived ambiguity temporally; but obviously the reverse temporal sequence cannot be the case. This kind of humour theory sounds Gestalt psychological—that is, insight or closure in problem-solving can prove 'reinforcing' in a manner whose happy by-product is amusement. More recent jargon than Gestalt called the perceived incongruity *cognitive inconsistency* (imbalance, cognitive dissonance, cognitive incongruity etc.) and older jargon sometimes named it *conflict*. Resolution of conflict, dissonance reduction, restoration of balance etc. apparently could, under specified conditions, amuse.

Involved, in addition to perceived incongruity, is a 'reinforcement' or happiness increment and a type of happiness increment is a feeling of superiority or heightened self-esteem. The insight which amuses typically (perhaps invariably) is *sudden*. Thus a useful humour formula might be: amusement results from a *sudden happiness increment consequent to a perceived incongruity*. Superiority, nonetheless, may get stretched too thin if it is equated with, rather than treated as a type of, happiness increment. It seems safe to say though that many of these resolutions of a perceived incongruity are dependent upon a feeling of superiority. (Perhaps this fact helps explain why 'jokes' whose resolutions seem too obvious fail to prove very amusing—little increment in self-esteem accrues from successfully coping with apparently Mickey Mouse challenges.)

A closely related humour area that also relates perceived incongruity and superiority humour theory involves so-called *sense-in-nonsense humour*. Here the noticed nonsense part is the perceived incongruity. Consider, for instance, Bertrand Russell's conjugation of an irregular verb: 'I am firm. You are obstinate. He is a pig-headed fool'.

Here we have denotative sense in connotative nonsense—since the denotative meaning is held relatively constant with respect to the predicate (referring to an individual who is resistant to attitude change) while the connotative meaning varies. However, the connotative meaning varies systematically, not randomly, in such manner as to flatter the speaker and insult his enemies (even though they share the same trait). We thus see through the speaker's 'unjustified' ego-enhancement technique and to him feel superior.

Two quasi-experiments (La Fave and co-workers, 1973), though not on humour *per se*, substantiated hypotheses which add some support to the above analysis. Ss tended to assign items of positive connotation to their own position and negatively connoted items to the enemy camp (regardless of denotative meaning).

Amusement apparently can also result from the superiority involved in perceiving *connotative sense in denotative nonsense*. A politician from the Southern U.S.A., addressing an audience believed to be opposed to homosexuals, Negroes and communists, describes his opponent as 'a queer, nigger-loving commie'. The incongruity here is that his opponent is assigned to categories seemingly unrelated; yet connotative sense is perceived in the common negative affect towards all these categories. One sees through the propagandistic tactic and feels superior to his audience which presumably does not.

Earlier we suggested that under specifiable circumstances an extreme insult is less insulting than a mild insult—since the extreme 'insult' would cognitively restructure as a 'left-handed insult' or compliment in disguise. Such an irony of ironies would furnish another bridge between the islands of superiority and incongruity humour theory.

Previously, La Fave (1965, 1969) had suggested how such an incongruity could relate to the Sherif–Hovland social-judgement model (Sherif and Hovland, 1961; Sherif and co-workers, 1965; La Fave and Sherif, 1968). A psychosocial (or psychophysical) item 'way out' in S's latitude of rejection (i.e. very *discrepant*) from his own position or latitude of acceptance would probably be judged amusing. However, we have performed no research along such lines.

Fortunately Nerhardt (1970) and Deckers and Kizer (1974), mentioned earlier, have connected incongruity humour research to this important area. They found, consistent with predictions, that Ss laughed or smiled more frequently when presented with weights very discrepant from an established range or comparison weight than when presented with weights less discrepant. A problem with their designs is that they operationalize amusement in terms of laughter and smiling (and it seems possible, within the context of their experiments, that some emotion other than amusement, such as embarrassment, was expressing itself). It is also not entirely clear what role, if any, happiness increment or a feeling of superiority plays in the perception of such incongruity. Thus further experimental work in this area employing humour judgements as the operational measure of amusement is a prime necessity to determine if their results replicate under such conditions.

In the meantime (as their results seem consistent with what is known about 'slapstick' comedy) we very tentatively assume that very discrepant weights more often amuse than less discrepant. We also prefer Nerhardt's theoretic treatment (which emphasizes the expected *range*) to that of Deckers and Kizer—which focuses instead on a central tendency measure (point of subjective equality or adaptation level) because Nerhardt's approach articulates better with the Sherif–Hovland model and seems, consequently, more relevant to the social sciences, as indicated below.

Henri Bergson (1911) is sometimes classified as an incongruity humour theorist and sometimes as a superiority theorist. Hardly surprising, since his brilliant insights substantially bridge the two areas. One cannot merely treat Bergson literally: he was vague, inconsistent and sometimes wrong—as is pretty much the case for all the well-known humour theorists at his time.

However, a stroke of genius seems to tie together his humour writings.

Bergson's work also seems especially relevant to group dynamics and humour. Laughter (presumably amusement) was for Bergson the consequence of the 'mechanical encrusted upon the living'. The quintessence of his meaning seems to be that when one accidentally (i.e. automatically or mechanically) commits a *faux pas* (*incongruously* non-conforms to a social norm) he becomes the butt, generating laughter (amusement) in others, resulting from a feeling of superiority.

Combining Bergson, Nerhardt, the Sherif–Hovland social-judgement approach, and some social-control theory, we suggest the following. If an individual non-conforms to a social norm, the likelihood that members of the audience will be amused is enhanced if: (1) the norm in question is *not so sacred* or apparently important for the society's survival that non-conformity to it is 'no laughing matter'; (2) the non-conformity is apparently *accidental*, rather than deliberate; (3) the non-conformer is of *high prestige*; (4) the non-conformity is *very discrepant* from the norm or range of expectancy. [Conditions (1), (2) and (3) above seem more closely tied to superiority theory, and (4) to incongruity.]

The resultant laughter from the audience may prove especially embarrassing to the *involuntary non-conformist* if he values the society and his status within it. In such an instance the amused ridicule laughter will act as a negative social sanction, punishment, social control or censure mechanism (Hertzler, 1970), indicating that he is losing status, and thus motivate him to take care *not* to make a fool of himself again (i.e. to conform to the norm). Thus a sufficiently ego-involving social or group norm is a steady state since those who non-conform to it will either cease non-conforming or be excommunicated—and in either event the norm will tend to be protected against extinction.

Approaching humour theory from another direction, the 'causes' of that involuntary non-conformity forcing one to commit a *faux pas* become relevant. We have some suggestions and relevant experimental evidence along these lines (La Fave and Teeley, 1967; Mannell and Duthie, 1975; La Fave, 1972b). We witness there the involuntary non-conformist—his heart in the right place but his foot in his mouth—victim of a habit learned wisely but too well.

CONCLUSION

We have reviewed some of the experimental literature on superiority humour research. However, this area has been evolving from an emphasis on superiority to vicarious superiority to heightened self-esteem. Since amusement resulting from heightened self-esteem seems possible when the preferred reference–non-membership group is victorious over the membership group (as occurred in our Prof–Stud experiment), it is perhaps stretching the construct *superiority* too far to consider such results consistent with it (and such data surely contradict Hobbesian superiority theory).

The confusing, contradictory results in the humour and aggression experimental literature suddenly become sensible when reconceptualized within a superiority–self-esteem humour paradigm; the latter exposes important uncontrolled variables which seem largely to account for the inconsistencies in the aggression-and-humour literature.

Our own theoretic approach in the superiority–self-esteem tradition is not only relevant to the aggression and humour literature, but also to intra-group and inter-group relations and social control, as Martineau (1972) has very capably shown.

However, a superiority–self-esteem approach as heretofore conceived could not provide the sufficient conditions of a theory of humour. Consequently we have tried to suggest some connecting links between superiority and incongruity theory. In doing so we have observed a further way of extending the superiority–self-esteem approach into group dynamics, with substantial assistance from the brilliant insights of the too-neglected humour theorist, Henri Bergson.

It seems abundantly clear that myopic ethnocentrisms have prevented many humour theorists and researchers from coping with certain ironies with respect to humour, stifling constructive creativity and trapping such humour theorists in dead ends. One of the biggest barriers to constructive contribution has been the stubborn insistence on employing the terms humour and laughter interchangeably.

Necessary ingredients of an adequate theory of humour would seem to involve a (1) *sudden* (2) *happiness increment* (such as a feeling of superiority or heightened self-esteem) as a consequence of a (3) *perceived incongruity*.

REFERENCES

Bergson, H. (1911). *Laughter: An Essay on the Meaning of the Comic.* New York: Macmillan.

Berlyne, D. E. (1972). Humor and its kin. In J. H. Goldstein and P. E. McGhee (Eds.), *The Psychology of Humor.* New York: Academic Press.

Cantor, J. R., and Zillmann, D. (1973). Resentment toward victimized protagonists and severity of misfortunes they suffer as factors in humor appreciation. *Journal of Experimental Research in Personality*, **6**, 321–329.

Chapman, A. J. (1973a). Social facilitation of laughter in children. *Journal of Experimental Social Psychology*, **9**, 528–541.

Chapman, A. J. (1973b). Funniness of jokes, canned laughter and recall performance. *Sociometry*, **36**, 569–578.

Clément, R. (1974). Ethnicity, deservedness and contextual formality in humor. Unpublished Master of Arts thesis, University of Western Ontario.

Cooley, C. H. (1902). *Human Nature and the Social Order.* New York: Scribners.

Deckers, L., and Kizer, P. (1974). A note on weight discrepancy and humor. *The Journal of Psychology*, **86**, 309–312.

Dott, N. M. (1938). Surgical aspects of the hypothalamus. In N. E. Clarke, R. J. Le Gros, and D. M. Dott (Eds.), *The Hypothalamus. Morphological, Clinical and Surgical Aspects.* Edinburgh: Oliver and Boyd.

Druckman, R., and Chao, D. (1957). Laughter in epilepsy. *Neurology*, **7**, 26–36.

Eastman, M. (1936). *Enjoyment of Laughter.* New York: Simon & Schuster.

90

Flugel, J. C. (1954). Humor and laughter. In G. Lindzey (Ed.), *Handbook of Social Psychology*, Vol. 2. Reading, Massachusetts: Addison–Wesley.

Freud, S. (1928). On humor. *International Journal of Psychoanalysis*, 9, 1–6.

Freud, S. (1960). *Wit and Its Relation to The Unconscious*. New York: Norton. (Original German edition, 1905.)

Gutman, J., and Priest, R. F. (1969). When is aggression funny? *Journal of Personality and Social Psychology*, 12, 60–65.

Haddad, J., and La Fave, L. (in preparation). A vicarious superiority theory of humor: membership versus reference groups and identification classes.

Hertzler, J. O. (1970). *Laughter: A Socio-Scientific Analysis*. New York: Exposition Press

Hobbes, T. (1651). *Humane Nature*. London: Anchor.

Hobbes, T. (1968). *Leviathan*. Harmondsworth: Penguin. (Originally published 1651.)

Hollingsworth, H. L. (1911). Experimental studies in judgment: judgment of the comic. *Psychological Review*, 18, 132–156.

Kelley, H. H. (1973). The processes of causal attribution. *American Psychologist*, 28, 107–128.

Koestler, A. (1964). *The Act of Creation*. London: Hutchinson.

La Fave, L. (1961). Humor judgments as a function of reference groups: an experimental study. Unpublished doctoral dissertation, University of Oklahoma.

La Fave, L. (1965). Some supplemental variables to assimilation–contrast principles in psychosocial 'scales'. Paper read at a symposium on 'Social Judgment' at the annual convention of the American Psychological Association, Chicago.

La Fave, L. (1967). Comment on Priest's article: election jokes: the effects of reference group membership. *Psychological Reports*, 20, 305–306.

La Fave, L. (1969). Humor as a supplemental variable to assimilation–contrast principles in psycho-social 'scales'. *Symposium Proceedings 1969 Western Psychological Association Meetings*, Vancouver, British Columbia.

La Fave, L. (1972a). Humor judgments as a function of reference groups and identification classes. In J. H. Goldstein and P. E. McGhee (Eds.), *The Psychology of Humor*. New York: Academic Press.

La Fave, L. (1972b). Implications of subadditive fusions for complex motor skills. In I. D. Williams and L. M. Wankel (Eds.), *Proceedings of the Fourth Canadian Psycho-Motor Learning and Sport Psychology Symposium*. University of Waterloo.

La Fave, L., and Sherif, M. (1968). Reference scale and placement of items with the own categories techniques. *Journal of Social Psychology*, 76, 75–82.

La Fave, L., and Teeley, P. (1967). Involuntary nonconformity as a function of habit lag. *Perceptual and Motor Skills*, 24, 227–234.

La Fave, L., Billinghurst, K., and Haddad, J. (in preparation. Humor judgments as a function of identification classes: women's liberation.

La Fave, L., Haddad, J., and Marshall, N. (1974). Humor judgments as a function of identification classes. *Sociology & Social Research*, 58, 184–194.

La Fave, L., McCarthy, K., and Haddad, J. (1973). Humor judgments as a function of identification classes: Canadian vs. American. *The Journal of Psychology*, 85, 53–59.

La Gaipa, J. J. (1971). Social psychological aspects of humor. Paper presented before Midwestern Psychological Association, Detroit.

Mannell, R. C., and Duthie, J. H. (1975). Habit lag: when 'automatization' is dysfunctional. *The Journal of Psychology*, 89, 73–80.

Martineau, W. H. (1972). A model of the social functions of humor. In J. H. Goldstein and P. E. McGhee (Eds.), *The Psychology of Humor*. New York: Academic Press.

Mead, M. (1950). *Sex and Temperament in Three Primitive Societies*. New York: Mentor Books. (Originally published 1935.)

Middleton, R. (1959). Negro and White reactions to racial humor. *Sociometry*, 22, 175–183.

Nerhardt, G. (1970). Humor and inclination to laugh: emotional reactions to stimuli of

91

different divergence from a range of expectancy. *Scandanavian Journal of Psychology*, **11**, 185–195.

Nosanchuk, T. A., and Lightstone, J. (1974). Canned laughter and public and private conformity. *Journal of Personality and Social Psychology*, **29**, 153–156.

Pollio, H. R., Mers, R., and Lucchesi, W. (1972). Humor, laughter and smiling: some preliminary observations of funny behaviors. In J. H. Goldstein and P. E. McGhee (Eds.). *The Psychology of Humor*. New York: Academic Press.

Priest, R. F. (1966). Election jokes: the effects of reference group membership. *Psychological Reports*, **18**, 600–602.

Priest, R. F., and Abrahams, J. (1970). Candidate preference and hostile humor in the 1968 elections. *Psychological Reports*, **26**, 779–783.

Priest, R. F., and Phillips, W. (unpublished manuscript). Dyad composition, social perception, and the appreciation of jokes.

Priest, R. F., and Wilhelm, P. G. (1974). Sex, marital status, and self-actualization as factors in the appreciation of sexist jokes. *Journal of Social Psychology*, **92**, 245–249.

Reynolds, D. V. (1971). Brain mechanisms of laughter. Paper presented before Midwestern Psychological Association, Detroit.

Roberts, A. F., and Johnson, D. M. (1957). Some factors related to the perception of funniness and humor stimuli. *Journal of Social Psychology*, **46**, 57–63.

Sherif, C. W., Sherif, M., and Nebergall, R. E. (1965). *Attitude and attitude change: the social judgment-involvement approach*. Philadelphia: Saunders.

Sherif, M., and Hovland, C. I. (1961). *Social Judgment: Assimilation and Contrast Effects in Communication and Attitude Change*. New Haven: Yale University Press.

Shultz, T. R. (1972). The role of incongruity and resolution in children's appreciation of cartoon humor. *Journal of Experimental Child Psychology*, **13**, 456–477.

Stearns, F. R. (1972). *Laughing*. Springfield, Illinois: Charles C. Thomas.

Suls, J. M. (1972). A two-stage model for the appreciation of jokes and cartoons: an information-processing analysis. In J. H. Goldstein and P. E. McGhee (Eds.), *The Psychology of Humor*. New York: Academic Press.

Tibbets, S. L. (1973). What's so funny?: humor in children's literature. *California Journal of Educational Research*, **24**, 42–46.

Webb, E. J., Campbell, D. T., Schwartz, R. D., and Sechrest, L. (1966). *Unobtrusive Measures: Nonreactive Research in The Social Sciences*. Chicago, Illinois: Rand McNally.

Wolff, H. A., Smith, C. E., and Murray, H. A. (1934). The psychology of humor. 1. A study of responses to race-disparagement jokes. *Journal of Abnormal and Social Psychology*, **38**, 345–365.

Zigler, E., Levine, J., and Gould, L. (1967). Cognitive challenge as a factor in children's humor appreciation. *Journal of Personality and Social Psychology*, **6**, 332–336.

Zillmann, D., and Bryant, J. (1974). Retaliatory equity as a factor in humor appreciation. *Journal of Experimental Social Psychology*, **10**, 480–488.

Zillmann, D., Bryant, J., and Cantor, J. (1974). Brutality of assault in political cartoons affecting humor appreciation. *Journal of Research in Personality*, **7**, 334–345.

Zillmann, D., and Cantor, J. (1972). Directionality of transitory dominance as a communication variable affecting humor appreciation. *Journal of Personality and Social Psychology*, **24**, 191–198.

Chapter 5

A Disposition Theory of Humour and Mirth

Dolf Zillmann and Joanne R. Cantor

In this chapter, a theory is developed which posits that the intensity of the response to humorous presentations critically depends upon the respondent's affective disposition toward the protagonists involved. Specifically, it is proposed that humour appreciation is facilitated when the respondent feels antipathy or resentment toward disparaged protagonists and impaired when he feels sympathy or liking for these protagonists. The generality of the theory is established by demonstrating that alternative notions, such as the reference-group theory of humour, are specific cases of disposition theory. The disposition theory is also shown to cope effectively with a variety of conditions which alternative notions cannot account for. The explanatory power of the various models is discussed in the light of available research evidence. Finally, the disposition theory of humour is expanded into a disposition theory of mirth, in order to explain appreciation deriving from non-humorous entertaining presentations.

ON INFIRMITIES AND SUDDEN GLORY

In his cynical comment that 'we grow tired of every thing but turning others into ridicule, and congratulating ourselves on their defects', Hazlitt (1926, originally published 1826) seems to have expressed the essence of early conceptions of humour and mirth. In much of Greek philosophy, the specification of what constitutes the ludicrous makes humour appear to be a cruel and brutal affair. In *Philebus*, through the dialogue between Socrates and Protarchus, Plato categorically declared that there is nothing wrong in rejoicing at the misfortunes of enemies. The moral legitimacy of such behaviour was apparently so obvious that Plato restricted his discussion of the ludicrous to the enjoyment people derive from seeing their friends suffer misfortunes. Enjoyment of this sort was seen as motivated by envy, which made it, of course, morally inferior and reprehensible. Enjoyment of the ludicrous was characterized as a vicious habit, based on ignorance, and contrary to acceptable standards of conduct. Plato proposed that not to 'know thyself' leads to the vain conceit of beauty, wisdom or wealth. He declared this vanity to be ridiculous when expressed by friends who are weak and defenceless, and detestable when expressed by friends who are potent and capable of defending themselves. When Plato had Socrates argue that only 'powerless ignorance ... is ridiculous', he made humour a punishment for the conceited weakling, a social corrective which was to be applied gleefully when a counter attack was not likely. Since, following Plato's reasoning, the fear of retaliation prevents the ridicule of the strong and healthy, and since the weak, the ugly, the foolish and the poor have a much greater temptation to have an exaggerated self-appraisal, it appears that, in the final analysis, Plato made the weak and helpless a prime target of ridicule and a risk-free source of social gaiety. Aristotle, in his *Poetics*, showing less concern about the moral legitimacy of ridicule, came to a very similar assessment of the source of merriment. He simply asserted that weakness and ugliness are sources of the ludicrous—unless they are followed by grief or death.

The view that the infirmities of others constitute a principal source of laughter and mirth was revived and, in fact, made more extreme by Hobbes. In *Leviathan*, Hobbes declared that 'those grimaces called laughter' express the passion of *sudden glory*, which people experience 'by the apprehension of some deformed thing in another, by comparison whereof they suddenly applaud themselves'. Hobbes' position thus agrees with earlier infirmity notions in stipulating that the imperfections of others are necessary for the induction of laughter and mirth. However, it differs critically from these earlier notions in the specification of who does the laughing. Whereas, according to the suggestions of Plato and Aristotle, the spotless and powerful laugh at the infirmity-stricken, Hobbes says that it is imperfect people, those who presumably have the greatest need to build up their own self-confidence, who laugh at those who are a bit more imperfect. In fact, Hobbes suggested that laughter was an activity of the weak, not of the spotless. In the *Leviathan*, he wrote, 'And it is incident most to them, that are conscious of the fewest abilities in themselves; who are forced to keep themselves in their own favour, by observing the imperfections of other men', and,' ... of great minds, one of the proper workes is, to help and free others from scorn; and compare themselves onely with the most able'.

Hobbes' conception of amusement and laughter as a self-glorifying, triumphant gesture has entered, in one way or another, many of the more recent notions of humour and mirth (cf. Bain, 1880; Carus, 1898; Dunlap, 1925; Leacock, 1935; Rapp, 1947, 1949; Sidis, 1913; Stanley, 1898; Wallis, 1922). All these notions, which are typically classified as superiority theories, build upon the idea that the triumph of superiority derives mainly from the comparison of oneself to inferior others. Those others, of course, tend to be ugly, dumb, clumsy, weak, poor, and so on. The shallow morality of such a triumph has generally been accepted as an undeniable part of human nature. At times it has been pointed out triumphantly (presumably because it made its proclaimers feel somewhat superior); at other times, it has been only grudgingly admitted. The philosophers' value position on this aspect of human nature was best articulated in Baudelaire's (1961, originally published 1855) view that laughter is the most reliable indication of the satanic spirit in man.

THE AFFILIATION FORMULA

The superiority propositions discussed above seem to be at variance with personal observations and, for that matter, with common sense. People may burst out in laughter when they see their enemies embarrassed, humiliated or injured, yet it appears that they do not enjoy witnessing their close friends suffer these experiences. Apparently, we do not enjoy the infirmities of others indiscriminately. Ugliness, stupidity, weaknesses and other inadequacies appear funnier in those we hate than in those we love. Misfortunes and setbacks seem more amusing when they befall the 'right people'.

The apparent dependency of mirth upon the individual's affective disposition toward the agent or the object displaying infirmities or undergoing maltreatment was first formally proposed by Wolff, Smith and Murray (1934). Wolff and co-workers developed a conceptual distinction between affiliated and unaffiliated objects from James' (1890) notion of the 'empirical self'. According to James, all 'things' a person *can* call his, such as his body, his abilities, his wife, his children, his clothes, his house, his ancestors, his friends, his reputation, his yacht and his bank account, constitute the larger self. And, according to Wolff and co-workers, all these things constitute *affiliated objects*. Affiliations were conceived of as acquired (e.g. beloved friends), created (e.g. offspring), or imposed (e.g. members of one's race), and of these, the acquired ones associated with intense positive sentiments were considered the most important. Whatever the type of affiliation, Wolff and co-workers proposed that '*affiliated objects* are those objects towards which a subject adopts the same attitude as he does towards himself'. This notion derives from James' statements about the individual's feelings toward elements of his larger self: 'If they wax and prosper, he feels triumphant; if they dwindle and die away, he feels cast down' (1890, p. 291). In these terms, the disparagement of an affiliated object amounts to the disparagement of the person holding the affiliations. Such a situation, in the assessment of Wolff and co-workers, cannot possibly constitute an optimal condition for mirth. In contrast, mirth should be unhampered when disparagement is directed at *unaffiliated objects*—those things to which a person is not bound by affection. Following from this reasoning, Wolff and co-workers delineated a realm in which infirmities and mishaps could be uninhibitedly enjoyed, and coined the formula for the following mirth-evoking thema: '*an unaffiliated object in a disparaging situation*'.

Essentially then, Wolff and co-workers have extended the superiority theory of humour by proposing an interaction between the enjoyment derived from superiority and the individual's affiliative disposition toward the object threatened with devaluation. They have created a dichotomy for all objects of the world: those we cherish and those we do not care about. And they have proposed that *witnessing the disparagement of those things we do not hold dear is enjoyed because it gives us a moment's glory of superiority*. The ridicule of esteemed objects, in contrast, cannot possibly be enjoyed because it is considered degrading and debasing to the self.

Wolff and co-workers put their proposition to the test with a degree of rigour unknown at the time in research on humour appreciation. They explored the effects of imposed affiliations, such as those based on ethnic group and sex, on the appreciation of disparagement humour. Specifically, they predicted that jokes disparaging Jews would be appreciated less by Jews than by non-Jews, and their findings bore out this prediction. Similarly, they found that men appreciated jokes ridiculing women more than women did, while women exceeded men in their appreciation of jokes disparaging men. More recently, Middleton (1959), also using imposed affiliations as a basis for making predictions, brought only partial support for the notion of Wolff and co-workers. In his study, Negroes surpassed Whites in their appreciation of anti-White jokes, but Negroes and Whites did not differ in their appreciation of anti-Negro jokes.

REFERENCE GROUPS AND IDENTIFICATION CLASSES

Clearly, Wolff and co-workers (1934) had started a research tradition in which affiliated and unaffiliated objects were *operationalized* in *de facto* group affiliations. For a Jew, other Jews were classified as affiliated objects, and non-Jews were considered unaffiliated. Similarly, to Catholics, Protestants, the Scottish and others, people of their own kind were considered affiliated and all others were not. Group membership, either imposed or acquired, served as the criterion for affiliation and non-affiliation. Such a procedure is hazardous in that it leads to the misclassification of those who do not feel affiliative bonds to a group they belong to in the eyes of an outside observer. Although *de facto* membership and affiliation in psychological terms tend to go hand in hand (cf. Sherif, 1948), some people may feel no closer to their particular ethnic or cultural group than to others, and some people may actively dissociate themselves from their own group and even develop a feeling of hatred for their own kind. The misclassification problem can be circumvented, however, by involving the concept of reference groups. This concept, which was originally introduced by Hyman (1942), defines reference groups as *'groups to which the individual relates himself as a part or to which he aspires to relate himself psychologically'* (Sherif, 1953, p. 206). In terms of this concept, only the pro-Jew Jew, in contrast to the plain Jew, will fail to see the humour in anti-Jewish jokes. Or to be more precise, this type of joke should appear less funny to the pro-Jew Jew than to the plain Jew.

Some research findings are relevant here. Middleton's (1959) failure to find differential appreciation of anti-Negro jokes by Whites and Negroes may have been due to the fact that he sampled according to group membership without considering the attitudinal component of membership. Middleton speculated that the middle-class Negroes in his sample had the tendency to make a marked distinction between themselves and the stereotypical lower-class Negroes depicted in the jokes. His data, which showed middle-class Negroes to enjoy these jokes as much as middle-class Whites and lower-class Negroes to enjoy them less, support this interpretation. Similarly, Cantor and Zillmann (unpublished data, University of Pennsylvania, 1970) found that although males tended to exceed females in their appreciation of jokes in which a female was disparaged by a male, males and females did not differ in their appreciation of the same jokes when they were manipulated to depict the female disparaging the male. Both males and females appreciated the joke versions in which a male dominated a female significantly more than those in which a female dominated a male. Apparently, the *de facto* distinction between subjects on the basis of sex did not adequately reflect dispositional tendencies on the part of males and females.

Priest (1966) has reported data which show that attitudinal assessments are superior to simple group distinctions in predicting humour appreciation. He used party preference (which presumably meant *de facto* membership) and candidate preference in predicting the appreciation of jokes disparaging presidential candidates. Although both measures correlated significantly with differential humour appreciation in the predicted direction, candidate preference, the more directly attitudinal measure, was the better predictor of appreciation.

La Fave, McCarthy and Haddad (1973) also used attitudinal measures of affiliation rather than simple group membership in making predictions of humour appreciation. All of their jokes depicted either a Canadian disparaging an American or an American disparaging a Canadian. The subjects were Canadian and American students, who had been recruited on the basis that they were considered pro-Canadian Canadians or pro-American Americans by participant observers. In addition, only subjects who indicated on a post-experimental questionnaire that they preferred to consider themselves as belonging to their home country were included in the data analyses. The data from the Canadian subjects selected in this manner confirmed predictions. The data from the American subjects did not predominantly emerge as predicted, however. La Fave and co-workers attributed the weakness of the findings to inaccuracies in the assessment of attitudes by the participant observers.

The involvement of the reference-group concept, no doubt, has helped to make the classification of affiliation and non-affiliation more precise conceptually (see Chapter 4). It has promoted a valuable empirical check on subjects' actual affiliations with the people shown in disparaging situations. But it has gone no further than that. It is occasionally implied that the so-called reference-group theory of humour has gone beyond the affiliation formula of Wolff and co-workers, but this is simply not the case. On the contrary, it seems that the older formula can readily accommodate reference-group theory, but not vice versa. Obviously, the unaffiliated-object construct, which gives prime consideration to attitudes and sentiments, can handle objects, any individual person, *and* groups of people. The reference-group construct, in contrast, is restricted to readily identifiable groups of people only. Thus, the reference-group theory of humour is nothing but a highly restrictive version of the affiliation formula. Reference-group theory has not gone beyond the older formula on any count. It has just helped to correct what had proved to be an unsatisfactory operationalization of group affiliations. This, of course, is a matter of method and procedure, not of theory.

Recently, the affiliation formula and the reference-group theory of humour have once more been reconceived and rephrased. La Fave (1972) replaced the reference-group concept with the concept of identification classes. Following Kelley (1947), he contended that the reference-group concept is used to denote the processes of both identification and comparison, and he sought to escape this ambiguity by modifying Turner's (1956) term 'identification group' to 'identification class'. However, for all intents and purposes, an identification class is precisely what Sherif has defined as a reference group and what Kelley has referred to as a normative reference group: an identifiable social aggregate to which the individual relates or aspires. The reasons given by La Fave to justify the relabelling of reference-group theory, for example, that a one-man group would be a contradiction in terms, whereas a one-man class would have legitimacy, appear highly contrived. Both 'group' and 'class' denote social aggregates of variable size, and a person's reference group or identification class is, in the more inclusive terminology of Wolff and co-workers, the aggregate of affiliated objects. Similarly, the newly introduced labels 'positive' versus 'negative' identification classes, referring to affiliated and unaffiliated objects, fail to carry superiority theory beyond Wolff and co-workers.

At one point in his theoretical discussion, La Fave expressed his reasoning concerning superiority theory in purely attitudinal terms, talking about 'objects of affection' and 'objects of repulsion' (p. 198). However, in creating a formula of his own, he avoided this nomenclature in favour of positive and negative identification classes. He thus arrived at the following model: a 'joke' is humorous to the extent that it enhances a positive identification class and/or disparages a negative one. Clearly, the second part of La Fave's proposition is the old thema of Wolff and co-workers, but the first part is an extension of the old thema. Wolff and co-workers went so far as to say that a person 'laughs at his own success and his neighbor's failures', but they did not suggest what La Fave proposed, namely that humour results from seeing people of one's own kind receive gratifications. A competitive student, for example, should no doubt respond joyfully when receiving a superior grade. Such an expectation would be in line with superiority theory. (To consider his mirth a humour response is another matter.) It would also be in line with superiority theory to believe that such a student would enjoy seeing others flunk the course. But why should he respond mirthfully when he learns that others of his kind have got good grades too—or even better ones? In terms of jokes rather than personal experiences, it seems impossible to construct anything minimally funny which would depict nothing but the enhancement of one's own kind. What, for example, could pro-American Americans find humorous in a cartoon showing their favourite ultra-American astronauts, after returning from the moon, receiving a new car, a dream house and a million dollars? In extending the formula of Wolff and co-workers, La Fave has broken with tradition. He has involved an element in his 'superiority humour assumption' which is alien to superiority theory. In fact, it is not only alien to superiority reasoning, but truly counter to it. This element is, instead, consistent with the assumption of an altruistic motivation toward friends. Such an assumption may seem acceptable as far as close friends are concerned. But then, those friends are never the subjects in standard, non-spontaneous jokes. The characters we encounter in such standard comic offerings, no matter how well they fit our positive identification classes, seem affectively too remote to mobilize any altruistic inclinations, if such inclinations ever exist (cf. Krebs, 1970), which could promote mirth. But even if mirthful behaviour were to occur in response to the good fortunes of friends, there seems to be some consensual reluctance to accept the idea that witnessing these events is 'funny'. This reluctance shows that it has been generally implied that enjoyment does not amount to humour unless someone or something is somehow disparaged or victimized.

In terms of research evidence, La Fave's proposition that the enhancement of positive identification classes is an autonomous factor in humour appreciation and, as such, a sufficient condition to induce a humour response, has received no support whatsoever. In studies which have assessed appreciation of the depicted success of one's own kind, the depicted triumph has always been at the expense of a less closely affiliated group (Cantor and Zillmann, 1970 unpublished; La Fave and co-workers, 1973; Wolff and co-workers, 1934; Zillmann and Cantor, 1972). Because of this confounding of the enhancement of one party with the disparagement of another, there is no evidence that the success of a positive identification class is amusing in itself. Although many studies have investigated humour involving disparagement without explicit enhancement (cf. Cantor and Zillmann, 1973; Middleton, 1959; Priest, 1966), there seem to be none which have involved enhancement without disparagement. The conspicuous absence of enhancement as a thema of humour attests to what has been called a disparagement bias (cf. Zillmann and Cantor, 1972). As far as humour is concerned, then, Hazlitt seems to have been right when he asserted that man derives more pleasure from hating than from loving!

A DISPOSITION MODEL OF HUMOUR

The affiliation formula, reference-group theory, and the notion of identification classes, all involve a dichotomization of disparaged entities. As discussed, entities are objects to which a person is affiliated or not, or people who are or are not members of their reference groups or identification classes. Once the disparaged entities are classified as fitting one or the other category, predictions of humour appreciation can be made. Thus, affiliation and non-affiliation are not conceived of in terms of degrees. Additionally, all these notions have emphasized a *positive disposition* toward a disparaged entity versus the *absence of a positive disposition*—rather than a negative one. This emphasis started with the involvement of James' reasoning concerning the larger self, which very clearly dissects the things of the world into those we 'own' and therefore cherish, and those toward which we display indifference (at no point is it said that we despise unaffiliated objects). It continued with the notion of identification classes, where 'positive' means that a person 'can identify with' the members of a class and 'negative' means that he cannot. It could be contended that 'negative' means more than indifference or the lack of identification. Particularly in view of the attitudinal phrase 'object of repulsion' used by La Fave (1972, p. 198), it may be suggested that negative classes involve members who are rejected, condemned or hated. However, a look at the way in which the concept has been operationalized shows that La Fave did not, other than in an isolated statement, desert the dichotomy of positive versus *non*-positive. In his research which contrasted Americans and Canadians (La Fave and co-workers, 1973) for example, the classification check was for pro-American Americans and pro-Canadian Canadians, not for anti-Canadian Americans and anti-American Canadians. In spite of changes in terminology, then, these notions predict humour appreciation on the basis of the dichotomization of affiliation and non-affiliation.

In developing a disposition model of humour appreciation, we have departed from such conceptualizations (Cantor and Zillmann, 1973; Zillmann, Bryant and Cantor, 1974; Zillmann and Cantor, 1972). First, we have dismissed the dichotomization of affiliation, groups, or classes, and have instead employed a conceptual *continuum of affective disposition* ranging from extreme negative affect through a neutral point of indifference to extreme positive affect. In contrast to dichotomy-based models, the disposition model is thus made sensitive to degrees of affect. Mirthful behaviour in response to a humorous presentation is then conceived of as a *function of affective disposition*. More specifically, in this disposition model of humour, the following two basic propositions are advanced:

(1) The more intense the negative disposition toward the disparaged agent or entity, the greater the magnitude of the humour response.

(2) The more intense the positive disposition toward the disparaged agent or entity, the smaller the magnitude of the humour response.

Since the disparagement of an agent or entity characteristically involves another agent who successfully applies the disparaging treatment, and this successful disparagement typically improves the status of the agent applying it (cf. Cantor and Zillmann, 1973), two further propositions are necessary:

(3) The more intense the negative disposition toward the disparaging agent or entity, the smaller the magnitude of the humour response.

(4) The more intense the positive disposition toward the disparaging agent or entity, the greater the magnitude of the humour response.

Thus, it is posited that *humour appreciation varies inversely with the favourableness of the disposition toward the agent or entity being disparaged, and varies directly with the favourableness of the disposition toward the agent or entity disparaging it.* Appreciation should be maximal when our friends humiliate our enemies, and minimal when our enemies manage to get the upper hand over our friends.

Clearly, all these propositions relate directly to disparagement, that is, to put-downs, belittlement, debasement, humiliation, hostility, and destruction. They all relate to superiority and dominance. Enhancement is involved only to cope with a side-effect of disparagement. There is thus no claim whatsoever that a humour response could result from witnessing the enhancement of an affiliated person or thing in a purely benevolent and beneficial manner. As far as this disposition model of humour is concerned, something malicious and potentially harmful must happen, or at least, the inferiority of some-one or something must be implied, before a humour response can occur. In this sense, the model is in the tradition of infirmity and superiority theories.

The emphasis on disparagement (rather than enhancement) brings with it an emphasis on negative sentiments (rather than affection). Disparagement seems to be a laughing matter only when the person or thing being debased is disliked or despised by the person witnessing the maltreatment. At the very least, the witness has to be in an affective position where he 'couldn't care less' about the vicitimized entity. Affection for it could only impair the fun. In developing the disposition model, Zillmann and Cantor (1972) have stressed the role of *resentment* as a motivating factor in humour appreciation. They accepted the individual's dispositions toward his social and physical environment and toward himself as given, and proposed that, in the framework of his dispositions, the individual pursues his own interests—even in responding to humorous presentations:

> It is assumed that the individual who attempts to bring about a certain state of affairs, or who at least sympathizes with those who attempt to bring it about, will respond antagonistically to any agent obstructing the achievement of the valued goals, and that this *resentment will motivate him to respond euphorically when witnessing the goal-blocking agent undergo undesirable experiences and suffer misfortunes.* (Copyright (1972) by the American Psychological Association. Reprinted by permission.)

The involvement of resentment as a humour-motivating factor should not be interpreted as an unrestricted belief in man's natural propensity for evil (cf. Baudelaire, 1961) or as a belief in the supreme pleasure of hating (cf. Hazlitt, 1926). Negative sentiments, which may be directed toward persons or objects, are not conceived of as potentially closer to 'human nature' than positive sentiments. Instead, all sentiments are conceived of as *acquired* in any of a variety of ways. Once acquired, a person's negative sentiments (and he may have many of them) are expected to determine the dose of fun he receives from seeing those he despises punished and set back. A person is thus 'malevolent' to the extent that he enjoys *witnessing* the misfortunes of his opponents and antagonists—without actively helping to bring about the setbacks. In a selfish manner, he enjoys seeing things come his way rather than theirs. In terms of the classic notions concerning superiority theory, this idea seems to relate best to

Hobbes' thoughts in *Leviathan* on the desire for power. 'So that in the first place, I put for a generall inclination of all mankind, a perpetuall and restlesse desire of Power after power, that ceaseth onely in Death'. If a person is so oriented, he will respond antagonistically to anyone who succeeds because the other's success potentially endangers his power to control matters at will. Only the other's setback assures power and wellbeing, and the power gain which comes with the competitor's loss makes for the 'exultation of the mind which is called *glorying*'. This puts man against his fellow men—all of them. But even in Hobbes' system of political philosophy, arrangements could be made to integrate the power interests of some, so that groups of friends, rather than individuals, would rival for power. At any rate, this is a very free interpretation of Hobbes. He himself never linked elements of his political philosophy with the casual remarks on joy, glory and laughter for which he is famed as a humour theoretician. Be this as it may, it seems that a bit of Hobbesian power struggle and malevolence in superiority humour cannot be denied. This becomes clear when an attempt is made to apply James' notion of the larger self to negative rather than non-positive sentiments. James suggested that we enjoy seeing our own cherished things prosper, and suffer seeing them dwindle, but he did not suggest that we either enjoy or suffer whatever happens to the things we do not care about. It thus follows that when, for example, our neighbour backs his brand new car into his mailbox, damaging both, we should not smile or chuckle—no matter how little we think of him and how much better his car is than ours. The fact that people can enjoy seeing the things their neighbour owns and cherishes dwindle, and resent seeing them prosper, attests to the involvement of malevolence in humour, which has gone largely unnoticed in recent treatments of superiority theory.

In addition to the conceptual differences discussed, the disposition model contrasts in another critical way with other models, in particular with the reference-group theory of humour and its reformulation in terms of identification classes. Concerning the decoding of humorous stimuli (Zillmann and Cantor, 1972) it was proposed that:

(1) 'the individual interpreting a humorous communication recognizes and labels relevant roles and aspects of behavior exhibited by protagonists', and that (2) 'he responds discriminately to these roles or activities either by empathizing more readily with those protagonists whose roles and behavior activate cognitions that reinstate salient activities of his, by reacting antagonistically to protagonists whose roles and behavior are associated with negative experiences of his, or both'.

It was explicated that the labelling process under (2) refers to 'the discriminatory identification of a particular role or type of behavior', and that 'it does not imply that the decoder has a verbal label for that role or behavior at his disposal'.

The disposition model thus stipulates only that a person *responds discriminately* to the display of roles or activities and that, by so doing, he takes sides.

Specifically, it is proposed that a person will 'take the side' of another person who is, according to the perception of his role and behaviour, experientially close to him in the sense of *sharing* relevant experiences, and/or that a person will 'take a position against' another person when this other person characterizes roles and behaviours which in the past have been associated with negative sentiments. In contrast to reference-group theory and the notion of identification classes, which explicitly require that the person must have some symbol—'such as a noun or a noun phrase' (La Fave, 1972, p. 209)—at his disposal to represent a reference group or an identification class to himself, the disposition model does not rely on classifiable entities which can be readily handled with a dictionary. By jointly involving a mechanism of empathy and a paradigm of affective or emotional reaction, the model can accommodate the interpretation of humorous stimuli without making any assumptions concerning groups or classes, the individual's awareness of them, or his awareness of self-classifications. The model can readily handle, for example, a joke depicting the ridicule of an acne-stricken teenager. The person who acutely suffers such an obtrusive handicap should readily empathize with the victim—even if he is totally unable to represent the class of such youngsters to himself in a label. Moreover, he need have no awareness whatsoever of the fact that, besides himself and the joke's protagonist, there are other acne-stricken people in the world. The same reasoning applies, of course, to empathetic affiliation with more positive features of agents involved. The case of 'anti-affiliation' by affective reaction seems even more direct. All the disposition model requires is that the interpreter of a humorous presentation identify and recognize roles and things. If he is able to understand and follow what is happening, he can display his 'gut response' to a group of people, to a single person, to an animal, to an object—in fact, to anything—without having labels for, or an awareness of, their conceptual or empirical existence in categories.

The disposition model, in short, renders conceptualizations in terms of groups or classes superfluous. The classification of people into racial, national, political, religious or socio-economic categories is a helpful tool to the analyst. But, as La Fave (1972) has stressed, it is valid only when the dispositions that group or class members are supposed to hold do, in fact, exist. Since, as discussed earlier, dispositions need not coincide with actual group or class membership, the empirical assessment of dispositions has become typical in recent research (cf. La Fave and co-workers, 1973; Priest, 1966). The adherents of group or class theory have thus come to place the disposition concept above the group or class concept. Since dispositions are used to validate classifications, it would appear that reference-group theory and the notion of identification classes are valid only as long as they adequately *classify dispositions*. The reliance on the more inclusive disposition construct, together with the fact that the disposition model effectively handles everything the group and class models can handle, renders the group and class theories of humour special cases of disposition theory.

The disposition model of humour contrasts with the other models discussed in still another way. Reference-group or identification-class affiliations are conceived of as relatively stable over time. In the terminology of Wolff and co-workers, imposed affiliations are permanent and acquired ones are of considerable duration. Affiliations are thought of as the manifestation of some trait or disposition of personality. In contrast to the supposition of such relatively stable personality characteristics, in the disposition model a disposition is conceived of as arbitrarily variable over time. It can assume the form of a personality trait, but it can also change with a spontaneous flare of temper. By conceiving of a disposition as free to vary over time, the disposition model accommodates the affective dynamics of individuals (cf. Zillmann and Cantor, 1972). This, in turn, empowers the model to cope with situations which place alternative models in a dilemma. For example, the disposition model can readily handle a situation in which someone is angry at his closest friend. His anger, as a transitory state of resentment, may well motivate him to laugh uproariously when he sees his friend fall off his chair. Since in this dyad, positive group or class affiliation remains unchanged, intense humour is not predictable from group or class theories. Moreover, with the accommodation of affective dynamics, the disposition model can cope with humorous stimuli to which the other models simply are not applicable. In many standard jokes, the protagonists are only scarcely described. There may be no cues as to their role in life, their socio-economic status, or other social characteristics. Or if there are such cues, the protagonists may all be of the same kind, status, conviction, etc. Yet, there may be much disparagement between these protagonists, resulting in much laughter. Characteristically, however, in this kind of joke, one character first commits a provoking act. It may be assumed that the depicted transgression creates an affective disposition toward the transgressor, so that when he finally gets what he deserves in the punchline, the appreciation of his disparagement is motivated by negative sentiments toward him. Furthermore, the disposition model can be related to intuitive considerations of justice (cf. Heider, 1958). An affective disposition may create expectations about what should happen to the resented agents. It may guide the evaluation of how much 'punishment' is fair and therefore enjoyable, and the assessment of what constitutes too little or too much (cf. Zillmann and Bryant, 1974a).

Finally, in developing the disposition model, Zillmann and Cantor (1972) stipulated that, for disparagement to be funny, the individual must recognize the type of an incident or the format of a presentation as humorous. This recognition was considered necessary in order to remove the social sanctions usually demanding the inhibition of the expression of euphoria upon witnessing others undergo misfortunes. It was proposed that only if the individual is thus freed from inhibitions, will he be free to respond mirthfully to such events. This proposal was derived mainly from Freud's (1960) insistence that tendentious humour, and disparagement humour would be tendentious, needs to be be comouflaged by what he called joke work, in order to function as legitimate humour. Apparently, counter to much of what was suggested in Greek philosophy, the blunt display of infirmities, hostilities, and aggression, even if it victimizes the 'right people', does not produce humour responses with any regularity. The popular club-over-the-head is funny when it happens to clowns and cartoon figures, not when police officers do it to rioting students— even if the students are resented. A blunt insult may be effective disparagement but, in general, it is considered deplorable. The same insult dressed up as a pun is equally effective but, in addition, it is socially sanctioned and *funny*. Plays-on-words, incongruities, unexpected contrasts, minimal surprises, exaggerations, extended facial features, or simply the announcement that something funny is to come are all elements of joke work. They may be trivial by themselves, but when combined with disparagement and hostilities, they become the excuse for being malicious in our pleasures. After all, who hasn't laughed heartily at a mishap, found his laughter brutal and cruel on second thought, and then blamed a trivial piece of joke work in it for his (mis) behaviour? As Freud (1960) put it:

> A good joke makes a total impression of enjoyment on us, without our being able to determine at once what share of the pleasure derives from its joke characteristics and what share from its apt thought-content. We are constantly making mistakes in this apportionment; sometimes we overestimate the quality of the joke because of the content's appeal, at other times we overestimate the appeal of its content on account of its joke-embodiment. We do not know what it is that gives us pleasure and what we laugh about. This uncertainty in our judgement, which must be assumed to be a fact, may have provided the basis for the development of the joke *per se*. The content seeks camouflage in joke work because in that way it recommends itself to our attention and can seem more significant and more valuable, but above all because this wrapping bribes and confuses our critical abilities. (p. 107; author's translation).

VALIDITY AND SCOPE OF THE DISPOSITION MODEL

Several studies have been published which provide support for the disposition model of humour while at the same time producing findings that remain unexplained by the more restricted notions concerning reference groups and identification classes. Zillmann and Cantor (1972) have demonstrated that humour appreciation can be accounted for on the basis of the individual's experiential similarity or dissimilarity to a joke's protagonists and on the basis of dispositional tendencies that are assumed to be a by-product of his experiential background. Samples were drawn from two populations, college students and middle-aged business and professional people. Subjects gave ratings to humorous communications in which one protagonist got the better of another by successfully committing physical aggression, by making an insulting remark or, in general, by 'having the last laugh'. All of the protagonists in the communications were white males with no outstanding ethnic characteristics, but each communication involved an interaction between a superior and a subordinate. Three types of superior–subordinate relationships were represented: father–son, professor–student and employer–employee. Two versions of each communication were created. In one, the superior got the better of his subordinate and, in the other, the subordinate had the final word over his superior. It was expected that students' experiences with such interactions would be predominantly from the subordinate side and that professionals' experiences would be predominantly from the superior side. Under the assumption that interactions between superiors and subordinates typically produce some perceived inequities (cf. Adams, 1965), it was further hypothesized that the protagonists not sided with would constitute objects of at least moderate resentment. It was predicted that subjects who saw the versions in which a protagonist sharing relevant experiences disparaged a member of the dissimilar group would show greater humour appreciation than subjects who saw the versions in which the experientially alien protagonist disparaged the experientially affiliated one. The results were as predicted. Students gave higher ratings of funniness to the communications in which the subordinate disparaged his superior than to those in which the superior disparaged his subordinate. The ratings of the professionals exhibited precisely the opposite relationship. Thus, in the domain of family interactions, students sided consistently with sons and professionals sided consistently with fathers. In educational settings, students gave their support to students and professionals were on the side of professors. In the domain of business, students rooted for the young employees and professionals were partial to their employers. Apparently, then, subjects had more sympathy for, and reacted more empathetically to, those protagonists who were experientially similar to themselves. They also seem to have reacted to the protagonists on the opposite side of the superior–subordinate dichotomy with some negative feelings. Disposition theory thus readily accounts for the findings. Theories based on the concepts of reference groups and identification classes can deal with the findings only with great difficulty, however. If these concepts are used in the strict sociological sense, referring to acknowledged sociological groupings only (such as ethnic or religious groups or socio-economic strata) the findings remain a mystery. In this narrow use of the concept, all the protagonists were representatives of the same reference group (White, American, upper middle-class), as were, no doubt, most of the subjects. The reference-group concept could, of course, be applied more loosely in an attempt to account for the data. It could be argued that students recognized the protagonists as 'sons', 'students', and 'employees', that they represented these protagonists to themselves with appropriate labels, and that they thought of themselves as members of these reference groups. It could also be argued that the professionals respond in the same way to the protagonists who were fathers, professors and employers. But even if the reference-group concept is stretched this far, it seems particularly odd to imagine students choosing employees and professionals choosing professors as reference groups. To circumvent this problem, advocates of a reference-group theory of humour might posit the functioning of reference groups based on even broader distinctions, such as age. They might argue, for example, that 'the younger generation' constituted the reference group for students and 'the older generation' served this function for professionals. If such an interpretation of the concept of reference groups is endorsed, the reported data can, of course, be accounted for. It seems, however, that with this interpretation, the concept becomes so vague and general as to lose most of its predictive power.

In a second study Cantor and Zillmann (1973) gave evidence for the enhancement of appreciation of disparagement humour when the disparaged protagonist is *resented*. They also produced evidence that accurate predictions of the appreciation of disparagement can be made even though the protagonists do not belong to readily identifiable social groupings. In this study, college students were used as subjects, and the implied occupations, opinions or accomplishments of the protagonists in the humorous communications were manipulated so as to cause the protagonists to be either resented or liked by the subjects. It was expected, and later validated in ratings, that, for example, students would have sympathy for a man expressing support for students' rights and antipathy for an opponent of students' rights, and that they would have generally positive sentiments toward such people as musicians and zoo-keepers and generally negative sentiments toward wealthy bankers and heavily armed policemen. In each cartoon used in the study, a protagonist was seen to undergo a misfortune. The misfortune was shown to be brought about by accident, by chance or by 'neutral agents' so that the humour response produced by witnessing the disparagement of a protagonist would be independent of the effect of witnessing the dominating triumph of another (liked or resented) agent. Figure 5.1 illustrates the manipulation of one of the cartoons used in this study. The results showed that, as expected from disposition theory, mishaps occurring to resented protagonists were much funnier than the same mishaps befalling favoured ones. The protagonists in question did not fit into readily identifiable groups or classes of which the subject either was or was not a member or an aspirant. Instead, they represented simply types of people which the subjects had the tendency either to like or dislike.

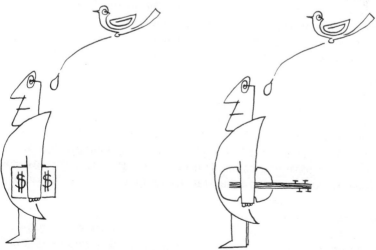

Figure 5.1 Example of cartoon used depicting musician/banker. (Cantor and Zillmann, 1973).

A study by Zillmann and co-workers (1974) is relevant to the same point. Political cartoons depicting physical assaults against candidates were created and manipulated so that the assault was perpetrated either upon Richard Nixon or George McGovern, the major contenders in the 1972 U.S. presidential election. These cartoons were seen and rated by college students during the week before the election. Predictions of appreciation of the cartoons were made on the basis of the subjects' statements of the degree to which they were opposed to or in favour of the policies of the depicted candidate. Consistent with predictions, when the depicted assaults were not inordinately brutal, subjects who were opposed to the depicted candidate appreciated the cartoons more than those who favoured him. This study went beyond the findings of Priest (1966) by making predictions not just on the basis of candidate preference, but on the basis of negative as well as positive sentiments toward candidates. The superiority of measures of attitudes toward candidates over simple measures of candidate preference is illustrated in the following comparison: subjects were included in the candidate-favoured category only if they preferred the depicted candidate over his opponent *and* gave him a positive evaluation on the attitude scale. Similarly, subjects were placed in the candidate-rejected category only if they preferred the opponent of the depicted candidate *and* gave the depicted candidate a negative evaluation. Those subjects who preferred the depicted candidate but nonetheless expressed disliking for him, and those subjects who did not prefer the depicted candidate but still evaluated him positively were excluded from the original data analysis. The mean appreciation score of the subjects who held a negative disposition toward their non-preferred candidate was sharply differentiated from that of the subjects who held a positive disposition toward their preferred candidate. The data of the excluded subjects revealed, however, that relative preference alone was not a basis from which accurate predictions of appreciation could be made. The means of the two groups of subjects whose attitudinal ratings were not consonant with their candidate preference fell in an intermediate position between the mean of the candidate-favoured condition and that of the candidate-rejected condition. More importantly, the means of these excluded groups differed only trivially from each other.

Studies by Gutman and Priest (1969) and Zillmann and Bryant (1974a) illustrate the point that affect toward a particular protagonist may be conceived of as dynamic and manipulable rather than static. In both of these studies, affective dispositions toward protagonists were manipulated by varying their *behaviour* prior to the punchline. Gutman and Priest used jokes involving two persons of the same sex and equal status, with no prominent ethnic characteristics. In each joke, acceptability versus unacceptability of the initial behaviour of the protagonist who delivered the disparaging punchline was factorially varied with acceptability versus unacceptability of the initial behaviour of the recipient of the final attack. Thus, the affective dispositions of the subject towards the aggressor and the victim were manipulated independently by having each protagonist behave either nicely or obnoxiously. Consistent with disposition theory, the jokes were considered funnier when the victim of the final disparagement had behaved poorly than when he had behaved well. Also as predicted from disposition theory, those squelches in which the disparaging agent had been characterized as 'good' were found funnier than those in which he was characterized as 'bad'.

Zillmann and Bryant (1974a) conducted a related study in which five different degrees of negative sentiment toward the recipient of a final attack were produced by varying the severity of the act of provocation he performed. The retaliatory action of a second protagonist was kept constant, and was roughly equivalent in severity to the provocation which occurred in the third, or middle, condition. As predicted from disposition theory, appreciation of the jokes increased as the level of provocation increased—up to the point where provocation and retaliation were at equivalent levels. Beyond this point, in the conditions where provocation exceeded retaliation, humour was impaired, possibly because the depicted under-retaliation was not perceived as a successful attack on a resented agent.

Apparently, in both the Gutman and Priest (1969) and Zillmann and Bryant (1974a) studies, subjects responded discriminately to the various protagonists on the basis of their behaviour and formed dispositions toward them in the absence of verbal labels which would permit their categorization into relevant groups or classes. In these studies, any classification of protagonists according to non-dispositional social strata which the analyst may attempt seems to be utterly irrelevant as far as humour appreciation is concerned.

A DISPOSITION MODEL OF MIRTH

Freud's (1960) proposal that tendentious humour requires both (a) an 'offence' which makes it tendentious and (b) joke work, and that there is considerable ambiguity in the partitioning of pleasure to the two contributing components, not only helps resolve the problem of the unfunniness of blunt disparagement, but may prove to be a key concept in separating humour appreciation from the appreciation of dramatic presentations. Humorous disparagement and disparagement in drama could be distinguished conceptually by the fact that humorous situations involve joke work and dramatic ones do not. This would mean that witnessed disparagement can be 'maliciously' enjoyed only under humorous conditions because only then can the individual attribute his enjoyment to the joke work involved. This joke work may contribute only trivially to the respondent's fun, but the attribution of the pleasure he derives from witnessing an assault upon a resented agent to this joke work, erroneous though it may be, makes his response socially proper. Social and self-generated objections to his behaviour seem groundless. And should moral considerations ever arise to spoil the fun, the joke work provides a ready-made vehicle for their refutation and dismissal. Apparently, we do not want to believe that we are cruel enough to enjoy, for example, our neighbour's misfortune of backing his new car into his mailbox. If, nonetheless, negative affect has made us burst out in laughter, we can always tell ourselves that it happened because of the peculiar way in which the mailbox was deformed, the peculiar expression on our neighbour's face, the peculiar squeaking noise of the impact, or a dozen other peculiar things. All of these things *save us from a moral dilemma and permit us to be malicious with dignity*. In fact, they permit us to vent negative sentiments with dignity. And this may well characterize what, precisely, humour can do for us.

Drama, in contrast, does not offer moral amnesty. Because drama does not have a genuine equivalent for joke work, the enjoyment of disparagement, hostility and violence cannot readily be attributed to certain elements of the presentation. The respondent thus cannot misattribute his behaviour and, in this sense, he has to take full responsibility for his affective responses. If he finds himself laughing or crying, he has only the dramatic events as such to blame. Clearly, when witnessing debasement he is more restricted in venting his negative sentiments through mirth. He is caught in the narrow framework of moral considerations. If, under the circumstances, debasement is indicated and justified, he is free to enjoy it (cf. Zillmann and Bryant, 1974b). If debasement is entirely unwarranted, he must hold back his enjoyment. And if he should fail in this and should find himself having gone too far in his enjoyment of infirmities and assaults, he is forced to justify his enjoyment to himself. He will, as in humour, have to find an excuse for his (mis)behaviour, and attribute it, at least in part, to something in the presentation other than socially condemned behaviour. But unlike in humour, the excuse is not readily available. Nonetheless, he may end up telling himself that what he really enjoyed was the way the movie was edited, the way music, lighting or slow motion was used, or simply the film's all-around aesthetic magic. In doing this he resorts to the ingenious solution invented by mediaeval gentlemen who, when prevented by strict Christian morality from decorating their homes with paintings of women in the nude, got their way by declaring such paintings pieces of art.

In all, mirthful behaviour particularly when it seems 'out of proportion', can come about more readily in response to the humorous depiction of disparagement than to its purely dramatic display. However, *humour and drama appreciation seem to be similarly influenced by affect toward disparaged persons or objects*. Bad things happening to a resented agent, whether they are considered funny or not, should be pleasing. The same things happening to a neutral or liked agent should not be pleasing, but rather displeasing or saddening.

A recent investigation of empathy (unpublished data obtained by Zillmann and Day, Indiana University, 1974) has revealed that mishaps are, in fact, appreciated only when they befall resented people. In this study, six versions of a film were created. A boy was shown to interact with friends, with his dog and with his younger brother in an obnoxious, neutral, or very friendly manner, so that children viewing the film would develop negative, neutral or positive sentiments towards him. The movie ended by showing the boy either in a painful bicycle accident or euphorically receiving a new bicycle from his

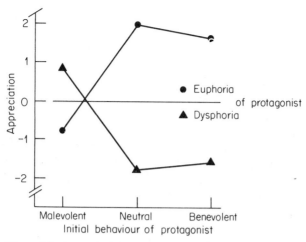

Figure 5.2 Appreciation of positive and negative outcomes to others, according to their likeability generated by initial behaviour

parents. As expected from the disposition model, the mishap in the drama was found to be truly appreciated only when the agent undergoing it was resented. When he was liked (and he was similarly liked when he was friendly and when he behaved in a neutral manner), the mishap led to displeasure. Concerning the boy's reception of benefits, this relationship was reversed: the presentation was pleasing when the liked agent was benefited, and displeasing when he was resented—the latter condition creating irritation in the viewers with considerable regularity. The conditions which involve the protagonist's reception of gratifications are, of course, alien to humour theory. However, since witnessing the rewards or enhancement of an esteemed person or object can nonetheless induce mirthful behaviour presumably through empathetic participation, it cannot be considered alien to a theory of drama appreciation or to a general theory of mirth.

If mirth is conceived of as the expression of euphoria, humour may be conceived of as mirth which the respondent attributes, fully or in part, to those stimuli of a more complex stimulus situation which make 'funny' a generally accepted qualifier of that situation. This is not to say that humour is a property of situations, or that being humorous is a quality which inheres in events. It means rather that *humour is the result of an appraisal process in which the individual can explain his mirthful behaviour to himself as fully or partly caused by stimuli which are considered funny in his cultural environment* (and only to the extent that there is consensus in this assessment of something being funny can we talk about 'humorous situations'). If witnessed disparagement lacks these stimuli, the individual's positive affective reaction is the pure enjoyment of witnessing maltreatment. Such enjoyment is likely to be expressed in mirth, but the situation cannot be labelled humorous. In this terminology, an infant who laughs at mishaps displays 'a sense of mirth', not a sense of humour.

The sense of humour develops with intellectual maturation—specifically, with the emergence of sophisticated moral considerations (cf. Piaget, 1932; Kohlberg, 1963, 1964) which threaten the unrestricted expression of mirth (cf. Zillmann and Bryant, 1974b). It comes into being when the child learns to bypass inhibitory stipulations concerning enjoyment of the misfortunes of others by singling out a potentially trivial cue to laugh at when he is, in fact, enjoying the mishap. Humour is thus nothing other than a particular interpretation of mirth to oneself.

If mirth is accepted as a most inclusive term for the expression of positive affect, a theory of mirth deriving from witnessing events and situations must incorporate both the debasement and the enhancement of persons and objects. In contrast to humour, drama has room for benefaction as a thema. It appears that mirth resulting from witnessing either malice or benefaction is critically dependent upon sentiments toward those persons or things which are debased or enhanced. A general disposition model of mirth (of which humour is a part) should thus include benefaction. This, of course, is easily accomplished by treating benefaction as the inverse of debasement in the basic propositions of the disposition model:

(1) The more intense the negative disposition toward the benefited agent or entity, the smaller the magnitude of mirth.
(2) The more intense the positive disposition toward the benefited agent or entity, the greater the magnitude of mirth.

The integration of disparagement and benefaction is a general disposition model of mirth leads to the following proposal:

(I) *Mirth deriving from witnessing the debasement of an agent or object increases with negative sentiments and decreases with positive sentiments toward the debased agent or object. Mirth deriving from witnessing an agent or object accrue benefits decreases with negative sentiments and increases with positive sentiments toward the beneficiary.*

At this point it could be speculated that mirth is a joint function of affective disposition and the degree of debasement or benefaction. It could be suggested that, when disposition is held constant, mirth increases with the extent to which a resented agent is debased and decreases with the extent to which this agent is enhanced, and it decreases with the extent to which an attractive agent is debased and increases with the extent to which this agent is enhanced. Such suggestions have not been confirmed by recent findings, however. Concerning disparagement, Cantor and Zillmann (1973) and Zillmann and co-workers (1974) failed to observe greater humour appreciation as the magnitude of a mishap befalling a resented agent increased. Also, when debasement in humorous communications and in drama was perceived as too severe under the circumstances, appreciation was impaired rather than facilitated (Zillmann and Bryant, 1974a, 1974b). The demonstrated dependency of mirth on moral considerations should also be expected for enhancement. As with debasement, it seems that benefaction can easily be perceived as inappropriate and, once the witness's sense of justice is thus disturbed, his enjoyment should be impaired.

The intricacy of the relationship between mirth and moral considerations is evidenced further by considering the viability of an inversion of the secondary propositions of the disposition model of humour. Substituting 'benefactor' for 'disparaging agent or entity', and inverting the functional relationship, the third proposition reads: The more intense the negative disposition toward the benefactor, the greater the appreciation. The fourth proposition becomes: The more intense the positive disposition toward the benefactor, the smaller the magnitude of appreciation. These derived propositions seem counter-intuitive; and they should because they are in conflict with the general model. In principle, *the disposition model asserts that loss of value inflicted upon our enemies and gain of value obtained by our friends is appreciated, and that gain of value obtained by our enemies and loss of value inflicted upon our friends is deplored.* If, in terms of moral judgement, being benevolent is meritorious, behaving in such a manner should bring value gain. Consequently, in accord with the general model, we should enjoy witnessing our friends as benefactors and deplore seeing our enemies in such roles. The secondary propositions concerning benefaction should therefore not be derived by inversion of those concerning debasement. They instead have to be kept parallel. Since, however, the primary propositions for benefaction were arrived at by inversion, the model seems to involve an inconsistency. In fact, it does. If, in terms of moral judgement, being malevolent is deplorable, behaving in such a manner should bring value loss to the person so behaving. Consequently, we should deplore seeing our friends behave in this manner and enjoy witnessing our enemies doing so. It would appear, then, that the secondary propositions concerning disparagement, which claim precisely the opposite, make for the inconsistency in the model. If, as discussed, being beneficial were a value and being malevolent were a vice, the initial proposition would have to be changed to assure consistency. Yet, and this is most revealing, *in our cultural situation, both benefaction and successful debasement seem equally meritorious.* He who successfully disparages someone else enhances himself by doing so. And witnessing such self-enhancement in friends seems less deplorable—or more worthy of appreciation—than witnessing it in enemies. The glory-through-malevolence phenomenon shows once more the disparagement bias and the pervasiveness of malevolence in humour and drama appreciation. If witnessed disparagement only (and not witnessed benefaction) can produce a venting of negative sentiments through mirth, this phenomenon would be explained psychologically.

The parallel secondary propositions may be integrated in the following proposal:

(II) *Mirth deriving from witnessing an agent debase or benefit another entity increases with positive sentiment and decreases with negative sentiment toward this agent.*

114

The theory of mirth expressed in propositions I and II accounts satisfactorily for all relevant experimental findings on the appreciation of humorous and dramatic presentations. These propositions effectively subsume alternative, but more restrictive models.

The remaining problems concern mainly the relative contributions to mirth of the various elements involved in the model. Is witnessing disparagement indeed more effective in the induction of mirth than witnessing benefaction? How critical is the display of the disparaging acts as such, and to what extent does the perception of the disparaging agent's glory, implied or explicit, facilitate the mirth response? Experimental investigations will have to address such questions; and the refinement of a disposition model of mirth will have to await the answers.

REFERENCES

Adams, J. S. (1965). Inequity in social exchange. In L. Berkowitz (Ed.), *Advances in Experimental Social Psychology*. Vol. 2. New York: Academic Press.

Aristotle. (1812). *Treatise on Poetry*. London: Luke Hansard & Sons.

Bain, A. (1880). *The Emotions and The Will*. (3rd ed.). London: Longmans Green.

Baudelaire, C. (1961). De l'essence du rire. In *Oeuvres Complètes*. Paris: Gallimard. (Original French edition, 1855.)

Cantor, J. R., and Zillmann, D. (1973). Resentment toward victimized protagonists and severity of misfortunes they suffer as factors in humor appreciation. *Journal of Experimental Research in Personality*, **6**, 321–329.

Carus, P. (1898). On the philosophy of laughing. *Monist*, **8**.

Dunlap, K. (1925). *Old and New Viewpoints in Psychology*. St. louis: Meaby.

Freud, S. (1960). *Jokes and Their Relation to The Unconscious*. New York: Norton. (Original German edition, 1905.)

Gutman, J., and Priest, R. F. (1969). When is aggression funny? *Journal of Personality and Social Psychology*, **12**, 60–65.

Hazlitt, W. (1926). *On the pleasure of hating*. In *Essays*. New York: Macmillan. (Original edition 1826.)

Heider, F. (1958). *The Psychology of Interpersonal Relations*. New York: Wiley.

Hobbes, T. (1968). *Leviathan*. Harmondsworth: Penguin. (Originally published, 1651.)

Hyman, H. H. (1942). The psychology of status. *Archives of Psychology, No.* 269, 5–38, 80–86.

James, W. (1890). *The Principles of Psychology*. Vol. 1. New York: Henry Holt.

Kelley, H. H. (1947). Two functions of reference groups. In G. E. Swanson, T. M. Newcomb, and E. L. Hartley (Eds.), *Readings in Social Psychology*. New York: Holt, Rinehart & Winston.

Kohlberg, L. (1963). The development of children's orientations toward a moral order: I. Sequence in the development of moral thought. *Vita Humana*, **6**, 11–33.

Kohlberg, L. (1964). Development of moral character and moral ideology. In M. L. Hoffman and L. W. Hoffman (Eds.), *Review of Child Development Research*. Vol. 1. New York: Russell Sage Foundation.

Krebs, D. L. (1970). Altruism—An examination of the concept and a review of the literature. *Psychological Bulletin*, **73**, 258–302.

La Fave, L. (1972). Humor judgments as a function of reference groups and identification classes. In J. H. Goldstein and P. E. McGhee (Eds.), *The Psychology of Humor: Theoretical Perspectives and Empirical Issues*. New York: Academic Press.

La Fave, L., MaCarthy, K., and Haddad, J. (1973). Humor judgments as a function of identification classes: Canadian vs. American. *Journal of Psychology*, **85**, 53–59.

Leacock, S. B. (1935). *Humour: Its Theory and Technique*. London: John Lane.

Middleton, R. (1959). Negro and White reactions to racial humor. *Sociometry*, **22**, 175–183.

Piaget, J. (1932). *The Moral Judgment of The Child*. London: Kegan Paul.

Priest, R. F. (1966). Election jokes: The effects of reference group membership. *Psychological Reports*, **18**, 600–602.

Rapp, A. (1947). Toward an eclectic and multilateral theory of laughter and humor. *Journal of General Psychology*, **36**, 207–219.

Rapp, A. (1949). A phylogenetic theory of wit and humor. *Journal of Social Psychology*, **30**, 81–96.

Sherif, M. (1948). *An Outline of Social Psychology*. New York: Harper.

Sherif, M. (1953). The concept of reference groups in human relations. In M. Sherif and M. O. Wilson, (Eds.), *Group Relations At The Crossroads*. New York: Harper.

Sidis, B. (1913). *The Psychology of Laughter*. New York: Appleton.

Stanley, H. M. (1898). Remarks on tickling and laughing. *American Journal of Psychology*, **9**, 235–240.

Turner, R. H. (1956). Role-taking, role standpoint and reference group behavior. *American Journal of Sociology*, **61**, 316–328.

Wallis, W. D. (1922). Why do we laugh? *Scientific Monthly*, **15**, 343–347.

Wolff, H. A., Smith, C. E., and Murray, H. A. (1934). The psychology of humor: 1. A study of responses to race-disparagement jokes. *Journal of Abnormal and Social Psychology*, **28**, 341–365.

Zillmann, D., and Bryant, J. (1974a). Retaliatory equity as a factor in humor appreciation. *Journal of Experimental Social Psychology*, **10**, 480–488.

Zillmann, D., and Bryant, J. (1974b). Viewer's moral sanction of retribution in the appreciation of dramatic presentations. Unpublished manuscript, Indiana University.

Zillmann, D., Bryant, J., and Cantor, J. R. (1974). Brutality of assault in political cartoons affecting humor appreciation. *Journal of Research in Personality*, **7**, 334–345.

Zillmann, D., and Cantor, J. R. (1972). Directionality of transitory dominance as a communication variable affecting humor appreciation. *Journal of Personality and Social Psychology*, **24**, 191–198.

Chapter 6

Physiological and Verbal Indices of Arousal in Rated Humour

Michael Godkewitsch

The term 'humour' can be used to describe a process initiated by a humour stimulus, such as a joke or cartoon, and terminating with some response indicative of experienced pleasure, such as laughter.

In any stimulus situation giving rise to some emotion in a given person, three factors probably interact to establish affect: first, the person's momentary level of central arousal; second, the net sum of the arousal-inducing and arousal-moderating properties of the stimulus situation; and third, the person's expectancies and habitual ways of reacting with regard to the given stimulus situation.

In this chapter the relation between funniness judgements and arousal is investigated. The main purpose of the experiments is to demonstrate that verbal humour responses are strongly related to fluctuations in the arousal level, as measured by physiological and verbal indices. The nature of this relation and its significance for a broader theory of affect and motivation are discussed.

MOTIVATION

What motivates humour responses? Why do people enjoy listening to jokes? Whatever the answers, the factors that make for experienced humour should fit into a more general theory of motivation.

This century has witnessed a rapid succession of theoretical views attempting to describe what initiates, what directs and what reinforces behaviour. Initially, the rise of empirical determinism, Darwinism and historical materialism replaced the rationalist tradition: reason and free will no longer dictated the direction and purpose of human acts. Organisms came to be seen as naturally inert, while behaviour was considered to result from 'special enlivening forces' such as incentives, needs and need drives (cf. Rethlingshaefer, 1963). Soon the Behaviourist revolution claimed that all motivating factors should be sought in the biochemical interaction between the organism and its environment. The aim of behaviour came to be regarded as the reduction of primary or learned drives. The control of learning processes was seen in reinforcements through pain or pleasure.

Neither this simple drive-reduction view of motivation, nor its refined successor, the homeostasis concept, could account for all motivated behaviour: spontaneous, creative, altruistic and aesthetic acts, including humour, remained unexplained. A great deal of experimental evidence collected after 1950 (cf. Fowler, 1965) forced behaviour theorists to admit that some acts did not seem to be aimed at the assuagement of tissue needs, but instead appeared to be carried out for their own sake. These 'exploratory' acts had certain drive-inducing aspects. Some theorists, for instance Hunt (1963), argued that information processing itself, and the interchange of information between the organism and environment, contains motivating power. Exploratory acts could result from incongruities between present inputs and past constancies in receptor stimulation. In other words, if an organism cannot match its perception of reality to its expectation about that reality, the organism becomes 'curious' — incongruity leads to exploration.

A convenient and plausible intervening variable that seemed to qualify as the chief mediator between stimulus conditions and the motivated response of the organism was found in the concept of 'arousal' (e.g. Berlyne, 1960). This term refers to the position of an organism's internal state of general activation on a continuum ranging from deep sleep to violent frenzy; and it indicates how alert or excited an organism is. Exploratory behaviour has the power to monitor the intake of stimulation and can thus regulate the arousal level of the organism. When arousal level is low in relation to an organism's optimal level, the organism explores; when it is too high, the organism will try to bring it down by withdrawing and thus decreasing stimulation (cf. Hebb, 1955).

The essence of this viewpoint is that states of very low arousal and states of very high arousal are both experienced as aversive, and that the organism consequently tends to reduce this unpleasant state of affairs by striving to optimize its arousal level. This contrasts with the more traditional drive-reduction viewpoint in that the latter claimed that organisms tend to *minimize* their level of arousal. Neither viewpoint succeeds satisfactorily in accounting for affective states. Feelings of drowsiness representing a state of low arousal, for instance, are not necessarily uncomfortable, nor do they automatically lead to exploratory acts. A tired person, about to doze off, is seldom eager for distraction or amusement.

Berlyne (1960, 1963, 1967) has attempted to synthesize these diverse views into a more general theory of collative motivation.

BERLYNE'S THEORY OF COLLATIVE MOTIVATION

This theory describes, among other things, how changes in the momentary level of arousal play a part in determining the quality and the intensity of affective responses. Earlier competing views held the arousal level *per se* responsible for the intensity of affect.

The overall power of a stimulus to affect the nervous system, to command attention and to influence behaviour (Berlyne, 1973) is called the stimulus situation's arousal potential (AP). It is determined by three classes of stimulus properties.

The first class contains *psychophysical* properties, depending on distributions of energy in time and space. They determine the size, frequency, duration, shape and other such attributes of the stimulus array that are independent of the observer. In humour these properties play a minor role. An example is the cartoon sequence effect: regardless of how cartoons are ordered, the second in a pair is usually rated funnier than the first (Lee and Griffith, 1962).

The second class involves *ecological* properties that are associated with events or experiences that were noxious or beneficial for the survival of the organism. For example, a picture of a broiled turkey gives rise to a motivational state different from that induced by a picture of a live turkey, by virtue of the associations with the respective contents alone, irrespective of other factors. In humour, content variables, for instance the theme of a joke, surely form an important component of what makes them funny.

The third class contains the *collative* properties of stimuli. These are defined in 'relations between physico-chemical and statistical properties of stimulus patterns on the one hand, and conditions of the organism on the other' (Berlyne, 1967). These properties 'depend on the collation, or comparison, of information from different sources' (Berlyne, 1963, p. 290). The collative value of a stimulus results from its comparison with others that are close in time or space, or with stimuli that have already been stored in memory. Some examples of collative properties in general are complexity, novelty, change, ambiguity, incongruity, redundancy and uncertainty. These stimulus properties have in common that they involve conflict between incompatible response tendencies. In humour, collative properties play a very important role. Godkewitsch (1974a, 1974b), for instance, worked with *tendency* jokes, that is, jokes in which themes and events occur that, if they were presented in a non-humorous context, might be shocking or evoke feelings of anxiety. He found that the funnier these jokes are rated the better the punchlines can be predicted, while the opposite is true for non-tendency jokes (1974a), and that greater semantic distance between members of adjective–noun pairs evokes higher ratings of humorousness, funniness and wittiness, and more facial reactivity (1974b).

The above three classes of stimulus properties together and in interaction determine how strongly a stimulus can affect an organism's arousal level. Of course, the impact of stimulation also depends on the organism's pre-stimulation state of arousal and its habitual ways of dealing with arousal changes.

Changes in arousal, effected by the interaction of arousal-raising or moderating stimulus variables, and the organism's state of arousal before it was confronted with the stimulus, show a complex relation to subsequent affective state.

Berlyne (1967, 1971) suggests that there are three different ways in which arousal changes may be rewarding and thus lead to feelings of pleasure and other positive affects.

First, when the arousal level greatly exceeds the optimal level, its reduction is experienced as pleasurable. Second, an event that initially raises arousal may be rewarding because it is followed by a prompt arousal reduction and thus may come to signify such reduction. An example is specific exploration: an ambiguous stimulus induces conflicting response tendencies because it has multiple meanings, associated with different behaviour sequences. This conflict arouses the organism. Exploration of the stimulus affords selecting the proper response, whereby the conflict and accompanying arousal are mitigated. In time that kind of stimulus may acquire the property of being pleasurable because its perceived ambiguity has become a signal for subsequent arousal reduction. Third, moderate increases in arousal may be rewarding in their own right, if one assumes that they only activate a 'primary reward system' in the brain and not the 'aversion system'. This latter system is reputed to have a higher threshold than the reward system, and is presumably only activated by large arousal increments.

So, if a stimulus has a very low arousal potential, the organism's affective state is indifferent. When the reward system becomes activated at moderate AP levels of the stimulus, resulting affect is positive. At even higher AP levels the aversive system is also activated and the sum of positive and negative affect brings its net effect back to indifference. When, finally, the stimulus's AP is very high, the activity of the aversive system 'overpowers' that of the reward system and net affect is negative. Berlyne's inverted-U-shaped curve, relating the intensity of affect and the AP of the stimulus situation, is much like the one proposed by Wundt (1893) for the relation between pleasure and stimulus intensity.

HUMOUR AND AROUSAL

Jokes are usually pleasurable stimuli. If pleasure is a joint function of the momentary arousal level and the net sum of the arousal-inducing and arousal-moderating stimulus properties, then the humour experience should similarly vary with such stimulus conditions. In other words, the working hypothesis is that perceived properties of humorous stimuli such as jokes or cartoons effect changes in central arousal which, in turn, result in pleasure.

Shellberg (1969) has proposed that humour and arousal are related according to an inverted-U: at low and very high arousal levels little humour is experienced, but at intermediate levels humour is enjoyed most. Godkewitsch (1972) pointed out a number of difficulties with this and related positions. The main problems are that authors linking arousal and humour meant by *arousal* the activating effects of treatments independent from the humour stimuli (such as the social situation) and not the arousal-inducing effects of the stimuli themselves. Additionally, independent measures of physiological arousal were seldom taken, so that there was no unity in the use of the term.

Empirical data

The experimental research bearing on the arousal question is quickly summarized. Guthrie (1903) and Piddington (1963) emphasized the lack of biological needs and activity in humour enjoyment. Lloyd (1938) noted that mirth results in a pulmonary gas deficit, which Fry and Stoft (1971) failed to replicate. Levi (1963), examining urinary output of adrenalin and noradrenalin during mirth and other emotions found increased sympathico-adrenomedullary activity during mirth.

Heart rate (HR) has been a favourite: Martin (1905) reported increased HR (and respiration) in subjects who found cartoons amusing. Averill (1969) found mirth-associated HR increases and concluded that the humour experience results in arousal of the sympathetic nervous system. Fry (1969a, 1969b) agreed, and demonstrated HR and electrocardiogram (ECG) increases during mirth. Jones and Harris (1971) similarly reported that cardiac acceleration was correlated with experienced amusement. Langevin and Day (1972) found HR changes and maximum responses, as well as galvanic skin response (GSR) recovery time and amplitude positively related to rated funniness of cartoons. Finally, Schachter and Wheeler (1962) demonstrated that pre-injection of arousal-inducing and arousal-reducing substances produced increased and decreased laughter, respectively, in subjects viewing a slapstick comedy. In the Schachter and Wheeler study the state of arousal helped determine the intensity of resulting affect, but neither in that study nor in any of the others could it be established whether or not arousal was a consequence of the stimulus properties.

In fact there is no empirical evidence that humour depends upon changes in arousal, owing to characteristics of the humour material itself. Langevin and Day (1972) concluded that arousal increases accompany the humour response, but their design was not equipped to test the present working hypothesis because they used cartoons as stimuli. A cartoon contains all the information and properties of what can be called the 'joke-problem' and its 'solution', so that physiological reactivity and humour responses are simultaneous. One cannot therefore conclude whether physiological reactivity to cartoons is concomitant to humour or an antecedent to it.

The basic questions

At this point, the basic questions are:

(1) Are changes in arousal level systematically related to the appreciation of humorous stimuli? And if so, in what way?

In accordance with Berlyne's hypotheses about the three ways arousal changes may result in pleasure, arousal and experienced humour can also be related in any of three ways:

(a) If humorous stimuli induce very much arousal, then its reduction should be rewarding and increasing funniness of jokes should be associated with decreases in arousal. This hypothesis is compatible with various traditional viewpoints concerning why humour is enjoyed, as for instance Freud's (1960) position that the release of surplus energy, originally mobilized for inhibition, is pleasurable.

(b) If humorous stimuli represent events that initially raise and then promptly reduce arousal, as Berlyne (1972) has proposed, then the funniest jokes should cause large arousal boost–jags, and very dull ones none.

(c) If humorous stimulus events cause only moderate increases in arousal, then within that class of stimuli a monotonically increasing relationship should obtain between rated funniness and arousal increments in the recipient.

(2) Can changes in momentary arousal level act as an intervening variable between stimulus conditions and responses?

The purpose of the two experiments reported in this chapter was to present some tentative answers to these questions.

EXPERIMENT I

With regard to the first question, whether changes in arousal are related to enjoyment of humour, the fragmentary evidence from the studies in which any physiological responses to humorous stimuli were recorded led to the expectation that greater reported funniness of jokes would be associated with increases in momentary arousal.

The second question, concerning the intervening role of arousal in affect, could be tackled by employing written jokes. These can be divided into joke-bodies and punchlines, and arousal changes in response to both parts can be recorded. If there is any physiological reactivity during the presentation of joke-bodies that is commensurate with subsequent funniness ratings of the jokes after the punchlines have been presented, then such physiological responses intervene in time between joke-properties and humour ratings. Obviously, such arousal changes cannot be mere consequences of the humour response itself, simply because the receiver has not yet read the punchline.

Method

Stimuli

Twenty-four jokes were used: 12 sex jokes, in which the main theme involved a description of or a reference or allusion to heterosexual non-perverse sexual behaviour and 12 non-tendency jokes involving 'harmless wit' and verbal put-ons. These classifications are fully described elsewhere (Godkewitsch, 1974a). In previous research these jokes were found to represent a wide range of funniness.

White-on-blue slides were made of all joke-bodies and all punchlines separately. Type, colour and projected letter size were uniform.

Subjects

Twenty-four female undergraduate students enrolled in an introductory psychology course volunteered to serve as Ss. Female rather than male Ss were chosen because they are physiologically somewhat more responsive (Duffy, 1962). Also, there may still be some social restraint on women, prohibiting their overt enjoyment of sex jokes, so that for them blatant sexual content may represent stimulation having greater AP than the same material would have for male Ss. Such an extension of the range of AP might allow a more valid picture of the empirical relationship between physiological and verbal reactions to jokes on the one hand, and their thematic properties on the other. All Ss were informed in advance about the nature of the stimuli and the experimental measures.

Apparatus and procedure

The slides were projected through a wire screen into the shielded and grounded room in which the S was seated. Three channels of a Grass-7 Polygraph recorder were continually in use during the experiment. One channel recorded slide changes (every 15 seconds), a second processed dermal conductance and a third channel graphed HR. Dermal conductance was picked up by means of electrodes placed on the palm and back of the non-preferred hand, while HR was derived from the two wrists. All recording, projecting and monitoring equipment was located in an adjoining room and instructions were given via an intercom system after S was hooked up. S was told that every joke would appear on the screen in three stages of 15 seconds each. First, the joke-body, describing the situation and the protagonists in the joke, and what led up to the punchline; then the punchline itself, finally followed by a dark period in which S was to give two verbal ratings. For the first rating S indicated on a seven-point scale, ranging from 'not at all funny' to 'extremely funny,' how much she appreciated that joke. The second rating on a four-point scale consisted of a verbal self-report of arousal in response to the punchline.

Design

The 24 jokes and 24 Ss were randomly assigned to the columns and rows of a 24 × 24 doubly balanced Latin Square, constructed following an algorithm by Williams (1949). Not only was every joke presented once to every S and once in each presentation order position across Ss but it was also preceded and followed equally often by every other joke. This within-Ss design affords an estimate of the variance associated with the presentation order affect which is probably important in humour responses. Byrne (1958), for instance, found that, regardless of the order of presentation, funniness ratings tended to increase from the start to the end of a 22-cartoon series. An even more important argument for the balancing of presentation order is that psychophysiological responses tend to flatten out over time, regardless of the experimental treatment, because of habituation (cf. Sokolov, 1963).

Dependent variables

Funniness ratings

Although mean funniness ratings for the jokes were available from earlier studies, these ratings were collected again in this study to estimate their reliability. Mean funniness, although formally a dependent variable in this experiment, was to be used as the independent variable with which the psychophysiological responses were to be compared, similar to the procedure used by Langevin and Day (1972). The result was that average rated funniness in the present experiment correlated better than 0·90 with ratings in previous work. This good stability justified the use of average funniness as levels of an independent variable because these levels were manipulated by the experimenter in the sense that they were known before the experiment.

Verbal self-reports of arousal

Thayer (1967, 1970) has contended that verbal self-reports of arousal reflect 'general activation' more accurately than do individual peripheral measures, if such self-reports correlate more highly with a composite of peripheral psychophysiological indices than these indices are themselves intercorrelated. If supported, this would be of obvious value in experimental aesthetics including humour research, because it would permit assessing a measure of the receiver's central state as a potential mediator between stimulus properties and affective or exploratory responses—one of the aims of this chapter.

Self-reports of arousal have rarely been used in humour research. Wolff, Smith and Murray (1934) found GSR responses less sensitive than funniness ratings, but Cattell and Luborsky (1947) noted that GSR readings and verbal or written responses to jokes discriminated equally well among them. No evidence was presented, however, of a statistical relationship between funniness and reactivity. Rickwood (1973) found that rated funniness of cartoons was positively related to self-reports of 'general activation'.

In general, values for phenomenological intensity of emotions are probably quite reliable. High correlations have been found with objective indices of activation (McCurdy, 1950; Traxel, 1960) supporting a direct relationship between stimulation intensity and arousal level (Schoenpflug, 1969). Of course, to define an individual's state of arousal in terms of subjective reports of intensity of feelings is recommendable only if there is substantial covariation between perceived and directly recorded autonomic activity (as found by, for instance, Frankenhaeuser and Jaerpe, 1962).

'Defensive style', a personality characteristic, can create discrepancies between self-report and autonomic arousal indices (e.g. Averill and Opton,

1968). 'Repressors', for instance, may show greater autonomic than self-report reactions to arousing stimuli, while 'sensitizers' tend to show the opposite. Lazarus (1966, p. 334) admits that shaping of verbal statements of affect by defence or social manoeuvre introduces error into the measurement of affect, but then notes that, nevertheless, such introspective reports can be of great value. They can yield information that is otherwise inaccessible, mainly because non-verbal behaviours cannot provide satisfactory indices of affective states.

Other arguments can be advanced favouring self-reports of arousal. Maltzman (1968, p. 332) argues that verbal indicators of emotional state are more valid than are physiological measures because they are more appropriate: 'the subjects enter the laboratory with a highly differentiated verbal response system, and a relatively undifferentiated physiological response system'. Self-reports of transient levels of arousal also make sense in view of other limitations of physiological measures (Thayer, 1967). These may compensate one another (such as blood pressure and pulse rate), reflect tissue depletions rather than intended motivational effects to which tissue needs are not relevant, and are probably differently patterned for every individual. Phenomenological awareness of general bodily functioning may well provide measures that make Ss more comparable than do physiological assessment techniques. Moreover, single peripheral measures are difficult and expensive to record reliably and can only be used in an experimental laboratory (with the exception of the palmar sweat index), while verbal measures are easy and cheap to collect. Finally, verbal measures probably interfere less than do physiological measures with Ss' natural aesthetic responses in that Ss are not physically restrained. Nor do the verbal measures evoke much anxiety, as do procedures such as hooking up electrodes, abrading the skin, hydration and calibration time of sensitive equipment, and the prohibition to move limbs.

According to Thayer (1971) 'general activation', the most stable of four activation dimensions, can be assessed by having Ss rate their momentary feelings of arousal on a small number of four-point bipolar rating scales, labelled by adjectives such as 'active', 'energetic', 'lively', and 'peppy'. This activation factor best discriminates cognitive, affective, psychomotor or general behaviour patterns 'not influenced by unusually strong stimulus conditions (i.e. intense shock, strong drugs, high anxiety-evoking instructions etc.)'. The adjectives that correlated most highly and consistently with physiological composites were 'active' and 'lively' (Thayer, 1967, 1970) and were therefore selected for use in the present study.

Physiological measures

Peripheral psychophysiological measures of arousal are assumed to indicate the level of the central arousal state, the 'amount of cortical bombardment by the ascending reticular activating system' (Malmo, 1959). There is widespread evidence to expect 'the immediate response to stimulation to have some relationship to the state of the organism . . . at the time of stimulation' (Lykken and Venables, 1971).

Heart rate parameters

(a) Initial HR, in beats per minute. This variable offers an opportunity to trace the arousal level in *S* during presentations of joke-bodies and punchlines.
(b) Latency to HR maximum.
(c) Latency to HR minimum, in seconds. These two measures were taken because there are no convincing arguments for tachycardia or bradycardia as the expected response. Lacey, Kagan, Lacey and Moss (1963) argue that bradycardia (deceleration of HR) is a consequence of attending to the environment, while concentration, intellectual tasks and other such inwardly turned behaviours cause tachycardia (acceleration of HR). But Lacey (1967) found that when *S*s were confronted with a problem to be solved, bradycardia ensued. Jennings, Averill, Opton and Lazarus (1970) found bradycardia following perceptual attention while Jennings (1971) found that cognitive tasks produced bradycardia followed by tachycardia.
(d) Average HR peak.
(e) Average HR trough. These two measures were considered separately because Lacey and co-workers (1963) posit that pleasure is associated with bradycardia and negative affect with tachycardia. A peak was defined as an HR level, preceded and followed during the exposure time of a given stimulus, by an HR level at least 2 beats per minute slower (or faster, for the HR troughs).
(f) HR range, representing the difference between (g) and (h), in beats per minute.
(g) HR maximum, in beats per minute.
(h) HR minimum, in beats per minute.

Skin conductance parameters

(i) Basal skin resistance (BSR) in ohms. This variable indicates general activation and is relatively uninfluenced by the task, or components of the orienting reaction (Warwick, 1970) and fluctuates as a function of adaptation to the experimental situation (Montagu, 1963).
(j) Galvanic skin response (GSR), defined as the largest single change upwards in conductance during the presentation of a joke-body or punchline, excluding the first second, in micromhos. This measure weighs the BSR in that a given change in resistance represents a larger proportion of a low BSR than of a high BSR. The method is fully described by Wilder (1962). The measure was taken because conductance is almost certainly more simply related to arousal than is resistance (Lykken and Venables, 1971) and represents responses to specific stimuli rather than a general arousal state (Warwick, 1970).
(k) The logarithm of the GSR (Log GSR). This transformation normalizes the otherwise skewed distribution of most psychophysiological measures, thus

increasing the probability that the measure is a reliable index of arousal (Lykken and Venables, 1971).

(l) The sum of the downward changes in conductance, in hundreds of ohms, during presentation of a given stimulus. The use of this measure was explorative.

(m) The number of GSRs, that is, the number of times during the presentation of a stimulus, excluding the first second that a GSR of at least 300 ohms occurred.

Results

All data, except the ratings for funniness and the self-reports of arousal, were corrected for individual differences in range. The ranges for physiological reactivity differ greatly across individuals, and some correction of the data is usually in order (Lykken and Venables, 1971) because the limits within which a physiological variable varies for a given S in response to a given stimulus is determined by structural, motivational, and physiological factors unrelated to the variable of interest—arousal state (Lykken, Rose, Luther and Maley, 1966). The error variance due to inter-individual differences in range can be removed in several ways. The method followed here was to obtain ipsative measures by changing the scores for each S on each variable separately to standard scores, so that the impact of the stimuli on one dependent variable could be compared with that of other stimuli within the same S (Sidman, 1960).

Physiological responses

Analyses of variance and planned trend analyses across the mean funniness levels were performed over the normalized data for both joke-bodies and punch lines. Orthogonal polynomials for the unequal distances between funniness levels were calculated following the method described by Robson (1959).

In all physiological measures of reactivity to joke-bodies and punchlines the order of presentation of the jokes was a highly significant source of variance, as expected. Ss clearly became progressively more habituated to the experimental situation. Skin resistance increased and HR parameters decreased over time, independently of any effect of the jokes.

Joke-bodies

Although the average HR peak, average HR trough and the sum of the conductance differences showed significant joke effects, neither their linear nor quadratic components across funniness levels were significant (see Table 6.1). In other words, differences between jokes for these dependent variables were not related to funniness.

Initial skin resistance (BSR) of the joke punchlines, which was, of course, an effect of the joke-bodies, appeared to be a negative linear function of rated funniness. Skin resistance went down during the presentation of the joke-

Table 6.1 Summary of analysis of variance main effects of jokes, and of their linear and quadratic components of trend across mean funniness levels, for physiological measures taken during the presentation of joke-bodies and their punchlines; and the same effects for verbal self-reports of arousal. Non-significant F values are not reported.

	Joke-bodies			Punchlines		
	Anova-effect			Anova-effect		
	Main $F[23,506]$	Lin. $F[1,506]$	Quad. $F[1,506]$	Main $F[23,506]$	Lin. $F[1,506]$	Quad. $F[1,506]$
Heart rate						
Initial HR	—	3·98*	—	—	—	—
Lat. HR max.	—	—	8·05†	—	—	—
Lat. HR min.	—	—	—	—	—	—
Av. HR peak	1·62*	—	—	1·54*	4·85*	—
Av. HR trough	1·69*	—	—	—	—	—
Max.–Min. HR	—	—	—	—	—	—
HR maximum	—	—	—	—	—	—
HR minimum	—	4·19*	—	—	—	—
Skin conductance						
BSR	—	—	—	2·80‡	15·24‡	—
GSR	—	—	—	2·79‡	15·32‡	4·25*
Log GSR	—	—	—	2·37‡	8·65†	7·80†
Sum cond. diff.	1·55*	—	—	1·56*	—	—
#of GSRs	—	—	—	—	—	—
Verbal self-report of arousal				2·27‡	44·43‡	—

*$p < 0·05$
†$p < 0·01$
‡$p < 0·001$

bodies to the extent that the jokes were later rated as funny (see Figure 6.1, top part). This tendency, implying that joke-bodies generate an amount of arousal that is closely related to how much pleasure the whole joke will provide, was stronger for sex jokes than for non-sex jokes.

Joke punchlines

There was more physiological reactivity in response to punchlines than to joke-bodies. Average HR peak went up linearly with funniness, and so did GSR amplitude and the Log GSR (Table 6.1, and Figure 6.1). GSR amplitude and Log GSR were slightly, but significantly, curvilinearly related to funniness because there were relatively large changes in conductance in response to one very dull joke (Figure 6.1). Langevin and Day (1972) similarly found greater GSR activity in response to very unfunny jokes in comparison to moderately funny jokes. Sex jokes evoked greater GSR and thus more arousal than the other, non-tendency, jokes.

The 'latency of response' measures of HR were not related to funniness.

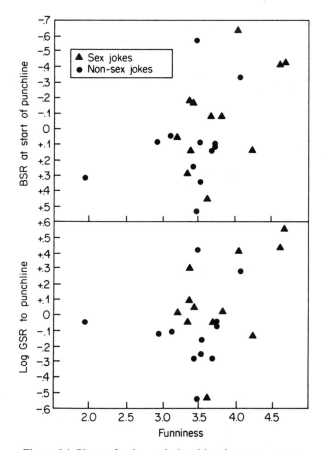

Figure 6.1 Plot of the relationship between mean
funniness ratings of 12 sex jokes and 12 non-sex jokes,
and initial skin resistance at the start of the presentation
of the jokes' punchlines (top part); and the same relationship for the logarithm of the galvanic skin response
(bottom part)

Although Goldstein (1970) found that latencies of humour responses became
shorter with funnier jokes this was not replicated in this experiment, just as it
was not in Langevin and Day's (1972) study. But the studies observed different
behaviours. Goldstein measured skeletal muscle response, while in the Langevin and Day study and in the present experiment peripheral psychophysiological
indices were recorded that have different build-up times.

Finally, Lacey and co-workers' (1963, 1967) suggestion that pleasant
experiences are accompanied by cardiac deceleration received no support.
On the contrary, funniness of jokes was related to tachycardia.

In conclusion, physiological responses to punchlines were associated with
their funniness in the predicted direction. The more arousal the punchlines
evoked, the funnier the jokes were rated in general. The relationships between

funniness and amount of arousal-increase, however, were significant for sex jokes and not for non-sex jokes (see Table 6.2) but the sets of product-moment correlations for the two kinds of jokes showed no significant differences. There was no indication that any decrease in arousal during punchline presentations was related to subsequent funniness ratings.

Table 6.2 Product–moment correlations between mean rated funniness of 24 jokes, four significant physiological response measures to joke punchlines, and verbal self-reports of arousal

	Av. HR peak	BSR	GSR	Log GSR	Self-reports of arousal
With funniness					
Sex jokes $(df = 10)$	0·58*	0·55*	0·67†	0·51*	0·93†
Non-sex jokes $(df = 10)$	0·49	0·33	0·23	0·10	0·87†
All jokes $(df = 22)$	0·37*	0·49†	0·49†	0·40*	0·91†
With self-reports of arousal					
Sex jokes $(df = 10)$	0·48	0·56*	0·67†	0·52*	
Non-sex jokes $(df = 10)$	0·53*	0·36	0·32	0·17	
All jokes $(df = 22)$	0·29	0·52†	0·54†	0·47†	

$*p < 0.05$
$†p < 0.01$

Verbal self-reports of arousal

An analysis of variance and planned trend analysis across the mean funniness levels showed that mean self-reports of arousal increased linearly with mean funniness ratings (Table 6.1, bottom). Further, Ss expectedly reported to feel more strongly aroused after reading sex jokes than non-sex jokes. As Table 6.2 shows, both verbal and physiological parameters of arousal were signifinantly correlated with funniness ratings.

Discussion

According to Berlyne's (1960, 1969) arousal–jag hypothesis of humour, a great jag should lead to higher funniness ratings. In other words, the more transient arousal is induced by properties of the joke-body, the more can be rapidly reduced by the punchline, making for stronger feelings of pleasure. Little support for this hypothesis was found in the present study, only that funniness was associated with a high HR minimum in response to joke bodies.

An alternative expectation was formulated for this experiment. Experienced humour, that is, rated funniness, was predicted to vary positively with the amount of arousal *induced* by the punchlines, rather than *reduced* by them. This prediction was confirmed: HR and skin conductance parameters indicating increased arousal were linearly and positively related to judged funniness.

These main results replicated the findings of Langevin and Day (1972) and extended them in three main ways:

(1) In the present study the linear component of the joke-variance was demonstrably related to the independent variable funniness, while the categorization of funniness in Langevin and Day's study was much cruder.

(2) Punchlines rather than joke-bodies were found to be the major source of humour-associated arousal. Since Langevin and Day used cartoons as stimuli they were unable to distinguish the contributions to the overall arousal level of the 'joke-problem' and the 'solution', respectively.

(3) Two distinct kinds of jokes were used in the present study while Langevin and Day used only one kind (cartoons depicting aggression). This distinction permitted the finding that the relations between physiological reactivity and rated funniness are very strong in sex jokes but not in non-sex jokes. But it must be noted that the two kinds of jokes were not matched in funniness; sex jokes were on the average significantly funnier than the others. Differences in response patterns may therefore be due to differences in funniness rather than to different characteristics of the two kinds of jokes.

Arousal as a mediating response

Elliott (1969) and Elliott, Bankart and Light (1970) suggest that while collative stimulus properties are distinctly effective in stimulating increased skin conductance, the instigation and initiation of responses effectively control heart rate increases. The present finding that BSR at the start of punchline presentations decreased (and arousal thus increased) with funniness is compatible with Elliott's suggestions, especially since at that moment subjects could not be actively preparing for any response. Increases in HR and skin conductance measures in response to punchlines may then be interpreted as arousal increments stimulus properties, and in preparation of responding on the part of the subjects. Further, smiles and vocal reactions to the punchlines occurred after the HR peak and greatest GSR.

Although these bits of evidence support the conclusion that arousal may operate as a mediator between stimulus properties and affective responses, several reservations must be entertained. Arousal, evoked by joke-bodies, may have been a response to collative and thematic properties of the jokes, but there may also, especially in sex jokes, have been arousal in anticipation of pleasure. Godkewitsch (1974a) found the funniness of sex jokes to be positively related to the rated plausibility, appropriateness, expectedness and predictability of their punchlines, and negatively to their surprisingness. Such anticipations may result in central processes conditioned to cues preceding and signalling reward or pleasure (cf. Fowler, 1971). In turn, central responses probably affect peripheral indices of arousal. Moreover, overt affective behaviour may feed back on arousal indices: laughing leads to increased respiration, which conceivably could have led to increased HR and GSR. In the present experiment this probably did not occur because physiological reactivity preceded overt behaviour in time.

EXPERIMENT II

In Experiment I all subjects gave their verbal self-reports of arousal after they rated the jokes for funniness. Because the funniness ratings corresponded closely to judgements of the same jokes in earlier studies they probably were not strongly contaminated by the self-reports of arousal. The self-reports of arousal, however, may have been contaminated by preceding funniness ratings, notwithstanding subjects' retrospection confirming that the two rating tasks bore no relation to one another at all. The purpose of Experiment II was to collect independent and unbiased self-reports of arousal in order to establish unconfounded relationships between funniness and verbal as well as physiological indices of arousal.

Method

Stimuli and design

These were identical to those employed in Experiment I.

Subjects

Twenty-four female undergraduate students enrolled in an introductory psychology course volunteered. As in Experiment I, they were informed in advance of the nature of the stimuli and the procedure. Three prospective Ss declined to take part.

Apparatus and procedure

All details were identical to those of Experiment I, with three exceptions. First, although electrodes were properly placed, no physiological responses were actually recorded. This hoax was necessary to keep conditions identical across experiments. Second, Ss were to rate their feelings of arousal on a seven-point scale, ranging from 'I definitely do not feel active and lively' to 'I definitely feel active and lively', rather than a four-point scale as used in the first experiment. Third, funniness ratings were not requested.

Results

The two sets of mean self-reports of arousal in response to the 24 jokes collected in Experiments I and II correlated significantly ($r = 0.84$; $df = 22$; $p < 0.001$). Also, although the correlations between the present, independently derived self-reports of arousal and funniness were somewhat different from the contaminated correlations reported in Table 6.2, they were not significantly lower.

An analysis of variance and planned trend analysis across mean funniness levels of the self-reports of arousal resulted in a highly significant main effect for jokes ($F = 3.55$; $df = 23/506$; $p < 0.001$), and a strong linear component ($F = 46.16$; $df = 1/506$; $p < 0.001$). In short, self-reports of arousal increased linearly with rated funniness.

Self-reports of arousal in relation to psychophysiological measures

Thayer's thesis that self-reports of arousal reflect 'general activation' more accurately than do separate physiological measures, was rendered testable by selecting those physiological measures that significantly varied with mean rated funniness: average HR peak, average HR trough, BSR, GSR amplitude and Log GSR. Their multiple correlation with self-reports of arousal was 0.58 ($p < 0.001$), while their average absolute intercorrelation was non-significant at 0.28. Thus, the results support Thayer's hypothesis: verbal self-reports of arousal indeed correlated strongly with a composite of individual physiological indices, while these were not significantly correlated among themselves.

The question of predictive validity of the verbal self-reports of arousal, and the step beyond Thayer's work, now became: can verbal self-reports of arousal account for experimental humour less well, or as well as a composite of peripheral psychophysiological measures? That question was answered by comparing, on the one hand, the variance common to the mean funniness ratings and independent self-reports of arousal of Experiment II with, on the other hand, the variance common to the composite of physiological measures and the mean funniness ratings of Experiment I. The simple correlation between mean funniness and independent self-reports of arousal was 0.75 ($p < 0.001$), so that the overlap of variance was about 56 %. The multiple correlation of the five significant physiological measures with mean funniness was 0.66 ($p < 0.001$), so that overlap in variance was about 44 %. The difference between the two overlaps was not large and one may conclude that the percentage of variance in mean funniness ratings accounted for by verbal self-reports of arousal is at least as great as that accounted for by physiological indices. In other words, Ss' phenomenological awareness of how aroused they feel as a consequence of reading the jokes is at least as strongly related to experienced humour as is an optimally weighed combination of actual physiological measures that tap the central state of arousal.

Verbal self-reports have thus reasonable predictive as well as construct validity, which warrants their use as legitimate indices of the central state of activation. If replicated, this finding would be a valuable extension of Thayer's work. Thayer (1970, 1971) used verbal self-reports to collect information about the central arousal states associated with diurnal rhythms, while the present study suggests that these measures may also be employed to record momentary central reactions in an experimental situation where arousal levels change at a much more rapid rate and are superimposed on diurnal fluctuations.

CONCLUSIONS

Arousal, as indexed by peripheral indices such as parameters of heart rate and skin conductance, increases with the intensity of the humour response, as evident from funniness ratings. Subjects are accurately aware of such arousal, because verbal self-reports of arousal were strongly associated with physiological indices of arousal on the one hand, and with funniness ratings on the other. There is some evidence, but it is not conclusive, that upward changes in arousal, commensurate with subsequent humour responses, act as mediating agents between perceived properties of jokes and the humour response. Such a process for affective responses in general has been suggested by Duffy (1962), Berlyne (1967) and others.

The findings indicate that arousal is necessary for humour and that humour cannot be explained simply in terms of cues that operate independently of arousal.

Aside from arousal, some cues do, of course, play a major part in generating experienced humour. The operation of such cues may help to fit the main findings of these experiments to Berlyne's hypothesis about the relation between arousal-increments and affect. While Berlyne suggested an inverted-U-shaped curve for that relation, the data reported in this chapter show a linear relationship.

Some situations, including those labelled 'play' or 'entertainment', in which stimuli such as 'art' or 'jokes' are presented are likely to contain cues that lead to inhibition of aversive responses through prior conditioning. For instance, knowing that someone is about to tell a funny story at a party probably precludes its interpretation as something very tragic or sad. If the cues had been absent the same story might have been interpreted quite differently. It is, in short, possible that the arousing properties of such stimuli activate the 'primary reward system' and produce a feeling of pleasure in a receiver of a joke, while leaving the 'aversion system' unaffected. When the primary reward system is the only one operative, experienced humour can increase with the arousal potential of the joke up to some asymptote. So, the findings are compatible with the suggestion that cues in the environment (for instance, the social situation) operate similarly to switches that channel arousal-increments; sometimes they steer arousal-increments so that only the reward system is affected, as for instance in jokes, and at other times perhaps the aversion system alone is activated, as for example in grief. If this model is valid, then an inverted-U-shaped curve representing the relationship between arousal increments and affect intensity and quality of affect may still be valid *in general*. However, for a given affect, such as humour, the quality (positive or negative, pain or pleasure) is determined by environmental cues while arousal changes determine the intensity of the affective state. In that case non-monotonicity in the relation between arousal-increments and the intensity of the affective response should not be expected. In summary, while environmental cues may determine the first stage of a two-stage process by defining which affective state shall result as a response to the stimulus, arousal-increments or -decrements consequent upon stimulus properties of a collative or ecological nature determine the intensity of the resulting affect.

The present studies and others (cf. Godkewitsch, 1974a, 1974b) have demonstrated that experienced humour increases when stimulus properties are more arousing. Thus, humour as a motivational state is not solely based on arousal-reduction. This finding contrasts with traditional ideas such as Freud's (1960) in which humour is the result of the reduction of surplus energy. In more general terms, the present findings suggest that the 'genuine cosmic principle' (Arnheim, 1971) of tension reduction as the source of all reward and pleasure is not so universal, and is at least not valid for humour responses. Those rather seem to be motivated by, among other things, arousal-increments.

ACKNOWLEDGEMENTS

The research reported in this chapter was supported by a Canada Council Doctoral Fellowship awarded to the author, and by grant A-73 of the National Research Council of Canada, awarded to D. E. Berlyne. The author wishes to thank Dr. R. Langevin, then at the Clarke Institute of Psychiatry of Toronto, Ontario, Canada, for his help in completing Experiment I.

REFERENCES

Arnheim, R. (1971). *Entropy and Art*. Berkeley: University of California Press.

Averill, J. R. (1969). Autonomic response patterns during sadness and mirth. *Psychophysiology*, 5, 399–414.

Averill, J. R., and Opton, E. M. (1968). Psychophysiological assessment: Rationale and problems. In P. McReynolds (Ed.), *Advances in Psychological Assessment*. Vol. 1. Palo Alto, California: Science and Behavior Books.

Berlyne, D. E. (1960). *Conflict, Arousal and Curiosity*. New York: McGraw–Hill.

Berlyne, D. E. (1963). Motivational problems raised by exploratory and epistemic behaviour. In S. Koch (Ed.), *Psychology: A Study of a Science*. Vol. 5. New York: McGraw–Hill.

Berlyne, D. E. (1967). Arousal and reinforcement. In D. Levine (Ed.), *Nebraska Symposium on Motivation*. Lincoln, Nebraska: University of Nebraska Press.

Berlyne, D. E. (1969). Laughter, humor and play. In G. Lindzey and E. Aronson (Eds.), *Handbook of Social Psychology* (2nd ed.), Vol. 3. Reading, Mass.: Addison Wesley.

Berlyne, D. E. (1971). *Aesthetics and psychobiology*. New York: Appleton–Century–Crofts.

Berlyne, D. E. (1972). Humor and its kin. In J. H. Goldstein and P. E. McGhee (Eds.), *The Psychology of Humor*. New York: Academic Press.

Berlyne, D. E. (1973). The vicissitudes of aplopathematic and thelematoscopic pneumatology (*or* The hydrography of hedonism). In D. E. Berlyne and K. B. Madsen (Eds.), *Pleasure, Reward, Preference*. New York: Academic Press.

Byrne, D. (1958). Drive level, response to humor, and the cartoon sequence effect. *Psychological Reports*, 4, 439–442.

Cattell, R. B., and Luborsky, L. B. (1947). Personality in response to humor. *Journal of Abnormal and Social Psychology*, 42, 402–421.

Duffy, E. (1962). *Activation and Behavior*. New York: Wiley.

Elliott, R. (1969). Tonic heart rate: Experiments on the effects of collative variables lead to a hypothesis about its motivational significance. *Journal of Personality and Social Psychology*, **12**, 211–228.

Elliott, R., Bankart, B., and Light, T. (1970). Differences in the motivational significance of heart rate and palmar conductance: Two tests of a hypothesis. *Journal of Personality and Social Psychology*, **14**, 166–172.

Fowler, H. (1965). *Curiosity and Exploratory Behavior*. New York: Macmillan.

Fowler, H. (1971). Implications of sensory reinforcement. In R. Glaser (Ed.), *The Nature of Reinforcement*. New York: Academic Press.

Frankenhaeuser, M., and Jaerpe, G. (1962). Psychophysiological reactions of a mixture of adrenalin and noradrenalin. *Scandinavian Journal of Psychology*, **3**, 21–29.

Freud, S. (1960). *Jokes and Their Relation to The Unconscious*. New York: Norton. (First German edition, 1905.)

Fry, W. F. (1969a). Humor in a physiologic vein. *News of Physiological Instrumentation*, Beckman Laboratory.

Fry, W. F. (1969b). Instinctual and physiologic bases of the humor experience. Paper presented at symposium proceedings of the meeting of the Western Psychological Association, Vancouver, September, 1969.

Fry, W. F., and Stoft, P. (1971). Mirth and oxygen saturation levels of peripheral blood. *Psychotherapy and Psychosomatics*, **19**, 76–84.

Godkewitsch, M. (1972). Arousal potential and funniness of jokes. In J. H. Goldstein and P. E. McGhee (Eds.), *The Psychology of Humor*. New York: Academic Press.

Godkewitsch, M. (1974a). Verbal, exploratory and physiological responses to stimulus properties underlying humour. Unpublished doctoral Thesis, University of Toronto.

Godkewitsch, M. (1974b). Correlates of humor: Verbal and nonverbal aesthetic reactions as functions of semantic distance with adjective–noun pairs. In D. E. Berlyne (Ed.), *Studies in the New Experimental Aesthetics: Steps Toward an Objective Psychology of Aesthetic Appreciation*. Washington, D. C.: Hemisphere.

Goldstein, J. H. (1970). Humor appreciation and time to respond. *Psychological Reports*, **27**, 445–446.

Guthrie, W. W. (1903). A theory of the comic. *International Quarterly*, **7**, 254–264.

Hebb, D. O. (1955). Drives and the C. N. S. (Conceptual Nervous System). *Psychological Review*, **62**, 243–254.

Hunt, J. McV. (1963). Motivation inherent in information processing and action. In O. J. Harvey (Ed.), *Motivation and Social Interaction: The Cognitive Determinants*. New York: Ronald Press.

Jennings, J. R. (1971). Cardiac reactions and different developmental levels of cognitive functioning. *Psychophysiology*, **8**, 433–450.

Jennings, J. R., Averill, J. R., Opton, E. M., and Lazarus, R. S. (1970). Some parameters of heart rate change: Perceptual versus motor task requirements, noxiousness and uncertainty. *Psychophysiology*, **7**, 194–212.

Jones, J. M., and Harris, P. E. (1971). Psychophysiological correlates of cartoon humor appreciation. *Proceedings of the Annual Convention of the American Psychological Association*, Vol. 6, 381–382.

Lacey, J. T. (1967). Somatic response patterning and stress: Some revisions of activation theory. In M. H. Appley and R. Trumbull (Eds.), *Psychological Stress: Issues in Research*. New York: Appleton–Century–Crofts.

Lacey, J. T., Kagan, J., Lacey, B. C., and Moss, H. A. (1963). The visceral level: Situational determinants and behavioral correlates of autonomic response patterns. In P. Knapp (Ed.), *Expression of the Emotions in Man*. New York: International University Press.

Langevin, R., and Day, H. I. (1972). Physiological correlates of humor. In J. H. Goldstein and P. E. McGhee (Eds.), *The Psychology of Humor*. New York: Academic Press.

Lazarus, R. S. (1966). *Psychological Stress and the Coping Process*. New York: McGraw–Hill.

Lee, J. C., and Griffith, R. M. (1962). Time error in the judgment of humor. *Psychological Reports*, **11**, 410.

Levi, L. (1963). The urinary output of adrenalin and noradrenalin during pleasant and unpleasant emotional states. *Psychosomatic Medicine*, **27**, 403–419.

Lloyd, E. L. (1938). The respiratory mechanism in laughter. *Journal of General Psychology*, **10**, 179–189.

Lykken, D. T., Rose, R. J., Luther, B., and Maley, M. (1966). Correcting physiological measures for individual differences in range. *Psychological Bulletin*, **6**, 481–484.

Lykken, D. T., and Venables, P. H. (1971). Direct measurement of skin conductance: A proposal for standardization. *Psychophysiology*, **8**, 656–672.

Malmo, R. B. (1959). Activation: A neuropsychological dimension. *Psychological Review*, **66**, 367–386.

Maltzman, I. (1968). Theoretical conceptions of semantic conditioning and generalization. In T. R. Dixon and D. L. Horton (Eds.), *Verbal Behavior and General Behavior Theory*. Englewood Cliffs, New Jersey: Prentice–Hall.

Martin, L. (1905). Psychology of aesthetics: Experimental prospecting in the field of the comic. *American Journal of Psychology*, **16**, 35–116.

McCurdy, H. E. (1950). Consciousness and the galvanometer. *Psychological Review*, **57**, 322–327.

Montagu, J. D. (1963). Habituation of the psycho-galvanic reflex during serial tests. *Journal of Psychosomatic Research*, **7**, 199–214.

Piddington, R (1963). *The Psychology of Laughter: A Study in Social Adaptation*. New York: Gamut Press.

Rethlingshaefer, D. (1963). *Motivation as Related to Personality*. New York: McGraw–Hill.

Rickwood, L. V. (1973). The arousal mechanism of humor activity and humor appreciation under stress. Unpublished Master's Thesis, University of Victoria, Victoria, B.C., Canada.

Robson, D. S. (1959). A simple method for construction of orthogonal polynomials when the independent variable is unequally spaced. *Biometrics*, **15**, 187–191.

Schachter, S., and Wheeler, L. (1962). Epinephrine, chlorpromazine and amusement. *Journal of Abnormal and Social Psychology*, **65**, 121–128.

Schoenpflug, W. (1969). Phaenomenologische Indikatoren der Aktiviertheit. In W. Schoenpflug (Ed.), *Methoden der Aktivierungsforschung*. Bern: Huber.

Shellberg, L. G. (1969). Arousal and humor preference: A theoretical formulation and empirical test. Paper presented at the meeting of the Western Psychological Association, Vancouver, B.C., Canada.

Sidman, M. (1960). *Tactis in Scientific Research*. New York: Basic Books.

Sokolov, E. N. (1963). Higher nervous functions: The orienting reflex. *Annual Review of Physiology*, **25**, 545–580.

Thayer, R. E. (1967). Measurement of activation through self-report. *Psychological Reports*, **20**, 663–678.

Thayer, R. E. (1970). Activation states as assessed by verbal report and four psycho-physiological variables. *Psychophysiology*, **7**, 86–94.

Thayer, R. E. (1971). Studies of controlled self-reports of activation. Terminal Progress Report, National Institute of Mental Health, Public Health Service, MH-14248–01.

Traxel, W. (1960). Die Moeglichkeit einer objektiven Messung der Staerke von Gefuehlen. *Psychologische Forschung*, **26**, 75–90.

Warwick, R. J. (1970). A bi-polar theory of the relationship between drive level and skin conductance. Unpublished doctoral Thesis, University of Nebraska.

Wilder, J. (1962). Basimetric approach (law of initial value) to biological rhythms. *Annals of the New York Academy of Sciences*, **98**, 1211–1228.

Williams, E. J. (1949). Experimental designs balanced for the estimation of residual effects of treatments. *Australian Journal of Scientific Research*, **2**, 149–168.

Wolff, H., Smith, C., and Murray, H. (1934). The psychology of humor: A study in responses to race-disparagement jokes. *Journal of Abnormal and Social Psychology*, **28**, 341–365.

Wundt, W. M. (1893). *Grundzuege der Physiologischen Psychologie* (4th ed.). Leipzig: W. Engelmann.

Chapter 7

Cognitive Aspects of Humour in Social Interaction: A Model and Some Linguistic Data

Howard Giles, Richard Y. Bourhis, Nicholas J. Gadfield,
Graham J. Davies and Ann P. Davies

In a field which is as ramifying and expansive as that of laughter and humour, it is not a little disconcerting to discover that there have been few attempts to integrate the various research topics chosen by psychologists within this area. Recently, however, a theoretical structure has been formulated by Rothbart (1973, see Chapter 2) primarily concerned with children's laughter, which at last attempts to describe the humorous situation *in toto*. She suggests that when a young child is stimulated intensely and suddenly by another person, or receives information that is discrepant from his expectations, this is liable to arouse the child's fear. However, should such stimulation be seen by him to be harmless at that time, then the relief from tension thus experienced would find expression in laughter. It is claimed that this 'arousal–safety' model may be useful in understanding adults' laughter at jokes. For this, Rothbart relies upon notions of incongruity by suggesting that a joke involves the presentation of two seemingly unrelated ideas, the novel congruence of which has to be solved before the humour can be appreciated. And so, 'when a joke is understood but the resolution is a "silly" one, that is, it does not lead to any instrumental activity, the tension from the effort of solving the joke, and probably also the positive excitement at having solved the joke, result in laughter' (Rothbart, 1973).

It is our contention that Rothbart's ideas are an extremely useful starting point for an understanding of adult humour and as such deserve further elaboration. For instance, we now need a greater understanding of the complexity of the decoding processes of humorous material, and also an insight into the cognitive operations underlying any humour which is *not* appreciated, nor perhaps even understood. In the first part of this chapter, we propose a model of adult humour as an initial attempt to take into account these problems. Moreover, we also take into consideration the processes underlying the intentional communication of humour between one individual and another.

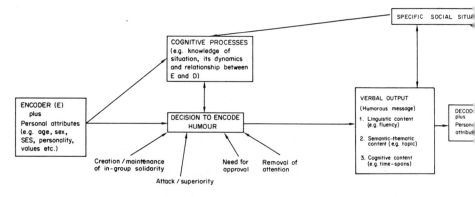

Figure 7.1 A dynamic model of humour in social interaction. (Dashed lines indicate loops in the system. All 'end responses', of course, feed back into the specific social situation)

In this way, we are presenting a tentative dynamic model of the encoding and decoding of humour in social interaction which will not only lead to important empirical hypotheses, but will also have the advantage of linking together theoretically a wide variety of the research interests in laughter and humour (see Figure 7.1).

The attempt to inject humour into social interaction occurs obviously in a specific social situation in a particular cultural context (Victoroff, 1969) and at a particular moment in time. The characteristics of, and the events occurring in, the situation not only determine why, when and how an individual encodes a humorous communication to another, but also how this message is interpreted by the recipient and his subsequent reactions to it. In turn, the behaviour of these participants often affects the nature of the situation itself as defined prior to the initiation of the humour, perhaps making it more relaxed or even more tense. (A desire for visual simplicity in a schematic representation of the model has meant that many of these feedback loops are not incorporated in Figure 7.1.) Let us now examine the encoding and decoding processes of humour in social interaction, concentrating initially on the deliberate situation.

THE ENCODING PROCESS

We have assumed that the encoder (E) has two possible decisions to make— whether to encode (and if so, when) and what to encode. He may decide that an ideal opportunity for humour has arisen and then have to decide on the type of humour to encode. Alternatively, a joke may first occur to him, perhaps following some previous humour, and E then has to decide whether to encode at all, and if so, when to do so for the most effect. Interesting personality differences may exist between those who think of encoding first and those who

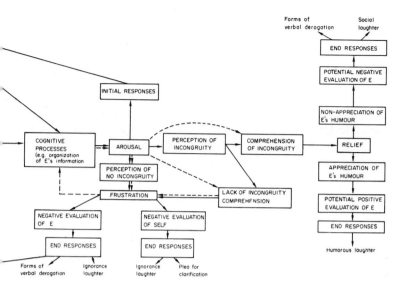

think of a joke first. We shall concern ourselves with the former for the present. Decisions regarding timing and topic for encoding will require knowledge of the social situation. This knowledge would include an understanding of the intimacy of his relationship with the decoder (D), their relative social statuses and so forth, and its validity would depend on a variety of E's defining attributes such as his age and values. We consider there to be four main reasons why E would want to encode humour at a given time. These reasons are:

(1) *Creation or maintenance of in-group solidarity.* In forming a group or interpersonal friendship, humour may serve as an effective alleviation of initial tension which may create an atmosphere conducive for the formulation or evolution of group norms and structures. Even when group cohesiveness has been established, humour may, particularly in times of stress with competing out-groups, serve as a device to maintain in-group solidarity (and 'keep the spirits up').

(2) *Attack or superiority.* Humour can often be used as a strategy to derogate an individual or group and belittle them in the eyes of others, thereby enhancing the instigator's own self-esteem. It often involves the victim of the humorous attack being made to look inferior and in this sense being laughed at is an indirect form of aggression (Berkowitz, 1970). Indeed, Harlow (1969) claimed that 'most humour lies in the physical or social derogation of others. Actually even the ideal or playful humour often carries with it some direct or implied derogation'. Humour as a form of attack can just as well be directed at D himself as at some third party outside the interaction (see Chapter 4).

(3) *Need for approval.* E's humour could serve the function of gaining D's approval of him. The rationale here might be that if D can be made to laugh—a pleasurable experience—this may dispose him to evaluate E's character and his viewpoints more favourably (Gruner, 1967).

(4) *Removal of attention.* Humour could be used by E as a means of diverting D's attention from an unfavourable verbal or physical act that E has committed or is about to commit. By making his misfortunes or misadventures humorous to D, E may succeed in disguising the potential negative aspects underlying his actions.

This is not, of course, meant to be an exhaustive list of the factors which may dispose E to initiate humour; undoubtedly others exist. In addition, these categories should not be regarded as mutually exclusive since E's reasons for introducing humour may be multidimensional. It could well be that all four factors operate simultaneously. For example, it could be that a fictitious governmental body has made a blunder in foreign policy. Its representatives may wish to minimize their apparent inadequacy by means of a public attack delivered in a humorous but direct manner on the integrity of the opposing political party. This speech, which would encourage people to laugh at the opposition, could serve to divert attention away from the real issue of the moment, enhance the government's rating at the polls and create a sense of solidarity within that political party.

The structure of E's humorous message will depend on both the reason for encoding it and E's knowledge of D and the situation. Three aspects of this message are considered here:

(1) *Linguistic content.* This refers to the speech patterns in which a humorous message is encoded. This facet of the encoding process is given empirical attention in the latter half of the chapter. Suffice it to say at the present, that the non-content aspects of speech accompanying a humorous message may be quite different from those accompanying a more serious message.

(2) *Semantic-thematic content.* This refers to the topic and theme of the humour. Often the reason for encoding humour (such as an attack on an out-group) defines the topic of humour; but E's knowledge of D's characteristics and preferences also determines the topic. For instance, Victoroff (1969) has shown that various social groups in France prefer different themes in their humour and so information of D's group membership might allow E to encode an 'appropriate' topic. Moreover, E's own mood and characteristics would also affect the type of theme chosen. Spiegel, Keith-Spiegel, Abrahams and Kranitz (1969) found that patients who had attempted suicide told significantly more jokes with a self-punishing theme than non-suicidal control patients.

(3) *Cognitive content.* This refers to the cognitive complexity of the humour. Giles and Oxford (1970), using the notions of Koestler (1964), suggested that jokes and humorous situations could be analysed into bisociative events: the setting of the scene and the punchline. They called the 'cognitive distance' between these events the 'time-span' of the humour. Short time-span humour occurs when the setting of the scene is made quite explicit at the time of the punchline as in slapstick or sarcasm. When time-spans become longer, as in puns or satire, the scene setting is made less explicit and D has to evoke this event himself in order to make the punchline meaningful in any humorous

sense. In this way D's cognitive operations become far more complex the longer the time-span of the humour. Giles and Oxford suggested that people's preferences for a particular time-span were related to their perceptual and cognitive style, and perhaps social class as well. Thus, E's supposed knowledge of D's attributes determines the cognitive complexity inherent in the humour, and in particular its time-span character.

Naturally, E's message would be sequentially decoded so E would be continually monitoring his linguistic, semantic-thematic and cognitive strategies on the basis of D's initial responses to the message. Except for research on creativity and humour (see Chapter 11), little attention has been paid to the encoding processes in humour. For instance, at what stage in conversation between strangers is it most advantageous for humour to be introduced? Are there different optimal levels of humour in formal and informal situations? What interpersonal and contextual cues does E use which suggest that a certain form of humour would be appreciated by D at any particular time? Does the relative status of E *vis-a-vis* D affect when and how much humour can be encoded? Is there a hierarchy of humorous topics used in interaction between strangers in the sense that some are 'safer' to joke about initially than others?

THE DECODING PROCESS

Firstly, we shall discuss the sequence of processes involved in a *successful* decoding of E's humour, that is, when it is appreciated by D. We shall assume at the outset that D is aware that E's message is a humorous one, although obviously in everyday life we are not always aware of whether the communication we are receiving was intended to be humorous or not. How often have we said of someone, 'I sometimes don't know whether he's joking or not'? It would be interesting to discover what cues a decoder uses which signal to him that the incoming message is humorous when this has not been made verbally explicit by the encoder.

It is proposed that the first reaction to humour is one of arousal as suggested in Rothbart's model Indeed there is psychophysiological evidence to support the view that perceiving humorous material induces arousal (see Chapters 6 and 8). Moreover, it is possible that such arousal may stem, at least in part, from an anticipatory fear of not being able to decode the humour effectively and from the consequent threat of losing self-esteem. Together with this arousal, and at many subsequent stages while E is relating a joke, D may emit initial responses such as smiling.

The next phase involves D in seeking out the incongruity in the humorous message. Many theorists agree that perceived incongruity between two unrelated ideas is at the core of every humorous experience (see Chapter 3) and that laughter is a behavioural response to resolving this incongruity (see Chapter 2). However, two distinct processes are conceived of here in the decoding task, namely the *perception* of incongruity and its *comprehension* (cf. Suls, 1972). For instance, a D may be able to perceive that the two elements of a joke are somehow conceptually discrepant from each other yet may not be able to resolve the incongruity. And so, D, believing the message to be humorous, seeks out the cognitive incongruity and, having once perceived it, attempts to organize E's information in such a way as to understand it. Having resolved the novel incongruence, the reaction is one of psychological relief at having successfully decoded the input. The next phase is one of evaluating the humour. If E has encoded the message well and gauged D's sense of humour correctly, the humour will be appreciated; in other words, it is considered funny. It can be suggested that this would lead D to positively evaluate E and his viewpoints (see Chapter 13). This positive evaluation is more likely to occur when the encoding is spontaneous and original, rather than when it is a mere recantation of someone else's humorous creation. The magnitude of the increased positive evaluation is likely to depend upon the relationship between E and D. If the relationship is considered to be an intimate one by D, positive evaluation is not likely to increase as much as if they are initially strangers. Indeed, the characteristics of the E–D relationship which influence evaluation at this point deserve closer investigation.

Finally, the end result of this decoding sequence lies in the behavioural response of 'humorous laughter'. This was a term adopted by Giles and Oxford to distinguish it from laughter emitted by D when he has not found a humorous message funny. An example of the latter might be when a person does not appreciate another's humour at all but nevertheless laughs in order not to embarrass him. The magnitude of the humorous laughter can be influenced by factors in the social situation such as the presence of others and the distance of D from them (see Chapters 8 and 9). However, this response in turn affects the nature of the situation itself probably making it more relaxed and less formal. Indeed, the function of humour in many social situations such as in industrial, educational and clinical settings needs far more researching than has hitherto been accomplished (see Chapters 14 and 15).

Let us now return to the commencement of the decoding process and discuss the various points at which the aim of E to elicit humorous laughter from D can be unsuccessful. The first occasion where this could occur is if D *fails* to perceive the incongruity in the humorous message. This might be in the situation where the punchline does not *appear* incongruous, or where a pun is not understood in its dual role. This leads to frustration, a reorganization of the material in order to detect the incongruity, and continued arousal. D is liable to maintain this cyclic movement until he eventually perceives the incongruity. Nevertheless, there is likely to be a maximal time before D is pressurized to respond in some fashion. And so, if at this point the incongruity is still not perceived, there will be either a negative evaluation of self or a negative evaluation of E. The inability to decode the humour is more likely to be blamed on E if D negatively evaluated him previously and E was aware of this fact. In this case the blame is 'externally attributed' by E (cf. Hastorf, Schneider and

Polefka, 1970). On the other hand, he is more likely to blame himself if E is of a higher status, or if observers are present and laughing. Here, the blame is 'internally attributed' by E. The exact behavioural responses to these situations are likely to depend upon the specific nature of the relationship between E and D. In the case of the external attribution of blame, if there is a need for E's approval or a desire not to embarrass him, laughter is still likely to ensue. Giles and Oxford have termed this type of response, 'ignorance laughter'. If D is not concerned for E on these accounts or if the relationship is somewhat intimate, verbal derogation of E or his humour, or a somewhat aggressive plea to clarify the humour, may occur.

When the attribution of blame is internal, either ignorance laughter or a polite plea for clarification is likely to result. In most situations, the former is more probable since the latter strategy involves D in a loss of face. Certainly a plea for clarification is unlikely, because of social conformity pressures, if others are present and laughing. The nature of the E–D relationship is therefore crucial in determining how the inability to decode is attributed and what form the subsequent reactions take.

The next stage at which the decoding process could break down would be a failure to resolve the perceived incongruity. This again results in frustration and sustained arousal, and undoubtedly there is a maximal time in which D can comfortably reorganize the input before making a definitive reaction. The length of this latency period is again a matter for further research. If there is ultimately a lack of comprehension of the incongruity, this leads once more to either internal or external attribution of blame and to one of the previous responses. It could be hypothesized that a lack of incongruity comprehension is more likely to lead to self- than other-derogation. This decoding failure could be empirically investigated to determine the important variables by presenting subjects with supposedly humorous material which was cognitively incongruous but comprehensibly unresolvable.

The last stage at which the intentions of the encoder may break down is at the level of evaluation (or appreciation). D may well understand the humour, and psychological relief may ensue. Yet for a number of reasons the message may not be considered funny. These reasons include:

(a) E's relating of the humour may be inadequate particularly with regard to the linguistic and cognitive aspects.
(b) The humorous message may be very familiar to D and hence there is limited pleasure at resolving the incongruity. Neither of these reasons is likely to induce D to evaluate E very negatively particularly if their relationship is intimate.
(c) The humour may be perceived by D to be in bad taste (or 'sick'), especially if it is an attack on a close associate of D or directed at D himself. Under these circumstances, negative evaluation of E is possible (see Chapter 5).

The precise behavioural response at this stage is again complex. If D requires E's approval then laughter (termed 'social laughter' by Giles and Oxford) will still ensue despite the non-appreciation. Indeed, even if social approval is not required by D and the humour is at the latter's expense, he may still laugh to display his broadmindedness. On the other hand, should approval not be required and the humour be at D's expense, then D is liable to respond with verbal derogation of that type of humour and possibly of E himself. As in all these decoding failures, D's responses are likely to change the nature of the situation quite markedly. It would be interesting to determine whether encoders can actually differentiate between humorous laughter, ignorance laughter and social laughter in everyday life when the laughter response of the decoder is the only cue available, and to determine what the distinguishing features are. A confounding variable is the possibility of self-persuasion (Bem, 1967) following one's own laughter. One may perhaps be 'coerced' into laughing and then actually attribute something funny into the situation. Thus one may perceive the situation as more humorous and pleasurable than if one had not laughed.

The model then to some degree reflects the complexity associated with the encoding and decoding processes of humour in social interaction. Although the model was conceived to account for humour intentionally communicated by E to D, it can nonetheless be useful in understanding the *decoding* of spontaneous humour unintentionally encoded. Similarly, even when there is no encoder physically present (e.g. when reading a humorous book or watching a comedy film), the same decoding processes are likely to be operating as in the model just presented.

Many suggestions for further research have been proposed and many assumptions made that could be empirically tested. Our own empirical work on humour has been concerned with the encoding process and in particular with the linguistic strategies employed by the joke-teller.

AN EXPERIMENT

Ervin-Tripp (1969), Hymes (1972) and Giles and Powesland (1975) have shown in reviews of the sociolinguistic literature how a person's speech style is influenced by the nature of the topic discussed, the person spoken to, and the context in which the conversation takes place. With regard to topic, people speak in a grammatically more complex manner the more abstract the topic of discourse (Lawton, 1965) and are verbally more productive the more salient the issue is to them (Matarazzo, Weins, Jackson and Manaugh, 1970). Other aspects of topic such as emotionality (Kasl and Mahl, 1965) and technicality (Moscovici, 1967) have also been shown to produce their own characteristic speech patterns. One dimension of topic mentioned by Rubin (1962) which has received little empirical attention is that of seriousness–humorousness.

As was mentioned earlier, we have little insight into how a humorous message is encoded by an individual. Our particular interest in the present investigation was to determine whether, and in what ways, the linguistic strategies an individual employs when encoding a humorous message are different from those adopted for more serious topics. Is there in Western societies a speech style peculiar to the verbal presentation of humorous material? The aims of the study were to determine firstly what speech modifications, if any, occur when a speaker moves from a serious to a humorous topic and back again and, secondly, whether speakers themselves are aware of change that occur in their speech when moving from topic to topic.

The experiment itself was divided into two distinct phases: *Phase* 1, the elicitation of subjects' spontaneous speech and their reactions to it under three stimulus topics. *Phase* 2, the analysis of these speech data.

Method: phase 1

Subjects

Twenty-five British male students between 18 and 28 years of age volunteered as naive subjects for the experiment; they were not recruited for their joke-telling skills. From a post-experimental questionnaire, their mean self-rated joke-telling ability was 6·28 on a nine-point scale (a rating of 1 indicating a good joke-teller), and their mean frequency of joke-telling was 5·96 (a rating of 1 indicating that they told jokes frequently). There was a strong positive correlation between subjects' frequencies of joke-telling and their self-reported ability ($r = 0·74; p < 0·002$).

Materials

The materials for the experiment consisted of typewritten stories of 314 words each, a questionnaire, and a Tandberg tape-recorder with microphone.

Stimulus topics

Two of the stories were serious and the other was humorous. One of the serious stories (S1) was an account of a football match while the other (S2) was an account of a non-fatal car accident. Both were devised in such a manner as to reflect a definite logical progression of events resulting in an outcome. It is believed that this sequencing of events is similar to the structuring of information in a joke. Moreover, it was felt that the subject matter of the serious stories would not be dissimilar from that related by men in everyday life. It was found subsequently that there was no difference in the interest value of the two serious topics.

The humorous topic (a joke, written in reported speech) concerned two elderly ladies, a vicar and two parrots. The subjects perceived the joke as moderately funny on a nine-point rating scale with a mean score of 4·84 (a rating of 1 indicating that it was extremely funny). The three stimulus stories were written in an equally informal style by the same author. It is suggested on the basis of post-experimental information that the three topics were equivalent in interest and recall difficulty; no differences emerged between the three stories in terms of how easy they were to recall and how satisfied subjects felt about their performances.

Questionnaire material

The questionnaire was divided into three separate sections: (1) ratings of the interest value of the serious stories and the funniness of the joke (nine-point rating scales were used throughout the questionnaire); (2) ratings of performance satisfaction, task comfort and ease in recall of material; (3) ratings of subjects' abilities and frequencies in joke-telling plus open-questions about joke-telling.

Procedure

Subjects were asked to attend for one hour and were individually tested. On arrival, they were handed a typed sheet of standard instructions informing them that we were interested in how well people could tell humorous and non-humorous stories. They were told that they were required initially to read typewritten copies of three stories, and when this was done they were to reread them one at a time and evaluate them separately on a short questionnaire form. Later they would be required to tape-record these stories in their own words, and their efforts would be evaluated by other students. Subjects were handed the three stories in a set sequence of serious, humorous and serious topics, but with half the subjects receiving S1 first and the other half receiving S2 first. When the subjects had read the stories twice and evaluated them, they left the laboratory to return after 20 minutes. (In everyday life we more often than not relate a tale or joke some while after we have heard it, and so we have the chance to process the information prior to relating it to others. So, allowing subjects the opportunity to leave the laboratory before the recording session better simulated reality.) Subjects were informed of this rationale.

Upon their return subjects were shown into another experimental room where the recording apparatus had been set up. The experimenter explained to subjects how to operate the equipment, and handed back the typewritten stories in the same order as previously presented, as well as the second section of the questionnaire. Subjects were told to read through the first story again, put it aside, and relate the tale in their own words into the microphone; they were then required to rate their performances on a number of scales. Subjects were to repeat this reading–recording–rating procedure for the joke and second serious topic in turn. The experimenter left the subjects to self-administer this phase of the experiment telling them that this was to enable them to be more relaxed. They were assured, however, that they were not being observed in any way during their recordings. They were reminded that their recordings would be subsequently evaluated by other students. All appeared to conform well to the instructions and poor recordings did not eventuate. This 'social isolation' technique of imagined others was adopted to control for audience effects and thus make the procedure replicable. It was thought impossible for an experimenter to be present and act as an effective audience, standard for all subjects. This emphasis on control naturally enough meant that without a live audience providing audio-visual feedback the atmosphere was somewhat sterile and artificial. When subjects had recorded the three stories and evaluated their performances, they were handed the third section of the questionnaire. Finally, they were debriefed and their comments invited in discussion. This second section of the procedure always lasted for at least half an hour.

Method: phase 2

Listener-judges

Three male undergraduate students volunteered as paid judges. They were not selected for any specialized linguistic decoding skills. We employed linguistically-naive, peer judges rather than linguists so as to increase the social reality of the analyses. A number of sociolinguists have recently advocated the use of untrained judges for the discrimination of shifts in speech style from tape-recordings (Robinson, 1972; Giles, 1973; Clément and Taylor, 1974). It has been argued that just because a speech expert may be able to detect subtle variations in an individual's speech patterns, it does not necessarily follow that such modifications will have meaning for the phonetically unsophisticated. Moreover, Frender and Lambert (1972) have found inter-rater reliability between two independent linguists who were assessing taped speech samples to be fairly low (cf. also Buck, 1968).

Rating scales

From impressions gained in a pilot study in which we asked subjects to relate jokes, humorous speech seemed to be more non-standard in accent usage, less precise in enunciation, and more fluent and varied in both tempo and pitch than in a serious topic. On the basis of such impressions, seven nine-point scales were adopted for analysis of the subjects' speech. They appeared in a questionnaire booklet in the following order: (1) enunciation: precise–imprecise; (2) accent: standard–regional; (3) tempo: slow–fast; (4) pitch of voice: stable–varied; (5) loudness: varied-stable; (6) hesitancy: fluent–hesitant; (7) variety of tempo: stable–varied.

Analysis tapes

By editing the master tape, three analysis versions were available for rating: tape A included each subject's speech on the first serious topic with which he were presented; tape B included each subject's telling of the joke; and tape C included each subject's speech on the second serious topic. The mean length of subjects' stories was 114·4 seconds; there were no differences in subjects' story length between topics.

Procedure

Three judges were assembled on three separate occasions to rate the analysis tapes. The ratings of tape A took two hours while those of tapes B and C took a further $1\frac{1}{2}$ hours each. The judges were familiarized with the three typewritten stories beforehand and told that they would hear 25 speakers relating each of these, but they were not told the specific aims of the inquiry. They were handed a questionnaire booklet containing 29 pages on each of which were seven rating scales. The experimenter explained how to use the scales and four 'practice' voices (appearing later on tape A) were played to the judges. They were required to evaluate these voices and discuss the merit of their ratings amongst each other. They reported the use of the scales to be quite straightforward and there appeared to be a considerable degree of agreement between them on these practice voices. The experimenter then proceeded to play tape A telling them that they would hear only serious stories on this occasion. These were rated by the judges without discussion. Tapes B and C were analysed on subsequent occasions and, before each of these, the judges were again required to evaluate four practice voices and to discuss their ratings with one another. Each judge then made 525 evaluations. After tape C had been assessed, the judges were debriefed and their comments invited.

Results

Subjects' evaluations of their own speech

No significant correlations emerged between speakers' ability to tell a joke and how they rated the stimulus joke or felt during the course of the experiment. As would be expected, subjects felt more comfortable taping the second than the first serious story ($t = 3·22$; $df = 24$; $p < 0·01$).

Subjects did consider that they had modified their speech styles from one topic to another; only one subject denied so doing. The mean shifts perceived in their speech styles from the first topic to the joke was 4·60, and from the joke to the third topic was 4·80 (a rating of 1 indicating a very large shift and 9 no shift at all). There was a significant correlation between the amount speakers shifted from the first story to the joke and the amount they shifted from the latter to the third story ($r = 0·49$; $p < 0·05$). However, no relationship was found between the magnitude of these shifts and either subjects' ability to tell jokes or how often they told them. In addition, there was no correlation between how funny the joke was rated and how much people shifted their speech style.

Subjects appeared able to specify the nature of the changes that occurred in their speech. The changes subjects mentioned when moving from the serious to the humorous story tended to be mirror-images of those mentioned when moving subsequently from the latter to the second serious story. The following are typical of subjects' comments of a shift from the serious to the humorous topics: 'a more relaxed tone, more intimate, friendly, animated ... '; 'quicker, more confident, not as toneless, more emphasizing certain words ...'. The following are typical of the shift from the humorous to the second serious topic: 'more formal speech, less animated, friendly etc. Less familiar, fewer colloquialisms ...'; 'it became slower, less emphasis, less confidence ...'. In short and with subject frequencies in parentheses, they perceived the humorous speech to be less concerned with factual precision (12), more informal (9), fluent (7), varied in tone of voice (4), colloquial and non-standard accented (2) than their more serious speech.

Prior to self-evaluation, subjects were asked to describe the qualities of a good joke-teller. According to these descriptions and with subject frequencies in the brackets again, a good joke-teller is a person who has flexibility in his speech style (25), a sense of timing (6), and brevity (2) and is sensitive to the nature of his audience (6). He is a quick thinker (4), self-confident (6), extraverted (2), with a good memory (6) and a sense of humour (7). Interestingly enough, over one-third of these statements (39 %) made reference to linguistic changes and, of those, half referred to tone of voice and fluency.

Judges' evaluations

Multiple-comparison t-tests were used to determine whether inter-judge differences occurred in ratings on the seven dependent measures. Discrepancies between the judges' assessments did in fact emerge on the scales of enunciation and variety of tempo. The three judges' ratings were then averaged for each of the five remaining scales, and one-way analyses of variance applied to these data to determine whether shifts in speech appeared between the topics. On the scales of hesitancy and variety of pitch, such differences did occur and t-tests were computed to specify where these lay. It was found that the speakers were perceived as more fluent when relating the joke than telling the first serious story ($t = 3.26$; $df = 24$; $p < 0.01$), and less fluent when relating the second serious story than when telling the joke ($t = 2.68$; $df = 24$; $p < 0.05$). Speakers were perceived as having more pitch variety in the second than the first serious story ($t = 2.73$; $df = 24$; $p < 0.05$). (This trend parallels subjects' changes in self-rated comfort in the first and third topics.) Changes in fluency were not correlated with subjects' joke-telling ability nor with the magnitude of subjects' self-rated shifts.

Discussion

The results suggest that people when moving from a serious to a humorous topic (or vice versa) do tend to modify their style of speaking. All but one of the subjects in this study were aware in retrospect of their speech changing from topic to topic and were able to some degree to specify these changes. However, from the analyses of the linguistically-naive judges such changes appeared to be related only to hesitancy; speakers were more fluent relating humorous than serious material. The fact that modifications in speech style were perceived at only *one* linguistic level may possibly have been due to the limitations in the experimental procedure. For instance, the socially-sterile nature of the setting which was devoid of interpersonal feedback cues may have inhibited expression of a linguistically-rich, humorous speech style. In addition, the nature of the joke which was emotionally-neutral and perceived by subjects as moderately funny may also have had an inhibiting effect. Certainly had the humour been of an ethnic or minority group variety where the characters in the joke had speech styles which would be distinct from those of the joke-tellers, a greater variety of speech modifications may have accrued. Moreover, the speakers' subjective impressions of their speech styles suggest that when a linguistically-rich, humorous speech style is elicited, it is characterized by informal and non-standard speech patterns. And so, the humorous situation may well be one where it is socially disadvantageous and communicatively ineffective to encode a prestige speech style (cf. Bourhis, Giles and Lambert, 1975). Undoubtedly, there is a real need to conduct further research in less artificial settings with a variety of humorous topics if we are to discover whether a humorous speech style can involve linguistic peculiarities other than fluency. In addition, there would seem to be a need to analyse other linguistic levels such as the lexical, grammatical and syntactical since these were mentioned by a few subjects. Nevertheless, a fluent (or 'snappy') presentation would seem to be one of the salient features of the effective humorous message. As all subjects mentioned the fact that an important aspect of good joke-telling was a flexible speech style, it would seem that the study of linguistics and humour deserves far more research attention.

Some general questions in this respect may also be posed. If a person knows he cannot tell a joke well (probably because he has not the flexibility in linguistic encoding skills) how does he convey to others that he may have a sense of humour? Would his appreciative reactions to others' humour convey this fact? Can he nevertheless make his conversations witty and lively, and if so, how? If people are aware of their own speech styles, as this study suggests, is the introvert in informal social interactions one who knows he is unable to encode a lively, humorous speech style?

SUMMARY

We have proposed a model suggesting a number of the complex processes underlying the encoding and decoding of humour in social interaction, and it is hoped, that future work may be concerned with revising and elaborating it with a view to producing a tentative framework for the psychology of humour and laughter. We have also attempted to show that, among a variety of areas needing empirical attention (particularly with regard to the encoding processes), the sociolinguistics of humour should no longer remain a barren field of inquiry.

REFERENCES

Bem, D. J. (1967). Self-perception: an alternative interpretation of the cognitive dissonance phenomenon. *Psychological Review*, **74**, 183–200.

Berkowitz, L. (1970). Aggressive humor as a stimulus to aggressive responses. *Journal of Personality and Social Psychology*, **16**, 710–717.

Bourhis, R. Y., Giles, H., and Lambert, W. E. (1975). Social consequences of accommodating one's speech style: a cross-national investigation. *International Journal of the Sociology of Language*. In press.

Buck, J. F. (1968). The effects of Negro and White dialectal variations upon attitudes of college students. *Speech Monographs*, **35**, 181–186.

Clément, R., and Taylor, D. M. (1974). Normative reactions to styles of Quebec French. *Anthropological Linguistics*. In press.

Ervin-tripp, S. M. (1969). Sociolinguistics. In L. Berkowitz (Ed.), *Advances in Experimental Social Psychology*, Vol. 4, 91–165.

Frender, R., and Lambert, W. E. (1972). Speech style and scholastic success: the tentative relationships and possible implications for lower social class children. *23rd. Annual Round Table Monographs on Language and Linguistics*, **25**, 237–271.

Giles, H. (1973). Accent mobility: a model and some data. *Anthropological Linguistics*, **15**, 87–105.

Giles, H., and Oxford, G. S. (1970). Towards a multidimensional theory of laughter causation and its social implications. *Bulletin of the British Psychological Society*, **22**, 97–105.

Giles, H., and Powesland, P. F. (1975). *Social Evaluation Through Speech Characteristics*. London: Academic Press.

Gruner, C. R. (1967). Effect of humor on speaker ethos and audience information gain. *Journal of Communication*, **17**, 228–233.

Harlow, H. (1969). The anatomy of humor. *Impact of Science on Society*, **19**, 225–239.

Hastorf, A. H., Schneider, D. J., and Polefka, J. (1970). *Person Perception*. New York: Addison–Wesley.

Hymes, D. (1972). Model of interaction of language and social life. In J. J. Gumperz and D. Hymes (Eds.), *Directions in Sociolinguistics: The Ethnography of Communication*. New York: Holt, Rinehart & Winston.

Kasl, S. V., and Mahl, G. F. (1965). The relationship of disturbances and hesitations in spontaneous speech to anxiety. *Journal of Personality and Social Psychology*, **5**, 425–433.

Koestler, A. (1964). *The Act of Creation*. New York: Macmillan.

Lawton, D. (1965). *Social class language difference in individual interviews*. Mimeograph: Sociological Research Unit, Institute of Education, University of London.

Matarazzo, J. D., Weins, A. N., Jackson, R. H., and Manaugh, T. S. (1970). Interviewee speech behaviour under different content conditions. *Journal of Applied Psychology*, **54**, 15–26.

Moscovici, S. (1967). Communication processes and the properties of language. In L. Berkowitz (Ed.), *Advances in Experimental Social Psychology*, Vol. 3, 225–270.

Robinson, W. P. (1972). *Language and Social Behaviour*. Harmondsworth: Penguin.

Rothbart, M. K. (1973). Laughter in young children. *Psychological Bulletin*, **80**, 247–256.

Rubin, J. (1962). Bilingualism in Paraguay. *Anthropological Linguistics*, **4**, 52–58.

Spiegel, D., Keith-Spiegel, P., Abrahams, J., and Kranitz, L. (1969). Humor and suicide: favorite jokes of suicidal patients. *Journal of Consulting and Clinical Psychology*, **33**, 504–505.

Suls, J. M. (1972). A two-stage model for the appreciation of jokes and cartoons: An information-processing analysis. In J. H. Goldstein and P. E. McGhee (Eds.), *The Psychology of Humor*. New York: Academic Press.

Victoroff, D. (1969). New approaches to the psychology of humor. *Impact of Science on Society*, **19**, 291–298.

Chapter 8

Social Aspects of Humorous Laughter

Antony J. Chapman

The prime purpose of this chapter is to provide an integrated summary account of the author's research on social aspects of children's 'humorous laughter'. The experimental studies so far completed relate to two distinct areas of social psychological theory. Most have been concerned with the *social facilitation* of laughter and have been designed to investigate important companion variables, while some of the most recent have been concerned with the ways in which humorous laughter may promote *social intimacy*. The concept of 'arousal' is common to both types of theory and is referred to also in relation to humour and laughter theory.

The chapter begins by describing in some detail three concurrent but separate lines of research interest which have converged in the studies on children's laughter. In the order presented here, they are: problems of measuring humour appreciation, associated initially with an inquiry into the efficacy of canned laughter in promoting humour appreciation and memory for jokes (*Starting-point* 1); attempts to discriminate empirically between opposing drive hypotheses in social facilitation theory (*Starting-point* 2); tension-reduction aspects of laughter and attempts to identify psychophysiological correlates of humour perception and appreciation (*Starting-point* 3). A new electromyographic study is reported in the latter context.

Three other studies which have not previously been published are reported in the section on social aspects of children's laughter. They investigate: (1) the elusive nature of laughter, specifically its tendency to diminish and evanesce under an experimenter's gaze; (2) laughter as a function of the social intimacy of a dyad, defined through prearranged seating orientations; and (3) facilitation effects engendered by a laughing companion encroaching upon a child's psychological body space. The first of these three studies has major implications for methodology and the latter two, in conjunction with others, have encouraged us to focus attention ever more intently on social dimensions of laughter and to study social interaction through humorous situations. Studies along these lines are under way at UWIST in collaboration with Hugh C. Foot and Jean R. Smith. (Our present programme of research is discussed in the following chapter.)

STARTING-POINT 1: MEASURING HUMOUR APPRECIATION

It is common knowledge that the broadcasting side of the entertainment industry sometimes adds 'canned laughter' to the soundtrack of radio and television programmes when comedy shows have been recorded without a 'live' audience or when audiences have been too quiet and restrained. The immediate and longer-term effects of this practice have received scant attention and the initial interest in social aspects of laughter developed in association with an experiment designed specifically to examine some of the gross facilitative effects of such laughter (Chapman, 1973b).

The findings of the experiment vindicated the utilization of dubbed laughter, showing that when adults are solitary recipients of humour, they laugh more if there is laughter accompanying the presentation. Solitary student subjects (Ss) who heard tape-recorded jokes with a canned laughter background engaged in more overt mirth than other solitary Ss who heard the jokes without the laughter background. However, contrary to expectations, the addition of laughter to the soundtrack did not significantly enhance ratings of funniness (on a 10-point scale), nor did it enhance ratings of cleverness. The canned laughter probably constituted additional laughter stimuli which Ss were able to discriminate from the jokes when making cognitive evaluations of the humour. In a memory test administered two weeks later, the jokes best remembered were those which had originally been rated as funniest and which had prompted most mirth. These relationships between recall and humour appreciation were strongest when jokes were presented without the canned laughter background.

The most intriguing psychological questions raised by this study, and others on canned laughter (Fuller and Sheehy-Skeffington, 1974; Leventhal and Mace, 1970; Nosanchuk and Lightstone, 1974; Smyth and Fuller, 1972), relate to the ways in which social influences are mediated. These questions are taken up later in the chapter when fresh data are introduced, derived mainly from 7-year-olds, and when other studies on children are reviewed.

Other questions relate to fundamental methodological issues pertaining to the scaling of mirth behaviours and to relationships between subjective humour ratings and expressive responses. Overt mirth responses were scored by the experimenter on a four-point scale ranging from *no response* (*blank face*) to *laugh* (*responses rater could hear*). This scale has been used in other studies (e.g. Leventhal and Mace, 1970; Zigler, Levine and Gould, 1966a, 1966b, 1967) and confirmed as reliable, but it is a crude and insensitive measuring technique, based tacitly upon a number of untested and implausible premises and paying no heed to crucial problems of quantification.

The mirth scores were significantly correlated with humour-ratings for both males and females under both the *with-canned-laughter* and *without-canned-laughter* conditions, but there was no treatment effect for subjective ratings corresponding to that for mirth: that is, Ss in the condition with canned laughter did *not* rate the jokes significantly funnier. The correlational data support Leventhal and Mace's (1970) notion that laughter and ratings are related in a dynamic causal fashion. This relationship may be a function of exposure to one's own enhanced responsiveness (Bem, 1967) or it may be a function of dissonance (Festinger, 1957). Some of the experiments with children have given rise to similar results in that boys and girls who give the highest ratings also laugh most (e.g. Chapman, 1973c, 1974b; Chapman and Chapman, 1974) and sometimes smile most (e.g. Chapman and Chapman, 1974), but other experiments using the same scales, similar procedures and identical humorous material have *not* always generated statistically significant relationships (e.g. Chapman, 1975b; Chapman and Wright, 1976). Therefore attitudinal reactions and affective expressions at least under some circumstances are not equivalent indices of humour responsiveness.

The humour rating-scale used by the children is simple through practical necessity: it merely requires them to say whether they considered the stimulus material 'not very funny', 'quite funny' or 'very funny'. However, it has been employed in studies producing significant correlations, and equivocal or inconsistent sets of data collected subsequently cannot reasonably be attributed to its insensitivity. Moreover, other studies have used more elaborate scales and a number of these (e.g. Dresser, 1967; Scofield, 1921; Shellberg and Brown, 1968; Young and Frye, 1966) have also failed to generate data substantiating relationships between the two types of measures. On the other hand, a number of other papers have reported significant correlations (Martin, 1905; Shultz, 1972), and it is not likely that deficiencies in the measuring technique are at the root of these disparate sets of findings. A more parsimonious view is that the expressive responses are more susceptible to changes in social variables than are attitudinal reactions. Schachter and colleagues have contended that the latter are more dependent upon previous experiences (Schachter and Singer, 1962; Schachter and Wheeler, 1962).

The opinion has been expressed by Berlyne (1969) that laughter is 'too insensitive as an indicator of appreciation of humor in most experimental situations'. Measures of laughter have been incorporated in fewer than 15% of studies published to date, and this may be evidence that Berlyne's view is shared by a good proportion of other humour researchers. The findings from empirical studies which have employed both types of measure imply either that subjective humour-ratings are *less* sensitive than behavioural measures or, more likely, that the latter are not adequately refined. In other words, behaviours may be registered by experimenters as mirth responses when elicited or augmented by non-mirthful and/or non-experimental stimuli. Ratings are almost certainly less prone to contamination by such extraneous influences and they are therefore more valid than conventional measures of laughter and smiling.

Laughter and smiling probably have different phylogenetic origins (cf. Eibl-Eibesfeldt, 1970; van Hooff, 1972), but they clearly converge functionally as non-verbal expressions of humour appreciation. There is usually a high correlation between laughter and smiling duration scores in our studies and, as one would expect, subjects frequently vacillate between laughter and smiling.

Nevertheless, laughs and smiles may sometimes be indicative neither of humour perception nor comprehension, either or both behaviours being emitted in the total absence of humour.

Bergler (1956) has drawn up a 'partial list' of fifty-six different types of smiles and other authors have also devised taxonomies of various kinds of smiles. Our operational definition of smiling is broad and embraces each of these sub-classifications. A smile is specified as being an upward stretching of the mouth occurring without vocal sound but possibly accompanied by loud exhalations of breath, particularly at the inception.

We are beginning to draw the simplest of conceptual dichotomies between those smiles which are mirthful and smiles which are non-mirthful, but it is evident from the definition that we are not ready as yet to distinguish empirically between them. The distinction has to be operationalized, of course, if non-mirthful smiling is to be excluded from mirth scores; but even then a major problem remains, and that is how mathematically to aggregate laughter and mirthful smiling in order to arrive at a composite mirth or humour appreciation score. No doubt mirthful smiles are attenuated laughs on occasions, but this is not always the case. Laughter and smiling are indubitably alternative responses under other circumstances and therefore these expressive responses cannot be conceptualized along a single continuum.

Problems of scaling are rendered especially acute in this area because laughter and smiling can each vary in physical characteristics on a number of dimensions, and movements along any one of them might be described in a number of ways (cf. Brannigan and Humphries, 1972; Grant, 1969; van Hooff, 1972). Considering just the sound of one laugh, Pollio, Mers and Lucchesi (1972) broke new ground by adopting three independent measures: the latency of the laugh from the humour stimulus or punchline; the duration of the laugh; and its peak amplitude. No one has explored how the general patterns of sound vary according to social aspects of the situation, and it remains to be demonstrated formally that, for example, people laugh louder and are quicker to respond to humour when in company. For operational purposes, we define laughter as inarticulate vocal sounds of a reiterated *ha-ha* variety and, so far, for both laughter and smiling, we have extracted only duration and frequency scores and then generally for sessions as a whole.

The development of a satisfactory mirth scale embodying valid and reliable measures of (mirthful) laughter and smiling demands systematic research into each of the complex issues mentioned above. In the complete absence of investigations into questions of psychological scaling and measurement, we have avoided arbitrarily defining an unequal weighting for smiling and laughter, and the two behaviours have been treated as equivalent responses in our computations of mirth behaviour scores (i.e. 1 second of laughter plus 1 second of smiling totals 2 seconds of mirth). In each experiment, separate statistical analyses have been conducted on laughter, smiling and composite mirth scores and, in studies where subjective ratings have been elicited, these also have been analysed separately.

STARTING-POINT 2: SOCIAL FACILITATION THEORY AND SOCIAL AROUSAL

Our fascination with social facilitation processes and mechanisms continues unabated today. Interest has grown out of a dissatisfaction with the empirical literature comprising studies which contrive to test the major rival drive hypotheses against one another.

The term *social facilitation* refers to some of the behavioural effects arising from the presence of another individual. In a classic paper, Zajonc (1965) drew attention to a consistency amidst the confusing and apparently conflicting social facilitation data with the result that we now recognize that, within standard social facilitation situations, a companion's presence is beneficial to a subject providing that the latter is not under an unusual degree of stress or engaged in a learning exercise.

Working within Hull–Spence behaviour theory (Spence, 1956), Zajonc proposed in his paper that the 'mere presence' of a companion is sufficient to increase general non-specific drive and hence facilitate dominant responses. Cottrell (1968) and Henchy and Glass (1968) took issue with Zajonc's hypothesis in postulating that it is not mere presence as such but evaluation apprehension which augments drive and thereby enhances the performance of well-learned responses and impairs learning. Considerable attention continues to be devoted by experimenters to separating and appraising the relative merits of these hypotheses (cf. Cottrell, 1972; Crandall, 1974; Weiss and Miller, 1971; Zajonc, 1972). There is no definitive study in support of the mere presence hypothesis for humans, and behavioural studies favouring evaluation apprehension have in practice done nothing more than demonstrate that evaluation apprehension can influence task performance under conditions where psychological presence effects are minimal.

The first two social facilitation experiments outlined in this chapter were not specifically related to humour but one did involve the presentation of comedy material and out of it was conceived the electromyographic (EMG) study of humour appreciation detailed below. These initial experiments were psychophysiological in character and they went beyond previous findings in demonstrating that *both* the psychological presence of a companion (Chapman, 1974a) *and* evaluation apprehension (Chapman, 1973a) enhance autonomic arousal.

Isometric muscle tension recorded from the frontalis muscle was taken as the index of arousal (cf. Goldstein, 1972). In the first of these EMG experiments, students who had experience of participating in psychophysiological studies listened to a comedy recording (Shelley Berman's *Morning After*, EMI Records # MFP 1269) in the presence of an inattentive experimenter who sat reading a book. They were tested individually while lying on a couch and they underwent a relaxation schedule before the humour recording was presented. *S*s were divided into two groups, matched for EMG resting levels and EMG gradients obtained on previous occasions. One group listened privately on headphones and the other listened to an external speaker.

Mere presence effects, by definition, were constant in the two conditions, and it was hypothesized that the latter group would experience greater evaluation apprehension and therefore greater isometric muscle tension because of the nature of the material: Ss listening to the external speaker would be concerned that the experimenter was expecting them to laugh and smile when audience laughter was prominent on the recording. Ss wearing headphones were expected to experience less evaluation apprehension because they knew that the experimenter could not hear the recording and therefore could not match stimuli and responses.

The EMG data supported the prediction: Ss who listened privately experienced significantly lower levels of muscle tension during the first 4 minutes of the 7-minute recording, and subjective ratings confirmed that they had experienced less evaluation apprehension.

In the second experiment, students listened on headphones, once only, to a tape-recorded Somerset Maugham story, 11·25 minutes in duration. They were tested in a solitary situation (*alone condition*), in the company of an inattentive experimenter (*audience condition*), or with the experimenter known to be behind a one-way viewing screen (*concealed-audience condition*). Groups were again matched and the same relaxation schedule was introduced prior to testing. The mere presence hypothesis predicted lower levels of muscle tension in the 'alone condition' than in the 'audience condition', and this was found to be the case. The evaluation apprehension hypothesis predicted no difference because Ss were not making behavioural responses which might be evaluated.

Data from these two experiments therefore support a drive theory of social facilitation and they indicate that a distinction can be drawn empirically between evaluation apprehension hypotheses and psychological presence hypotheses. However, the mean EMG levels of Ss in the 'concealed-audience condition' were significantly higher at some points than those of the 'alone' Ss and numerically, but not significantly, lower than those of 'audience condition' Ss. These results suggest that psychological presence should be described along a continuum and not considered an all-or-nothing phenomenon inextricably tied to physical presence. In the second experiment, therefore, the experimenter's presence in the Ss' psychological environment is seen as being variable across the three experimental conditions.

Further evidence favouring the view that there are degrees of psychological presence comes from a new experiment on electroencephalographic (EEG) correlates of interpersonal distance and eye-contact in male dyads (Gale, Spratt, Chapman and Smallbone, 1975). A confederate stood facing student Ss at distances of 2, 4, 8, 16 or 32 feet, and either gazed directly at the Ss' eyes or averted his gaze. Ss looked continuously into the confederate's eyes during several blocks of trials and closed their eyes between trials while the confederate repositioned himself. EEG arousal was shown to diminish with distance and to be greater for direct than averted gaze.

There are other studies also affirming that physiological changes incorporated within the arousal construct are related to various aspects of a companion's presence and behaviour (cf. Christie and Todd, 1975). Such studies provide essential information for the conclusion at the end of this chapter concerning the social functions of laughter. It is suggested there that 'social arousal' induced by eye-contact, proximity and other social aspects of the situation may be reduced indirectly through humour, primarily because the ensuing laughter affords an opportunity to withdraw attention from the companion.

STARTING-POINT 3: PSYCHOPHYSIOLOGICAL CORRELATES OF HUMOUR APPRECIATION

The third concurrent starting-point was an interest in laughter as a tension-reducer and the notion that increases in arousal accompany humour perception and humour appreciation.

It is evident from a review by Stearns (1972) that psychologists have barely begun to study the physiology of humour appreciation and laughing. Some informative and valuable studies have already been published however. Schachter and Wheeler (1962), for example, have found that pre-injection of epinephrine produces increased laughter from subjects presented with a slapstick comedy film and Levi (1965) has found increases in epinephrine excretion with both comedy and aggressive films.

Averill (1969) took various physiological measures of sympathetic activation, cardiovascular changes and respiratory changes from independent groups of subjects viewing a comedy film, a sadness-inducing film and a control film. He found that only respiratory changes were unique to the comedy group. Although five additional measures discriminated the comedy from *either* the control *or* sad film, only two of these, log palmar conductance and maximal increase in heart rate, were positively correlated with subjects' ratings on a sadness–mirth scale. Langevin and Day (1972) took various indices of heart rate (HR) and galvanic skin response (GSR) while subjects were presented with a series of cartoons. They found that subjective evaluations of humour were postively related to GSR amplitude, GSR recovery time, mean change in HR and maximum HR response.

Other studies also suggest, but without appropriate statistical confirmation, that enhanced autonomic arousal is concomitant with humour experiences (e.g. Fry, 1969; Fry and Stoft, 1971; Martin, 1905; Wolff, Smith and Murray, 1934). Theoretical and descriptive accounts of humour by Spencer (1860), Koestler (1964) and others, and an early experiment by Paskind (1932) in which muscle tone was apparently measured by a system of gears, pulleys and a shaft, give grounds to suspect that muscle tension in particular may be altered in humorous situations. Moreover, observations of children (cf. Leuba, 1960; Williams, 1945) and discussions of cataplexy and narcolepsy symptomatology (cf. Bateson, 1953; Fry, 1963) also point towards there being a build-up of muscle tension during the presentation of humour.

An EMG study of humour

In this study, the frontalis muscle tension of 18 female, university students was monitored every tenth second as they listened through headphones to tape-recordings incorporating the following joke:

A father went to consult a child psychologist about his twin sons. 'One of them is ridiculously optimistic', he reported. 'And the other is equally pessimistic. They are both quite irrational in their attitude. Have you any suggestions as to how I could encourage them to approach life in a more balanced way?'

The psychologist thought for a while and then he said, 'I note that your sons' birthday is only a few days away. Why not present your pessimistic lad with some splendid gift, but give the optimist some miserable and completely unacceptable object—say a box of manure?'

On the morning of their birthday the optimistic twin leaped gaily out of bed. 'Many happy returns, Fred!', he carolled. 'What did Daddy give you?' The pessimist lethargically examined the leather box on the beside table. 'It looks like a gold watch', he replied suspiciously. 'Bet it doesn't go. What did you get?' 'A pony!' shrieked his brother ecstatically. 'But I don't know where it's hiding!' (Reprinted by permission of Wolfe Publishing Limited)

Ss were tested alone while lying on a couch in a small, darkened room. Each had previously participated in at least three EMG sessions and each was familiar with the laboratory and with important aspects of the procedure. A pair of surface silver–silver chloride electrodes were located 10 centimetres apart and 2·5 centimetres above either eyebrow; a grounding electrode was sited on the neck. All three electrodes were secured to the skin with collodion and subsequently filled with Cambridge electrode jelly by means of a syringe. Muscle action potentials were amplified and integrated through a Beckman type R dynograph and an integrator input coupler (Type 9852). Chart paper was driven at 2·5 millimetres per second and scores obtained directly from the paper in microvolts.

The 15-minute relaxation schedule used in previous experiments preceded the material on the tape-recordings. The stimulus material was 7 minutes long with four 1-minute periods of silence separating three 1-minute sound items: viz., the joke, an uninteresting financial news passage, and the regular beating of a metronome. The sound items were equated for peak levels of loudness, and order of presentation was balanced through the use of six separate tapes, each tape being played to three of the Ss chosen at random. At the end of sessions, Ss were required to rate laboratory experiences and the sound stimuli along a number of dimensions. A humour-rating for the joke was elicited on a 10-centimetre scale which was marked 'not at all funny' at one end and 'extremely funny' at the other.

Subsequently Ss were divided into high (above median) raters and low (below median) raters and their EMG levels compared at the 10-second intervals by means of two-tailed t-tests. High raters had significantly greater ($p < 0.05$) EMGs at 30, 40 and 50 seconds into the joke, and they were also greater 20 seconds after the joke. (A comparison was not feasible at the punchline, nor

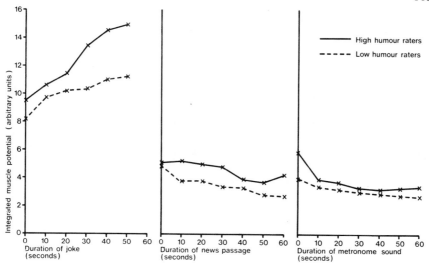

Figure 8.1 Changes in EMG as a function of time into joke, news passage and metronome sound

10 seconds afterwards, because laughter and/or head movements invariably occurred between these points and rapid EMG changes caused the ink trace on the chart paper to become indecipherable.) There were no differences in EMGs between high and low raters at other times of silence, nor during the news passage or metronome. Mean EMGs were numerically greater for the high raters at every comparison point, but the only additional points at which the group differences approached significance were at the beginning of the joke and 10 and 20 seconds beforehand ($p < 0.10$, in each case). Ss were presumably anticipating the onset of the joke: they knew of its position within the material from instructions studied before the relaxation schedule. No laughter ever occurred before the final 10 seconds of the joke. This is an important point because increased respiration and muscle activity accompanying laughter affects such arousal indices as HR, GSR and, in this case, EMG.

EMG levels rose regularly during the joke, for high raters particularly. There were no corresponding increases during the metronome sound, the news item or the periods of silence; nor were there increases across sessions as a whole. However, it is pertinent to note that in at least two other listening experiments (Chapman, 1974a; Wallerstein, 1954), regular increments in EMG levels have been found with *non-humorous* recordings. On the other hand, these have been smaller increases materilizing over appreciably longer periods of time.

A main finding in this EMG experiment, therefore, is that a positive association exists between subjective evaluations of a joke's funniness and muscle tension. This finding adds credence to the notion that heightened levels of arousal are associated with humour appreciation. A second main finding is that arousal increases during the presentation of humour.

SOCIAL ASPECTS OF CHILDREN'S LAUGHTER

The above studies precipitated several interrelated questions meriting extensive systematic research. Of special interest are those relating to the social functions of humour and laughter, the contagious nature of laughter and the behavioural changes in humour appreciation which are concomitant with the presence of a companion.

These questions are addressed through behavioural analyses of situations in which children attend to auditory humour. In exploring the children's responsiveness to one another in these situations, their reactions to the humour stimuli *per se* are exposed to experimental scrutiny. Additionally, in an unpublished study mentioned below, attention has been directed fleetingly towards the adult population and, currently, our school subjects are being shown cartoon films (see Chapter 9).

Experimental methodology

Laughter is especially important in the social interactions and play of young children and as a consequence children are potentially the most interesting of possible Ss for study. However, reasons of expediency also governed the choice of children as Ss in these studies. Painstaking preliminary testing of students, adolescents and children of various ages strengthened preconceived ideas that, under controlled and contrived conditions, it is easier to elicit natural and spontaneous behaviour from children than from adults. In particular, it is appreciably less difficult with young children to stimulate laughter in standardized small group conditions, always providing that the situations are pleasant and not in any sense anxiety-inducing. Within their school environment, children are remarkably uninquisitive about the purpose of their participation, and they are considerably less curious than adults about the nature of the research work.

The Ss in this series of experiments were pupils in state coeducational junior schools catering for 7–11-year-old children of mixed abilities. The schools' catchment areas border on one another and they are of predominantly middle-class socioeconomic status, although several embrace working-class neighbourhoods. Eligibility for registration at these schools is dependent only upon the age of children and the geographical location of their homes. Within each school, boys and girls were selected for experiments solely on the basis of age. They were 7 and 8 years old and were the youngest boys and youngest girls in the school.

Equal numbers of boys and girls were tested in each experimental treatment group. They were tested once only, under standard physical conditions in independent groups, sometimes in isolation and occasionally in like-sex triads, but usually in like-sex dyads: in dyads, they sat face-to-face 2·7 feet apart (expect where otherwise stated). Assignment to treatment conditions was random and experimental group sessions were sequentially randomized as far as possible. Children were labelled *subjects* (*S*s) and *companions* according to their spontaneous choice of seats on entering the laboratory (except when companions were accomplices of the experimenter). In coaction sessions, members of a pair were treated identically, but the distinction between *S* and companion was necessary for analyses of data. (Tables present scores for *S*s only.) Several of the experiments outlined in this chapter involved the training of 9-year-old confederates who then acted as companions to *S*s; special procedures attached to their employment are outlined later.

The children were tested on school premises, during teaching hours, in a children's dual-compartment mobile-laboratory, and they were observed through a one-way viewing screen by either one or two observers, equipped in all but the first main study (i.e. Chapman, 1973c) with an event-recorder. *S*s appeared not to contemplate the possibility of being watched in this way and, in part, this no doubt reflected their naivety about the content matter of Psychology and its methodological techniques. The base of the viewing screen was approximately 30 centimetres above the seated eye-levels of 7-year-olds.

*S*s were played tape-recorded humorous material through headphones. The material was 13 minutes 4 seconds long and comprised a story (*The Funny Green Hair* from H. E. Todd's book, *Bobby Brewster's Camera*. Leicester: Brockhampton Press, 1959) and a song (*The Laughing Policeman* performed by Charles Penrose on Columbia Records # SEG 7743). Also included on the composite tape in the first of the following social facilitation experiments (Chapman, 1973c), was the laughter of two children recorded as they listened to an extended version of the song. The modified song constituted a just-audible background, and the total recording was then 17 minutes 42 seconds in duration. In terms of a 10-category classificatory system for children's humour developed by Kappas (1967), the humour in the story and song is in part based upon 'surprise' but relies more upon 'incongruity' and 'absurdity'. Opening, closing and link comments on the tape were as brief as possible (for instance, *Well, that was the story. Now here is 'The Laughing Policeman'*).

The story was picked from 13 preselected for this research by two professional narrators of children's stories. They recorded each of them, firstly, alone in an anechoic chamber and, secondly, in a small classroom with an audience of a dozen children. The song was an extra item. Selection of material from within the 14 items was based upon data collected from 240 children aged 6–8 years. They listened individually or in like-sex dyads to various pairs of the recordings. The experimenter remained with them and surreptitiously recorded their laughs and smiles with the aid of a second tape-recorder and cumulative stop-watches. The song and the story (recorded without an audience) which were finally chosen satisfied the following criteria: they were not known to these children; they were easily understood; laughter and smiling occurred relatively frequently throughout their duration; and they induced no large-scale individual differences.

After observational sessions *S*s were engaged briefly in conversation by the experimenter who asked them about the comedy material and about their favourite fictional characters and television programmes. Post-test conversations were sometimes designed to disguise the administration of verbal rating scales but, more than this, they fortified a cover story. In the days or weeks immediately preceding the onset of an experiment, while children were habituating to the presence of the experimenter and mobile-laboratory, the Ss-elect were led by their teachers to believe that their opinions were to be sought in connection with the stocking of a new children's library.

Inhibition of laughter as a function of knowledge of one-way viewing screen: an experiment

A variety of reasons in combination could account for the paucity of psychological research into laughter. One of the most important single causes is no doubt the sheer difficulty of generating laughter in a laboratory. Pollio and co-workers (1972) noted that up to their time of writing no researchers, including themselves, had ever claimed to have created 'explosive laughter' under laboratory conditions: the term 'explosive laughter' was used to refer to laughter occurring with 'profound body movements, changes in respiration, tears, etc.' (p. 213).

However, explosive laughter, without tears, has been a very common phenomenon in our sessions. This consistent and apparently unprecedented success is probably attributable to the unusually relaxed atmosphere prevailing in the mobile-laboratory. Some of the key elements contributing to the congenial testing environment are as follows: children are in the playroom compartment without an adult; they do not know that they are being 'tested' or that any aspect of their behaviour is under study; and, perhaps most important of all, they are not aware that they are observed. In all our observations of children and in all our conversations with them, their teachers, and their parents, not one sign has been detected suggesting that a child is suspicious that he might be visible through the one-way viewing screen. Like all such screens, it has the appearance of an ordinary looking-glass; it is an integral part of the partition dividing the laboratory into the two compartments.

In post-test interviews conducted at the embryonic stage of this research, a high proportion of student Ss stated that they were inhibited because they perceived the situations as artificial, and they were certain that their behaviour was under study. In most cases, laughter was not vented at all when Ss suspected that this was the behaviour under investigation. If laughter was not suppressed totally in adults, its expression tended to be tranquil, private and transitory, bearing none of the attractive, infectious qualities usually inherent in everyday displays of laughter. In marked contrast, the laughter of children was generally indistinguishable inside and outside the laboratory.

The present experiment was designed to assess whether it was necessary to withhold information about the one-way screen and to observe Ss without their knowledge. In a *with knowledge* condition, eight pairs of children were informed of the viewing screen facility but told that the experimenter would not be watching them since he was 'working on something else'. To prevent their being discouraged from laughing freely through fear of disturbing the experimenter, he went on to say that the 'wall between the two rooms' was completely soundproofed. (He would know when the tape ended by an alarum-clock sounding in his room.) Eight pairs of children in a *without knowledge* condition received instructions differing in one critical respect: the screen was not mentioned. Otherwise the two groups were treated identically. *S*s in the 'without knowledge' condition were tested first. They had no contact with the other *S*s during the course of the experiment, the entire test schedule being run in a single day.

The general expectation was that the 'with knowledge' group who knew that it was possible to be seen would behave differently from the 'without knowledge' group who had no such awareness. It was predicted specifically that they would engage in less laughter during sessions as a whole. Other dependent measures were duration of eye-contact (EC) and duration of smiling. (Eye-contact is defined as reciprocated looking in the region of the eyes.)

The findings demonstrate convincingly that 'humorous laughter' is apt to vanish from the repertoire of laboratory behaviours if *S*s realize that their reactions are open to inspection. The data are summarized in Table 8.1 and were analysed statistically with *t*-tests. The 'with knowledge' *S*s laughed considerably less than the 'without knowledge' *S*s (1-tailed $p < 0.005$), and group differences on the other two dependent behaviours were highly significant in the opposite direction: *S*s in the 'with knowledge' condition engaged in more smiling (2-tailed $p < 0.005$) and EC (2-tailed $p < 0.001$).

There is some suggestion in the data that girls were affected more than boys by awareness of potential observation. Large percentage differences emerged in pairs of means for 'with knowledge' boys and girls which were not evident in the corresponding 'without knowledge' means. In the former condition especially, girls tended to smile more and engage in more EC, but the small numbers of *S*s precluded a statistical confirmation of sex differences in these behaviours.

This experiment adds weight to the notion that a principal reason why laughter has been sparsely researched is that it is inhibited by standard laboratory procedures and environments. The findings attest to the ephemeral,

Table 8.1 Mean laughter, smiling and eye-contact scores in seconds

| | 'Without knowledge' condition (Subjects not known to be visible to experimenter) | | 'With knowledge' condition (Subjects known to be visible to experimenter) | |
	Boys	Girls	Boys	Girls
Laughter	19·6	21·1	6·3	3·5
Smiling	71·1	77·3	118·9	141·3
Eye-contact	135·3	150·2	211·5	278·0

enigmatic and elusive nature of laughter. Perhaps if Ss detect even the most intangible of hints that their laughter is being observed then the natural expression of the researcher's dependent behaviour is liable to be suppressed or lost altogether, so sensitive is laughter to social aspects of situations.

Included in the standardized conversations which conveyed preliminary instructions to children was the sentence, *Now, you're going to hear two things that will make you laugh.* It was embedded amongst several others and was not emphasized. If greater stress had been placed on laughter in this period then the findings for laughter might have been reversed. This is pure speculation but Ss, particularly children, might respond to demand characteristics of the experiment and obligingly laugh more, especially if they know their reactions are visible to the experimenter. This form of deliberate laughter would no doubt be qualitatively different from that generated under more relaxed circumstances.

The smiling data highlight the measurement problems discussed earlier. The experimenter was in no doubt that most of the smiling in the 'with knowledge' condition was non-mirthful. Although children in this condition smiled appreciably more than children in the 'without knowledge' condition, the impression was gained that less of their smiling was associated with mirth stimuli in the recordings. When there was an obvious link, the humour often seemed, in the 'with knowledge' condition in particular, to provide an excuse for Ss to share EC with companions and engage in a form of sociable smiling. These and other informal observations coupled with the higher EC in this condition suggest that the children were not comfortable in the situation but gained reassurance from the other's presence. The end result of this experiment was that no Ss in other studies had their attention drawn to the one-way viewing screen.

Social facilitation of laughter

Laughter is an explosive, spontaneous, expressive behaviour and as such is an unusual behaviour to introduce into the literature on social facilitation as conventionally demarcated. It is nonetheless an appealing behaviour to study in this context because, in the case of children, it can be generated through naturalistic situations in which evaluation apprehension effects are minimal, arguably non-existent, and in which consequently the salience of psychological presence effects may begin to be assessed satisfactorily. The demonstration in even one behavioural setting that the psychological presence of a companion has effects independent of those emanating from evaluation apprehension is of considerable significance theoretically, offering support for Zajonc's position and compelling the retention of the two distinct types of drive hypotheses. Thus, there is potentially a major advantage to be gained in testing social facilitation theory in experimental situations where Ss' evaluation apprehension is minimized.

We have set about this through studying the facilitation of 'humorous laughter' because, unlike responses emitted in typical learning and performance tasks, laughter cannot be judged objectively by companions or experimenters according to criteria such as good–bad and right–wrong. Although quantitative and qualitative aspects of an individual's laughter are inevitably influenced by personal characteristics of that individual, they also reflect the quality of the humour especially if, as in these studies, it is inoffensive and not complex or difficult to comprehend.

Clearly, our Ss are engaged in an experimental task: they are expected to attend to the auditory humour recordings (or films). However, it has already been emphasized that the children are not aware they are observed, and in this major respect these experiments differ from previous studies of social facilitation in human Ss. From their exuberance in the laboratory and from teachers' comments it is evident that with precious few exceptions the children greatly enjoy the test sessions and, as implied earlier, the vast majority appear oblivious to the fact that they are participating in any form of special activity or research.

Since they do not know that their responses are being recorded it is safe to deduce that, while attending to the humour, Ss are not experiencing apprehension about evaluation by the experimenter. Also, there is evidence that in coaction conditions children endeavour to share the social situation maximally and even to react to the humour in unison. Under these circumstances, because they are unable to extricate themselves from the joint activity, they are probably not capable of inducing evaluation apprehension within one another. Evaluation apprehension associated with the presence of companions in these coaction situations is presumably minimal therefore. In audience situations, objective evaluations of Ss' mirth responses by companions is out of the question. The companions are not able to perceive the stimuli because they are not provided with headphones: hence, they cannot form objective judgements about the appropriateness of Ss' responses.

The opening experiment in the series on socially facilitated laughter (Chapman, 1973c) was modelled upon the traditional audience and coaction paradigms of social facilitation research. Children were presented with tape-recorded humour through headphones in the company of a non-listening companion (*audience condition*) or a companion who could also hear (*coaction condition*); others listening in the absence of a companion (*alone condition*) provided baselines scores. As indicated above, the audience condition was implemented by indicating to companions that the second set of headphones was temporarily defective. (They were assured that they would have an opportunity to hear the material on the day following.)

Time scores were corrected for heterogeneity of variance by means of log $(1 + X)$ transformations prior to applying parametric statistics. Analyses of variance were computed, together with Kramer's extension to Duncan's multiple range tests for unequal cell frequencies: for reasons which do not concern us here, 10 children were tested in the alone condition and 10 pairs in the coaction condition, compared with 20 pairs in the audience condition.

Ss in the coaction condition laughed more ($p < 0.05$) than Ss in the audience condition, and they also smiled more ($p < 0.05$): this finding has since been replicated (Chapman, 1975a). Solitary children responded least of all. In fact, though they could not hear the humour material, the audience-companions laughed and smiled approximately four times as much as children in the alone condition. Highly significant differences between Ss' laughter scores in alone and audience conditions ($p < 0.001$) are difficult to explain except by reference to the mere presence concept and the experiment thereby offers some of the strongest behavioural evidence to date for the concept and for Zajonc's mere presence hypothesis. The fact that a companion was present in the audience condition may have been *sufficient* to augment laughter beyond the alone level.

In both audience and coaction conditions there were statistically significant associations between Ss' and companions' laughter ($p < 0.01$) and smiling ($p < 0.01$). These correlational analyses strengthened an impression, derived from informal observations, that the level of social intimacy between members of dyads is a crucial factor influencing 'humorous laughter' and that the more shared the situation, the more children laugh.

It was resolved that this impression should be put to the test in due course. However, in the first instance, research activity was directed towards demonstrating that highly significant behavioural differences between audience-companions and coactor-companions could have contributed substantially to the difference in Ss' responses, both within and between conditions.

Confederates

In virtually all subsequent experiments until the most recent, 9-year-old confederates of the experimenter have performed as companions to Ss in the two-person (and three-person) situations. These accomplices were required to behave in various ways according to their assignment to the different experimental conditions. They usually acted as coactors but in one experiment they also performed as audiences. Five boys and five girls were chosen for each experiment so that each was paired with one of the Ss in every experimental condition, there being five boys and five girls tested in each condition.

The selection and training procedures were the same for all experiments. Education Authority rulings precluded the drawing of confederates and Ss from different schools, but prior familiarity and friendship were controlled satisfactorily by selecting confederates from the schools' third-year pupils: first- and third-year children generally have very little contact within schools. However, it was feared that the use of older children in this way might have contaminated results since younger pupils tend to ascribe high status to more senior children. Status of companions was not varied during the following experiments but as a check that status does not influence laughter and smiling to an unacceptable degree, independent groups of first-year boys and girls were tested in like-sex dyads with first- and third-year companions (Chapman and Wright, 1976); test sessions were procedurally identical to the coaction sessions above. Because in this case the third-year children were not confederates, no child was taken into the experimenter's confidence. Results showed that the first-year Ss' mean scores and ranges were barely affected by the companion's seniority in the school. There was therefore no reason to suppose that there would be any differences between first- and third-year confederates on Ss' laughter and smiling.

Form teachers and headmasters were responsible for the final choice of confederates, but the following criteria were recommended as guidelines: (1) confederates should have no siblings in the school; (2) they should be 'trustworthy' and capable of maintaining confidences; (3) they should enjoy acting and be relatively proficient at it; (4) they should be likeable, cooperative and enjoy performing as companions.

In coaction sessions, the confederates received pre-recorded on-line instructions through one set of headphones, and just audible as a background was the humour material. Ss received the humour material through a second set of headphones, the two sets being connected to independent channels of a Heathkit stereophonic tape-recorder. Ss were generally led to believe that companions listened simultaneously to the same recordings although in two experiments, half were explicitly instructed that companions were listening to different humorous material. In the latter circumstances, the instructional set was given authenticity through encouraging Ss (and confederates) to inspect the two (or three) sets of headphones for up to 90 seconds prior to testing. Ss assigned to the audience situation heard two different pieces of music from the sets, while a single piece of music was played in synchrony through the headsets for Ss in coaction situations. The taped directions were derived from the response profiles of children in naturalistic pairs and, since all smiles were intended to be interpreted as mirthful, each concurred with an amusing event in the material.

Because the confederates were not required to memorize any complex series of activities, the training procedures were not complicated. Nevertheless, training extended over 4–5 days, most of it taking place in small groups or with solitary children. It was designed to ensure that confederates appeared to behave naturally during test sessions whilst in fact complying with directions dictating their laughter, smiling and looking behaviours. The confederates were first invited into the laboratory as one group and the general nature of the particular study in which they were to become involved was revealed to them. Only hypotheses of a non-specific and non-directional nature were ever disclosed, but all confederates were told of the one-way screen.

Further objectives underlying the instigation of meetings prior to formal training were, firstly, to accustom confederates to the laboratory, equipment and experimenter and, secondly, to assist them in maintaining the deception outside test sessions. Success in the latter revolved around Ss remaining ignorant of the confederates' frequent participation. To this end the laboratory was always stationed out of sight of classrooms: therefore, pupils were not able to witness the toing-and-froing of confederates. Also, it was carefully arranged that Ss and confederates should arrive simultaneously at the laboratory door after having approached it from opposite directions. There is no reason to suppose that any S suspected that companions were confederates.

Analyses of companion variables

The first of the social facilitation studies employing confederate-companions (Chapman and Wright, 1976) was primarily concerned with examining the facilitative effects upon an S's laughter induced, (a) by the amount of attention paid to him by a coactor, and (b) by the coactor's own mirthful behaviour.

The differences in laughter in the original experiment for Ss in alone, audience and coaction conditions may have been principally a function of there being more laughter stimuli in some situations than in others: the same material was played to all Ss but coactors laughed more than audience-companions.

Unquantified observational data in that experiment indicated that coacting-companions looked much more at Ss than did audience-companions. Coactors therefore seemed to pay more attention to their partners than did audiences. Coaction Ss may consequently have laughed more than audience Ss through sensing that their companions were paying a great deal of attention to them: this may have induced feelings of sharing the social situation which possibly enhance laughter, or it may have given rise to social conformity effects.

The confederates' levels of mirth and looking in the first study were as follows: (1) MIRTH: *Frequent mirth*—58 seconds laughing, 131 seconds smiling; *Intermediate mirth*—33 seconds laughing, 78 seconds smiling; *Zero mirth*. (2) LOOKING: *Frequent looking*—463 seconds; *Intermediate looking*—318 seconds; *Low looking*—157 seconds. By 'looking' is meant glancing or gazing at the face of the other child.

Increments in the confederates' mirth prompted additional laughter ($p < 0.005$), smiling ($p < 0.005$) and looking ($p < 0.005$) from Ss. Duncan's new multiple range tests confirmed that response levels on each of the dependent behaviours were significantly different between pairs of conditions ($p < 0.01$, in each case). Increases in looking at Ss also tended to result in more smiling ($p < 0.05$) and looking ($p < 0.05$) at confederates. Ss in 'low looking' conditions smiled less than Ss in the other two 'looking' conditions, and Ss in the 'frequent looking' conditions looked more than Ss in the other 'looking' conditions ($p < 0.05$, in each case). Duncan's range tests indicated that there were no other significant differences between means. A tendency for Ss to engage in more laughter as companions looked at each other more was not statistically significant ($p < 0.25$).

Thus, a coacting-companion's mirth is a determinant of the S's mirth. There are two possible reasons, neither exclusive of the other. It may be that the companion's laughter and smiling directly facilitate the same responses in the S through their infectious nature, or it may be that they do so indirectly through their informative value for the S in showing that someone else finds the stimulus material funny.

In one of two experiments (Chapman, 1974b; Chapman and Wright, 1976) designed to explore these two possibilities, the companions' mirth was varied systematically across pairs of audience and coaction conditions (Chapman and Wright). If the former factor is at work, we expected a similar relationship to exist between the mirth of Ss and companions in the audience condition, and we expected no difference is Ss' mirth between audience and coactions conditions when the companions' mirth was held constant between them.

Strictly speaking of course, if no difference were found between audience and coaction conditions, companions' mirth held constant, it does not necessarily follows that the informational value of the companion's mirth in the coaction condition has not had a facilitative effect; for it is obviously possible that some additional factor intrinsic to the audience situation has a similar and compensating facilitatory effect. But it does mean that the differences found between coaction and audience conditions in the original experiment cannot be attributed to the informational factor. If the informational factor is of significance, however, we might anticipate that it would show up in a potentially inhibitive situation. We might reasonably expect that a silent and serious coacting-companion would tend to reduce the S's mirth more than a similarly taciturn audience-companion. Some supplementary conditions introduced into this next experiment confirmed that this was the case.

It was found in analysing the main coaction conditions that, as before, increases in the companions' mirth up to the highest level produced regular increases in the Ss' laughter; and it seems reasonable to assume that further increments would have continued to enhance humour responsiveness. Successive increments in the audiences' mirth ceased to enhance Ss' laughter as the former's mirth level approached that of coactors in the original experiment; Ss' mirth tended then to decline. The data suggest that a curvilinear (inverted-U) relationship exists between audiences' and Ss' mirth. This may be a function of distraction in that Ss may be unable to comprehend the cause of a companion's high level of mirth. Also, they may become inhibited if they suspect, for example, that their companion is laughing *at* them rather than *with* them.

The facilitative value of knowledge that coacting-companions are known to be attending to the same humorous material also received attention in experiments in which instructional set was manipulated (Chapman, 1974b, 1975b). One half of Ss were given to believe that their companions were listening to the same humorous material and the other half of Ss were under the impression that companions were listening to different humorous material. In Chapman (1974b) mirth was systematically varied across pairs of conditions, and increments in the confederates' mirth again promoted significant increases in laughter, smiling and looking. This was so whether Ss thought they were listening to the same or different recordings. The instructional set was found not to affect any of the dependent measures and this is a clear indication that information to the effect that others are listening to the same humour is of little or no relevance to the facilitation of laughter: it is *not* the sharing of humour *per se* which is important. However, there was some suggestion in the looking data that the sharing of the social situation may have been important. Ss looked most at companions who laughed most, and looking is presumably an index of sharing. It is possible, therefore, that companions' mirth made Ss especially reactive to the humour, through promoting the feeling that social situations were shared. This received further attention in Chapman (1975b), discussed below.

An interesting question at this stage of the research concerned whether the increased smiling of coacting-companions was contributing to the facilitation of responses or whether it was solely their laughter which was responsible for the incremental effects. A coaction experiment was run to investigate whether laughter, smiling and subjective evaluations of funniness are differentially facilitated by the companion's smiling and laughter (Chapman and Chapman, 1974). Although the companion's attentiveness to Ss had not been found to produce significant effects on laughter, there were significant effects on measures of smiling and looking. Thus, control over confederates' looking was warranted. For ease of enforcement in this experiment, it was maintained at a constant, zero level across all conditions. A $3 \times 3 \times 2$ factorial design was adopted, there being 3 levels of laughing and 3 levels of humorous smiling for confederates in male and female dyads. In *frequent laughter* conditions, confederates engaged in 18 laughs totalling 60 seconds; *intermediate laughter* conditions—13 laughs totalling 36 seconds; *zero laughter* conditions—no laughter at all. In *frequent smiling* conditions, confederates engaged in 19 smiles totalling 126 seconds; *intermediate smiling* conditions—19 smiles totalling 74 seconds; *zero smiling* conditions—no smiling at all. Sometimes Ss failed to notice the confederates' smiles: on average, they observed 71 seconds of smiling in 'frequent smiling' conditions and 42 seconds in 'intermediate smiling' conditions.

Increased smiling from the companion tended to enhance scores on each of the dependent measures but the effect was significant only for smiling ($p < 0.005$). Increased laughter augmented Ss' scores on all measures: that is, on smiling ($p < 0.005$), looking ($p < 0.05$), funniness ratings ($p < 0.05$), and laughter ($p < 0.005$), although there was no significant difference between duration of laughter in 'intermediate' and 'frequent laughter' conditions ($p < 0.10$). After giving their own humour-ratings, Ss were asked to guess what their 'friend' (the confederate) was about to say; a positive association was found between confederate's level of laughter and the ratings expected from them. A similar relationship was found in Chapman (1974b) between expected ratings and amount of mirth displayed.

There are a number of possible mechanisms which may account for the facilitation of the behavioural responses. Following Tolman's (1968) identification of four principal social facilitation processes, it has been suggested elsewhere (Chapman, 1973c) that the companion's mirth may enhance an S's responses to humour by making the S more reactive to the humorous material, by acting as an eliciting stimulus for laughter, by disinhibiting responses and by drawing the S's attention to humour stimuli which would otherwise escape unnoticed. However, the companion's mirth is not likely to have operated according to the two latter processes during the course of these experiments.

The audiences' mirth in the Chapman and Wright study could not have served a direct attention-drawing function, and even naturalistic coactors are unlikely to have been successful in this respect because one major criterion for the selection of material was that it should be easily understood by children of this age. Similarly, there is little reason to suppose that responses are disinhibited in these experiments; children appear to be totally at ease. On the other hand, the sight and sound of the companion's laughter probably does seem funny to Ss on occasions and it may augment mirth scores. There was never any evidence indicating that Ss deliberately imitate confederates, or that they engage in any form of competition, but the companions' laughter may induce social conformity effects. However, its strongest facilitative property may be its propensity to make Ss more reactive to the humour material.

The supplementary conditions of Chapman and Wright indicated that a companion possesses the capacity to enhance overt humour responses, even when he displays zero laughter and smiling and is apparently insensitive to the presence and behaviour of S. Companions never once looked at Ss in the extra dyadic conditions and so the latter may initially have used laughter in an attempt to gain attention and show their willingness to share the situation. Effects due to other psychological mechanisms must have been negligible under these circumstances, and the data have therefore been interpreted as supporting the notion that the psychological presence of a companion is sometimes sufficient to enhance humorous laughter. However, in the case of adults, the presence of a second person does not appear to be sufficient to enhance laughter. In an unpublished study, Chapman and Osborne found that the presence of an unresponsive confederate-companion significantly lowered laughter below the level of alone adults.

The experiments on children described so far combine to show that the differences in coactors' and audiences' behaviour, especially laughter, go a long way towards accounting for the significant differences in Ss' laughter in the original audience and coaction conditions. Somewhat surprisingly, however, it does not seem to matter that the coacting companion's laughter is supposedly evoked by the material heard by Ss. The fact that the companion's laughter was known, or believed, to be a response to laughter stimuli, whether exposed to S, or not, appears to be the crucial factor.

Audiences laughed much less than the coacting-companions in the original experiment but the results of Chapman and Wright suggest that audiences could not have facilitated as much laughter in Ss even if they had laughed as much or more than the natural coactors. In any case, audiences' laughter in the original experiment was usually a response to Ss' laughter, rather than vice versa.

Some of the audiences' responses in naturalistic situations may have been evoked by laughter-provoking stimuli which were present in the expressions of a laughing S, but probably much of their laughter and smiling behaviour was of a sociable nature. This form of behaviour almost certainly helped maintain the Ss' interest in their companions and it was undoubtedly conducive to a friendly atmosphere. Probably the companions who appeared most amiable, particularly in an audience condition, were most successful in facilitating laughter.

On the other hand, the subsidiary conditions in Chapman and Wright indicate that neither a display of laughter nor friendly/responsive behaviour is an essential ingredient for the facilitation of laughter. Moreover, it appears that when companions laugh and smile very little their facilitatory influence is greater if they pay minimal attention to Ss.

Perhaps the most interesting result, however, is that children in two-person conditions tended to laugh more than solitary Ss even when the audiences and coacting-companions engaged in little or no laughter, smiling and looking. The low scores of solitary Ss were not due to the novel environment causing them to be apprehensive: the mean scores of Ss tested alone after having been made thoroughly familiar 3 days earlier with the laboratory and accoutrements during a 90-minute session were no greater than those of more naive alone Ss (Chapman, 1975b).

The final experiment in this social facilitation series was designed specifically to investigate whether sharing humour or sharing the social situation was crucial to the facilitation of laughter (Chapman, 1975b). The experiment had origins in the everyday observation that although a person may be a member of a small group in physical terms, he may feel an outsider because of subtle cues that operate or fail to operate. The main independent variable was the amount of interaction between pairs of confederate-companions. Other variables known to be potentially important were held constant across conditions: the amounts that confederates laughed, smiled and looked at Ss were constants across all treatment groups. They looked at Ss for 30% of the time in each session, but they looked at one another 0%, 15%, 30%, 45% or 60% of the time according to experimental conditions.

Results showed that as confederates looked less at one another, so Ss' laughter ($p < 0.01$) and smiling ($p < 0.05$) increased. Sharing the social situation rather than sharing the humour *per se* was again the crucial factor, since degree of interaction between confederates had similar effects whether they were thought to be listening to the same or to different humorous material. Finally, through the inclusion of two dyadic conditions, in which single confederate-companions engaged in the same amounts of laughing, smiling and looking at Ss as in triadic conditions, it was shown that the mere addition of a *second* companion is not sufficient to enhance children's responses to humour.

Laughter and social intimacy

Until the experiment outlined below (Chapman, 1975a), laughter had not been studied in the context or Argyle's heuristic model of social intimacy.

In part, this is probably because it was not specifically listed as an 'intimate' behaviour in Argyle and Dean's (1965) original theoretical exposition.

The model asserts that the intimacy level of any dyadic encounter is dependent upon a variety of mutually compensatory variables. The variables named are eye-contact (EC), interpersonal distance, smiling, body orientation and topic of conversation, but this is by no means intended to be an exhaustive list.

States of equilibrium are said to exist for the various signals of intimacy. In the case of EC, for example, affiliative needs and the demand for feedback are positive forces tending to promote EC, while excessive EC is avoided through concomitant anxiety leading to gaze aversion. Of course, social signals interact and, according to the model, if an optimum level of intimacy is disturbed by a change in intensity on one dimension (e.g. EC) then a reciprocal change results along at least one other dimension (e.g. proximity). In this way, the level of intimacy is maintained in a dynamic state of balance throughout any two-person interaction.

The experiment on laughter (Chapman, 1975a) calls into question the fundamental assumption underlying this equilibrium model, namely, the assumption that there is a single level of intimacy for any particular dyadic encounter. In a review of the empirical literature pertaining to the model, Patterson (1973) draws an analogy with 'a hydraulic model in which the total pressure in the system, while remaining constant, can be differentially distributed'. However, there is no evidence to corroborate the view that intimacy is static: on the contrary, a study by Scherer and Schiff (1973) using photographic slides suggests that people find situations less intimate as interpersonal distance increases.

Studies which have found EC and proximity to be inversely related provide some of the strongest evidence for the 'Intimacy Model' and, in an unpublished study by Chapman and Conyngham, the relationship has been shown to hold for children in non-humorous situations when they are engaged in both listening and conversational activities. However, preliminary observations of children listening to humour suggested that those who laughed and smiled most also sat closest together on the floor *and* engaged in most EC. Consequently, an experiment was run in which pairs of Ss in independent groups were tested at two interpersonal distances (2·7 feet, 5·5 feet) in audience and coaction conditions. No child was a confederate of the experimenter.

The results for the coaction conditions are striking. Children sitting closer together engaged in significantly *more* EC (2-tailed $p < 0.01$), and this is the converse of the model's prediction. They also engaged in more laughter (2-tailed $p < 0.01$) and more smiling (2-tailed $p < 0.01$). Moreover, other social signals such as body posture and seating orientation, though not included as dependent measures, seemed also to covary with proximity, EC, smiling and laughter: informal observations suggested that the most responsive of children on the dependent measures tended also to lean forwards in their seats with their heads raised for long periods, and they tended to move their legs and arms more.

In audience conditions, distance had no effect on EC, smiling or laughter. Significant differences in laughter and smiling for Ss in audience and coaction conditions closely resemble those obtained in the first social facilitation experiment (i.e. Chapman, 1973c). There were sex differences in EC corresponding to those found in older Ss (cf. Aiello, 1972; Libby and Yaklevich, 1973): girls engaged in more EC than did boys.

The most plausible explanation for the covariation of social signals in this experiment is that intimacy was *not* static during sessions but rose steadily, especially in coaction conditions and at the more proximate distance, since there was then greater potential for participants to share experiences. There was a tendency for laughter, smiling and EC to increase within sessions but the trends did not attain statistical significance ($p < 0.10$).

In demonstrating for the first time that a *direct* relationship can exist between EC and proximity, the study indicates that extreme caution is necessary in predicting from the model if there is any suspicion that its basic axiom, concerning static intimacy, may be contravened.

Other experimenters (Jourard and Friedman, 1970; Kleck, 1970) have also provided evidence contrary to the compensatory notion although their unusual dependent measures have set their studies apart from the main body of literature. Jourard and Friedman's measure of 'distance' was a composite of touching and interviewer self-disclosure, and Kleck measured non-verbal agreeing responses. However, the results of their studies are also explicable in terms of intimacy rising during sessions. The rapport between interviewer and Ss presumably developed during testing in both studies and it is likely to have grown most at the nearer distances because close proximity is especially disarming and conducive to the growth of a shared and friendly or confidential atmosphere.

Overt mirth and social intimacy: An experiment varying seating orientations

In this experiment the 'intimacy' of social situations is manipulated across conditions by varying systematically the relative seating positions of Ss and confederate-companions in dyadic coaction situations. It was argued that greater intimacy between Ss and companions would be reflected in greater laughter and smiling (Chapman, 1974c).

Four seating arrangements and a single variation in confederate-companions' looking behaviour define five conditions of intimacy. In ascending order of intimacy, as conceived by the writer, they are:

(a) *Back-to-back*, where confederates turned to glance at Ss at the beginning and end of sessions but not while Ss were listening to the humour recordings. [Conditions (b) and (c) involved the same pattern and incidence of minimal looking.]

(b) *Seated-at-right-angles*, where the chairs faced outwards at right angles.

(c) *Side-by-side without gazing*, where Ss and companions sat alongside one another.

(d) *Side-by-side with gazing*, which was the same as condition (c) except that confederates looked at Ss for a total of 318 seconds in each session.

(e) *Face-to-face*, where Ss and models sat as in all previous experiments, the confederates looking being the same as in condition (d).

The distance between the centres of the 2 chairs was approximately 2·7 feet under each arrangement. Ss were asked not to move their chairs or turn around in them. When absolutely necessary, confederates conveyed similar messages in a gentle manner during the course of the session. The confederates' taped instructions directed them to laugh on 20 occasions for a total of 59 seconds. They were encouraged to be explosive in their laughter: that is, it was to be loud and sudden, its ending as abrupt as its onset. It was impressed upon confederates during their training that they were never to smile during sessions. Fifteen girls and 15 boys were tested in each of the five conditions.

Mean scores are reported in Table 8.2. Analyses of variance indicated main treatment effects for Ss' laughter ($p < 0.01$), smiling ($p < 0.01$) and mirth ($p < 0.01$), and these were in the directions predicted. Also, girls smiled more than boys ($p < 0.01$) and their mirth scores were greater ($p < 0.05$). There were no other significant effects.

It can be seen from Table 8.2 that laughter and smiling (and, therefore, mirth) scores tended to increase regularly through conditions (a) to (e) with the one exception that the mean laughter score of Ss in the back-to-back condition was numerically greater than that of Ss tested in the seated-at-right-angles condition; this is because the back-to-back arrangement was sufficient to cause laughter in a few Ss. However, multiple range tests revealed no significant differences in mean laughter scores for any pair of adjacent conditions although there were some significant differences in smiling scores: smiling means for conditions (a) and (b)($p < 0.05$), (b) and (c)($p < 0.05$), and (c) and (d) ($p < 0.01$), were significantly different from one another. (c) and (d) were the only adjacent conditions for which there was a significant difference in Ss' mirth scores ($p < 0.01$).

The mean laughter score of Ss tested in the face-to-face condition (e) was significantly greater than that of Ss tested in conditions (a), (b) and (c)

Table 8.2 Mean laughter and smiling scores in seconds

Experimental conditions	Boys		Girls	
	Laughter	Smiling	Laughter	Smiling
(a) Back-to-back	2·9	8·1	7·7	7·8
(b) Seated-at-right-angles	3·6	13·8	6·2	19·1
(c) Side-by-side without gazing	4·9	17·3	8·3	34·5
(d) Side-by-side with gazing	11·2	33·8	10·0	40·6
(e) Face-to-face	13·6	42·8	15·5	42·1

($p < 0.01$). Similarly, the condition (d) mean laughter score was greater than that of Ss tested in conditions (a) and (b) ($p < 0.05$), but these were the only significant differences between the mean laughter scores obtained from the five experimental conditions. Ss' smiling was more susceptible than their laughter to changes in seating arrangements. The mean scores obtained from conditions (d) and (e) were significantly greater than those from conditions (a), (b) and (c) ($p < 0.01$). Similarly, the mean smiling score from condition (c) was greater than that from (a) ($p < 0.01$), but there were no other significant differences. In the case of mirth scores, there were significant differences between condition (e) and conditions (a), (b) and (c) ($p < 0.01$), and between (a) and (c) ($p < 0.01$). Overall, therefore, this study provides support for the notion that as intimacy of a social situation is increased so overt responsiveness to humour is enhanced.

Overt mirth and social intimacy: An experiment on invasion of psychological body space

As noted earlier, during the preliminary observational phase of this research, the most responsive of children were observed informally to sit closer together and engage in relatively high levels of EC. They also appeared to touch one another a good deal and generally to encroach more upon one another's body spaces. This experiment arises from the latter observation and is designed to test whether overt responsiveness to humour is enhanced through the invasion of body space by a laughing companion.

Independent groups of Ss were tested in two dyadic coaction conditions distinguished by confederate-companions' trunk movements. The confederates' laughter, smiling and looking instructions were identical for the two conditions: they were directed to engage in 18 laughs totalling 58 seconds, 19 periods of smiling totalling 131 seconds, and 463 seconds of looking. Under the *intrusion* condition, confederates moved backwards and forwards in their seats as they laughed and they came within inches of the Ss' faces. In the second (*standard*) condition, confederates remained relatively upright when they laughed. It was predicted that the 'friendly' infringement of psychological body space by a laughing companion would augment laughter and smiling scores because the effect of such action, it was postulated, is to enhance intimacy. The prediction was upheld: Ss in the 'intrusion' condition displayed more laughter ($p < 0.01$) and more smiling ($p < 0.01$). Looking scores were similar in the two conditions.

Table 8.3 Mean laughter, smiling and looking scores in seconds

	'Standard' condition	'Intrusion' condition
Laughter	42·9	57·3
Smiling	122·0	148·8
Looking	192·1	199·0

SUMMARY AND CONCLUSIONS

The experiments in this chapter demonstrate that social aspects of situations are crucial determinants of so-called 'humorous laughter'. Given the same humour stimuli, there are vast differences in a child's laughter and smiling according to whether a companion is present, what role is occupied by that companion and how he responds to the subject and humour.

One series of experiments has revealed that the following are some of the important features of the companion's presence and responsiveness: the amount of time he spends laughing; the amount he engages in humorous smiling; the amount he looks at the subject's face; whether he is an 'audience' and therefore unable to hear the humour, or whether he listens to humour (though it does not matter whether it is the same humour); how close he sits to the subject; his seating orientation relative to that of the subject; and whether or not he encroaches upon the subject's psychological body space while laughing. The mere addition of a second companion is not sufficient to enhance laughter and smiling, but the degree to which two companions look at one another can be an important determinant of responsiveness to humour.

In experiments which were in fact run principally to check the appropriateness of methodology in other studies, it was demonstrated that a two-year age/status difference between seven-year-old subjects and nine-year-old confederates had no effect on laughter and smiling, and that knowledge of a one-way screen suppressed laughter severely whilst augmenting smiling and eye-contact.

In studies on adults it has been shown that canned laughter facilitates overt expressive responses, and that the presence of an unresponsive adult companion inhibits humorous laughter and smiling. The latter finding contrasts markedly with findings for children for whom the effect of a companion, at least in the above studies is always to enhance laughter no matter how taciturn he may appear.

These experiments were designed and have been discussed within an intermeshed framework of social facilitation theory, social intimacy theory and laughter-arousal theory. Some of the behavioural effects are explicable in terms of the sharing of social situations and the companion's variable psychological presence; other effects are explicable in terms of reflexive, disinhibitory, motivational and perceptual models of social facilitation; and other effects may be the result of social conformity and social desirability processes.

Two major social functions of laughter have been inferred from the above studies: (1) it serves as a 'safety value' against excessive 'social arousal' (cf. Chapman, 1975a); (2) it alleviates various forms of motivational arousal in a way that is socially acceptable and physically harmless to others (cf. Chapman, 1975b). Superimposed upon these functions are a number of others of a secondary nature: for example, laughter can attract attention and it can convey information.

Summarizing the first of the two major functions, 'social arousal', which is built up through the psychological presence of others and through social signals and a variety of interpersonal factors, can reach uncomfortable proportions during everyday encounters. However, the injection of humour into interactions invariably prompts laughter and this permits the withdrawal of attention from the companion; the momentary reduction of the companion's presence in the subject's psychological environment alleviates social arousal. Not only humorous laughter but other types also may reduce social arousal: 'nervous laughter' in a stressful interview situation is but one example.

The electromyographic humour study reported in this chapter, and psychophysiological data supplied by other investigators, indicates that arousal in enhanced during the presentation of humour. According to the second of the major functions of laughter referred to above (and detailed in Chapman, 1975b), arousal relating to the theme of the humour is alleviated when a threshold level is attained and laughter is triggered. Berlyne and others have suggested that increments and decrements in arousal are pleasurable in themselves, and it is clear from observations of children attending to humour that social cues can be utilized to promote changes in arousal during humour experiences. It has been reported elsewhere the children 'stare continuously at one another's eyes during the build-up to a punchline and/or just before they burst into laughter. At the onset of laughter a child would usually avert his/her gaze. Sometimes children threw their heads back laughing, and occasionally they gestured extravagantly with their arms and hands' (Chapman, 1975b).

Taken as a whole, this research demonstrates in an unambiguous fashion that 'humorous laughter' is an important social behaviour. We may conclude that a thorough examination of humour is not possible unless it incorporates studies on the social dimensions of humour. Also, it is evident that more systematic investigations into the social functions of humour and laughter are required in order to understand better our everyday social interactions.

REFERENCES

Aiello, J. R. (1972). A test of equilibrium theory: visual interaction in relation to orientation, distance and sex of interactants. *Psychonomic Science*, **27**, 335–336.

Argyle, M., and Dean, J. (1965). Eye-contact, distance and affiliation. *Sociometry*, **28**, 289–304.

Averill, J. R. (1969). Autonomic response patterns during sadness and mirth. *Psychophysiology*, **5**, 399–414.

Bateson, G. (1953). The role of humor in communication. In H. von Foerster (Ed.), *Cybernetics* (Trans. 9th Conf.). New York: Macy Foundation.

Bem, D. J. (1967). Self perception: an alternative interpretation of cognitive dissonance phenomenon. *Psychological Review*, **74**, 183–200.

Bergler, E. (1956). *Laughter and the Sense of Humor*. New York: Grune & Stratton.

Berlyne, D. E. (1969). Laughter, humor and play. In G. Lindzey and E. Aronson (Eds.), *Handbook of Social Psychology*. Vol. 3. Cambridge, Mass.: Addison–Wesley.

Brannigan, C. R., and Humphries, D. A. (1972). Human non-verbal behaviour, a means of communication. In N. Blurton Jones (Ed.), *Ethological Studies of Child Behaviour.* Cambridge, England: University Press.

Chapman, A. J. (1973a). An electromyographic study of apprehension about evaluation. *Psychological Reports,* **33,** 811–814.

Chapman, A. J. (1973b). Funniness of jokes, canned laughter and recall performance. *Sociometry,* **36,** 569–578.

Chapman, A. J. (1973c). Social facilitation of laughter in children. *Journal of Experimental Social Psychology,* **9,** 528–541.

Chapman, A. J. (1974a). An electromyographic study of social facilitation: a test of the 'mere presence' hypothesis. *British Journal of Psychology,* **65,** 123–128.

Chapman, A. J. (1974b). An experimental study of socially facilitated 'humorous laughter'. *Psychological Reports,* **35,** 727–734.

Chapman, A. J. (1974c). Laughter and social intimacy. Paper presented to the Social Psychology Meeting of the British Psychological Society London Conference, December.

Chapman, A. J. (1975a). Eye contact, physical proximity and laughter: a re-examination of the equilibrium model of social intimacy. *Social Behavior and Personality.* (in press).

Chapman, A. J. (1975b). Humorous laughter in children. *Journal of Personality and Social Psychology,* **31,** 42–49.

Chapman, A. J., and Chapman, W. A. (1974). Responsiveness to humor: its dependency upon a companion's humorous smiling and laughter. *The Journal of Psychology,* **88,** 245–252.

Chapman, A. J., and Wright, D. S. (1976). Socially facilitated laughter: an experimental analysis of some companion variables. *Journal of Experimental Child Psychology.* (in press).

Christie, M. J., and Todd, J. L. (1975). Experimenter-subject-situational interactions. In P. H. Venables and M. J. Christie (Eds.), *Research in Psychophysiology.* Chichester: Wiley.

Cottrell, N. B. (1968). Performance in the presence of other human beings: mere presence, audience and affiliation effects. In E. C. Simmel, R. A. Hoppe and G. A. Milton (Eds.), *Social Facilitation and Imitative Behavior.* Boston: Allyn & Bacon.

Cottrell, N. B. (1972). Social facilitation. In C. G. McClintock (Ed.), *Experimental Social Psychology.* New York: Holt, Rinehart & Winston.

Crandall, R. (1974). Social facilitation: theories and research. In A. Harrison (Ed.), *Explorations in Psychology.* Monterey: Brooks-Cole.

Dresser, J. W. (1967). Two studies on the social function of joking as an outlet for aggression. *Dissertation Abstracts,* **28 (2-A),** 778–779.

Eibl-Eibesfeldt, I. (1970). *Ethology: The Biology of Behavior.* New York: Holt, Rinehart & Winston.

Festinger, L. (1957). *Theory of Cognitive Dissonance.* Evanston: Row, Peterson.

Fry, W. F. (1963). *Sweet Madness: A Study of Humor.* Palo Alto: Pacific Books.

Fry, W. F. (1969). Instinctual and physiologic bases of the humor experience. Paper presented at symposium proceedings at the meeting of the Western Psychological Association, Vancouver, September.

Fry, W. F., and Stoft, P. (1971). Mirth and oxygen saturation levels of peripheral blood. *Psychotherapy and Psychosomatics,* **19,** 76–84.

Fuller, R. G. C., and Sheehy-Skeffington, A. (1974). Effects of group laughter on responses to humourous material, a replication and extension. *Psychological Reports,* **35,** 531–534.

Gale, M. A., Spratt, G., Chapman, A. J., and Smallbone, A. (1975). EEG correlates of interpersonal distance and eye contact. *Biological Psychology,* **3,** 237–245.

Goldstein, I. B. (1972). Electromyography: a measure of skeletal muscle tension. In N. S. Greenfield and R. A. Sternbach (Eds.), *Handbook of Psychophysiology.* New York: Holt, Rinehart & Winston.

Grant, E. C. (1969). Human facial expression. *Man,* **4,** 525–526.

Henchy, T., and Glass, D. C. (1968). Evaluation apprehension and the social facilitation of dominant and subordinate responses. *Journal of Personality and Social Psychology*, **10**, 446–454.

Hooff, J. A. R. A. M. van. (1972). A comparative approach to the phylogeny of laughter and smiling. In R. A. Hinde (Ed.), *Non-Verbal Communication*. Cambridge, England: University Press.

Jourard, S. M., and Friedman, R. (1970). Experimenter–subject 'distance' and self-disclosure. *Journal of Personality and Social Psychology*, **15**, 278–282.

Kappas, K. H. (1967). A developmental analysis of children's responses to humor. *Library Quarterly*, **37**, 67–77.

Kleck, R. E. (1970). Interaction distance and non-verbal agreeing responses. *British Journal of Social and Clinical Psychology*, **9**, 180–182.

Koestler, A. (1964). *The Act of Creation*. London: Hutchinson.

Langevin, R., and Day, H. I. (1972). Physiological correlates of humor. In J. H. Goldstein and P. E. McGhee (Eds.), *The Psychology of Humor: Theoretical Perspectives and Empirical Issues*. New York: Academic Press.

Leuba, C. (1960). *Man: A General Psychology*. New York: Holt, Rinehart & Winston.

Leventhal, H., and Mace, W. (1970). The effect of laughter on evaluation of a slapstick movie. *Journal of Personality*, **38**, 16–30.

Levi, L. (1965). The urinary output of adrenalin and noradrenalin during pleasant and unpleasant emotional states. *Psychosomatic Medicine*, **27**, 80–85.

Libby, W. L., and Yaklevich, D. (1973). Personality determinants of eye contact and direction of gaze aversion. *Journal of Personality and Social Psychology*, **27**, 197–206.

Martin, L. J. (1905). Psychology of aesthetics. I. Experimental prospecting in the field of the comic. *American Journal of Psychology*, **16**, 35–118.

Nosanchuk, T. A., and Lightstone, J. (1974). Canned laughter and public and private conformity. *Journal of Personality and Social Psychology*, **29**, 153–156.

Paskind, H. A. (1932). Effect of laughter on muscle tone. *Archives of Neurology and Psychiatry*, **28**, 623–628.

Patterson, M. L. (1973). Compensation in nonverbal immediacy behaviors: a review. *Sociometry*, **36**, 237–252.

Pollio, H. R., Mers, R., and Lucchesi, W. (1972). Humor, laughter, and smiling: some preliminary observations of funny behaviors. In J. H. Goldstein and P. E. McGhee (Eds.), *The Psychology of Humor: Theoretical Perspectives and Empirical Issues*. New York: Academic Press.

Schachter, S., and Singer, J. E. (1962). Cognitive, social, and physiological determinants of emotional state. *Psychological Review*, **69**, 379–399.

Schachter, S., and Wheeler, L. (1962). Epinephrine, chlorpromazine, and amusement. *Journal of Abnormal and Social Psychology*, **65**, 121–128.

Scherer, S. E., and Schiff, M. R. (1973). Perceived intimacy, physical distance and eye contact. *Perceptual and Motor Skills*, **36**, 835–841.

Scofield, H. A. (1921). The psychology of laughter. Unpublished Master's Thesis, University of Columbia.

Shellberg, L. G., and Brown, S. (1968). Some methodological problems in humor ratings. Paper presented at Western Psychological Association Meeting, San Diego.

Shultz, T. R. (1972). The role of incongruity and resolution in children's appreciation of cartoon humor. *Journal of Experimental Child Psychology*, **13**, 456–477.

Smyth, M. M., and Fuller, R. G. C. (1972). Effects of group laughter on responses to humorous material. *Psychological Reports*, **30**, 132–134.

Spence, K. W. (1956). *Behavior Theory and Conditioning*. New Haven, Connecticut: Yale University.

Spencer, H. (1860). The physiology of laughter. *Macmillan's Magazine*, **1**, 395–402.

Stearns, F. R. (1972). *Laughing: Physiology, Pathophysiology, Psychology, Pathopsychology and Development*. Springfield, Ill.: Thomas.

Tolman, C. W. (1968). The role of the companion in the social facilitation of animal behavior. In E. C. Simmel, R. A. Hoppe, and G. A. Milton (Eds.), *Social Facilitation and Imitative Behavior*. Boston: Allyn & Bacon.

Wallerstein, H. (1954). An electromyographic study of attentive listening. *Canadian Journal of Psychology*, **8**, 228–238.

Weiss, R. F., and Miller, F. G. (1971). The drive theory of social facilitation. *Psychological Review*, **78**, 44–57.

Williams, J. M. (1945). An experimental and theoretical study of humour. Unpublished Master's Thesis, University of London.

Wolff, H. A., Smith, C. E., and Murray, H. A. (1934). The psychology of humor. *Journal of Abnormal and Social Psychology*, **28**, 345–365.

Young, R. D., and Frye, M. (1966). Some are laughing: some are not—why? *Psychological Reports*, **18**, 747–754.

Zajonc, R. B. (1965). Social facilitation. *Science*, **149**, 269–274.

Zajonc, R. B. (1972). Compresence. Paper presented to the Midwestern Psychological Association, Cleveland, Ohio.

Zigler, E., Levine, J., and Gould, L. (1966a). Cognitive processes in the development of children's appreciation of humor. *Child Development*, **37**, 507–518.

Zigler, E., Levine, J., and Gould, L. (1966b). The humor response of normal institutionalized and noninstitutionalized retarded children. *American Journal of Mental Deficiency*, **71**, 472–480.

Zigler, E., Levine, J., and Gould, L. (1967). Cognitive challenge as a factor in children's humor appreciation. *Journal of Personality and Social Psychology*, **6**, 332–336.

Chapter 9

The Social Responsiveness of Young Children in Humorous Situations

Hugh C. Foot and Antony J. Chapman

Most situations that evoke laughter are social. As Hertzler (1970) has put it, 'Laughter is a social phenomenon. It is social in its origin, in its processual occurrence, in its functions, and in its effects'. Yet despite the widespread acknowledgement that laughter is subject to social influence, little systematic attempt has been made to explore the social situations which instigate and modify laughter. Both the processes and the responses are poorly understood.

Our current research is concerned with the experimental investigation of children's responsiveness to one another in humour situations. Responsiveness to humour *per se* is not our primary interest although we shall be concerned at a later stage with attempting to relate particular humour responses with particular stimuli. Because of this orientation we define responsiveness in broad terms, to include not only laughter but other interactive behaviours such as smiling, looking, eye-contact, physical proximity, posture, and other related responses.

In this chapter we discuss some of the social functions which laughter serves; we review previous empirical investigations on the effect of social influences upon children's laughter; we describe in some detail the general methodology and outline the theoretical context adopted for the current research; we give an account of two experimental studies recently completed; finally we provide a brief overview of some of our future studies planned within the context of a three-year project.[1]

THE SOCIAL FUNCTIONS OF LAUGHTER

Berlyne (1972) has stated that since laughter can occur in a solitary individual, 'it seems doubtful that its prime significance is a social one'. However, the possibility of laughter occurring in solitary individuals hardly justifies this inference. The same *non sequitur* exists in the proposition that because buses can be driven around the city streets empty their primary purpose is not to ferry passengers around. It is equally plausible to take the view that what may be learned as an appropriate response in a social situation may carry over to solitary situations and that we laugh on our own because we recognize the situation as one where we would have laughed in company. Be that as it may, the fact remains that we usually do laugh in company and indeed we may have difficulty remembering the last occasion when we laughed on our own.

Giles and Oxford (1970) have sketched out some of the varied categories of laughter which occur in different situations and the presence of others is implicit in virtually all of them. Firstly, Giles and Oxford draw attention to what they regard as the most common category of laughter 'humorous laughter', occurring when we are amused by a joke or a funny incident which we have experienced. In fact the presence of others is not necessarily implied in humorous laughter situations: the only prerequisite appears to be the humour stimulus. However, common experiences, together with our own observations, suggest that the elicitation of laughter, as distinct from merely smiling, in response to a humour stimulus is relatively rare and infrequent unless others are present and able to share the humour (see Chapter 8). No doubt other social factors, such as whether the humour is perceived to be intended or not, may serve to modify the response.

A second more functional category of laughter which Giles and Oxford define as 'social laughter' is used 'to integrate the individual within a particular social group'. Typically this occurs in the absence of any specific humour stimulus and is a means of gaining social approval, bolstering group cohesiveness and signalling our affiliative motives. It is also used for maintaining the flow of interaction in our daily encounters: filling in pauses in our conversations and maintaining the interest and attention of our conversational partner. It is in fact highly probable that we use laughter for these social purposes much more frequently than we use it in response to actual humour stimuli—unless we happen to be gainfully employed as scriptwriters for Eric Morecambe and Ernie Wise. Middleton and Moland (1959) report that in the natural environment the frequency of jokes as occasions for laughter is low relative to other forms of stimuli.

A third category is 'ignorance laughter' and this implies both the presence of humour stimuli and the presence of others. It can best be illustrated by the social situation in which we recognize that a joke has been told but wish to disguise our ignorance or inability to comprehend. Clearly it has much in common with social laughter in as much as it is a product of the same social motivational factors directed towards maintaining group acceptance and group harmony.

In other social situations we may use laughter as a weapon to ridicule others. 'Derision laughter' is undoubtedly most prevalent amongst children who will often laugh *at* another child in a mocking scornful way for some unusual physical characteristic or for being rejected by others because of some disapproved, foolish or cowardly act. Such laughter is often a form of 'scapegoating', drawing attention away from the child's own shortcomings and inadequacies and to a more acceptable (to the child) target. Carried to extremes the persistent derision of a particular child by his classmates may be both very distressing and potentially harmful to his social development. Used aggressively by adults, derision laughter is normally more subtle and indirect: it may take form of a controlled chuckle following a sarcastic or derogatory remark and is aimed quite clearly at taking the sting out of the remark. Skilful users of derision laughter well know that a victim who shows offence can always be countered with the claim that the remark was merely meant in jest.

The other three categories of laughter outlined by Giles and Oxford are 'anxiety laughter', 'apologetic laughter' and laughter in response to tickling. Anxiety laughter is seen almost as an autonomic response which occurs as a consequence of a stressful experience. It may accompany feelings of relief after the sudden ending of a period of acute tension. This is comparatively rare, of course, and as a concomitant of the release of tension it may not be affected in any way by the presence and absence of others. Apologetic laughter is totally a response to the social situation. It occurs, for example, when we wish to excuse our own lack of action or indecision with respect to our past behaviour or when we wish to play down the possibility of future failure by appealing to our inadequacies or lack of experience. Laughter in response to tickling has remained an enigma to most humour and laughter theorists and we shall not make any attempt to deal with it here. Suffice it to say that, whatever its aetiology, it is also a highly social behaviour: the same quality of touch produces different reactions according to whether the touching agent is inanimate or animate (Weiscrantz, Elliott and Darlington, 1971). No doubt the social and, in the case of adults, possibly sexual context in which tickling between two persons occurs is fundamental to the instigation of laughter.

To this list of social categories of laughter two more can be added. Firstly, the relationship of laughter to joy must not be overlooked and much of children's laughter, particularly during play, might be regarded as a pure expression of *joie de vivre*. We suggest, therefore, that laughter serves not only as a functional means of maintaining in-group relations (as in social laughter) but as a spontaneous and possibly non-functional reaction to pleasurable, exhilarating experiences. In theory such laughter does not imply the need for a social situation. In practice it probably occurs only in the presence of others, as when a child engages in energetic rough-and-tumble play. Secondly, and somewhat akin to a mild form of anxiety laughter, we often use laughter to rescue us from embarrassment in social encounters. It gives us time to decide what the appropriate response should be in a situation which is ambiguous, out-of-the-ordinary, or possibly threatening as when we are insulted or criticized. The great virtue of laughter in many of these kinds of situations is that it is itself an *ambiguous* response to a potentially ambiguous situation. The person laughing is relieved, at least momentarily, from having to commit himself to an interpretation of the meaning behind the comment addressed to him, and is giving himself time for clarification.

We have defined a number of important functions which laughter serves in order to highlight the social nature of its evocation. Many of these functions have been taken up in more detail in other chapters of this book. We do not suggest that we have exhausted the possible functions, nor have we attempted to discuss their aetiology. An exposition of the causation of some of the forms of laughter is given elsewhere (cf. Giles and Oxford, 1970).

SOCIAL ASPECTS OF CHILDREN'S LAUGHTER: PREVIOUS STUDIES

Some reasons for choosing to study the laughter of children rather than that of adults are set out in the previous chapter. Firstly, since laughter and smiling are such important ingredients of the everyday interactions of children, we regard the study of such behaviour as essential for the proper understanding of children's interaction. Secondly, there has been very little research into the effects of the social situation upon children's responsiveness to humour. Most of what has been done with children has been concerned with what constitutes laughter provoking stimuli (e.g. Justin, 1932; Sroufe and Wunsch, 1972) or cognitive–developmental aspects of humour appreciation (e.g. McGhee, 1971, 1974; Shultz, Chapter 1). Thirdly, and at a practical level, the study of laughter is easier and more rewarding in young children than it is in older children or adults. Children under the age of 10–11 years do act in a more natural and unrestrained manner than do their elders, when exposed to a test environment. They are much less aware that they are in any sense being observed and possibly evaluated.

Our research essentially bridges the gap between what Giles and Oxford call humorous and social laughter. They regard their seven categories of laughter as mutually exclusive. Our view, at least as far as social and humorous laughter are concerned, is that they are not mutually exclusive categories. We are studying the ways in which the social situation modifies by enhancement or inhibition the expression of laughter in response to humour stimuli. In this context, therefore, the extent of a child's laughter may be simultaneously a function of both humorous and social laughter. Indeed what few other studies have been conducted on the effects of social variables upon children's laughter have also sought to demonstrate how the level of responsiveness to humour stimuli is enhanced or inhibited as a function of the social situation. Ding and Jersild (1932) found that the presence of another child or an adult enhanced laughter more with older than younger preschool children, and Enders (1927) found that young children's laughter was enhanced more by the presence of other children than by the presence of adults. Kenerdine (1931) reported that, in her study of nursery school children, subjects very seldom laughed except when in the presence of others. The evidence from these and other early studies (e.g., Blatz, Allin and Millichamp, 1936; Brackett, 1933, 1934; Gregg, Miller and Linton, 1929; Wilson, 1931) suggests that laughter is rarely elicited from children unless there is some form of social stimulation accompanying the more obvious laughter-provoking stimuli. Some of these studies highlight the social significance of laughter. Gregg and co-workers, for example, investigated a suggestion that laughter is an indication of social awareness: they concluded that nursery school children laugh and smile more in social situations than when alone. Similarly, Brackett found a high correlation between the frequency of a child's laughter and the frequency of his presence in situations where other children laughed. Jacobson (1947), in a theoretical exposition, has put forward the view that laughter grows as a social response during childhood.

It is evident, however, that the main intention of these studies was to demonstrate the influence of rather gross social situational variables upon children's laughter. They achieved little more than the drawing of attention to behavioural differences due to the presence or absence of a child or adult companion. Very few studies, with the notable exception of Pollio, Mers and Lucchesi (1972), have attempted to explore more detailed aspects of social influence, but this is no doubt a reflection of the almost total neglect of the social aspects of laughter in more modern times. Morrison (1940) and Andrus (1946) examined the effects of group size the obtained high positive correlations between size of theatre audiences and number of laughs per performance. Malpass and Fitzpatrick (1959) and Young and Frye (1966) have measured laughter in small groups presented aurally with humour. However, this work was conducted entirely with adult subjects.

In a series of recent studies Chapman has explored more systematically the effects upon children's laughter and smiling of a variety of interpersonal factors and forms of social influence. His basic research paradigm and main results are reviewed in the previous chapter. One of the advances represented in this work is the more objective form of measurement used in terms of the *duration* of laughter rather than in terms of the ubiquitous rating-scale which has traditionally been used for gauging amounts of humour appreciation. In fact judgements of funniness, like behavioural responses, have themselves been found to be influenced by the social situation. Social facilitation effects have been found in some studies (e.g. Calvert, 1949; Chapman, 1973a; Malpass and Fitzpatrick, 1959) while decrements in funniness evaluations have been associated with the suppression of laughter in studies by Martin (1905) and Leventhal and Mace (1970). However, humour ratings have proven to be less consistently susceptible to social influence than behavioural responses, and the presence of companions has not always promoted assessments of funniness (e.g. McKibben, 1969; Young and Frye, 1966). The discrepancy may be at least partly attributable to the early researchers failing to control their own presence and behaviour; socially desirable responses may thus have been emitted. However, it appears from Chapman (1975a) that ratings may not be enhanced when subjects are aware that their laughter and smiling have been socially facilitated.

THE CURRENT RESEARCH

The programme of research upon which we are currently engaged in designed to extend the scope and theoretical implications of previous work. Our intention is to explore a wider range of social variables which have a potential influence upon children's responsiveness in humorous situations and to develop more sophisticated measures of responsiveness. We emphasize that it is the responsiveness of children *to each other* with which we are fundamentally concerned rather than responsiveness to the humour *per se*, and this is why we define 'responsiveness' in broad terms, referring not only to laughter and smiling but also to looking, eye-contact, physical proximity, posture and other related behaviours. The interaction of children is so complex that we do not believe it is sufficient to examine just one kind of behaviour to the exclusion of others. Such a procedure, while often adopted in the past, cannot hope to provide the insights into the interactive process that the analysis of several interrelated processes can give us.

In this section we discuss some of the theoretical issues we are tackling; we outline our general methodology and describe two preliminary studies already completed.

Theoretical perspectives

There is little theory upon which to base experimental studies on social aspects of laughter. Our work arose initially out of an interest in social facilitation processes and social interaction. We have set out to draw together within a single framework several theoretical strands, in order to produce a more comprehensive and, it is hoped, more illuminating analysis of children's interactive behaviour than can be achieved by any single approach. Many of these theoretical views are set out in the preceding chapter in relation to particular experimental studies. For present purposes we shall merely highlight briefly some of the main aspects of theory which we seek to develop.

Social facilitation theory

One of the basic problems we are tackling concerns what forms of social influence are engendered by the presence or absence of a companion. Previous research has demonstrated unequivocally that overt responsiveness in humorous situations is readily modified by a companion's presence and behaviour. But just what *forms* of facilitative influence are operative? Tolman (1968) has identified at least four forms of influence defined in terms of 'reflex', 'perceptual', 'motivational' and 'disinhibitory' models. Translated into the context of a laughter situation these models would suggest that the companion's laughter may serve in the following ways: it may serve as an eliciting stimulus for the subject; it may focus the subject's attention upon some aspects of the humour stimuli which he may otherwise have missed; it may make him generally more reactive to humour; it may serve as a means of disinhibiting his responses. It is possible that in a given social situation any or all of these sources of influence are operating simultaneously. The kind of detailed, micro-analysis of sequences of interactive behaviour which we intend making will enable us to differentiate between at least some of these potential sources of influence.

A basic problem in social facilitation research which our studies largely overcome is the dilemma posed by the 'mere presence' versus 'evaluation apprehension' controversy. This again is discussed in the last chapter. Briefly, it is our view that laughter experiments constitute ideal vehicles for examining and developing social facilitation theory, because the effects of apprehension are minimized. From a practical point of view the problem of putting the children at their ease and relieving their general apprehension can be overcome by familiarizing them with the test environment and experimenter. From a methodological point of view laughter and smiling are not the kinds of behaviour which the children are likely to regard as being under study or monitored for the purposes of comparison in the way that the 'performance' of a task usually is. Because we have minimized both types of apprehension effects we are free to conduct relatively pure investigations of the influence of 'mere presence' effects and companion variables. Companion variables include possible variations in the role, relationship and behaviour of the companion.

Social intimacy theory

Laughter is a cue to intimacy—like smiling, physical proximity, posture, eye-contact and so on. The way in which it is expected to vary reciprocally in relation to other intimacy behaviours during a given period of interaction [according to Argyle and Dean's (1965) model] has already been described in the preceding chapter. Chapman (1975b) has found, contrary to most other evidence, that laughter, smiling, eye-contact and proximity all positively covary, and takes this as grounds for challenging the basic underlying assumption of Argyle and Dean that there is a static level of intimacy for any given social encounter. Our view is that the level of intimacy is in a dynamic state, even during relatively short-term interactions. One of our major theoretical aims is to examine interactive sequences during the course of a humorous situation and plot the changes in level of intimacy that occur. In particular we shall be interested in examining the role and function of laughter in such changes.

Underlying many theories of laughter is the fundamental notion that humour and laughter are tension-reducing. Berlyne (1960, 1969), for example, has noted propensity of a joke to build up an unfulfilled expectation creating increments in arousal. He suggests that arousal jags are quickly resolved or dissipated and that arousal–relief sequences are satisfying *per se*.

Chapman (1975b) has argued that the primary function of laughter is to serve as a 'safety-valve' to protect the individual against excessive social arousal. In dyadic interactions there may be a sustained trend towards heightened intimacy, but laughing may reduce tension at moments when the level of social interaction momentarily becomes uncomfortable: that is, when either individual's level of social arousal is out of step, and therefore incompatible, with the prevailing level of intimacy which is then tolerated by both parties.

As they stand these theories may appear to suggest rather different approaches to the study of social responsiveness in humorous situations. Social facilitation theory raises questions concerning the nature of the processes in the social situation which modify the subject's behaviour. Social intimacy theory addresses itself to the problem of the relationship between behaviours both at inter-subject and intra-subject levels. The arousal theory of laughter is concerned with the internal state of the subject and is therefore appropriate for considering the way in which this state is modified by the presence and behaviour of a companion. But these approaches should not be regarded in any sense as mutually exclusive. They share many concepts and rely heavily upon each other. Social facilitation theory and social intimacy theory, for example, draw upon the notion that the presence of a companion has an influence upon the internal state of the subject. Social facilitation effects generally presuppose a boost in the subject's arousal as a direct consequence of the presence of his companion leading to enhanced motivation, attention or perception. The social intimacy model takes as its central theme the notion of forces of equilibrium which are, by definition, homeostatic processes directed towards eliminating discomfort or tension. Between themselves social facilitation and social intimacy processes overlap considerably by virtue of defining various forms of social influence brought about by the behaviour and role of the companion.

We are proposing to pursue a more micro-analytic approach than has hitherto been adopted for studying humour responsiveness. It is our view that it is only by exploring the temporal patterning of behaviour sequences and the interplay of responses between the subject and his companion that particular processes can be isolated and identified. An analysis of this kind should enable us to make theoretical modifications and advances, and we are hopeful that it will enable us to draw social facilitation, social intimacy and laughter (arousal) theory into a more unified framework rather than merely develop them as separate theories.

General Methodology

As has already been indicated the main aim of this research is concerned with children's responsiveness to each other. Humour stimuli are introduced, not so much in order to determine what makes children laugh (although it is our intention to investigate this aspect), but as a vehicle for creating a congenial psychological climate in which children are likely to display a variety of interactive behaviours including laughter and smiling (Foot and Chapman, 1975).

At UWIST we have laid the foundations for a series of studies of social responsiveness in children by designing and equipping a mobile-laboratory for on-location studies in schools. The shell of a 5·2 metre long Bailey caravan provides the basis for a children's playroom, 3·9 × 2·2 metres, with a separate experimenters' room.

The children's playroom is decorously carpeted and curtained in bright colours and designs. Fitted cupboards along the sides contain a selection of toys which can be produced as necessary. At the far end is hung a projection screen, and immediately above this are mountings for two Shibaden video-cameras concealed inside an eye-level cupboard. The camera lenses are inset behind slots in the cupboard doors, and are therefore inconspicuous. At the near and, in the wall dividing the playroom from the experimenters' room, is a one-way viewing screen above which is the mounting for a third concealed camera.

The room also contains a selection of children's furniture and a table specially constructed to conceal microphones and a mixer unit. Lighting and heating are maintained at a standard level.

The experimenters' room contains Shibaden video-recording equipment and monitors, and a super-8, cassette-loaded, film projector with an automatic rewind facility for showing comedy films. A push-button device enables the selection, at any given moment in time, of the camera from which to record onto tape. Three cameras, two with wide-angles lenses, are sufficient to cover the whole of the children's playroom. Should a child change his position or orientation and face away from the camera filming him he can immediately be picked up on another camera. The cameras are connected independently to corresponding monitors, and a fourth monitor displays the output from the video-recorder. A split-screen facility enables simultaneous recording from two separate cameras, when necessary.

The stimulus material which we are using in this research consists of movie cartoon films (e.g. Tom and Jerry), or single-frame cartoons. Some comic material will also be presented aurally. As far as the studies reported in this chapter are concerned, comedy cartoon movies were used. Prior pilot work indicated that these produced greater responsiveness in children than non-cartoon comedies such as Charlie Chaplin or Laurel and Hardy. Despite the apparent violence in Tom and Jerry cartoons it is interesting to note, from a study on television audience perceptions (Howitt and Cumberbatch, 1974), that factor scores were obtained reflecting the opposite pole of the violence factor in relation to these cartoons. The violence is clearly seen as an integral part of their humorous content and justified accordingly.

We have deliberately chosen to work primarily with film material in this research rather than with aural material. Whilst the listening tasks used previously by the second author have proved perfectly suitable for eliciting differences in responsiveness according to the social situation, they are not as naturalistic as the watching of film material. This is particularly true in relation to those listening situations which require the children to receive different inputs over headphones. It is largely for this reason that we have shifted to film material to which children are much more frequently exposed in the natural environment.

General procedure

A major procedural consideration is to ensure that, when the child enters the laboratory, he is not made unduly anxious or nervous either by a confrontation with experimenters who are strangers to him, or by a novel, and possibly threatening, environment. To prevent this happening, we set up our laboratory in the school at least a week before testing begins. Once parents' permission has been obtained the children to be used in the studies visit the playroom in groups with or without their teacher in order to play or to watch a film. In this way they quickly become familar with the experimenters (*E*s), with the interior of the playroom, and with the kinds of activities in which they are expected to engage (Foot, Smith and Chapman, 1975). Experimental sessions are conducted by one or other of the two authors with a Research Assistant. (Only the authors participated in the two studies to be described in the next section.)

During the period of testing one *E* fetches children from the classrooms, by arrangement with the teachers, and accompanies them to the laboratory. The pilot work has shown the importance of maintaining a friendly informal manner towards the children at this crucial stage immediately after leaving the classroom and prior to entry into the playroom. Once in the playroom the children (in some cases a single child) are seated, usually on stools, facing the projector screen. *E* continues chatting informally with them for a few moments and then tells them what is about to happen: for example, they are to be shown a comedy film. *E* tells the children that he is interested in finding out what children 'think of' various kinds of films, or whatever, and that he will ask them a few questions afterwards to find out how they had enjoyed it. Then *E* leaves the children, enters the experimenters' room and joins the second *E* who is operating the video-equipment and projector.

Sessions are typically brief, the duration of the stimulus material being about six minutes. One of the hallmarks of on-location studies of this kind is the relative ease with which a large number of children can be quickly handled with minimal disruption to the classroom activities for both teacher and child.

Measurement

The analysis of video-recorded behaviour could be an endless task. Clearly the researcher must start out with some hierarchical ordering of behavioural categories in terms of their relevance to the behaviour under investigation. Taken in its widest sense social responsiveness covers a wide array of interactive behaviours. Laughter, smiling, looking, mutual eye-contact, posture, distancing, gesticulations, facial expression and verbal behaviour are all cues of intimacy which may be taken to indicate a more or less responsive set towards the companion. We are investigating most of these measures during the course of the research programme. For the purposes of the two studies to be described, however, four measures were selected for analysis on the basis of previous work: laughing, smiling, looking and mutual eye-contact. In operational terms laughter and smiling have been defined in the previous chapter: laughter as inarticulate vocal sounds, of a reiterated *ha-ha* form, and smiling as an upward stretching of the mouth occurring without vocal sound but sometimes accompanied by a loud exhalation of breath at its genesis. Looking is defined here as gazes or glances at the companion's face, and eye-contact refers to a reciprocated gaze or glance in the region of the eyes, often incorporated into a longer period of looking.

Two principal forms of analyses are undertaken in the research as a whole:

(a) total durations over sessions of the different dependent measures exhibited by the children; (b) the sequential patterning of corresponding responses exhibited by the subject and his companion(s). In addition many of the studies involve securing simple verbal ratings in response to questions concerning the humour, the social situation and the children's emotional reactions.

The transcription of the tapes involves independent recordings carried out by all Es using a pen-recorder and a series of timers and counters designed for use in recording the parallel behaviours of the subject and his companion. These facilities are currently still being developed and will, in future studies, enable the coding of information concerning the temporal patterning of responses as well as durations and frequencies. The advantage of a micro-analytic approach is that it provides the basis for an interpretation of the relationship between responses generated by the subject and his companion, and of the subtle forms of influence which one child's behaviour experts upon that of another. [In drawing attention to the usefulness of this approach in the study of mother–child interactions, Schaffer (1974) has argued that 'psychology has in the past tended to neglect this two-way flow and instead concentrated on artificially isolated one-way units'.]

The two studies reported here were conducted in late 1973 and early 1974, and the analysis is purely in terms of the *duration* of the various dependent behaviours. Frequencies of occurrence of the different behaviours were found to be highly correlated with total durations (e.g. $r_s = 0.92$ for smiling), and were not therefore subjected to separate statistical analysis.[2] A very limited analysis of the patterning of looking and smiling is presented, for illustrative purposes, based upon the tapes of two sessions in Study II.

Reliability between the two independent analysers were assessed and found to be very high. Pearson's product–moment correlations between the two Es' recordings (over both studies) on measures of laughter, smiling and looking were 0.96, 0.98 and 0.93 respectively. The raw data for analyses are taken as straight averages of pairs of scores recorded by the two Es.

It should be noted that the Es, in recording these measures, analysed the video-tapes blind; that is, they did not know in which treatment group a child had been placed. This is a necessary control in view of the possibility of unintentional bias entering the cumulative recordings of time (cf. Rosenthal, 1966). The only clue to treatment evident from the tapes already obtained occurs in those for Study I in which half the children were seated close to each other and half more distantly (distance being an independent variable). However, since the children differed on at least one other independent measure which was not evident from the tapes, this was not seen as constituting a worrying source of bias.

Experimental work

The two preliminary studies reported here were designed essentially to confirm the appropriateness of the experimental setting and task for eliciting expressive and interactive behaviours which are sensitive to variations in the social situation. Independent variables were selected which have previously been investigated in the context of a listening task and which have been found to be susceptible to change in the social setting (see previous chapter).

In Study I children were tested in dyads. The main independent variables were: (a) the presence or absence of E during the test period and (b) the physical proximity of the children relative to each other and relative to E. Laughter, smiling and eye-contact have already been shown to be influenced by the dimension of physical proximity in a coacting *listening* situation (Chapman, 1975b). In Study II the main variables were: (a) the presence or absence of a child companion (to demonstrate the basic social facilitation effect) and (b) the humour stimuli: the differential effects of cartoon films with and without soundtrack. This latter variable has not been investigated before and was included partly for the purposes of determining optimum film material for future studies, and partly because of studies with canned laughter showing that responsiveness can be heightened by auditory augmentation of the humour stimuli (Chapman, 1973b; Leventhal and Mace, 1970; Nosanchuk and Lightstone, 1974).

Sex constitutes a separate factor in both studies. Previous research (e.g. Leventhal and Mace, 1970; Cupchik and Leventhal, 1974) has produced some interesting and marked sex differences in laughter and smiling, but results are not altogether clear. Chapman (1973a) has obtained some evidence to suggest that boys are more responsive to the humour stimuli while girls are more responsive to their companion. In Study I half the dyads comprised boys and half girls. In Study II mixed-sex dyads were used in addition to same-sex dyads in order to permit a comparison between the effects on boys and girls of either-sex companions.

Study I: Method

Subjects (Ss) were 100 7-year-old children (50 boys and 50 girls). They were drawn from the four youngest classes at the Llanedeyrn Junior School, Cardiff.[3] These classes are not streamed in any way and are equivalent in terms of their status within the school and variety of abilities. The children are from a range of low–middle socioeconomic backgrounds. The material used was one of a series of short colour comedy cartoon films (in sound and lasting 6 minutes) produced by Castle Films and featuring 'Woody Woodpecker'. This series is intermittently shown on British broadcasting networks. The procedure followed that set out in the General Methodology section except that all sessions were conducted by one or other E, rather than by both Es together. The children were tested in pairs of the same sex. Pairings were made randomly by the teacher, the only stipulation being that pair members should not be special friends. Inevitably most of the children would know each other quite well through living in the same district and through having possibly attended the same Infants' school. On arrival in the playroom the children were directed to two stools. They were allowed to choose whichever seat they wished, but in fact this choice determined which child became S and which child the 'companion' for the purposes of analysis. Since spatial proximity was a key independent variable in this study, the stools were either locked into place directly beside each other, ensuring that the children sat very close together (*children-near* condition) or 1 metre apart (*children-far* condition). Some conditions involved E being present during the test session. In these cases he returned to the children's playroom on the lead-in to the film and sat either on the bench seat immediately alongside the children (*E-near* condition) or slightly in front of the children and 1 metre to the side of S (*E-far* condition). S was thus seated between E and his companion.

The conditions thus formed a 2×2 independent groups design:

CONDITIONS

Children-near / Experimenter-near
Children-far / Experimenter-near
Children-near / Experimenter-far
Children-far / Experimenter-far

Forty subject/companion pairs were randomly assigned to one of each of these four treatment conditions (five pairs of boys and five pairs of girls in each) in all of which E was present. The two Es shared equally in the role of adult companion. They responded with brief, intermittent smiles and laughs of low intensity at various appropriate times throughout the film. A fifth (*E-absent*) condition, again with five pairs of either sex, was run in the absence of E with children near relative to each other.

Results

Mean laughter, smiling, looking and eye-contact scores of boy and girl Ss in the five conditions are given in Table 9.1. Analyses of variance were conducted on the data obtained in the four experimental conditions with E present in order to assess the overall effects upon responsiveness of the two distance conditions for both child and adult companions. Eye-contact scores were not analysed in view of the relatively high frequency of zero scores. Nor were the companions' scores analysed. For purposes of analysis, raw scores of Ss were subjected to the log $(1 + X)$ transformation recommended by Winer (1971) to correct for heterogeneity of variance.

No clear trends emerged in these analyses other than a general non-significant tendency for girls to laugh and look more than boys. There were no significant main effects or interactions. It appears, therefore, that distance, at least up to 1 metre, does not affect responsiveness on these measures, for film material and this applies both to distance between children and distance between subject and E.

Although it was not originally intended to study experimenter-effects, the data for smiling and laughter quite clearly reflected a difference attributable to the two Es. The children in all conditions smiled more and laughed more in the

Table 9.1 Mean laughter, smiling, looking and eye-contact scores (in seconds) of subjects according to variations in the distance between the child subject and his/her child and adult companions

			Boys		Girls	
			Near	Far	Near	Far
Laughing	Experimenter	Near	4·0	6·0	2·8	7·9
		Far	4·6	4·5	13·1	7·6
		Absent	8·4	—	8·9	—
Smiling	Experimenter	Near	58·8	67·0	60·2	44·1
		Far	44·5	53·9	64·6	42·5
		Absent	47·8	—	37·6	—
Looking	Experimenter	Near	2·6	1·5	2·2	3·5
		Far	1·7	1·7	3·6	2·0
		Absent	4·2	—	3·3	—
Eye-contact	Experimenter	Near	0	0·4	0·5	3·1
		Far	0	0·1	1·2	0·5
		Absent	0	—	0·4	—

presence of one E (A.J.C.) than in the presence of the other (H.C.F.). Mean smiling scores were 81·6 and 27·3 seconds respectively ($F = 19·33$; $df = 1,32$; $p < 0·01$) and mean laughter scores were 10·8 and 2·1 seconds respectively ($F = 13·06$; $df = 1,32$; $p < 0·01$). Therefore differences attributable to the presence or absence of E were not independent of whom E was. Children seated close to each other smiled more in the *presence* of A.J.C. than in his absence ($F = 5·96$; $df = 1,18$; $p < 0·05$). However, this effect did not extend to the presence or absence of H.C.F. With laughter the children laughed more in the *absence* of H.C.F. than in his presence ($F = 5·93$; $df = 1,18$; $p < 0·05$), but no such difference was found with the presence or absence of A.J.C.

These results strongly suggest that the adult companion has a crucial influence on the children's behaviour, despite attempts to standardize Es' behaviour and mode of interaction with the children during sessions.

Study II: Method

Ss were 92 7-year-old children (46 boys and 46 girls). They were drawn from amongst the same children as those used in Study I. Two colour comedy cartoon films were used from the 'Tom and Jerry' series produced by M.G.M. One film, *The Truce Hurts*, was silent while the other, *Cruise Cat*, had a sound accompaniment consisting mainly of an action-related musical score with occasional vocalizations. Both films when projected at 24 frames per second lasted for 6 minutes. The procedure followed that described in the General Methodology section except that, again, all sessions were conducted by one E only. Seventy-two of the children were tested in pairs: 12 boys pairings, 12 girl pairings and

12 boy/girl pairings. *E*s deliberately avoided using the same pairings as those formed for Study I, but apart from this constraint the children were paired on the same basis as before, and designated as *S* or companion according to which seat they occupied. The remaining 20 children were tested in isolation. All the children watched two films, projected in quick succession. Subject–companion pairs were divided between four conditions.

ORDER OF FILMS

CONDITION	FIRST	SECOND
Si/Si	Silent	Silent
So/So	Sound	Sound
Si/So	Silent	Sound
So/Si	Sound	Silent

There were thus nine pairs in each condition: three boy, three girl and three mixed-sex.

The 20 solitary children were divided into 10 who followed the Si/Si condition and 10 who followed the So/So condition.

The children in pairs were seated on two low stools locked close together throughout the presentation of both films. When solitary children were to be tested, one of the stools was removed. All the children were tested in the absence of *E*. After instructing the children, *E* retired to the experimenters' room, and stayed there for the remainder of the testing session. Between films, while the first film was being automatically rewound in preparation for the showing of the second film, *E* opened the door joining the children's and experimenters' room and reminded the children that the second film was about to be shown.

Results

Social facilitation effects and sex differences

Table 9.2 presents the mean laughter, smiling, looking and eye-contact scores for *S*s. The means shown are the averages for the two films to which *S*s were each exposed, and relate therefore to a 6-minute time period. (They are, therefore, directly comparable with the means in Table 9.1.) Separate means are presented for each of the sex pairings and for the solitary condition. It is important to note that the means for the sex pairings are based upon the pooled

Table 9.2 Mean laughter, smiling, looking and eye-contact scores (in seconds) for dyadic and solitary children

	Boy/Boy	Boy/Girl	Boy	Girl/Girl	Girl/Boy	Girl
Laughter	6·5	5·5	1·1	4·9	8·5	0·2
Smiling	60·7	62·3	14·4	35·7	59·2	17·2
Looking	3·4	2·8	—	5·6	4·9	—
Eye-contact	0·4	0·8	—	2·1	0·8	—

data for Si/Si, So/So, Si/So, and So/Si film combinations. The means in columns 3 and 6 for solitary boys and girls are based upon the pooled data for Si/Si and So/So film combinations only. They are not, therefore, strictly comparable with the other means in the table.

Several analyses of variance were undertaken to investigate differences in the dependent measures. Three points should be made concerning these analyses: firstly, as implied immediately above, those undertaken to compare solitary boys with boys in dyads, and solitary girls with girls in dyads, used the data drawn exclusively from Si/Si and So/So film combinations. Secondly, in relation to the boy/girl pairings *both* members of each pair were separately scored on the dependent measures. Thus, for one analysis, the boy was treated as S and the girl as companion, and for another analysis the girl was treated as S and the boy as companion. Thirdly, although the mean values of mutual eye-contact scores are included in the Table, they are omitted from further analysis, as in Study I, because of the high frequencies of zero scores.

From the analyses of variance, the following results emerged:

Laughter. Both boys and girls laughed more in the presence of a companion than when alone [F (boys) $= 10·64$; $df = 2,16$; $p < 0·01$. F (girls) $= 15·00$; $df = 2,15$; $p < 0·01$.] This held whether the companion was of the same or opposite sex. Moreover, whereas the sex of the companion did not affect the boys' laughter, it did affect that of the girls: girls laughed significantly more when with a boy companion than when with a girl companion ($F = 5·24$; $df = 1,21$; $p < 0·05$).

Smiling. A similar pattern emerged with smiling. Both boys and girls smiled more in the presence of a companion of either sex than when alone [F (boys) $= 8·39$; $df = 2,16$; $p < 0·01$. F (girls) $= 7·67$; $df = 2,15$; $p < 0·01$]. As with laughter the sex of the companion also made a difference to the smiling of girls but not to that of the boys. A girl with a girl companion smiled significantly less than she did with a boy companion ($F = 7·32$; $df = 1,21$; $p < 0·05$). Moreover, she smiled significantly less than a boy with a boy companion ($F = 4·80$; $df = 1,21$; $p < 0·01$) or than a boy with a girl companion ($F = 4·80$; $df = 1,21$; $p < 0·05$).

Looking. There were no significant differences in looking scores attributable to the sex of the companion, although the means in Table 9.2 suggest that girls looked at their companion more than did boys (supporting the non-significant result in Study I).

The humorous films and sex differences

Silent versus sound film. The mean scores of Ss for the silent and sound films separately are presented in Table 9.3 (these data ignore the order in which the films were presented). The means for the alone boys and girls are based upon the data for Si/Si or So/So film conditions alone, whereas the means for the dyads are based additionally upon data for Si/So and So/Si conditions. Statistical

Table 9.3 Mean laughter, smiling, looking and eye-contact scores for silent and sound films

		Boy/Boy	Boy/Girl	Boy	Girl/Girl	Girl/Boy	Girl
Laughter	silent	10·3	4·7	1·5	9·1	11·8	0·4
	sound	2·7	6·3	0·8	1·3	5·3	0·1
Smiling	silent	80·9	56·5	14·0	36·0	66·1	31·3
	sound	40·4	68·0	14·9	35·5	52·2	3·2
Looking	silent	1·0	2·6	—	6·8	5·7	—
	sound	5·8	3·1	—	4·7	4·1	—
Eye-contact	silent	0·1	0·7	—	2·9	0·7	—
	sound	0·6	0·8	—	1·4	0·8	—

comparison of the alone conditions with the dyads therefore made use exclusively of the data from conditions common to alone children and dyads. First and second films were analysed separately, since repeated measures were obtained for the same film from some groups, and for different films from other groups.

Laughter. An overall difference between silent and sound films presented to the children was noticeable: the silent film produced significantly more laughter than did the sound, whether it came first ($F = 12·00$; $df = 1,29$; $p < 0·01$) or second ($F = 6·06$; $df = 1,29$; $p < 0·01$). There was no significant interaction between film and sex, and therefore no differential effect of the films upon pairs of varying sex composition.

Smiling. Silent and sound films did not, however, have any differential effect upon smiling. Only in the case of the boy pairs did the difference in smiling reflect that found in laughter, but this difference was not significant ($F = 2·77$; $df = 1,10$; ns).

Looking. While there was no overall difference in amount of looking between silent and sound films, there was a significant interaction between film and sex pairings during the showing of the first film: boys looked more at a boy companion during the sound film than during the silent film, while girls looked more at a boy companion during the silent film than during the sound film ($F = 5·48$; $df = 1,20$; $p < 0·05$).

These results are unfortunately equivocal since two different films were used. The assumption was made that, soundtrack apart, the two films were similarly mirth-provoking in content, but they may not have been entirely so. This assumption could be validated through further research.

Warm-up effects. The extent to which responsiveness changed from the showing of the first film to the showing of the second film was also analysed independently of whether the film was sound or silent. Quite clearly there were no warm-up effects for laughter or smiling (F ratio probabilities > 0.10). For looking, however, the analysis yielded a significant difference in favour of the second film ($F = 5.15$; $df = 1,32$; $p < 0.05$). Mean looking scores were 3.6 and 4.6 for first and second films respectively. This difference appeared to be primarily attributable to those children who saw the *same* film twice rather than two different films.

Relationship between measures

The overall correlations between measures of laughter and smiling, laughter and looking, and smiling and looking were $+ 0.25$, -0.02 and -0.01 respectively. Only the coefficient between laughter and smiling approaches significance at the 0.05 level ($n = 47$). In Table 9.4 a more detailed breakdown of the relationships between these measures is given for each of the different sex pair combinations.

These relationships are very low on the whole. Laughter and smiling are only significantly related in the case of boys with a boy companion, and smiling and looking in the case of girls with a boy companion.

Correlating the total durations of these three measures is, however, not the only way of looking for relationships between them. The patterning of responses over time serves as a useful means of studying how they occur sequentially in relation to each other. As has already been mentioned in the section of General Methodology, no serious attempt has been made to analyse the video-tapes in this way, but the tapes of two sessions were so studied for illustrative purposes. The S (a boy) from pair 21 and the S (a girl) from pair 26 were selected, for no other reason than that both had scored relatively highly on smiling and looking (the two measures under scrutiny).

Table 9.5 gives some of the main descriptive data drawn from a sequential analysis of smiling and looking from these children's tapes. What is revealing about this method of analysis is the way in which looking is closely tied to periods of smiling, irrespective of the total duration of smiling. Both boy and girl rarely looked without simultaneously smiling at some stage. This is reflected

Table 9.4 Product–moment correlation coefficients between measures of laughter, smiling and looking

	Sex pair combinations			
Relationships	Boy/Boy	Girl/Girl	Boy/Girl	Girl/Boy
Laughter/Smiling	$+ 0.73$[†]	$+ 0.26$	-0.52	$+ 0.33$
Laughter/Looking	-0.06	$+ 0.16$	$+ 0.05$	-0.27
Smiling/Looking	-0.14	$+ 0.20$	-0.11	$+ 0.56$[*]

[*] $p < .05$
[†] $p < .01$

Table 9.5 Analysis of smiles and looks from a boy subject and from a girl subject

	Total number of looks	Total duration of looks (seconds)	Total number of smiles	Total duration of smiles (seconds)	Number of looks accompanied by smile at some stage	Percentages of time looking while also smiling	Number of looks occurring at onset of smiles
Boy	23	26·5	19	65·0	21	70%	15
Girl	28	37·5	14	108·5	23	77%	8

by the high percentages of time that they were looking while also smiling. The patterning of looks and smiles is also of interest. Looks, in the case of the boy, normally accompanied the onset of his smile, rather than occurring at a later period during the smile. Indeed, of the 15 looks occurring at the onset of a smile, 10 fractionally preceded and overlapped with the smile. This might suggest that the looking triggers the smiling. However, this was not the case with the girl who looked more during the course of the smile than she did at its onset.

Discussion of Studies I and II

Taking the two studies together the main results can be summarized briefly as follows:

(1) Children were very sensitive to the presence of a companion of either sex: both their laughter and their smiling were enhanced.
(2) Girls were more affected by the sex of their companion than were boys: girls laughed and smiled more in the presence of a boy than in the presence of a girl companion. Boys' laughter and smiling were, on the other hand, relatively unaffected by the sex of their companion.
(3) The effects of the presence of an adult companion upon the responsiveness of pairs of children were ambiguous, but there is no doubt that children's responsiveness is a function of an adult companion's responsiveness.
(4) Distance between pairs of children up to 1 metre did not appear to influence children's responsiveness to each other on the dependent measures in any systematic way nor did the distance of the adult companion from the children.
(5) Results with films accompanied or unaccompanied by a soundtrack suggested that the children laughed more in response to a silent film than in response to a sound film; no difference emerged with respect to amount of smiling. Nevertheless, the validity of this conclusion rests upon the assumption that the visual material in both sound and silent films was equally mirth-provoking.
(6) There appeared to be no warm-up effects upon the measures of laughter and smiling. There was, however, more looking in response to the showing of the second film than in response to the showing of the first film, whether accompanied by sound or not.

(7) The relationships between the total durations of laughter, smiling and looking during sessions were generally very low. Evidence from the recordings of two relatively responsive children, however, suggested that children rarely look at their companion without smiling at some stage.

An inherent danger in comparing the behaviour of a solitary person (particularly a child) with that of two or more together is that the former is likely to be more prone to apprehension when he does not have the social support of a similarly naive companion. This apprehension could be attributable to the novel experimental environment, the test procedures and/or a possibly unfamiliar E. The outcome may, therefore, be that one is studying not the facilitating effect of the presence of a companion, but rather the inhibiting effect of being alone and apprehensive.

Emphasis has already been laid in the General Methodology section upon the need for a naturalistic setting for this kind of research and for giving the children an opportunity, prior to the commencement of testing, of familiarizing themselves with the Es and with the testing environment. There were no signs whatever of any apprehension on the part of the children. They volunteered very eagerly when E visited the classroom to fetch Ss. The children were keen recruits and they were unaware that they were being filmed. There is little doubt that the task in which they were engaged (watching films) served admirably to draw their attention away from themselves as 'objects' of study. A warm-up effect due to initial apprehension should, unless it were of very brief duration, be reflected by an increase in responsiveness from the first to the second film. This did not occur on measures of laughter or smiling either for solitary children or for dyads. Members of dyads looked more at their companions during the screening of the second film than during the screening of the first, but this difference can be attributed to the increased responsiveness on the part of those children who were shown the same film twice, rather than those who saw two different films. This suggests that it is familiarity with the film material, not a warm-up effect, that served to increase responsiveness, at least on this measure of social interaction. It is probable that, on the second showing of the same film, the children were less attentive to it and more attentive to each other, whereas they were perhaps equally attentive to the second film when it was novel to them. In the light of this evidence it is unlikely that the increased responsiveness of pairs of children over solitary children was a function of apprehension at the testing environment.

The question concerning how the social facilitation is operating is not easy to answer. As has been noted elsewhere (Chapman, 1972), it is impossible in any operational sense, to distinguish reliably between humorous laughter and smiling and sociable laughter and smiling. Yet, in an aetiological sense, it is quite certain that there is a distinction between purely task-related responses (i.e. laughs and smiles produced by the humorous stimuli) and responses exhibited as a direct consequence of the companion's presence. No doubt social smiles often merge into humorous smiles and vice versa.

Some of the children's laughs and smiles may have served according to Tolman's (1968) perceptual, disinhibitory, reflexive and motivational models of social facilitation mentioned earlier. In reviewing the possible operation of these processes several points are relevant. The visual humour contained in cartoon comedies is very immediate and simple to understand. It seems unlikely, therefore, that increases in a child's laughter and smiling would result from his attention being drawn to the comic nature of particular scenes in the film which he would have otherwise have missed. It is possible that the companion's laughter motivates an inattentive child to look at the film when his gaze is directed elsewhere, thereby increasing his opportunity for responding to comic scenes. In practice, however, the children rarely do look away from the film except to glance at each other, so the extent to which this process could operate is very limited. A perceptual-informational model, therefore, seems to be inappropriate in the present context. The operation of a disinhibitory process makes the assumption that the child is under some kind of restraint from which he is released by the presence of a companion. In the light of what has already been said concerning apprehension, it is our view that this assumption is untenable. There is no evidence that the child is under any such restraints, except, as will be discussed shortly, when he is in the presence of an adult companion who is perceived to be unresponsive.

It is always possible that the companion's laughs and smiles themselves function as laughter-provoking stimuli. A sequential analysis of the patterning of laughs and smiles between each pair of coacting children might give some indication of the occurrence of this kind of reflexivity and indicate whether there are any competition or imitation effects such as might be inferred if one child, for example, appears to take his cue from the other by consistently responding fractionally later. Such an analysis is of great interest and is pursued in our current studies.

However, and as Chapman (1973a) argues in relation to humour presented aurally, it is much more likely that the companion's responsiveness made the child more reactive to the humour 'perhaps through promoting the feeling that the social situation was shared'. This notion of 'sharing' the social situation has been mentioned in the previous chapter and refers basically to the individual's conception of the psychological presence of his companion, very much akin to the degree of intimacy of the social situation. Support for this view is to some extent tangential on the basis of the analyses actually conducted here. We can assume that looking is a behavioural index of sharing; and it is then of some interest to note in the case of the two children's records over time that looking was related to smiling inasmuch as it rarely occurred in the absence of smiling. However, the overall relationships between durations of looking and durations of laughter and smiling were not significant, except in the case of girls in girl/boy dyads (Table 9.4).

The results of Study I indicate a very strong and unexpected experimenter effect upon the responsiveness of the children. The presence of A.J.C. significantly enhanced the children's smiling while the presence of H.C.F. significantly inhibited their laughter. Before the reader draws any conclusion concerning differences in our popularity with the children, we must emphasize that our behaviour as adult companions quite clearly differed during the testing sessions. The attempt to standardize our behaviour and mode of interaction was not successful. The video-tape-recordings indicate very consistent differences, in terms of both the frequency and intensity of our intermittent smiles and laughs. A.J.C. acted in a substantially more responsive way than H.C.F., and it is noticeable from the tapes how much more attention (i.e. looking) the children paid towards him, in addition to their enhanced smiling. It is, of course, possible that the differences obtained were at least partially a result of our different interactive styles with the children prior to commencement of testing sessions. This can readily be tested in future studies. Such differences are, however, unlikely to have as great an effect as the E's behaviour during sessions.

These results are in themselves very interesting and clearly demonstrate the extent to which children take their cue concerning what is appropriate behaviour in the situation from the adult. In an unpublished study on female adults designed deliberately to vary the interactive behaviours of a confederate companion, Chapman and Osborne obtained marked differences in the responsiveness of Ss corresponding to the responsiveness of the companion. In the case of children, the role and behaviour of the adult companion has a crucial influence upon behaviour and clearly merits further investigation.

Contrary to previous findings of Chapman (1975b), physical proximity had no effect upon responsiveness. Chapman found that in coaction *listening* sessions with children measures of laughter, smiling and eye-contact were all enhanced by close proximity. This discrepancy may be explicable in terms of several procedural differences, the most important of which is that the children in Study I were seated side-by-side for the purposes of watching the film rather than face-to-face as they were when listening to aural material in the earlier study. It is feasible that sitting face-to-face makes Ss more conscious of each others' proximity and more sensitive to changes in their proximity. This sensitivity may also be related to differences in the demands made on Ss' attention by visual and aural comic material. Another plausible explanation lies in the differences in the distances used. Chapman used 0·8 metre and 1·7 metre as his 'near' and 'far' conditions respectively, whereas in this study 1·0 metre represented the far condition and shoulder-to-shoulder the near condition. The far condition in this study is therefore similar to Chapman's near condition. Quite possibly effects of proximity upon measures of responsiveness are only demonstrable when comparing distances below 1 metre with distances well above 1 metre.

The correlations between measures of laughter, smiling and looking examined in Study II are generally very low. Where there are significant correlations (i.e. between laughter and smiling for boys in boy pairs, and between smiling and looking for girls in girl/boy pairs) the relationships are positive. These lend only modest support to results previously obtained by Chapman (1973a,

1975b) showing that in coaction situations expressive behaviours tend to vary together rather than inversely.

A novel feature of Study II is the inclusion of mixed-sex dyads, enabling the effects of an opposite sex companion to be studied. Both boys and girls laughed and smiled more in the presence of a companion that when alone. The effect on the boys was the same whether their companion was a boy or girl. Girls, however, responded with more laughter and smiling to the presence of a boy companion than to the presence of a girl companion (see Table 9.2). This differential sensitivity between the sexes is very interesting and has not been shown in any other study on laughter.

Other studies which have explored sex differences in laughter (e.g. Cupchik and Leventhal, 1974; Leventhal and Mace, 1970) have tended to focus on the relationship between overt mirth responses and evaluations of the humour stimuli. But these studies are with solitary subjects or same sex pairs and have not been concerned with responsiveness to the companion as such. Nevertheless some interesting differences between males and females have emerged: Leventhal and Mace, for example, found that boys exhibit a high degree of *independence* between mirth and evaluation; that is, the extent of their expressive behaviours in response to the humour does not affect their evaluations of that humour. In girls, on the other hand, there appears to be an *interdependence* between mirth and evaluation: the more expressive their behaviour is, the funnier they evaluate the stimulus. Leventhal and Mace argue that in evaluating a stimulus females take into account their own expressive reactions, via kinaesthetic feedback cues, as well as the 'primary appraisal' of the stimulus, whereas, with males, their own expressive reactions are irrelevant to their evaluations. This is consonant with the view that females tend to respond more to the *whole* situation than do males.

This line of reasoning has a bearing upon our observed differences between boys and girls. If girls take more account of the whole situation, then they might be expected to be more sensitive to the existing *social* situation. But while this appears to be true, it does not explain why the girls were found to be more responsive to the companionship of boys than to that of other girls. The increased sensitivity of the girls was revealed also in the context of an adult companion (Study I). Although these results were not significant, girls tended to laugh and look more than did boys when near to each other and when far from the experimenter.

Some sex differences also emerged in relation to responsiveness to silent and sound films. It might reasonably be postulated that a soundtrack serves to highlight the comic episodes in the film. If, as Chapman has argued, boys are more concerned than girls with sharing the laughter stimuli, then they should be more responsive to a sound than to a silent film. With girls, on the other hand, it might be expected that the soundtrack inhibits their interactive behaviour since it draws their attention away from the social situation with which they are primarily concerned. These expectations are borne out by the data on looking which indicate that girls look at their companion more during the silent film whereas boys look more during the sound film (particularly with a boy companion). Both sexes, however, laugh more and boys smile more, in response to the silent film. This result is contrary to expectation and cannot easily be explained. As already mentioned, the assumption was made that the two films were equally mirth-provoking and this may not have been entirely true. Ideally the same film should have been used with and without soundtrack, a control which will be adopted in a later study.

OVERVIEW OF CURRENT RESEARCH

It is not our claim that these two studies in themselves go very far beyond what has already been done. In empirical terms some new results have been obtained in relation to the responsiveness of the adult companion and sex of the child companion. Other results obtained here concerning the effects of the presence of a coacting-companion and changes in responsiveness over time confirm the findings of previous work in a novel stimulus environment and with a novel task. Additional results such as those relating to physical proximity do not bear out previous findings but may be explicable in terms of differences in task and procedures. In a sense, therefore, the studies raise more questions than they answer, but they point the way to some potentially fruitful lines of investigation, particularly in relation to the role and sex of the companion and the relationship between subject and companion. In theoretical terms the studies have generally confirmed the views expressed early in the chapter, although we have not attempted the more detailed analysis of behaviour sequences between subject and companion which, in our view, is crucial for the further development of social facilitation and social intimacy theories.

The primary purpose of the two studies was to enable us to evaluate the suitability of our new test situation for eliciting spontaneous expressive and interactive behaviour in children. The results obtained vindicate the task, the environment and experimental procedure as a sensitive medium for the study of social influences upon responsiveness.

The experimental studies planned for the current research programme fall into two broad groups, those primarily concerned with social facilitation processes and those concerned primarily with intimacy processes, drawing upon laughter (arousal) theory as mentioned earlier in the chapter. Clearly some of the independent variables may be regarded as factors influencing both processes, so no hard-and-fast distinction is made. Within a social facilitation context, the effects of both physical and psychological variations in the stimulus environment are studied. Psychological factors are all-important and include the role and responsiveness of the child or adult companion, variations in which have already been shown to exert a strong influence upon the subject's responsiveness. These variables, as also indicated earlier, need further exploration. Other factors are studied which might be defined as producing both physical and psychological variations in the testing environment. They include the nature of the film material, prior exposure to the laboratory situation, group size and the sex composition of groups or dyads. Variations in the types of film material screened are introduced in order to test whether patterns of responsiveness between a child and his companion differ according to the content of the humorous material. It will enable a determination of whether particular interactive behaviours are systematically associated with particular kinds of comic incidents. Single-frame cartoons will also be used to this end.

The second group of studies is concerned principally with signals of intimacy and is designed to investigate the implications of variations in social responsiveness for social intimacy theory. Their primary intention, therefore, is to determine whether variations in signals of intimacy can be shown to be related systematically to differences in levels of intimacy (as defined by our dependent measures) across conditions and during sessions. Variables influencing levels of intimacy include friendship and sex groupings, interpersonal distance, canned laughter, exclusion from a situation shared by others, and pre-play arousal. The relationship between coactors is without doubt a major determinant of the level of intimacy tolerated between them. We expect differences in intimacy levels to be reflected by differences in the dependent measures and by the patterning of responses between subject and companion. Particular interest lies in the responsiveness directed towards companions of the same or opposite sex whether friends or not, and in one study attention is focused on the child who has a same sex and an opposite sex companion. Triads may well produce situations in which a subject 'shares' humour with one companion (i.e. directs signals of intimacy towards that companion) but excludes the other. Chapman (1975a) has already shown what a gross inhibiting effect two confederate companions can have upon the subject when the latter sees them direct more interactive cues towards each other than towards himself. The consequences of exclusion are taken up more purposefully in another study in which one child is effectively prevented from sharing the humorous situation which his two companions are enjoying, by virtue of performing another task. The effect of their behaviour upon him and vice versa may give some indication of the psychological impact of being 'left out'. The subsequent exposure of the excluded child to the humorous stimuli which he was previously unable to share with his companions may produce carry-over effects in terms of an increment of responsiveness. Such a finding would be of interest in relation to the arousal-reducing model of laughter because it would provide evidence for the build-up of tension in the child which cannot be satisfactorily dissipated until triggered by the humour stimuli. The notion of a carry-over effect from one situation to another is explored in another study in which the level of intimacy between children is deliberately manipulated using canned laughter and non-humorous film material prior to their engaging in interactive play.

Two studies involving children from three to eight years of age are designed to search for developmental trends with respect to the potency of social facilitation and social intimacy processes.

As mentioned earlier, the research has methodological aims and in designed to provide a more detailed analysis of social responsiveness in humorous situations than has yet been attempted. If we are to advance theory we need to advance measurement. With the exception of the work of Pollio, Mers and Lucchesi (1972), the most sophisticated forms of measurement used have been cumulative measures of duration and total frequencies of particular behavioural events. These are, however, no more than summary data. They are useful only for comparing *amounts* of one form of activity or another between or within the experimental conditions.

When looking at the influence of one person upon another it needs to be stressed, as Schaffer (1974) has done, that 'any relationship is after all a two-way process, a kind of ping-pong game where the move of each partner is to some extent dictated by the previous move of the other partner'. To partition the behaviours of the two persons, therefore, and analyse them separately neglects totally the subtle interactive sequences occurring between them. Our aim in the current research is to explore the ways in which laughter and other responses to humour function in children's social encounters. To understand the processes involved we are adopting a micro-analytical approach which will enable us to examine in more detail the forms of social influence which underly interactions between children.

NOTES

1. This research is sponsored by a grant from the Social Science Research Council (HR 3043/1).
2. Previous work has indicated that duration and frequency tend to go hand in hand; however, duration scores are on a higher level of measurement and permit more powerful and sophisticated statistical analysis.
3. We are grateful to Mr. Eric E. Powell, Headmaster of Llanedeyrn Junior School, Cardiff, and to his staff for their kindness and cooperation in allowing us to carry out this research in their school. We are also grateful to the Director of Education for Cardiff for permitting us to approach headteachers within his Authority.

REFERENCES

Andrus, T. O. (1946). A study of laugh patterns in the theater. *Speech Monographs*, **13**, 114 (Abstract).

Argyle, M. and Dean, J. (1965). Eye-contact, distance and affiliation. *Sociometry*, **28**, 289–304.

Berlyne, D. E. (1960). *Conflict, Arousal and Curiosity*. New York: McGraw–Hill.

Berlyne, D. E. (1969). Laughter, humor and play. In G. Lindzey and E. Aronson (Eds.), *Handbook of Social Psychology*. Vol. 3. Reading, Mass.: Addison–Wesley.

Berlyne, D. E. (1972). Humor and its kin. In J. H. Goldstein and P. E. McGhee (Eds.), *The Psychology of Humor: Theoretical Perspectives and Empirical Issues*. New York: Academic Press.

Blatz, W. E., Allin, K. D., and Millichamp, D. A. (1936). A study of laughter in the nursery school child. *University of Toronto Study in Child Development, No. 7*.

Brackett, C. W. (1933). Laughing and crying of preschool children. *Journal of Experimental Education*, **2**, 119–226.

Brackett, C. W. (1934). Laughing and crying of preschool children: a study of the social and emotional behaviour of young children as indicated by laughing and crying. *Child Development Monograph, No. 14*.

Calvert, W. C. (1949). The effect of the social situation on humor. Unpublished Master's Thesis, Stanford University.

Chapman, A. J. (1972). Some aspects of the social facilitation of 'humorous laughter' in children. Unpublished Doctoral Dissertation, University of Leicester.

Chapman, A. J. (1973a). Social facilitation of laughter in children. *Journal of Experimental Social Psychology*, **9**, 528–541.

Chapman, A. J. (1973b). Funniness of jokes, canned laughter, and recall performance. *Sociometry*, **36**, 569–578.

Chapman, A. J. (1975a). Humorous laughter in children. *Journal of Personality and Social Psychology*, **31**, 42–49.

Chapman, A. J. (1975b). Eye-contact, physical proximity and laughter: a re-examination of the equilibrium model of social intimacy. *Social Behavior and Personality*. (In press).

Cupchik, G. C., and Leventhal, H. (1974). Consistency between expressive behavior and the evaluation of humorous stimuli: the role of sex and self-observation. *Journal of Personality and Social Psychology*, **30**, 429–442.

Ding, G. F., and Jersild, A. T. (1932). A study of the laughing and smiling of preschool children. *Journal of Genetic Psychology*, **40**, 452–472.

Enders, A. C. (1927). A study of the laughter of the preschool child in the Merrill–Palmer Nursery School. *Papers of the Michigan Academy of Science, Arts and Letters*, **8**, 341–356.

Foot, H. C., and Chapman, A. J. (1975). Laugh and the world laughs with you. *Psychology Today* (U.K. edition), No. 1, 42–45.

Foot, H. C., Smith, J. R., and Chapman, A. J. (1975). Investigating social aspects of children's laughter. Paper presented at the Annual Conference of the British Psychological Society, April, Nottingham.

Giles, H., and Oxford, G. S. (1970). Towards a multidimensional theory of laughter causation and its social implications. *Bulletin of the British Psychological Society*, **23**, 97–105.

Gregg, A., Miller, M., and Linton, E. (1929). Laughter situations as an indication of social responsiveness in young children. In D. S. Thomas (Ed.), *Some New Techniques for Studying Social Behavior*, New York: Teachers' College.

Hertzler, J. O. (1970). *Laughter: A Socio-Scientific Analysis*. New York: Exposition Press.

Howitt, D., and Cumberbatch, G. (1974). Audience perceptions of violent television content. *Communication Research*, **1**, 204–223.

Jacobson, E. (1947). The child's laughter. *The Psychoanalytic Study of the Child, Vol. 2.* New York: International Universities Press.

Justin, F. (1932). A genetic study of laughter provoking stimuli. *Child Development*, **3**, 114–136.

Kenerdine, M. (1931). Laughter in the preschool child. *Child Development*, **2**, 228–230.

Leventhal, H., and Mace, W. (1970). The effect of laughter on evaluation of a slapstick movie. *Journal of Personality*, **38**, 16–30.

McGhee, P. E. (1971). Cognitive development and children's comprehension of humor. *Child Development*, **42**, 123–138.

McGhee, P. E. (1974). Cognitive mastery and children's humor. *Psychological Bulletin*, **81**, 721–730.

McKibben, E. K. (1969). An experimental study of the effects and the variables of personality, sex and social situation upon the appreciation of humour. Unpublished Master's Thesis, University of Glasgow.

Malpass, L. F., and Fitzpatrick, E. D. (1959). Social facilitation as a factor in reaction to humor. *Journal of Social Psychology*, **50**, 295–303.

Martin, L. J. (1905). Psychology of aesthetics. I. Experimental prospecting in the field of the comic. *American Journal of Psychology*, **16**, 35–118.

Middleton, R., and Moland, J. (1959). Humor in negro and white subcultures. *American Sociological Review*, **24**, 61–69.

Morrison, J. A. (1940). A note concerning investigations on the constancy of audience laughter. *Sociometry*, **3**, 179–185.

Nosanchuk, T. A., and Lightstone, J. (1974). Canned laughter and public and private conformity. *Journal of Personality and Social Psychology*, **29**, 153–156.

Pollio, H. R., Mers, R., and Lucchesi, W. (1972). Humor, laughter, and smiling: some preliminary observations of funny behaviors. In J. H. Goldstein and P. E. McGhee (Eds.), *The Psychology of Humor: Theoretical Perspectives and Empirical Issues*. New York: Academic Press.

Rosenthal, R. (1966). *Experimenter Effects in Behavioral Research*. New York: Appleton–Century–Crofts.

Schaffer, H. R. (1974). Early social behaviour and the study of reciprocity. *Bulletin of the British Psychological Society*, **27**, 209–216.

Sroufe, L. A., and Wunsch, J. P. (1972). The development of laughter in the first year of life. *Child Development*, **43**, 1326–1344.

Tolman, C. W. (1968). The role of the companion in social facilitation of animal behavior. In E. C. Simmel, R. A. Hoppe and G. A. Milton (Eds.), *Social Facilitation and Imitative Behavior*. Boston: Allyn and Bacon.

Weiscrantz, L., Elliott, J., and Darlington, C. (1971). Preliminary observations on tickling oneself. *Nature*, **230**, 598–599.

Wilson, C. O. (1931). A study of laughter situations among young children. Unpublished Doctoral Dissertation, University of Nebraska.

Winer, B. J. (1971). *Statistical Principles in Experimental Design*. (2nd ed.). London: McGraw–Hill.

Young, R. D., and Frye, M. (1966). Some are laughing; some are not—why? *Psychological Reports*, **18**, 747–754.

Chapter 10

Comedians and Comic Style

Howard R. Pollio and John W. Edgerly

Whether in the colourful cap and bells of a medieval jester, the spotted silks of a circus clown or in the immaculate garb of a late night MC, there exists a unique class of people whose very actions and behaviour set them apart from everyone else and these are the comedians. Whether they dance and fall, act foolish or faggy, are hostile or mild, or give and/or get a pie in the face, it is clear that such a group does exist as a social and phenomenal reality and that although personally they may be treated somewhat ambivalently by their society they nonetheless are enormously well remunerated if successful in evoking that most precious of commodities—laughter on demand.

As if to accentuate their uniqueness, the personal life of a comedian or clown is often considered to be something special. Pagliacci, as well as the more contemporary Emmet Kelly, is always sad, and we are ever fearful of a melancholic existence lurking behind the painted clown's facade. On the other hand, we are exhorted, as the song says, to 'be a clown, be a clown, (for) all the world loves a clown ...', and we are ever perplexed by the question of whether the clown is melancholic or gay.

But clowns and comedians are not the only ones who make people laugh; rather they represent only the most highly skilled and professionally developed of a much larger group of individuals who are witty or funny in their everyday lives. On both a commonsense and empirical basis it is quite clear that the wit is often esteemed above other members of the group particularly in regard to such things as being likeable, helpful, influential, and so on (Goodchilds, 1972). As if to moderate such a highly flattering and effective self-picture, Smith and Goodchilds (1963) failed to find any special esteem for witty individuals in groups of long duration although such groups having deliberate wits were more satisfied with their situation and worked better on problem tasks than groups not having wits.

Being witty, however, represents not only a particular mode of social behaviour but a widely occurring cultural phenomenon as well, and the anthropological literature points this out quite clearly: of 136 cultures reported in a cross-cultural survey in 1940, 56 contained information about the social role of the clown or fool. Of these 56 cultures no single geographical locale seemed to have a monopoly: 'the distribution of clowning among primitives appears to be fairly even, with Asia, Africa, Oceania and North and South America all offering examples of high developments' (Charles, 1945).

Turning from so-called primitive to more technological–advanced societies, Enid Welsford (1935) has traced the history of Fools and Clowns from early medieval England down through to the invention of movies and records. On the basis of her work, she concludes that fools operate upon the stage of literature and history not because 'the fool is a creator of beauty, but (rather because he is the creator) of . . . freedom'. The clown is successful not because he gets slapped or degraded, but rather because he is none the worse for his slapping. Thus, the fool is 'not only physically, but morally and spiritually resilient' and for this reason he comforts us because he alone shows 'that Death is a hoax and that the whole world does not bear the tree on which (a clever fool such as) Marcolf can be hanged' (p. 315).

In a more contemporary vein, Klapp (1972) views the Fool as a social type of great importance; so great, as a matter of fact, as to be considered equal in stature to the Hero and the Villain. For Klapp, a social type never represents a real person; rather it is one way in which members of a particular society think about, and thereby categorize, other individuals in that society. The social functions assigned to the Fool are many, although the most important seems to be that by his negative example he tells us what is valued even if he himself cannot quite get it right. In this role of moralist-in-reverse the Fool acts as a control mechanism stressing what he violates by emphasizing what is beyond him. To call a non-fool, *fool*, is to put social pressure on that individual to conform to a social value.

What all of this seems to imply is that to talk of comedians and comic style we must take account of comic performance in a wide variety of situations; situations that vary from lived and living natural ones through to more contrived and staged ones. In the living natural situation, the comic event and its attendant laughter are usually incidental to other ongoing activities while in the created theatrical setting the comic event and its attendant laughter are brought about by the antics of specially trained performers. In this latter case, performers may be spontaneous as on late-night talk shows, partially pre-planned and partially ad libbed as in a circus, almost completely pre-programmed as in a night-club or TV monologue, or completely rehearsed as in a comic play or operetta. Comedy makes its appearance in the lived as in the contrived, and any analysis of comedians and their styles must take this complete comic spectrum into account.

Over and above the specific situation, and perhaps ultimately as important, is the larger social context within which comedy occurs. It is this larger context which is obvious in sociological and anthropological studies and which serves to moderate everything a comedian or clown says and does. It is quite one thing when a ritual Zuni clown drinks 'great draughts of urine amid the roaring merriment of the spectators' (Charles, 1945) and quite another when a psychotic patient does so in a hospital back-ward. In one case we have humour and laughter, in the other, only madness and woe. Because of the very strong effect social factors seem to play in defining what is permissible and/or appropriate, it seems necessary to look at such factors before we turn more directly to comedy and comedians. Our first act then begins with just such a social prologue, and it is to this matter which we now turn.

A SOCIAL PROLOGUE: CULTURE, COMEDY AND THE SOCIAL MEANING OF WHAT'S FUNNY

In his classic work *Childhood and Society* (1951), Erikson described two American Indian cultures in sympathetic and clear terms. In both cultures he noted the existence of a special mode of behaviour which appropriately can be called comic or clownish. So, for example, in the very highly regulated Yurok, their year-end festivities always include a period of licence: a period in which 'jokes, ridicule and abuse run riot'. For the Sioux, a vastly different group, an institutionalized clownish role is provided by the *heyoka*: a role which allows and sometimes even requires the person to behave as absurdly as possible.

Such situations and roles abound in American Indian culture reaching their most organized form among the Zunis. The Zuni tribe clowns (Koyemci) are not only clowns but also often form the priestly class ruling a given village. The double life of the Koyemci is perhaps best symbolized in terms of a very special ambience surrounding these clowns/priests; namely, that in many comic situations they are functionally equivalent to children (Levine, 1961). Within the context of certain religious festivals, the antics of the Koyemci clown often free him and his crowd from rational and moral restraints; and this only occurs because an unreal imaginary world has momentarily been created wherein priests are profane and the powerful are as children. All is possible as long as a humorous and, therefore, unreal attitude is maintained.

Although from our technological perspective such actions may seem anything but funny, we need only remember the public 'roastings' which surround such prestigious social clubs as the Gridiron Club in Washington, or the Friar's Club in New York. The Gridiron Club Dinner is given by newspapermen for the sole purpose of lampooning and satirizing the mighty in American political life. The Friar's Club at its annual dinner lampoons a person in the public eye; and here the cut is no less scabrous than at the Koyemci ceremonies.

Given the universality of such public roastings, how are they to be understood? Charles (1945), arguing from a Jungian point of view, sees the ritual clown as an archetype helping to put a society back in contact with fundamentally primitive matters: matters that have been under-emphasized or excluded by a given social grouping. Levine (1961), on the other hand, sees the ritual clown as expressing in an appropriately controlled, yet uncontrolled, form the repressed aspects of a given society. What is indisputable on the basis of either interpretation is that the clown, and his more verbally articulate counterpart, the comedian, handle something not quite proper—something 'embarrassing, astonishing and shocking ... Although the clown holds the licentious thing in his hand ... he knows, and his audience knows, and both he and his audience know that the other knows, that he is not the thing ... He is playing with fire; but he is not the fire, (and) in the moment he identifies himself with the fire he is no longer funny ... That fine delightful sense of balance and mastery is lost, and the clown becomes pathetic, ineffective, disgusting' (Charles, 1945).

This balance is, of course, the control a specially gifted person exhibits over a feared or tabooed event, and it is the mastery which reveals the clown and the comic as masters of the fire rather than as fuel for its consumption. Despite the importance of such mastery, not all literate commentators in the English-speaking world feel comfortable with humour as a saving grace. Ludovici (1932), following Hobbes, sees in laughter and comedy little that is worthy of the human spirit. As a matter of fact, despite a reasoned and reasonable analysis of the secret of laughter, Ludovici is convinced that such behaviour is an enemy to progress, frittering away man's creative fire in the trivia of laughter. As he put it somewhat heavily: 'had Napoleon recognized the overpowering disproportion between his absurdly inadequate personality and the stupendous task he was undertaking ... he would have had to crack some paralysing joke about it'. Or again: 'who could ever imagine Christ laughing?' (Ludovici, 1932).

Well, someone, G. K. Chesterton to be exact, could imagine Christ laughing and for this reason has earned Mr. Ludovici's everlasting scorn. The view that laughter and humour are more than just trivializing aspects of culture is perhaps best expressed by Konrad Lorenz in his book *On Aggression* (1966). Citing the Gospel According to Nature and Chesterton in equal measure, Lorenz sees in humour and laughter an appropriate vehicle whereby seemingly rational and serious schemes of unusual control and domination may be exploded by the pin-prick of a Will Rogers, a Charlie Chaplin or a Grock. It is *tierischer Ernst* that produces the paralytic effects of chauvinism and militarism and it is laughter which explodes these profane myths periodically. For Lorenz, the truth of the matter would seem to be that behind the comedian or clown's mask there often lurks a moralist ready to rebalance that which is upset, repressed or distorted in a society. For this reason the mask may hide a person who can be either melancholy or gay depending on whether or not the personal and/or social message does its critical and curative work.

ACT I: THE LAUGHING PLACES

In order to locate comedians within the total spectrum of laughing places it is necessary first of all to look at specific situations in which people laugh. There are two published sources of data from which to draw: (1) a questionnaire responded to by 100 male and 84 female college students (Young, 1937) and (2) a set of 'humor diaries' kept by 70 female Vassar students in 1926 (Kambouropoulou, 1926). Both sets of results have been categorized into five specific situations and these data are presented in Table 10.1. The specific codings used in this table represent a compromise between those suggested by Young and Kambouropoulou, with most of the changes involving a difference

Table 10.1 Natural situations in which laughter is evoked: Self-reports

Situation	Percentage of Total Events		
	Diaries[1]	Questionnaire[2] 1937	1973[3]
(1) Happy mood in general	4%	—	15%
(2) Physical actions and antics of other people	25%	12%	13%
(3) Wisecracks, put-downs, clever remarks, jokes, stupidity of others	53%	57%	31%
(4) Incongruous incidents and situations	18%	13%	21%
(5) Formally funny materials—plays, radio programmes, movies, etc.	—	18%	20%

[1] From Kambouropoulou (1926): 70 student diaries.
[2] From Young (1937): 100 male and 84 female respondents.
[3] From Edgerly and Pollio (1974): 40 male and 40 female respondents over a 5-day period.

in phrasing rather than in intent. Although there is a great deal of variability in the percentages obtained over both sets of data, one situation (3), that involving clever remarks made by one person at the expense of another, accounted for over half of the responses in both lists. This finding seems to suggest that aggression or hostility is often involved in those events contributing to laughter. None of the other situations, with the exception of (4), are sufficiently detailed as to allow for an exact specification of what might be at work in that situation. Situation 4, however, does convey the impression that in addition to hostility, funny situations must also include a class of events that can best be described as involving an incongruity of component ideas.

A more recent use of Young's (1937) questionnaire at the University of Tennessee (Edgerly and Pollio, 1974) is presented in the last column of Table 10.1. Basically, these new results showed far fewer examples of Category (3)—wise cracks, and so on—than in Young's original results and a somewhat greater proportion of Categories (1) and (4), both more begin types of humour. Also in agreement with earlier results, we found that on the basis of self-report, students estimated they laughed between 15 and 20 times per day, a figure that agrees quite closely with Young's value of 19 per day.

Thus, over an almost 50-year period there has been very little change in terms of what college students say they laugh about and how frequently they say they laugh. Generally speaking, they laugh at put-downs and incongruous activities. In the one case, where someone else is made to look from a bit to a lot foolish, and in the other, where there is very little in the way of putting someone else down, humour in the lived world seems to involve both targeted and whimsical events and this is as true today as it was 50 years ago.

The data provided by both Young, and Edgerly and Pollio, also show that college students laugh at formally funny material about 20% of the time and the major category here would seem to be that of the joke. For this reason it is not surprising to find that some investigators (Middleton and Moland, 1959) have attempted to track down how frequently, and what kind of jokes get told. In their study, 220 college students were asked to record jokes they heard other people tell during a one-week period. Following this, jokes were coded according to a rather straightforward system involving the categories of: (1) harmless jokes, (2) sexual and excrement jokes, (3) ridicule of minority group jokes and (4) ridicule of deviant behaviour jokes. The major results showed that most students heard between four and six jokes for the week and that sexual and excrement jokes were most frequent (49 %), followed by minority group jokes (21 %), ridicule of deviant behaviour jokes (19 %) and harmless humour jokes (11 %). In addition, Middleton and Moland found that men told more jokes than women: over the one-week period the total group heard 604 jokes of which 350 (59 %) were told by men. Although there were other aspects of this investigation, the important finding is the relative infrequence of jokes as occasions for laughter in the natural environment.

Since four to six per week do not equal 19 per day, it does seem that a good deal of laughter must be primarily a product of social interaction. For this reason it seems reasonable to ask what people laugh at in the context of a group setting and whether or not it is possible to see the emergence of natural comedians in such settings. One of the earliest studies dealing with laughter in groups was done by Goodrich, Henry and Goodrich (1954) who looked at the frequency and targets of jokes and wisecracks occurring within the context of 23 psychiatric staff conferences. Over all conferences, the median number of laughs was 7 ± 2 per session. A formal categorization of 174 witty remarks showed that 85 involved disparaging either oneself, someone else or the opinion of someone else; that 81 involved incongruity of words or ideas (as when a physician was telling of making clay tyres for a child patient and commented 'I had to give him more and more spares'); and that eight could not be coded. The major content-themes, as expected, dealt with doctors, patients, patients and doctors, and their respective problems: nurses, neuroses, patients and doctors.

Intrigued by the surprisingly large number of disparaging remarks, Coser (1960) examined the social functions of humour among the staff of a Boston mental hospital by looking at the origin and function of laughter occurring in 20 staff meetings. As in the Goodrich and co-workers study, Coser was a participant observer; in this situation, however, the group consisted of five senior staff members, six junior staff members and six paramedical staff. As in the prior study, most witticisms (90 of 103) were directed at some target or other. Of these 90 shots, 53 were made by senior staff, 33 by junior staff and four by paramedical staff, and this occurred despite the fact that junior staff members spoke more often than senior staff, especially since most sessions were devoted to case presentation by junior staff.

But what of the targets—the butts of these directed jokes? Of the 53 senior staff jokes, 21 were directed at junior staff, nine at patients, four at themselves and 14 at no easily determined target. Of the 33 junior staff jokes, 13 were directed at patients, 12 at themselves, two at senior staff (and then only when the specific staff person was absent) and two at no discernible target. Paramedical staff only told jokes about patients (2) and about themselves (2).

What all of this seems to mean is that within the context of a hierarchically ordered situation such as a teaching hospital, those at the top more often make use of humour than those at the bottom. In addition, top-dogs tend to target themselves and their peers only some of the time (13%), preferring instead to direct their wit downward much more often (50% of the time). Those at the (lower) resident level never direct it upward, focusing instead on themselves and others below them in the hierarchy almost 75% of the time. Although it is clear that witty remarks are valued and can and do serve to relieve tension, resolve role conflicts, and help promote teaching and learning, it must not be over-looked that humour—even when serving in any of these functions—always contains from a little to a lot of aggression. In discussing just this aspect, Coser notes that humour serves 'to reduce social distances between people in different positions (in the hierarchy) and, therefore, has an equalizing function ... Hence release of aggression in witty manner may do much to prevent the outbreak of hostility ... Humor helps to convert hostility and to control it, while at the same time permitting its expression' (Coser, 1960).

Thus far the implication seems to be that the witty person in a natural group is among the most powerful members of the group. In order to study how witty individuals emerge in less hierarchically structured situations, Goodchilds and Smith and their associates (see Goodchilds, 1972) attempted to define the characteristics of wits in much more socially ambiguous positions as well as to determine whether or not there is more there than one type of wit. When asked as to whether or not they used mainly sarcastic wit or clowning wit subjects uniformly opted for the clown category. In an admittedly complex and interpretatively difficult study, Smith and White (1965) also found that sarcastic wits tend to be under-nominated as witty, largely because being witty seems to mean being clownish or whimsical rather than dominant or aggressive.

This dichotomy between sarcastic and whimsical wit has been pursued most strongly by Goodchilds in a series of studies dating as far back as 1959 (Good-childs, 1959, 1972). In this research, fictional scripts were devised in which one of three actors consistently attempted to be funny, either by being sarcastic or whimsical. A group of students then read the scripts and were asked to tell which of three actors (a) had the most power to influence me, (b) would I like best, (c) had most group influence and (d) was best liked by the group. In general, results showed that clowning wits were well-liked but not very influential relative to sarcastic wits, although subjects did not choose the sarcastic wit where specific influence over them was at issue. When subjects were divided into three subsets according to whether or not they themselves were witty, results indicated that non-wits overvalued the clown and slightly undervalued the sarcastic wit on the influence dimension. Wits, on the other hand, definitely minimized a clown's ability to influence either themselves or the group. To the witty individual, sarcastic wits are powerful and not very well-liked while clowns are well-liked, but not very powerful.

This distinction between whimsy and sarcasm, or between nonsense and directed aggression, seems to appear in almost all attempts to assess the effect and effectiveness of naturally occurring wits; as indeed it occurs in any attempt to categorize the laughing places which seem to involve either incongruity or hostility. Interpersonal humour nearly always has some target and this target can be either gently prodded or forcefully exploded. It seems characteristic of hierarchical structures that gentle prodding is done to teach whereas outright aggression, at its best, is employed so as to allow for the expression of aggressive intentions without disrupting group order or structure.

The idea of a whimsical and a sarcastic wit also makes important contact with the dual status of institutionalized funny men—jesters and butts—and seems to explain how a clown can be both a clowning and a powerful religious figure. Only powerful individuals can handle the taboo topics of a society with poise and mastery, and only a clown who incorporates both the butt and the aggressor role will be able to get people to laugh and thereby increase their own freedom and mastery in dealing with taboo topics. According to these notions, a comedian (or professional wit) can take one of two roles, and at times perhaps both.

ACT II: LAUGHTER IN THERAPY GROUPS

Because humour seems such an important topic for any understanding of human interaction processes, Peterson (1973, 1975) reasoned that appropiate use and management of laughter and humour must have important implications for group psychotherapy. Much to his surprise, Peterson found that the topic of humour almost never occurred in the group therapy literature. It is as if everyone knows humour is important in group (and individual) psychotherapy; no one seems to know exactly how to teach would-be therapists what to do with it. In order to provide some data on laughter in therapy groups, Peterson video-taped five sessions in a 17-week group therapy experience. His tapes involved the first, fourth, eighth, thirteenth and seventeenth sessions of the group. The particular group observed had a somewhat changing membership over sessions, so that of the original ten group members only eight were there by Session 17. On the average, sessions lasted about 103 minutes: the longest session was 119 minutes, while the shortest was 89 minutes. The number of participants varied between eleven for Session 1, to six for Session 13, with the median number equal to eight.

Once video-records were obtained, independent raters continuously monitored three distinct behaviours for each participant: talking, smiling and laughing. These behaviours were recorded on an Esterline–Angus multi-channel event-recorder. Reliabilities were assessed for all three categories: median inter-rater reliabilities were 0.77 ($p < 0.01$; range 0.67 to 0.90) for smiling; 0.85 ($p < 0.01$; range 0.61 to 0.92) for laughing; and 0.96 ($p < 0.01$; range 0.93 to 0.98) for talking.

Given these very acceptable levels of reliability, Peterson focused on the amount and pattern of laughter within each of the therapy sessions. Figure 10.1 shows a typical pattern for the most representative session, Session 8. The

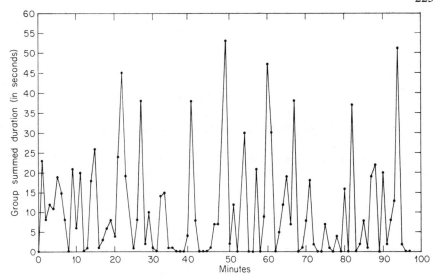

Figure 10.1 Typical pattern of laughter for a session of group psychotherapy

metric plotted in this figure is group summed laughter, a figure which is determined by adding up the total amount of time all eight individuals laughed during each of the 90 minutes of this session. A different measure of laughter, number of people laughing, was also examined and was found to correlate 0·87 ($p < 0.01$) with the metric used in Figure 10.1. Actually over all five sessions the median correlation between these two measures was 0·87 ($p < 0.01$; range 0·79 to 0·88). Comparable correlations for smiling ranged between 0·71 ($p < 0.01$) and 0·87 ($p < 0.01$) and produced a median value of 0·82 ($p < 0.01$). In addition to these measures it was also possible to do a minute-by-minute correlation across pairings of all three measures, and here the median correlation for laughing and smiling was 0·59 ($p < 0.01$; range 0·04 to 0·84); the median correlation between talking and laughing was 0·20 (range 0·07 to 0·76), while the median correlation between talking and smiling was −0·31 (range −0·55 to + 0·80).

An examination of Figure 10.1 shows that it is quite easy to locate points at which a good deal of laughter occurred. Perhaps more germane to the present context, it is also possible to look at individuals within the group and describe quantitatively and exactly how often each group member talked, laughed and smiled as well as to determine the pattern of intercorrelations between these three measures for group members across an entire session.

Largely because Peterson was interested in the effects of laughter on group process and therapeutic change, he did not look at these correlations, and it remained for Alan Childs and Howard Pollio of the University of Tennessee to re-use and extend Peterson's data so as to examine the occurrence of intentional wit in this setting. To do this, three independent raters first went through all five sessions and noted the number of tries at humour produced by individual group members whether or not laughter resulted from the attempt. Using a criterion of at least two of three raters agreeing on intent, it was found that there were a total of 111 attempts at humour over the five sessions studied. Of these, only four were not met with laughter.

The data made one fact immediately apparent—the number of people taking a shot at being funny was always less than the total number of people in the group: regardless of group size there were never more than five people producing more than a single attempt at humour with the median value falling at three.

With these joke-attempting data in hand, it was decided to see if there was any consistent relationship between joking and the other three measures—laughing, talking and smiling—recorded for individual group members. Although separate correlations were computed for each session, a matrix containing median values for these sessions seems to represent the data fairly well, and is presented in Table 10.2. The only correlation which failed to reveal a consistent pattern across all five sessions concerned talking and smiling, where two of the five correlations were $+ 0.80$ and $+ 0.41$, while the remaining three were -0.45, -0.31 and -0.55. For this reason a question mark appears in the appropriate cell in Table 10.2. Of the remaining correlations only those between talking and joking, and smiling and laughing, produced significant positive relationships. What this means is that people who joke also tend to talk a lot, although they do not necessarily smile or laugh a lot. Group members who smile a lot, however, also tend to laugh a lot, and tend to be different from those individuals who talk and joke. The total picture that emerges is that people who joke also tend to dominate in terms of talking, while those who smile also tend to laugh. There seems to be no relationship between enjoying a joke (laughing and smiling) and having the floor often enough to tell a joke (talking and joking).

In agreement with other studies (Coser, 1960; Middleton and Moland, 1959) women made far fewer attempts at humour in this situation although they did tend to laugh and smile more. So, for example, of the total of 111 attempts at being funny, women made only 15 as compared to 96 for men; (of these 15,

Table 10.2 Median correlations across all four response categories

Behavioural event	Joke	Talk	Smiles	Laugh
Number of jokes	×	0·64*	0·17	0·11
Amount of talking		×	?†	0·20
Amount of smiling			×	0·59*
Amount of laughter				×

*$p < 0.05$
†See text.

four were made by the female group leader). Since over all five groups 18 of the participants were women and 25 were men, this produces a mean value of 0·83 for women and 3·84 for men. Over all five sessions, the mean number of attempts made by men was greater than the mean number made by women on all five occasions. The positive correlation between joking and talking suggests that men ought to do more talking, and this was true for four of the five sessions. In terms of smiling, the picture reverses: for all five sessions women smiled more than men, and because of the correlation between laughing and smiling, we might expect and in fact did find, that women on the average laughed more than men in four of the five sessions.

The composite picture that emerges is this: men talk and joke; women smile and laugh; and this pattern is true for all five sessions. This same trend—for men to attempt to be witty and for women to smile and laugh—also appears in Coser's data dealing with psychiatric training sessions where it was found that of 103 attempts at humour women made only 4, despite the fact that there were more women than residents and that two of the senior psychiatrists were women. Without labouring the point, it is quite clear that women just do not attempt to be humorous in a mixed group setting and the reason seems to be that women are neither expected, nor trained, to joke in this culture. Without also being unduly psychoanalytic, it seems reasonable to propose that attempting a witty remark is often an intrusive, disturbing and aggressive act, and within this culture, probably unacceptable for a female.

Laughing and smiling, on the other hand, are both responsive behaviours indicating that an intrusion has been noted, understood and accepted. Such behaviour accords with the social stereotype of a clever as well as a dull woman— a stereotype described by Coser (1959) as 'passive and receptive'. Therefore, a woman who feels comfortable with humour is receptive and signals this by laughing and/or smiling and never (or hardly ever) by making a witty remark.

What are wits witty about, and who are their targets? Here it is well to begin with a very broad categorization—that between hostile and whimsical wit—and see how much of group wit is which. Of all 111 attempts at humour, 76% could be coded as hostile and only 12% as whimsical, with an additional 12% not fitting comfortably into either category. It was possible to subdivide the 84 instances of hostile wit according to target, and for present purposes three different types of targets seemed enough: (1) self, (2) other in the group and (3) generalized other. Of these 84 instances, 33 or 39% were self-directed; 35 or 42% were directed at a specific group member or the group as a whole; while 16 or 19% were directed at a generalized other such as University of Tennessee students in general, or relatives, or others not present in the group, and so forth.

Of the 15 attempts made by women, only 12 were easily classifiable, and of these 12, two (13%) were non-targeted while ten (65%) were targeted, with three directed at self, five at other group members and two at generalized others. These figures compare quite closely with those obtained for the total group and indicate that, while women may make far fewer attempts at humour than men, they do aim in roughly the same way, that is, 66% targeted for women, 76% for men.

These figures, however, are quite different from those reported by Goodrich and co-workers (1954) who found that 81/174 (47%) of all remarks were of the non-targeted, or incongruity type, and that 85/174 (49%) were of the disparagement variety. An examination of these 85 remarks indicated, by our figuring, that ten (or 6% of the total) were aimed at the self, 15 (8%) represented the disparagement of another's opinion while 62 (36%) represented disparagement of others. A different set of data, that reported by Coser (1960), provides values much closer to our own. Of the 90 attempts at humour noted, 16 (18%) had no 'manifest target'. Of the remaining 74 remarks, 18 (20%) were directed at oneself, 27 (30%) at a generalized other including the absent patient under discussion and 29 (32%) at someone else in the group.

Table 10.3 presents a summary of these three different sets of observations. As can be seen, results provided by Goodrich and co-workers (1954) seem a bit high in regard to non-targeted humour with both other samples producing values of less than 20%. The other major difference among these sets of data concerns the proportion of self-directed versus other-directed remarks. While both Goodrich and co-workers (1954) and the present study produced a value of about 45% 'Other' plus 'Generalized other' targets, Coser's data show a combined value of 59%. This latter value reflects the fact that senior staff targeted junior staff and patients about 60% of the time, while junior staff targeted patients 40% of the time. The relatively large proportion of self-directed remarks made by Coser's subjects almost all involved junior staff and paramedical staff targeting themselves (i.e. 16 of 18 self targets). The relatively high proportion of individuals targeting themselves in the present study is likewise accountable by the fact that they were patients who presumably were not completely satisfied with themselves and chose to show it by self-derogating humorous remarks.

Table 10.3 Targets of attempts at humour in three different settings

Source of data	N	Targeted			Non-targeted
		Self	Other	Generalized other	
Psychiatric staff conferences 1954[1]	174	6%	← 45%* →		47%
Mental hospital staff 1960[2]	90	20%	27%	32%	18%
Present study, 1974	111†	30%	32%	14%	12%

[1]Goodrich and co-workers (1954).
[2]Coser (1960).
*These figures cannot be separated from published data.
† Figures do not add to 100% since all attempts at humour were coded into more than the four categories contained in this table.

An examination of the number of self-directed remarks made by individuals in the present study revealed that one group member, Person M, made 14 such remarks, while no other member made more than six. In addition to these 14, Person M also made six other-directed and nine incongruity remarks. Person C, who made 29 attempts at humour, produced three that were incongruity remarks, six that were self-directed and 17 other-directed. Because of the large number of remarks made by these two group members (53% of the total) we decided to study their activities in greater detail. Of the approximately 30 remarks made by Person M, 47% were self-directed and only 20% other-directed; Person C made 21% self-directed and 59% other-directed remarks. On the basis of these data it seemed as if Person M provides a natural example of the butt role, while Person C provides a natural example of the hostile wit. For this reason we looked carefully at what both of them said and did in the time-period immediately surrounding any attempt at humour.

As should be obvious from these data, Persons C and M were markedly different from the rest of the group in terms of 'giving' (directing remarks at others) and 'getting' (being the target of group and self-remarks). For all 111 group members, Figure 10.2 presents a plot of 'giving' versus 'getting' and produced a correlation of 0·62 ($p < 0.05$). A careful examination of these data indicates that for all but Persons M and C (both so marked in the graph) most individuals 'got' slightly more than they 'gave'. Since the data for these two group members were so different from the remaining nine points, a correlation was computed excluding them; it produced a value of 0·92 ($p < 0.01$). Since

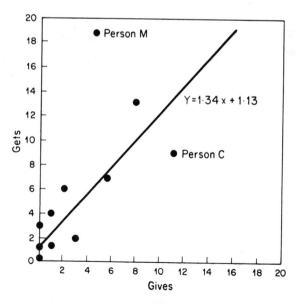

Figure 10.2 The relationship of 'giving' to 'getting' in the context of group therapy

this latter value seems to describe the data more accurately the regression line plotted in Figure 10.2 was estimated on the basis of these nine points.

Whichever way you look at it, Person M is getting it more than anyone else and more often than he's giving it, while Person C is giving it more and getting it less; on this basis the description of Person M as Butt and Person C as Hostile Wit seems appropriate. Closer behavioural observation of what both did almost every time they made an attempt at humour showed that Person M usually preceded each attempt by leaning forward in his chair, by moving his hands a great deal and by general body agitation. Each attempt at wit was followed by nervous laughter and then by looking down. Person C, on the other hand, most often maintained the position he was in prior to attempting a witticism (usually leaning back in his chair), his movements were slow and well controlled, and he tended to follow each attempt by maintaining eye contact with the primary listener and then by looking around at other members of the group during their laughter. He tended to smile and nod during this latter period.

If such schematic portraits sound familiar they should. In one way or another almost all comedy pairs make use of precisely these, or similar, behaviour patterns. We need only think of Laurel and Hardy and the behaviour of Persons M and C are duplicated fairly exactly. As a matter of fact, Laurel and Hardy's comic effect comes from at least two different sources both of which involve the roles of Butt and Wit: (1) the chronic put-down of Laurel by Hardy and (2) the chronic put-down of Hardy by the world. Like our two patients, one member of a pair may act superior to the other; in reality both are not making it and it is at this point that the comic again makes contact with that which is significant for each of us in our own very particular society.

ACT III: THE COMEDIAN'S WORLD

The world of lived and living events provides many, if not all, of the pieces out of which the comic artist must fashion the fragile and ephemeral world of comedy. From these events he takes the elements of aggression and superiority as well as those of whimsy and incongruity; elements which appear wherever there is humour. He also draws upon the articulated social role of the fool; a role which separates into jester and butt. Then, there is the differential status of men and women in regard to the humorous thrust; men joke, women laugh and smile. There is also the obvious significance of a social hierarchy both within and across a cultural context: a hierarchy which says who's on top (and therefore may joke at whose expense) as well as a social hierarchy in which certain minority groups find themselves in a less powerful social position *vis a vis* others. And finally there is always the fire—the taboo—which provides so much of the content of what it is that is laughed at, and laughable, in a given society or social setting.

Associative definition of the comedian's world

These elements represent the raw material a professional comedian has at his or her disposal and how and when he or she chooses to use these materials forms the topic of this section. Actually, such a question is probably best delayed a bit, at least until we discover the dimensions defining the comic worlds spun by contemporary comedians. But how is this to be done? In a first attempt at recovering the dimensions of these worlds, Pollio, Edgerly and Jordan (1972) began by compiling a list of contemporary comedians. This was done by asking a group of students to list the names of all comedians they could think of. The final list consisted of 37 names which were then given to a different group of students with instructions to 'write the name of any other comedian that each of the comedians on the list makes you think of'. Once such comedian associates were obtained, the number of comedians any two comedians had in common was computed as their agreement or overlap score. According to Deese (1965) such values are equivalent to correlation coefficients and therefore make it possible to uncover groups of comedians on the basis of factor analysing these scores.

The results of this analysis produced eight factors each of which was named and interpreted as follows:

Factor I was composed of the comediennes Diller, Burnette, Rivers and Ball. Insofar as these are all women, it appeared appropriate to label this factor 'Sex' with the female end of the scale most dominant.

Factor II contained only Black comedians, Wilson, Cosby, Gregory, Sammy Davis Jr. and Moms Mabley. This factor would seem best defined as a 'Black' factor.

Factor III included Carson and Cavett, most strongly, and Newhart and Steve Allen, less strongly. These four comedians all have done late-night talk shows and for this reason we labelled Factor III as a 'Night talk' or 'Verbal facility' factor.

Factor IV, which consisted of the Smothers Brothers and Pat Paulson, was considered a 'Contiguity' factor, largely because Paulson has often worked with the Smothers Brothers.

Factor V, which contained the comedians Dick Van Dyke and Morey Amsterdam, was called 'Contiguity factor II' largely because these two particular comedians also have often worked with one another. Although comedians contained in both of these last two factors may do the same kind of comedy, we felt that they were grouped together by the present word-association procedure largely because they worked together on the same TV shows, not necessarily because of any intrinsically similar comic style.

Factor VI showed heaviest loadings for Rickles and Leonard and seemed to be best described as a 'Hostility' factor. Further examination of those comedians who loaded less strongly, that is Winters, King, Adams, and Gleason etc., also substantiated this feeling.

Factors VII and VIII, because of a strong time reference, were labelled 'Generation I' and 'Generation II', respectively. Factor VIII, Generation II, was comprised of the oldest comedians in our analysis: Laurel and Hardy, Chaplin,

Fields and the Marx Brothers; while Factor VII was comprised of Comedians who were in vogue during the late 1950s and early 1960s: Hope, Benny, Skelton and Berle. Again, it might be possible to argue that each of these factors defines a comic style; unfortunately the data are sufficiently equivocal on this point as to warrant caution. Further analysis, involving older respondents, might help to clarify these factors.

On the basis of these results, Pollio and co-workers (1972) suggested that there are two different types of comic dimensions, with one reflecting the *surface* properties of a comedian and with the other reflecting his or her particular *style* properties. By surface properties, they simply meant those factors that have to do with the comedian's personal attributes [sex, colour or with whom he or she works regularly (see Factors IV and V)]. The overriding style factors emerging in their analysis were best defined by Factors III and VI, with III representing the 'urban, late-night talk comedian', and VI representing something they called the 'aggressive tone' of the comic best exemplified by Rickles and others. Taken together, these factors can be described as a verbal fluency factor and a personal hostility factor. Whereas not all comedians seem to have verbal fluency to as great a degree as Carson and Cavett, far more do seem to make use of hostility to a greater or lesser extent.

In one sense these results are quite satisfying—they reveal groupings that are intuitively meaningful—yet in another sense they are somewhat disappointing—no new information regarding the dimensions of comic art seem to have been uncovered. For this reason we decided to ask a different set of students to provide us with five adjectives describing each comedian on the previous list in the hope that this would provide us with some less obvious dimensions. Since results of a pilot study showed that *funny* almost invariably occurred as a response, we asked subjects not to include this particular adjective.

The first result of interest concerns the nature of the adjectives produced, and here we were absolutely amazed by the sheer quantity of unpleasant or negative adjectives such as fat, ugly, nasty, gross, clumsy, stupid, deformed, and so on. As a matter of fact, of the 32 adjectives produced 20 or more times in response to these comedians, we found that 17 or 53% were negatively toned. Of the remaining 15 adjectives, 11 (or 34%) could be coded as pleasant while four (13%) were ethnic words such as Jew or Black, which we coded as neutral. If we considered adjectives that occurred in these data 15 or more times, the percentage of negatively toned adjectives was about 54% (22/41) while the comparable figure for adjectives occurring 10 or more times was 42% (25/60). Considering only those 10 adjectives which occurred 50 or more times, 7 turned out to be negatively toned.

This predilection for negative adjectives is quite marked, and in order to determine whether or not it reflects the usual proportion of negative words in the language we looked at some earlier demographic work on word-association by Wilcox (1968). In this earlier work, Wilcox found that of the 360 words— including all parts of speech—contained in the Jenkins, Russell and Suci (1958) word norms, only 72 or 20% were negatively toned, 187 or 52% were

positively toned, and 101 or 28 % were neutral. A Chi-square test of these normative values against those reported for the comedian data produced a value of
18·63 ($p < 0·001$) indicating that comedian names, considered as stimuli, tend
to draw out far more negative adjectives than a simple random selection of
words in English ought to do. As a matter of fact, Wilcox reports that when he
attempted to draw a fairly equal representative sample of positive and negative
words the best he could do was to get 25 % unpleasant words. Comedians just
seem to bring out the worst in adjectives, and they seem to do it at well beyond a
chance level.

There were other interesting demographic aspects to the adjectives produced.
For one, ethnic and religious adjectives such as Black, Jewish and Italian, were
very much in evidence, as were sex-marked adjectives, such as female, effemi-
nate, and so on. Although this finding may seem surprising at first glance, an
examination of the specific comedians evoking ethnic, sexual or religious labels
showed that these comedians tend to make a point of, for example, their ethnic
background; that is, Rickles, Lewis, Hackett, and others as Jews; Dean Martin
as Italian, Flip Wilson as Black, and so forth. What was also interesting was
that no comedian was ever hit with the adjective Protestant, Methodist or
Church of England.

Does this mean that there are no male Protestant comedians or simply that
being Protestant is no way an occasion for laughter? As one way of examining
the ethnic background of the 42 comedians on the list (counting comedy pairs
as two comedians), we counted up the number of Jewish and Black comedians
and found easily 15 Jews (36 %, not counting Sammy Davis, Jr.), five Blacks
(counting Sammy Davis, Jr.) and two Catholics—Irish or Italian. Of the
remaining 21 comedians, 3 were Protestant women (plus 1 Jewish and 1 Black
woman) leaving a total of 16 *bona fide* Protestant male comedians. Either being
a White Anglo-Saxon Protestant (WASP) male is not funny or the majority
culture does not encourage or tolerate its children to become comedians.

Parenthetically, we ought to note that this particular sample of comedians
was culled from responses produced by students at the University of Tennessee.
Demographic data indicate that only some 500 out of roughly 20,000 students
checked their entrance blanks as being of the Jewish faith. Hence, any estimate
of the number of Jewish comedians provided by responses produced by this
particular sample of students is probably an underestimate, given the relatively
small proportion of Jewish students at the University of Tennessee. In support
of this, some of the Jewish comedians not appearing on the list were rather
surprising, to wit, the following well-known Jewish comics were never mentioned: Phil Silvers, Ed Wynn, Carl Reiner, Mel Brooks, Danny Kaye, Woody
Allen, Toodie Fields, Marty Feldman, Jack Carter and Harvey Korman.

The conclusion that seems clear is that certain groups, such as Jewish males,
are over-represented among comedians and that certain other groups, WASP
males, are under-represented. This, in turn, suggests that certain minority
groups reward comedy as a way of relating to the social world while others do
not. Erikson (1951), in commenting on one of his case studies, indicates how a

Jewish child when moved to a predominantly non-Jewish environment adopted his aggressive intelligence to become a teasing wit; a strategy which allowed him to express both his aggression and his intellect in a socially controlled and non-threatening manner. Although a complete characterization of what it means to be a Jew (or analogously a Black, an Irishman, an Italian, or perhaps even a woman) is beyond the scope of the present chapter, what does seem clear is that as a technique of acceptable social aggression humour represents an ideal strategy. Not only does it allow for an indirect expression of aggression it also affords an opportunity to deflate and thus to change the damaging prejudices and pretences of the majority society. As a matter of fact, comedy and humour meet so many diverse needs as to be a natural for non-majority group members; particularly for a non-majority group such as Jews which strongly endorses verbal and intellectual virtuosity.

Our original purpose in collecting adjectives was to discover how comedians tend to be grouped in terms of attributes and it is about time we got back to that job. Using an evaluation procedure identical to the one used in the Pollio and co-workers (1972) study, ten factors were extracted from the present data, with Table 10.4 presenting these results. Naming factors always presents the would-be factor-namer with a bit of a problem; in the present case, however, we did have the adjectives to go on. Basically all of the comedians comprising Factor I evoke, to a greater or lesser extent, the words *crazy*, *stupid*, *clumsy*, *ridiculous* and *dumb* and suggest the phrase, 'awkward clown'. Factor II involves the words *intelligent*, *witty*, *interesting*, *smart* and to a very small degree, *short*, and for this reason suggests the general factor 'intelligent wit.' Factor III contains the words *fat*, *bald*, *old*, *ugly*, *crazy*; Factor VI contains many of the same words, *fat*, *old*, *short*, *talented*, as does Factor X: *short*, *fat*, *old*, *nasty*. Taken together, these factors suggest that there are three types of fat comedians: those that are a little weird and a little nasty (III), those that are

Table 10.4 Factor loadings for the first comedian adjective study

Factor	Comedians (Factor loadings in parentheses)
I	Jerry Lewis (0·39); Don Adams (0·37); Lucille Ball (0·36); Phyllis Diller (0·26)
II	Dick Cavett (0·43); Johnny Carson (0·38); Morey Amsterdam (0·31)
III	Jonathan Winters (0·50); Jack E. Leonard (0·37)
IV	Milton Berle (0·34); Phyllis Diller (0·28); Danny Thomas (0·25); Lucille Ball (0·22); Jack Benny (0·22)
V	Bill Cosby (0·50); Dick Gregory (0·45)
VI	W. C. Fields (0·42); Jackie Gleason (0·35); Buddy Hackett (0·33)
VII	Pat Paulson (0·34); Laurel (and Hardy) (0·32); Don Knotts (0·30)
VIII	Steve Allen (0·38); Bill Cosby (0·33); Dick Van Dyke (0·22); Carol Burnette (0·21); Sid Caesar (0·21)
IX	Bob Hope (0·40)
X	Don Rickles (0·37); Morey Amsterdam (0·33)

chubby and pleasant (VI) and those that are not weird and not pleasant, just *fat*, *dumb* and/or *nasty* (X).

This same 'fat–skinny' factor emerged in slightly different forms in Factor VII where the only word in common is *skinny* as well as in Factor VIII where the major overlapping adjective was *thin*. Factor VIII also contained the words *tall* and *witty*, and suggests a general pleasant and attractive aspect to these comedians.

Of the remaining factors, Factor V is clearly a 'Black' factor, while Factor IV, more than anything else, is an 'age' factor with all comedians loading on this factor defined by the adjective *old*, or some variation thereof. Factor IX is overwhelmingly defined by Bob Hope and to a lesser extent by four other comedians. While no clear definition emerges from the adjective data—there is no neat overlap—Factor IX seems to be 'fat cat' factor although this is only a weak guess and not offered very strongly at that.

What now can we say of the two sets of results? As in the case of the Pollio and co-workers (1972) study, descriptive surface traits seemed to predominate: *old*, *fat*, *clumsy*, *Black*; although a 'hostility' factor (Factor X, and, to a lesser extent, Factor III) and a 'verbal intelligence' factor (Factor II and, to a lesser extent, Factor VIII) also do appear in the data. Unlike our first attempt at partitioning the comedian's world, no sex of comedian or work-contiguity factors appeared in this analysis. As in the first analysis, a strong time-marking did emerge once again probably best captured by the adjectives *old* or *old-fashioned*. The strong emergence of a *fat–skinny* dimension also appears clearly supported by the data.

Both of these analyses involved rather special procedures and it is possible to feel that some of the results specific to each can be accounted for on the basis of task demands. Both contiguity factors found in the first analysis seem best explained on the basis of asking for comedian-associations. That is, when you ask a respondent to give the first other comedian he or she thinks of in response to Comedian X, it is not unreasonable to expect that much of the time the response will be that other comedian, X works with most often. For this reason, both contiguity factors are probably artifacts of the association method. By similar reasoning, the particular constraints imposed by asking for adjectives seems to guarantee that the data will be forced in certain ways and here the ubiquitous adjectives seem to be *fat* and *skinny*, or some variation thereof. To be sure, there would seem to be quite strong body-typing for comedians, but just as surely, it may be a central rather than a trivial attribute only for a select few comedians: *fat* as a description for Rickles is probably nowhere as critical an adjective as *skinny* is for Don Knotts; yet the way in which overlap coefficients are computed fails to take centrality of trait into account.

In general, however, the two sets of data are in agreement, and somewhat contrary to common sense. Before we come to any conclusions, however, it seems best to report the results of one further analysis, this time by Pollio and Edgerly with Al Best of the University of North Carolina. In this last analysis we tried to replicate the preceding study, only this time making use of a larger number of respondents and a better format for presenting comedian names. As previously, student-subjects were asked to provide five adjectives for each comedian. Most importantly, however, we not only ran a factor analysis on the data, we also ran a hierarchical clustering and a multi-dimensional scaling analysis as well.

For reasons that are not easy to explain, results of the factor analysis did not yield an easily interpretable pattern, producing only two factors accounting for only about 15% of the variance. Although there were groupings similar to those produced by earlier work, the rather small percentage of the variance accounted for seemed to indicate that in the present case factor analysis was not a completely satisfactory analytic technique.

The results of a hierarchical clustering analysis, as well as that of multi-dimensional scaling, produced more reasonable and interpretable groupings and these data are presented in Figure 10.3. The 'swimming pools' appearing in the plot represent groupings uncovered by the clustering analysis, while the specific location of each comedian represents results uncovered by multi-dimensional scaling. The groupings provided by the clustering programme seem easily interpretable: Group I, appearing in the upper right-hand part of the figure, represents a cluster of Black comics. Moving counter-clockwise, Group II represents a Loud—Crazy, zany cluster, Group III a self-deprecating Skinny—Weird cluster, while Group IV represents a sarcastic or satirical old man cluster.

An analysis of proximities—that is, how close which comedian is to which

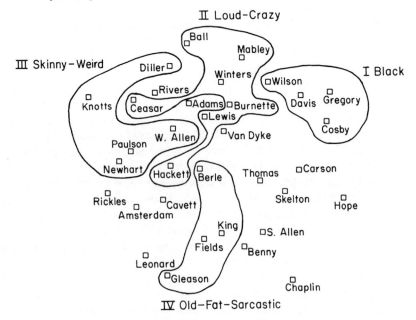

Figure 10.3 Groupings uncovered by hierarchical clustering and multi-dimensional scaling techniques

other comedian—presents a comparable picture and suggests that it is possible to label different regions of the figure. So, for example, if we overlay a clock face on Figure 10.3 it is possible to locate a *Black* neighbourhood between 1:00 and 2:00. At about 12:00 and going toward 11:00 is a *woman* neighbourhood, while a *skinny–weird* grouping appears at about 10:00. A *nasty* grouping makes its appearance between 8:00 and 7:00 with a *small* grouping (Amsterdam and Cavett) occupying a position closer to the centre at this same location. At 7:00 and going toward 6:00 a *fat* group appears followed by a loosely structured *old* group running from slightly past 5:00 to 4:00. Right above this group and right below the Black group there is a *rich* grouping which ends at about 3:00. The one neighbourhood that has yet to be specified seems to fall just to the left of the centre between 9:00 and 11:00 and seems best described as *loud and crazy*—that is, Jerry Lewis, Milton Berle, Carol Burnette, Buddy Hackett, Dick Van Dyke and others.

All of these nine or so neighbourhoods were named in accordance with the words used to describe the comedians falling in that locale. If we specify each of these neighbourhoods in terms of their major descriptors we find the following adjectives: *Black, women, skinny–weird, nasty, small, fat, old, rich* and *loud–crazy*. Almost all of these adjectives have appeared in earlier analyses and suggest that they represent the major dimensions serving to describe the *persona* of any presently active comedian. In addition we again note the relatively larger number of clearly deprecating adjectives as well as the occurrence of ethnic and sex-marked descriptors.

These three sets of data, involving as they do three different sets of respondents as well as three different analytic techniques, are remarkably similar. Comedians are thought about, associated about, and grouped about a relatively small number of attributes, with these attributes generally having something to do with what the comedian looks like (generally negative: *fat, old, small*) as well as with how he or she behaves (again generally negative: *clumsy, loud, zany,* etc.). More than either of our first two analyses, results obtained through the use of multi-dimensional scaling places *loud* and *zany* people at the centre of the comedian's world. If we look carefully at both the specific individuals occupying this region as well as at the specific adjectives used, we see that this centre is composed of a somewhat undesirable-looking set of fairly zany people; in short, a set of people who can best be described as clownish. Although each of these clown-like people has other attributes as well, their awkwardness and their generally benign (or at worst) self-deprecating actions lead us again to the conclusion that the basic form of comic art is that of the clown, and that all comedians, no matter how polished or articulate, draw their inspiration from this common comic centre.

The comedian's world: some behavioural definitions

Word-association and adjective studies provided a taxonomy of comedians based on a single subject's attitude toward a single set of comedians; nowhere do they take the crucial next step of seeing how such attitudes relate to behaviour. In order to take such a step it is necessary to observe groups of people responding to comedians in that special social setting known as an audience. Preliminary pilot observations involving audience response (Pollio, Mers and Lucchesi, 1972) seemed to indicate that whether you listened to a particular comedian within the context of a group of friends or a group of strangers made a big difference in how much you laughed or smiled. It was not an unusual event to find that comedians we thought hilarious would produce absolutely no response from an audience of randomly selected undergraduate students.

Then, too, there was the rather serendipitous finding that groups of people who waited together for a long time before listening to a comedian often produced more laughter than a group that did little or no waiting. One dramatic incident of this sort occurred on a very rainy Spring day when students came into the laboratory dripping wet and spent about half-an-hour bitching to each other about the weather and about how wet they all were from the walk over to the laboratory. Although no previous group of strangers had laughed more than two or three times at a particularly nasty routine by Don Rickles this group went into paroxysms of laughter and asked us to replay the tape again. Group cohesiveness seemed to be critically important, at least for Rickles, and occasioned the next set of studies.

In order to test the effects of group cohesion in a more systematic fashion, Murphy and Pollio (1973) and Murphy (1975) formed groups of friends and strangers, video-taped them, and then played them comedy routines performed by Bill Cosby and Don Rickles. An examination of these tapes showed marked differences between 'friends' and 'strangers' listening to Rickles and only small differences between 'friends' and 'strangers' listening to Cosby. Basically, 'friends' laughed and moved a lot while listening to Rickles, while 'strangers' seemed to move very little and to find the material, if not distasteful, then at least unfunny.

In order to quantify such intuitive observations, Murphy and Pollio (1973) developed a category rating system and counted the number of times each of the behaviours occurred for each comedian under the 'friend' and 'stranger' conditions. Table 10.5 presents these data; for ease of presentation the behavioural observation categories are divided into (a) those that deal with personal activity and group interaction and (b) those that deal specifically with laughing and smiling. Looking first at Category (a) the overall picture is that people listening to both Cosby and Rickles show less behaviour of almost any and all kinds when in a group of strangers. Although there are differences between both Cosby groups, the differences between friends and strangers listening to Rickles were much more marked, with Rickles strangers comparatively inactive and scarcely looking at one another.

Turning now to laughing and smiling, strong differences emerged between the two comedians. For laughing, the comedian difference was clearly significant as was the interaction of group by comedian. A comparison of means suggested

Table 10.5 Mean number of responses for all behavioural categories

Behavioural category	Comedians			
(a) Activity and group interaction responses	Cosby		Rickles	
	Friends	Strangers	Friends	Strangers
Hand Movement	20·04	15·35	19·22	8·85
Turning Head	3·86	1·75	5·95	0·80
Vocalization	2·36	0·55	2·59	0·16
Lowering Head	1·90	1·70	2·31	1·50
Head to Forehead, head lowered	0·27	0·05	0·77	0·15
(b) Humour responses				
Smiling	14·18	15·30	14·81	8·80
Laughing	16·04	20·50	18·00	8·95

that during Rickles, laughing was greatly augmented in the 'friends' groups while during Cosby, strangers tended to laugh only a bit more than friends. For smiling, a similar pattern emerged though there appeared to be little difference between the two Cosby conditions. The comedian effect was significant, as was the interaction of comedian by group. As was true of laughing, strangers presented with Rickles smiled far less than did friends.

In addition to these direct behavioural observations, audience members were also asked to fill out a questionnaire dealing with both comedians. The results of this questionnaire revealed no systematic differences between the 'friends' and 'strangers' groups in the amount of previous exposure to either comedian with most subjects reporting that they had not heard either of the records previously. The percentage of 'friends' indicating a preference for Rickles over Cosby was 0·35, as compared to 0·02 for 'strangers', implying that while one out of three friends expressed a preference for Rickles, only one out of 50 strangers did.

Although a number of further analyses were done (see Murphy and Pollio, 1974, for a more complete presentation) it seems better at this point to note what present results suggest about the comic worlds created by Rickles and Cosby. Here differences between comedians are striking: Cosby creates a world of the nice guy, ruminating about the misadventures of childhood and the perpetual battles a kid has with his arch-enemies—adults and school. Rickles, on the other hand, perpetuates a world of hostility where failure, incompetence and inferiority are focal points, with the scapegoat of this humour some unfortunate soul in the audience whose verbal competence is invariably microscopic compared to the quick-witted and acid-tongued Rickles. Laughing invariably comes at someone else's expense. Rickles is so good at this, that perhaps in order to laugh with him it is necessary to have group support. A group of people who do not know one another must find the situation unsettling and the material unfunny. Friends, however, presumably support one another thereby making it unlikely that any one individual would personally feel intimidated by the jokes of one man. A group's failure to laugh, typified in the 'Rickles–strangers' group, should, and does, have an inhibitory effect on any single audience member. Smiling, laughing and behaviour in general are inhibited and thus none of the conditions necessary for humour expression are present.

In terms of a taxonomy of comedians these results suggest that Cosby and Rickles serve to define two different types of comic styles: one that focuses the individual audience member on the here and now (Rickles) of his experiences, and a second (Cosby) which allows the individual member to transcend the situation and to roam about in a sensibly-nonsensical world. The terms usually applied to these differences would seem to be those that distinguish a comic from a humorist. The comic (and some of his near relatives—the nasty clown and the sarcastic wit) all focus the person on his immediate situation thereby making group structure and group solidarity a key issue. The humorist (and his relatives—the story-teller and the fabulist) all focus the audience member on himself and his experiences outside of the present context.

It is perhaps for this latter reason that there was slightly more laughing and smiling to Cosby under the 'strangers' condition than under the 'friends' condition. For Cosby, a situation or context other than the present one is crucial and, for this reason, little effect of audience composition was found. On the contrary, because Rickles does focus the individual audience member on the here and now of his experience, great differences were found in the responsiveness of 'friends' and 'strangers' groups and this also is to be expected.

In order to examine the effect of audience reactivity on a different sample of people, Murphy (1975) in his doctoral dissertation, made use of two 9-minute comedy routines done by George Carlin and the ever-useful Bill Cosby. For this experiment there were three different conditions: in Condition I student-shills were present who laughed and smiled all the way through a given routine; in Condition II, shills were present who neither laughed nor smiled during either routine, while in Condition III, there were no shills present, with this condition serving as a control against which to evaluate Conditions I and II.

Murphy trained his shills by having them study the behaviours produced by audience members in the earlier Murphy and Pollio (1973) experiment. For Condition I, the shills—who always consisted of one male and one female stooge—studied the behaviour of laughing subjects, while for Condition II, they studied the behaviours produced by audience members in the 'Rickles–strangers' group. Therefore, not only did shills not laugh and smile, they produced many constrained behaviours similar to those produced naturally by subjects in the earlier experiment.

Table 10.6 presents the mean number of smiles and laughs produced by non-shill audience members under all three conditions. As can be seen, shills potentiated a far greater number of laughs and smiles under Condition I relative to Condition III for both comedians. With the exception of smiles for

Table 10.6 Effects of shills on audience response to Cosby and Carlin

Shill	Mean number of responses			
	Smile		Laugh	
	Cosby	Carlin	Cosby	Carlin
I Present–laugh	15·61	13·76	12·72	20·29
II Present–no laugh	7·63	8·86	5·13	7·52
III Absent (control)	9·90	8·10	8·67	12·09

Data from Murphy (1975)

Carlin–Condition II, shills were able to depress laughing and smiling for all other conditions of the experiment. In general, however, results were quite clear: even for such a relatively not here-and-now comedian such as Cosby, shills were able to effect group responsivity to a marked degree thereby indicating again the enormously powerful role of audience peer behaviour upon response to humour.

In another condition of the same experiment, Murphy had shills switch from laughing to no-laughing as he switched from one comedian to the other. In the case of a Cosby to Carlin switch, subjects listening to Carlin produced 6·8 smiles and 7·2 laughs. This compares to 8·1 smiles and 12·1 laughs for Carlin under control conditions (Condition III). In the case of a Carlin to Cosby shift, subjects listening to Cosby produced 8·9 smiles and 8·8 laughs where control subjects had smiled 9·9 times and laughed 8·1 times. Such differences between control and experimental conditions indicate that changing from humorous to non-humorous behaviours on the part of shills produced a smaller change for subjects listening to Cosby than for subjects listening to Carlin. These findings agree with earlier results involving Cosby, where he was defined as a story-teller comedian, and therefore less subject to the vicissitudes of audience responsivity than other comedians. These new findings again support a taxonomy of comedians based on the distinction between here-and-now (Rickles) and there-and-then (Cosby), and suggest that such a taxonomy is probably quite general across comic performers.

Here, our behavioural data end. 'The time has come,' as the Walrus said, 'to speak of many things'; and one of these many things must be that audience factors can and do exert an enormous influence upon the response to comedy. This is true whether we assess the effects of group cohesion or the effects of specially trained shills. In a sense, this is as it should be, for it suggests that audiences have their own inner dynamics and that such dynamics are often as important as the material used by a particular performer in bringing about a desired artistic effect.

A certain class of comedians has always understood this and to a greater or lesser degree all comedians do make use of their crowds. More than any other performer, the stand-up comic needs, and uses, audience feedback so that it is incorrect, strictly speaking, to talk about here-and-now and there-and-then comedians in some absolute sense; rather, we need to recognize that all comedy depends upon certain here-and-now factors whether these involve group cohesiveness, shills, or the subtle (or gross) give-and-take that goes on in nightclub and stage performances.

Humour is a fragile phenomenon and the comedian as custodian of the phenomenon is, and must be, ever mindful of the fine, delicate balance existing between kidding and hurting, between social commentary and prejudice, between controlled fantasy and madness, as well as between all of those aversive states that comedy depends upon and their controlled comic counterparts. The comedian is an artist, and his or her artistry consists precisely in being able to produce in us experiences involving the most fundamental and significant of human passions in a way that is restorative and cathartic rather than destructive and regressive. In the end, as Welsford has suggested, the comedian, and all of his or her kin—the story-teller, the clown, the fool, the comic actor, as well as the naturally occurring witty person—provide a situation which allows each of us a bit of transcendance; a bit of transcendance designed to make sport of those situations, events and taboos that lie heaviest upon us if seen only from an earnest and serious perspective. Whether in cap and bells, spotted silks or immaculate garb, the comedian is often the author of such exhilarating moments of transcendance and for this reason a person of special worth and/or significance.

SUMMARY

The curtain falls on the final act, the last antic, the closing incongruity. The audience, the tribe, the viewer slowly file back to their respective realities, taking with them a sense of freedom and the acknowledgement that for awhile they have transcended. And the catalysts of that freedom—the comedians— return to their world satisfied that they were the momentary vehicles for that relief.

All that remains now is the job of the critics and summarizers, both of whom reluctantly assault their typewriters in an effort to reconstruct the complex web called *Comedians and Comic Style*. The first fact they must take account of is the universality of the comic as a social reality. But comedians, be they clowns or cocktail-party wits, cannot exist without their attendant audiences; and as our play has shown this interaction is vital for the successful evocation of laughter. A more analytic study of social contexts, be they psychiatric hospital staff meetings or group psychotherapy encounters, reveals that most attempts at humour involve an initiator (the Wit) and a target (the Butt); and that all attempts at being humorous contain from a little to a lot of aggression and/or hostility.

Again, it is an analysis of social settings which provides the conclusion that most laughter is initiated by men and that women much more frequently laugh or smile, but hardly ever joke, in these contexts.

Turning now to professional comedians, it is clear that they are usually described in terms of two primary properties: their surface and stylistic characteristics, and that most often their personal attributes tend to be negative, for instance, fat, skinny and crazy.

But, the comedian is not independent of his audience, and here findings are quite dramatic—group cohesiveness is critically important in determining who laughs at what, when, and under what conditions. Friends apparently support one another, while strangers can and often do inhibit laughter.

Regardless of the fact that comedians are most often described in negative terms, one fact remains clear: the social event of humour allows for the cathartic release of aggressions, hostilities and taboos and provides for a private–public affirmation that such activities are acceptable providing an appropriate balance is maintained. This balance is provided, of course, by the very special artistry of the Clown and all of his near and far relatives—the comic actor, the comedian, the story-teller, the fool and, finally, the naturally occurring witty person.

REFERENCES

Charles, L. H. (1945). The clown's function. *Journal of American Folklore*, **58**, 25–34.

Coser, R. L. (1959). Some social functions of laughter. *Human Relations*, **12**, 171–182.

Coser, R. L. (1960). Laughter among colleagues. *Psychiatry*, **23**, 81–95.

Deese, J. (1965). *The Structure of Associations in Language and Thought*. Baltimore: The Johns Hopkins Press.

Edgerly, J. W., and Pollio, H. R. (1974). Laughing and crying in college students. Unpublished paper, University of Tennessee.

Erikson, E. H. (1951). *Childhood and Society*. New York: Norton.

Goodchilds, J. D. (1959). Effects of being witty on position in the social structure of a small group. *Sociometry*, **22**, 261–272.

Goodchilds, J. D. (1972). On being witty: causes, correlates, and consequences. In J. H. Goldstein and P. E. McGhee (Eds.), *The Psychology of Humor: Theoretical Perspectives and Empirical Issues*. New York: Academic Press.

Goodrich, A. J., Henry, J., and Goodrich, D. W. (1954). Laughter in psychiatric staff conferences: a sociopsychiatric analysis. *American Journal of Orthopsychiatry*, **24**, 175–184.

Jenkins, J. J., Russell, W. A., and Suci, G. (1958). An atlas of semantic profiles for 360 words. *American Journal of Psychology*, **71**, 688–699.

Kambouropoulou, P. (1926). Individual differences in the sense of humor. *American Journal of Psychology*, **37**, 268–278.

Klapp, O. E. (1972). *Heroes, Villains, and Fools: The Changing American Character*. Englewood Cliffs, New Jersey: Prentice-Hall.

Levine, J. (1961). Regression in primitive clowning. *Psychoanalytic Quarterly*, **30**, 72–83.

Ludovici, A. M. (1932). *The Secret of Laughter*. London: Constable.

Lorenz, K. (1966). *On Aggression*. New York: Harcourt, Brace & World.

Middleton, R., and Moland, J. (1959). Humor in Negro and White subcultures: A study of jokes among university students. *American Sociological Review*, **24**, 61–69.

Murphy, B. (1975). *The Effect of Audience Composition on Response to Humor*. Unpublished Doctoral Dissertation, University of Tennessee.

Murphy, B., and Pollio, H. R. (1973). I'll laugh if you will. *Psychology Today*, **7**, 106–109.

Murphy, B., and Pollio, H. R. (1974). The many faces of humor. *Journal of Personality and Social Psychology*, submitted.

Peterson, P. (1973). An initial look at humor in group therapy. Paper presented at Southeastern Psychological Association, New Orleans, Louisiana.

Peterson, P. (1975). *Laughter in a Therapy Group.* Unpublished Doctoral Dissertation, University of Tennessee.

Pollio, H. R., Edgerly, J. W., and Jordan, R. (1972). The comedians world: some tentative mappings. *Psychological Reports,* **30**, 387–391.

Pollio, H. R., Mers, R., and Lucchesi, W. (1972). Humor, laughter and smiling: Some preliminary observations of funny behaviors. In J. H. Goldstein and P. E. McGhee (Eds.), *The Psychology of Humor: Theoretical Perspectives and Empirical Issues.* New York: Academic Press.

Smith, E. E., and Goodchilds, J. D. (1963). The wit in large and small established groups. *Psychological Reports,* **13**, 273–274.

Smith, E. E., and White, H. L. (1965). Wit, creativity and sarcasm. *Journal of Applied Psychology,* **49**, 131–134.

Welsford, E. (1935). *The Fool: His Social and Literary History.* London: Faber and Faber.

Wilcox, R. (1968). *The Structure of Meaningfulness.* Unpublished Doctoral Dissertation, University of Tennessee.

Young, P. T. (1937). Laughing and weeping, cheerfulness, and depression: A study of moods among college students. *Journal of Social Psychology,* **8**, 311–334.

Section II

Using Humour

Chapter 11

Humour as a Creative Experience: The Development of a Hollywood Humorist[1]

William F. Fry, Jr.
and
Melanie Allen

Creativity presents many faces to the world. We have recently been involved in a rather novel area of research, studying among other things the relationship between creativity and humour in the lives of professional comedy writers. These people are relative newcomers in the troupe of mirth-makers—the clowns, the comedians, the harlequins, the jesters, the humorists, the jokers.

During their brief time on stage, the professional comedy writers have experienced audiences of hundreds of thousands, sometimes millions. Through their productions for the entertainment world, they capture and articulate common values, conflicts, and current viewpoints on an international scale. The catharsis and coping function of their humour contribute powerfully to the trending of the world spirit, thus affecting significantly the evolution of our human society.

In this chapter we will present general comments on creativity and a discussion of humour as a creative process. These theoretical matters will receive extensive illumination by data drawn from our interviews with one of the eight subjects of our study.

We would like to be able to state simply and conclusively that humour is creative, let it go at that, and proceed immediately into a discussion of the psychology of professional comedy writers. However, this splendid simplicity is not possible since there are too many people who are sceptical about humour in particular, about psychology in general, and especially about humour being considered as creative. And so, it behoves us to begin this discussion with some definitions.

THE CREATIVE EXPERIENCE

A succinct, preliminary definition of creativity has been distilled from many sources in a book by Fabun (1969). Creativity is therein defined as 'the process by which original (novel) patterns are formed and expressed'. 'Patterns' is defined as 'original combinations of familiar or common items'.

A formula expression has been offered by Haefele (1962):

$$A + B \rightarrow C$$

A and B are designated as familiar or common items, and C is the original pattern resulting from their combination. The formula could, of course, read:

$$A + B + \ldots \rightarrow C$$

depending on the number of items combined.

Certain elements of this basic definition require further elaboration. The 'combinations' are specified as original to the individual creator's experience, but not necessarily new to the world—which they *may* be—for qualification as that individual's creativity. Also, it is important to emphasize the familiarity or commonness of the component items (A, B, etc.). This emphasis effectively eliminates those patterns which are made up of totally idiosyncratic, esoteric or incomprehensible items.

Some purists call for the creative product to be one which has a social value, one which solves problems in a practical and/or useful way, one which increases order or unity, and/or one which embraces a palpable reality. The net effect of these conditions is to eliminate vast numbers of creative products that might be acceptable under the basic definition. Any national Patent Office will have a magnificent collection of such curiosities.

The distinction between invention and discovery is to be considered. The basic definition does not have a place for that which is creatively discovered, only for that which is formed, or invented. This limitation is unacceptable, since it eliminates the major part of scientific creativity. So, an expanded definition states, 'Creativity is the process by which original patterns are formed and expressed, *or discovered.*' (Fabun, 1969). The formula represents this expansion by a double-headed arrow:

$$A + B \longleftrightarrow C$$

$\rightarrow$ represents creative synthesis, or invention; $\leftarrow$ represents creative analysis, or discovery.

There are those who proclaim that the *process* of invention, or of discovery—rather than the invented patterns of discovered combinations—is the true creativity. The characteristics of this creative process have been subjected to more intense study than most other aspects of creativity (Ghiselin, 1952). It is presented as consisting of several stages, summarized as: desire or motivation, preparation, manipulation, or playing around with the items, incubation, intimation, illumination, and verification or examination (Fabun, 1969).

Much attention has been given to describing the *affective* consequence of being involved in the creative process. Important affective elements are said to be a feeling of relief, pleasure, diminution of tension and climax—each being associated with attainment of the state of illumination. This element adds an exclamation mark to the formula:

$$A + B \longleftrightarrow C!$$

For those who argue that the process *is* the creativity, the patterns or combinations are seen merely as ephemeral way-stations in the process or by-products of it. They characterize creativity as the pursuit of an objective that must always elude complete realization. The reach is more important than the grasp. We may quote Picasso who, as he finished one painting, discovered how he would do the next one better. It can be pointed out that the first law of thermodynamics leads to the second law, which anticipates Einstein, whose ideas blend with those of Planck, etc.

Many enthusiasts of process creativity consider some forms more creative than others (Roe, 1963). Their ranking gives highest score to process and lowest to product. The purity and dedication of the pursuit is the measure of creativity.

Another ranking looks to the *creator* and rates the creativity on the basis of the knowledge and skill he brings to his mission. The argument is that the more knowledgeable the creator is, the larger is the array of items at his disposal in forming the original combinations and the more complex or original, therefore, will be the products. Skill is similarly treated: the greater the skill in dealing with the items, the better the creative product.

It is obvious that most of these elaborations of the basic formula are oriented to the limiting and the narrowing of that which is to be considered creative. Most eliminate, rather than include or expand. Contrast this tendency with that found in Erich Fromm's (1959) definition, 'Creativity is the ability to see (or be aware) and to respond', or Rollo May's (1959), 'Creativity is the encounter of the intensively conscious human being with his world'. Or consider Henry Adams' (1964) statement, 'Chaos often breeds life, when order breeds habit'.

HUMOUR AND CREATIVITY

Where does humour fit into all this? It is quickly apparent that there is no problem with humour conforming to the basic definition of creativity. Most delineations of humour call attention to the element of incongruity, unexpectedness, surprise, uncertainty or incompatibility derived from bringing together the components that make up the joke, or whatever has stimulated the humour response. In his book *The Act of Creation*, Arthur Koestler (1964) makes this a major point in affiliating humour and creativity. He writes, 'The pattern underlying (comedy) is the perceiving of a situation or idea in two self-consistent but habitually incompatible frames of reference'. He also writes, 'The creative act of the humorist consists in bringing about a momentary fusion between two habitually incompatible frames of reference,' which, he says, consists in, 'bringing about a momentary fusion between two habitually incompatible matrices. Scientific discovery ... can be described in very similar terms—as the permanent fusion of matrices of thought previously believed to be incompatible'.

Now consider the issue of the familiar or common items that are the components of the original patterns. It is obvious that the elements of comedy must be perceived and comprehended by the audience. One does not laugh at a joke told in a language foreign to one (unless that is the joke). A blind person will not be amused by a cartoon at which he is unable to look. If a person is observed to be laughing at something ordinarily incomprehensible, he must have given personal meaning to that incomprehensibility; or he may be engaged in laughter which is primarily associated with social process, rather than mirth.

Our next consideration is that of social value, usefulness, increased order or palpable reality. There can surely be no doubt that humour has social value and practical usefulness beyond measure. Most observers would agree that humour has an immense impact in easing social conflicts, relieving tensions and promoting order. Humour proves invaluable to mankind in contributing to the sort of interpersonal rapport that accelerates resolution of social injustices, racial or sexual exploitation and political oppression. It is hardly an opium; humour exposes injustice, exploitation and oppression in such a way as to afford opportunities for relief which are not available when more passionate emotions, such as anger and hostility, are aroused.

In humour we are not concerned with the distinction between invention and discovery. A joke may be invented by a humorist and then discovered over and over again by millions. Each of us invents humour, sometimes even daily, just as each of us discovers the humour invented by others.

However, we may begin to sense an important issue when we consider the case of a dedicated humour inventor—such a person as will soon be described. This consideration of the humour inventor immediately brings us to that qualification of the basic creativity formula emphasizing the process over the components and their combinations.

Those who emphasize process describe stages of creativity, as listed earlier—desire, preparation, manipulation, etc. The dedicated inventors of humour we have studied describe stages in the process of creating their humour which conform to the descriptions of the stages of creativity. They consistently endorse the presence of the exclamation mark in the formula.

The characteristic of pursuit in the creativity process—'the reach is more important than the grasp'—is recognized in these humorists' lives. They are indeed dedicated, perhaps even driven, persons. Many have had other choices of life work, many have even followed other occupations at times during their lives. But their pursuit in the creation of humour reveals dedication and intensity. And, like Picasso, most of them never look back; they are straining forward to the next punchline.

The matter of skill is also found relevant in the story of the humour inventor. Some humorists seem to have burst forth *de novo*, without the necessity of having developed knowledge or skill. This phenomenon is more apparent than actual; not taken into consideration is the multitude of experiences with humour in the humorist's pre-professional life that have each added their increment of refinement to his talent. And for all humorists, whether they have seemed to burst forth or whether they can be observed to move slowly into place, it is evident that they improve as they pursue their occupation.

At this juncture, we are confronted with the impression that there may be two different humour experiences to be considered when relating humour to creativity. There are the humour-inventing, creativity-process experiences of the dedicated humorist: this category conforms to even the more limiting, rigorous definition of creativity. And there are the humour-discovering and humour-inventing experiences of the rest of us who do not become so deeply involved in the humour experience, to the same degree as the dedicated humorist. The latter conforms to the broader, basic definition of creativity, with its patterns, combinations and familiar components.

One might ask if there may be some other element in the picture, to help clarify this difference between the two types of humour experiences. Studies of play offer valuable information in response to this question. One of the present authors (Fry, 1963, 1970) has reported research that reveals the essential role of play in humour. Each humorous experience is found to be contained within the context of play. In other words, a play frame must be established around each episode for its humorous potential to be realized. The nature of this play frame is delineated in Gregory Bateson's (1956) monograph *The Message—'This is Play'* and can be summarized as stating, 'This behaviour is different from the behaviour which it is meant to represent'. In other words, a joke is not a factual report of an actual event.

The context of play is essential to all humour, but play seems to have an additional role in the lives of the dedicated humorist. Berlyne has made extensive studies of humour and play, as well as creativity, and has some valuable comments to offer. In his review *Laughter, Humour and Play* (1969) he states, 'playful activities are carried on "for their own sake" or for the sake of "pleasure". They are contrasted with "serious" activities, which deal with readily identifiable bodily needs or external threats or otherwise specifiable practical ends'. He also writes of the tension, excitement, then relief of tension and relaxation associated with play.

In addition to the fact that these characteristics can be recognized in most theories about creativity and descriptions of the creative experience, they may also be recognized in accounts of and by dedicated humorists on the subject of their humour-inventing. Specific examples of this will follow.

Although the play frame is found universally as a component of the formal structure of humour, the humour experiences of most of us regularly have underlying association with Berlyne's serious activities, in the sense that they have some impetus or some consequence or some input from the sources Berlyne indicates as 'bodily needs or external threats or otherwise specifiable practical ends' On the other hand, aside from earning a living (which he could have done or may already have done in other ways), the dedicated humorist does not have the life-experience-coping orientation in his humour creation. It is coping of a broader, more perduring nature, comparable to play that is carried out for its own sake, for pleasure. To him, at the moment, it *is* living. To the rest of us, humour is not *the* primary life process, rather it is making significant contributions to the life process.

In summation, when we focus on the creative process, there seems to come into shape two different humour-creativity entities. There is the common, widespread, frequent humour discovery experience which happens to all of us, and which conforms to the basic definition of creativity; and there is the much less common experience of the humour inventor. This experience answers the requirements of even the more rigorous definitions of creativity. And the role of play in these assorted phenomena supports and confirms our viewpoint in this differentiation.

The elitist requirement of skill and knowledge lends further support to this differentiation: the humour inventor is recognized as a talented professional, often with many years apprenticeship to his credit before he gets to do his own thing. Ignore the fact that much of this skill may be unobserved in himself by the humorist—many of the professionals interviewed in our studies were not able to provide conscious insights about technique; some were even puzzled by our line of questioning, though it is quite apparent from examination of their material that technical skills are in operation. And, of course, there are other humorists who are quite aware of the technical skill in their creations.

The rest of us, if we are lucky, may be humorous and amusing. We may have practised timing, enunciation and so on, and we may even be semi-professional in our knowledge. But ours is not the refined and integrated set of skills that identifies the professional. These skills may identify him as uniquely as a personal fingerprint. One rarely has difficulty distinguishing between material created by such outstanding humorists as James Thurber, S. J. Perelman, and Robert Benchley.

Interviews with Hollywood humorists

Nathan, a single-case study

We devote the rest of the chapter to providing the reader with materials from one of the interviews done as part of our recent study of creativity and humour in the development of the professional humorist. The eight interviews we conducted in order to gather material to provide us with information concerning the place of humour and creativity in the growth of the individual, and in the course of his or her life, have proven to be a ripe and rich source for us. Through these interviews, we have been able to gain further insight into the main motifs dominating humour research (the interviews in total comprise a book now in press, *Make 'em Laugh*, Science and Behavior Books, 1975).

When we began these interviews, we started with some specific interests in mind. We were seeking to determine whether:

(a) humour was a part of the early life-style of the person
(b) the interviewee was cognizant of how humour began to develop in his or her life
(c) there were any early models upon whom the subject patterned his 'style of humour'

(d) the transition to professional humour was accidental or deliberate

(e) the humorist's professional product and humour as he utilizes it in his personal life show a similarity in style, or whether the humorist uses humour in his personal life at all

(f) the interviewee is a performer in real life, acting as a vehicle for his own creativity

(g) the interviewee is aware of internal or external reinforcement contingencies operative out of his being humorous or creating humour

(h) the interviewee is aware of the place humour plays in his life, or whether any purpose it may serve is one of which he is unconscious.

Despite the fact *we* were cognizant of what it was we were 'looking for' and though we were able to cover all of these areas within the scope of the lengthy sessions with subjects, our procedure was one designed to elicit responses from the subject more or less spontaneously. We seldom had to ask specific questions. Rather, we attempted to put the writers at ease, let them 'go at it in their own way' after we let them know the *basic* purpose of the interviews, thus enabling us to be reflectors of the mirror-image they showed us. We reaped abundant rewards from this 'informal approach' in that the humorists shared both the glories and the traumas of their lives with us, and in that each interview gave us further ideas as to the elaboration of our own structure and focus. For instance, we were initially very interested in the writer's knowledge of rhythm, metre, colloquial jokes and so on, but soon found that, within the frame of reference of these interviews, this was possibly one of the least fruitful areas. We therefore moved to concentrate more on the process of the development of the particular human being and what he or she went through in the act of creating, and gave secondary attention to development of particular techniques, etc.

The interviews were conducted, as mentioned previously, in rather informal settings, usually during breaks in the writer's studio, or in his or her home. The interviews ranged from 1½ to 4 hours in length. Six of the subjects were men. One of the women was a writer herself; the second was the wife of the subject we will treat in this section. She was able to give us added insight and detail concerning her husband as he utilizes humour in his work and as a part of his life-style.

As mentioned previously, we only had to ask on occasion such questions as: 'Do you consciously perform so as to get attention?' Usually the interviewees came up with such materials themselves. Therefore, we do not need to be heavily interpretive in our retrospective analyses of these interviews. On the other hand, most of our subjects showed a charming and convincing naivety about 'humour theory' *per se*. Thus, when we discuss in this chapter and in other contexts what our materials demonstrate theoretically, the interpretations are customarily our own, although based strongly on the materials our subjects provided.

The utilization of the single-case study rather than any attempt to lump the group together as a whole comes from our belief that, although we are able to make various generalizations about our group as a whole, such as: 'the Jewish ethos in America of the Depression years seemed to breed humour', this in-depth kind of study is new and forsakes the *zealous* generalizer. We simply do not have enough material yet to force everything into a group schema. And each case seen individually is amazingly clear, making it difficult to force or bend data towards an individual's particular bias. We hope we can demonstrate this in the case of our subject, fictitiously named *Nathan*.

Of further interest to behavioural scientists is that basic controversy between those humour theorists who, after Freud, see humour as largely a *tension-reducing* experience. The Freudian view is clearly antagonistic to (or not representative of the broad scope of) the material presented earlier in this chapter. Humour as an example of the creative act in its full range of potential, or humour as play, is a sensitive means of coping, an adaptive vehicle for making life's compromises, and is, therefore, a *growth experience*.

Most of our subjects were Jewish, out of New York or East Coast backgrounds. As we mentioned, something in this 'sub-culture' seems to breed humour or the humour response. Several of the humorists described humour as a means of 'getting through' the Depression. One told us of his family dinners, wherein a group of six children and their folks were all 'funny'. One-upping each other grew more important to them than the absence of food on their plates.

Nathan is a highly successful writer, producer and director. His current programmes are at the top of the Nielson ratings; he has won several Emmys; he is a major figure in the industry today. His humour is not, however, reserved for those scripts which must be knocked off rapidly once a week. And he claims the creation of humour is anything but a mechanical endeavour. Though one or two of our writers seem detached from their products in their *living* this man clearly indicates that humour is an integral part of his life-style, life-stance, philosophy of life. Indeed, his raps with us were tinged with humour; he often broke serious moments with funny ones, laughing at us, 'And what brings *you* here today, Doctor?' or turning the tables on himself, 'playing the fool'.

This was the first description of early life given us by Nathan:

I was always funny, they tell me, when I was a kid. I started off being funny physically, not wanting to write, but *being* funny. I think I was in pain; I think most of it comes out of pain. I came from a family who yelled a great deal. They lived at the top of their lungs always. The only defence against that was to laugh at it, find what was funny in it. Like somebody beginning somebody for something, for anything . . . Let that somebody crawl on their knees across a room following somebody, on their knees. That can be funny—and terrible. I had lots of those sights in my youth to frighten me, but also to make me laugh and learn to see what was funny.

This quote, the source of which was his mother begging her father for something in the midst of a family quarrel, shows the humorist as a young boy in that very act of *discovery* which we mentioned earlier as one *kind* of humorous and creative experience.

Nathan existed in a situation of suspended tension. Money was short, his father was a prolific dreamer, waiting for his ship to come in, and his mother had stopped waiting and started worrying. Nathan slapsticked around the place, turning his eyelids inside out (he did it for us, by the way, on the spot, becoming a child again, *playing* for and with us), distracting the others *and himself* from the trauma at home.

Within a couple of years. he had developed another defence. Listening to his mother and father fighting, he would no longer retreat or do his eyelid routine but:

> I used to sit in the kitchen in full view of them, and have a pad and pencil, and I would be scoring them. What *could* I do after all? They paid no attention to me. I became largely an observer.

And Nathan was later to incorporate this and other domestic situations from real life into his work, *rediscovering* them, *reliving* them, and always keeping an ear out for the funny moment in the midst of family chaos.

We can easily see that, even in his youth, Nathan was not just using humour as a vehicle for *escape* but as a means for establishing a firm *identity*, one more secure than it might have been, in the midst of constant explosions and instability.

Although he cannot remember any one person after whom he *consciously* patterned his humour, he remembers his grandmother as being the 'subtlest, loveliest influence' in his life. He claims that even as an elderly woman, terribly ill and blind in an institution, she never lost this sense of humour. He now recognizes that the two years he lived with her as a boy might have had a tremendous influence on him. On an occasion late in her life he was visiting the institution and, in leaving, he said, 'Bye-bye, Grandma, I'll see you soon', and her reply, 'I'll see *you*. I'll *be* here. If I'm here, I'll be here', even now touches something very basic in him. Freudians might exhibit this as an example of a death-instinct or death-wish. We see it as having the ability to laugh in the face of Death.

He remembers having an audience among both his family and his peers when he wrote plays in the neighbourhood during early adolescence, when he did his high school humour column, and in the practical jokes and pranks he remembers as exemplifying his chronic style at home and at school. His ambition was to do publicity in showbusiness. After military service he immediately got sharted in this arena through an uncle. Soon after he was one of Walter Winchell's gag ghost-writers, an early step in the careers of many of our group of humorists.

For a period before his first major break in the business, (after he migrated to the West Coast with the advent of television), he became involved in what he describes sentimentally as 'funny little business'; he manufactured a demi-tray, he sold baby pictures from door-to-door. Then he and a partner who were renting a small office and doing skits together came up with one they thought perfect for Danny Thomas. His description of the sale of this skit and his immediate entry into the entertainment business (he never had another kind of job after that) is typical of the playful way this man tells stories and lives his life:

> I had a boyhood friend back East by the name of Merle Robinson. I always loved that name so much I used it whenever I was stopped in the army by the Military Police. Or for all kinds of other situations. Like if I didn't want a girl to know my name, I would say I was Merle Robinson. So one day I called William Morris, who represented Danny Thomas. Because I didn't know how you reached a star like Danny Thomas from a little office above a delicatessen, I called up the agency and said, 'This is Merle Robinson and I'm out here for the *New York Times* ... I'm doing a couple of stories and there's some information I need for a piece on Danny Thomas'.

He went on to say that he had to reach Thomas immediately and states that he guesses the urgency in his voice and the fact that he was from the *Times*, made the girl give him a number.

> I called the number and Danny Thomas answered the phone. I then said, 'I have a fantastic piece of material for you—you don't know me, but I have a fantastic piece of material for you'.

Apparently, just at the moment, Thomas and one of his people were in the throes of trying to find some new material for the yearly Friar's Club Frolic at Ciro's in Hollywood. Thomas said, 'I've never done this before, but can you come over right away? How fast can you be here?'

> I thought up some excuse and said two hours, because though we had a great idea, it wasn't written ... but we sat down right away and wrote it, and I went there, and he read it aloud and just loved it and fell down.

The next day an agent phoned Nathan, sent him to New York, and he was signed for the Four Star Revue with his partner.

This semi-audacious, clearly assertive behaviour, one designed to open the doors, even given its almost absurd premise, exemplifies this person's approach to both his craft and his life. With this approach, he would frequently even surprise himself. Even now, his family life is a series of humorous encounters. Both Nathan and his wife describe all the members of their family as being funny. Many times, serious moments or moments of conflict are broken by twisting the situation toward the absurd. Asked if this kind of procedure is hurtful or painful to others, he responds that he does not think so, 'it's certainly not meant to be,' but that, as in his childhood, he is alert to situations which reveal their humour to him. He describes an entire life atmosphere in which most family and close friends are able to parlay the punches, to roll with them, and to elaborate upon them.

He is aware, however, by his own admission, that he still waits for the reinforcement. Often he worries that he is too aware of 'being on', that professionally and personally his 'sensitivity to audience' can kill his spontaneity. His performer self is *not* his favourite self. Yet, he feels that this very sensitivity, and his interest in what it is that people find funny, has made his writing a success.

Currently, he holds warm-up sessions previous to the filming of one of his weekly TV shows in which he questions the audience members directly as to which development of a scene seems most natural, what is right for certain characters, which of two climax lines they find funniest.

In this move, he is being analytical, trying to probe the essence of humour, but *essentially* he sees the art of humour and the making of it as a visceral reaction. He admits it *may* be learned, but it becomes 'like an instinct'. He claims he doesn't have a knowledge of his techniques, that 'my belly tells me that's the way it's supposed to be'. He thinks that people with good instincts for humour get into trouble trying to formulate or follow rules for writing, that the message comes in 'loud and clear' as to the phrases, words, gags, or situations that 'click'. (Herein, the essence of our exclamation point in the creativity formula!)

Asked to describe what usually happens to him while writing, he delineated this initial stage:

> This is hard to put into words, I've never done it before . . . the first feeling I have when I'm ready to write is like I'd like to have sex, or masturbate . . . it's physical, I want to make love, and if I'm not careful, I'll do the sex and then not be there to do the writing. In the middle, for me, there's a long, long period, seems endless — it's never short — which I identify as 'shit in the head' — that's the way I always describe it to myself. It's something like a sound. And I'm afraid nothing is going to come through this morass, nothing is going to escape or break through, and I can't motivate myself to do anything, least of all write, but I feel like I should be writing every second of it.

He *does* have techniques for breaking the blur of this period, though each time he feels they 'may not work this time around'. Examples of some of the modes he utilizes are his adopting a tape-recorder so that he can immediately record any fragment that occurs to him just to get started, even though it may seem as though it had nothing at all to do with the story. He calls this: 'finding a hairpin'. Before he breaks out of this initial period of true isolation and apparent non-productivity, he is always alone in the same setting, a stark, cloistered room with a tape-recorder and typewriter. He describes:

> . . . feeling mentally and physically terrible, like my posture's bad, my breath is bad, my feet smell, my beard is ugly . . . I'm very aware of all these things. When things start going well, they may all still be true, but I wouldn't be aware of any of them.

Interestingly enough, although Nathan does not *label* the period just referred to, his wife does. She identifies it as a kind of 'gestation' period, what creativity theorists often see as the incubation period. Similar to these theorists, she does not see this period as wasteful, for it is the time within which a fragment may touch off other associations, which may later integrate into an *apperceptive mass*. She describes him during this time as being totally preoccupied, non-communicative, irritable, and says he desperately needs to be left alone. This concurs with his own feelings. For instance, he states:

> If things aren't going well, I am thinking about sex, or a great many other things. When I'm writing a screenplay, I have the most wonderful ideas for plays, novels, short stories, which I never write. Also, I love to communicate with my congressman at such times . . . .

Nathan goes on to describe this, however, as a transition into:

> a wonderful period, also physical, which could last for a week or a month, when everything is going so well it's just, well, the only way to describe it is one extended orgasm . . . everything is gushing, everything is just gushing . . . When the muse is with you; once you're at this point, you just keep going and going, all the difficult problems are behind you. You know you're going to beat it, you are going to go around those trees or climb that mountain or whatever you call those obstacles and you can't wait to know just how you're going to do it.

It may seem obvious that Nathan has delineated the progress from *incubation* to an almost-subliminal period of *illumination* directly into the period of productivity. He further stresses that this feeling of elation, well-being, or 'soaring', as he has called it, can last for the *entire period* of production. 'You know', he says, 'I can get carried away completely. And *I can add time to my own life* (authors' italics)'.

We cannot equate Nathan's description as simply being a manifestation of tension-release. It seems to us that rather than the sudden and short-lived ecstasy of sexual orgasm, he has deliberately chosen a very different form of 'pleasure', that powerful pleasure given *by* him *to* him in the act of *invention* we spoke of previously. Albeit he utilized sexual metaphor, there is considerable scope to the multi-levelled and prolonged feeling of accomplishment, expansiveness, and self-fulfilment he experiences as creator–inventor. The full impact of this personal power is found in his statement: 'I can add time to my own life', for the human being with inventive power and an intimate relationship with this force is re-creating *himself* each time he breaks through the period of quicksand to clearly contact and bring to life his product.

Another clear example of the humorist–creator's continuous drive to create and to thereby *sustain tension* over long periods of time, defying a simplistic Freudian explanation is indicated in this statement of Nathan's:

> I was home. It was just three days after finishing a giant job, a film I'd written, produced and directed. I'd been on location across the States for three months. Anybody would have been happy to give himself a week's rest. I find myself standing in my living room, marrying my daughter off to a young man I adore. Suddenly, in the middle of the ceremony, I feel a strange sense of guilt. Then I realize what it is, it comes to me, 'I'm not working . . . I haven't worked in three days', and I was just flooded with this, the immensity of the void. The Rabbi is incanting, and I'm feeling, 'Why am I not writing?'

In his life-style of spontaneity and wit, and in his play with mundane absurdity,

Nathan exemplifies the creator as explorer and *discoverer*. In his professional work, he is the powerful creator–*inventor*. In both, humour plays a continuous role, as a *life-giving growth process*.

Our work with Hollywood humorists is satisfying and significant to us on several levels. Although it has not led to definite or definitive conclusions, it provides us with material for *single-case life-studies* justifiable scientifically because of their rich detail and attention to the unique individual. We are therefore able to do *meaningful, humanistic* research within the scientific arena. Furthermore, we hope to demonstrate to our traditionally-oriented colleagues the ripeness and 'fitness' of humour as an area of exploration for social and behavioural scientists. And, as a final factor, we find it a gratifying challenge to work both holistically *and* in detail with the *process of creativity*, an area shamefully neglected by the traditional scientist. In humour and in its integral relationship to creativity, to adaptation and to human growth, we find that same elusive key to the nature of man as did Hesse (1929) in *Steppenwolf*:

> Humour alone, that magnificent discovery of those who are cut short in their calling to highest endeavor, those who falling short of tragedy are yet as rich in gifts as in affliction. Humor alone (perhaps the most inborn and brilliant achievement of the human spirit) attains to the impossible and brings every aspect of human existence within the rays of its prism. To live in the world as though it were not the world, to respect the law and yet stand above it, to renounce as though it were no renunciation, all the favorite, commonly formulated propositions of an exalted, worldly wisdom, only humor has the power to make those paradoxes obvious ... it is a third kingdom wherein the spirit becomes tough and elastic, a way of reconcilement, of extolling the saint and the profligate in one breath, and making the two poles meet ... You should not take things too seriously ... the immortals will tell you that ... seriousness is an accident of time, it puts too high a value on time. Eternity is a mere moment, just long enough for a joke.

NOTE

1. This paper is a revision of materials presented by the authors as part of a panel on *Creativity and Humor*, Annual Meeting of the Association for Humanistic Psychology, Squaw Valley, California, September, 1972.

REFERENCES

Adams, H. (1964). *The Education of Henry Adams*. In E. N. Saveth (Ed.), New York: Twayne Publishing Co.

Bateson, G. (1956). The message—'this is play'. In B. Schaffner (Ed.), *Group Processes, Second Conference*. New York: Macy Foundation.

Berlyne, D. E. (1969). Laughter, humor and play. In G. Lindzey and E. Aronson (Eds.), *Handbook of Social Psychology*, Vol. 3. Boston: Addison–Wesley.

Fabun, D. (1969). *You and Creativity*. Beverly Hills: Glencoe Press.

Fromm, E. (1959). The creative attitude. In H. H. Anderson (Ed.), *Creativity and Its Cultivation*. New York: Harper.

Fry, W. F., Jr. (1963). *Sweet Madness: A Study of Humor*. Palo Alto: Pacific Books.

Fry, W. F., Jr. (1970). Now you see it, now you don't: The magic of humour. *Perspectives in Biology and Medicine*, **14**, 173–175.

258

Ghiselin, B. (1952). *The Creative Process.* Berkeley: University of California Press.
Haefele, J. W. (1962). *Creativity and Innovation.* New York: Reinhold Publishing Co.
Hesse, H. (1929). *Steppenwolf.* New York: Henry Holt & Co.
Koestler, A. (1964). *The Act of Creation.* New York: Macmillan.
May, R. (1959). The nature of creativity. In H. H. Anderson (Ed.), *Creativity and Its Cultivation.* New York: Harper.
Roe, A. (1963). Psychological approaches to creativity in science. In M. A. Coler (Ed.), Essays on *Creativity in the Sciences.* New York: New York University Press.

Chapter 12

Calypso Humour in Trinidad[1]

James M. Jones
and
Hollis V. Liverpool

PROLOGUE

Humour in Trinidad is a way of life. It is the currency of social exchange and the vehicle of psychological and cultural organization. There is no idea, event emotion or person who can rise above the common denominator—humour. In some ways it makes Trinidad one of the most egalitarian of societies. Not power, education, prestige or good looks can elevate you above the equalizer—humour. It can brutalize you if you are weak, and humble you if you are strong. It can ease the tension of a confrontation, or heighten the enjoyment of a happy time. It educates the masses and keeps the few in power educated to the prevailing mood of the people. (Jones, 1974)

Humour is no joke in Trinidad, because if you cannot appreciate it, you do not belong. The eternal sustenance of this humorous way can be found in the calypso. The quick tongue, *bon mots*, social and political satire, and general sharing of relief from tension are all part and parcel of the legacy of calypso humour.

This chapter will treat the subject of humour through the ample vehicle of Trinidad calypso. The basic thesis for this work is that Trinidad humour derives from the calypso humour prototype. The calypso emerged during slavery and, with the catalyst of Carnival, brought humour to everyday Trinidadian life, with a thoroughness rarely seen in other societies.

After a brief introduction, we will trace the development of calypso from its inception during slavery to the present. The role of the calypsonian and his uses of humour to forge the power of his presence will be highlighted here.

The next section will focus on calypso for 1974. Because calypso is such a dynamic process with an extensive socio-cultural specificity, it is important to bring the reader into Trinidad to 'experience' calypso. The analysis of humour which springs from these experiences will be gentle, and relatively open. We cannot box our subject into a neat analytical frame. We can let it loose for your careful regard, comparison and interpretation.

Finally, we will try to place the calypso humour of Trinidad within the broad domain of general humour theory. Certainly, if we can understand anything about humour and how it functions in human affairs, we ought to draw theoretical associations to prevailing views.

INTRODUCTION

Calypso in Trinidad is dance, music, song and poetry. It is also theatre, political analysis, satire, oration and verbal battle. It has a cultural tradition at least 150 years old. Born in slavery as an antidote to suffering and a whimsical entertainment for slave-masters, calypso has been the cornerstone of the Trinidadian cultural edifice.

Alterations from multi-racial and cultural influences have made the calypso even more distinctive. The music has changed over the years as Spanish *parang*, French *belé* rhythms and instruments have been incorporated. The language of calypso changed from the French patois to broken English. In one time elaborate high sounding words were *à la mode*, now it is basic language of the folk that dominates.

The political system has escaped the domination of slavery, slipped past colonialism and rests rather firmly now as an independent nation–island. The African people have shared their calypso and their island with East Indians, Chinese, Portuguese, Americans and Western Europeans. Through all this, the one thing that remains steady and unfailing as the essence of calypso is its humour.

Calypso has been a social force in Trinidad from the beginning. It is probably the flexibility of the humour that enables calypso to function effectively across such a sweep of time and changing circumstance. It is a most impressive monument to the power and necessity of humour in the everyday lives of people and nations.

An empirical study of a cultural tradition that is also an art form, a folk-feeling (it has been said that all Trinidadians are calypsonians inside) a business enterprise and a social role is not easy. Calypso steps onto centre stage at the beginning of Carnival season in early January, remains up to Ash Wednesday, and then virtually disappears until the following year. (This is less so now, but still basically the pattern.) Against this backdrop of 150 years of changing forms and influences, personnel and social and political conditions, it is important to realize the limitations of traditional research procedures. These limitations become even more acute when one comes to appreciate the legacy of an oral tradition, which feeds the social–psychological needs and desires of a people for two months of each and every year.

Most readers will be familiar with tunes like *Marianne, Dey-o,* and *Rum and Coca-Cola* which have been popularized by Harry Belafonte. These are original calypso compositions but Belafonte is not a calypsonian. In Trinidad, to understand calypso is also to understand the role of the calypsonian as a product of the society who has shared the experiences of the masses. He is the bard and poet who brings those experiences out for public scrutiny and catharsis. He is not just a singer but a composer and performer. The people must 'know' what the calypsonian is talking about. Conversely, the calypsonian must know what the people are thinking about. The humour is not 'intellectual' (an abstraction which is internally consistent and for which the point of the humour depends on a penchant for problem-solving), but it does require a certain cognitive ability to translate the *double entendre*. But as the subjects are always very well-known, the meaning of the humour is understood quickly. The good calypsos are added to the oral archives of the Trinidadian people and the tradition continues.

Before we begin delineating various aspects of calypso and calypso humour, an example from a popular calypso created by a popular calypsonian appropriately called *Lord Funny* will usher us gently into our study.

SOUL CHICK

Verse	Chorus
Mih neighbor Wimaly	How you could work so
Ask mih to build ah coob for she	How you could knock so
She couldn't stay she was busy	How you could groove so
So she leave she daughter home with me	How you could move so
But she daughter Jasemay	How you could wail so
Up under me de whole day	How you could nail so
And anything ah do you see	How you could do so
De girl only asking me	How you could screw so
. . .	. . .
Ah sorry dat ah take de job	How yuh could sweat so
Because ah know dat ah done get rob	How yuh skin wet so
With dis soul chick called Jasemay	Is how yuh strong so
Keep harassing me whole day	How yuh could pong so
And everything she want to know	How yuh could dip so
She want to know how de wood smooth so	How yuh could rip so
And through she ah build it wrong	How yuh could make so
And had to break it dong	How yuh could break so

Lord Funny (Donric Williamson) is a straight-faced comic calypsonian. He composed this calypso and sang it during the 1973 season. It was one of the most popular calypsos of the year and continues to have an impact on Trinidad. This calypso is a classic because it makes maximum use of the very colourful and exciting Trinidad vernacular language, to present two parallel stories, one about building a chicken coop, the other about a sex frolic. Beginning with 'wood' (vernacular for penis), the sex *double entendres* flow like water: hammer, pound, rip, screw, break and so on.

Important also about this calypso is the impact it has had on Trinidad language and humour. If one is driving a car and has occasion to make a fast or inept or especially clever move, it is likely that an onlooker will say, 'How yuh could drive so', with a characteristic Trinidadian inflexion. Or, if a good-looking woman passes a set of limers, 'How yuh could walk so', is sure to emerge.

Perhaps the most celebrated use of this phrase was presented in *The Bomb*, a satirical weekly newspaper, politically left of centre, but apt to detonate any person, place or thing with clever good humour. The occasion for the use of 'how you could——so' was the culmination of four months of political intrigue. It began in September when the then Attorney General, Karl Hudson-Phillips, returned from a trip to Africa to find that the Prime Minister, Eric Williams, was 'too busy' to see him. After a few days conjecture in the press, Hudson-Phillips tendered his resignation as AG, which was readily accepted by Williams. In October, Dr. Williams announced that he was retiring from public life, and would relinquish leadership of the People's National Movement (PNM), and hence the Prime Ministership. Immediately Hudson-Phillips and the Minister of Health, Kamal Mohammed, began vying for leadership of the party. A crisis developed as Karl clearly was the dominant choice by party members, but Kamal was next in line by seniority. The PM rejected a plea to reconsider at the party convention in early November so, at the reconvened convention in early December, it was expected that either Karl or Kamal would be elected to leadership (tipsters had Karl way-ahead). In a dramatic move, a resolution was circulated, voted and adopted to invite the PM to return to head the party until elections could be organized. Just as dramatically, the PM accepted this draft, and returned to the convention floor to address the rapturous party members.

All of that set the stage for the cover of *The Bomb* for Friday, 7th December. 'HOW KARL COULD EXPECT SO!' read the headline next to a photograph of a very pregnant bride dressed in white, the face of whom was unmistakeably that of Karl Hudson-Phillips. So calypso humour comes out of the folk culture, is sharpened, packaged, and given a public airing, then returns for use as common language, with common meaning available to all the people of Trinidad, from the poor of country districts, to the press and the politicians.

This interplay of calypso, politics and society with good humour is the core of our subject. We will now take a brief backward glance at the origins of calypso and the emerging role of the calypsonian.

Trinidad calypso—an historical sketch

The variety of explanations of the origins of calypso make it impossible to give an unequivocal history. Various writers see Spanish, Carib Indian, French and African influences (Crowley, 1959; Elder, 1971; Esponet and Pitts, 1941; Hill, 1972; Quevedo, 1962). It is not our purpose here to add another interpretation to the confusion. Rather, we shall try to paint a broad picture of certain aspects of the development of calypso and calypsonians so that the reader can bring more understanding to the texts and characteristics of today's humour in Trinidad calypso.

Very little is known authoritatively about calypso prior to the twentieth century. Apart from scattered entries in diaries and reports of English colonialists, and obviously emotional newspaper articles of the time, the most comprehensive information of early calypso in Trinidad is a short article by Mitto

Sampson edited and arranged by Andrew Pearse for the *Caribbean Quarterly* (1956). Pearse organized this article from three typescripts and a two-hour interview with Sampson who was then 31 years of age; this was in 1955.

Sampson's knowledge of the folklore of nineteenth century Trinidad was based on his relationship to his grandmother, Mrs. Florence Atherley, to Remmy Roberts who was 93 in 1944 and a noted 'mako' (gossip-monger) who hung around calypsonians and street people, to Shiffer Braithwaite who died in 1952 at the age of 82, and to a man named Jo-Jo who was the son of nineteenth-century calypsonian, *Thunderstone*, and lived to the age of 92.

The reader must understand that story-telling produces legendary and certainly exaggerated accounts of real events. Trinidadians are especially noted for story-telling proclivities and the tendency is toward humorous amusement. So the accounts of calypsonians, like the calypsos themselves, are subjected to a humour-licence which quickly takes them outside our customary standards of verifiability.

Pierre Begorrat came to Trinidad from Martinique with his son, St. Hillaire, in 1784. He purchased a large plot in Diego Martin and proceeded to make a name for himself as a rather eccentric scoundrel. He became a sort of king and held court in a cave on his property. At these courtly ceremonies his African slaves sang *Cariso* or *Caiso* extemporaneously in a flattering vein (for Begorrat and his friends) or satirical humour against unpopular neighbours. On several occasions, slaves would sing *mepris* or insults on each other to the amusement of other slaves, Begorrat and his friends.

The first known cariso singer was named *Gros Jean*. He was Begorrat's favourite 'chantwell' and was appointed Mait' Caiso. When Begorrat fell into one of his infamous foul tempers, they would send for *Gros Jean* to sing him out of it. It is alleged that the two men were inseparable and that eventually, one of Begorrat's wives poisoned *Gros Jean* out of jealousy for his favoured position.

A slave named *Soso* succeeded *Gros Jean* as Mait' Caiso and was noted as a lover of decrepit and wrinkled old women. However, he was also considered generous, humane, charitable and extremely religious. He once sang a caiso that destroyed the character of one of Begorrat's enemies. A year later he was found mutilated from tortures received at the hands of the offended person. As with the *Gros Jean* story, the facts are not as important as the attitude toward caiso singers, and function which they were seen to play in early Trinidad society.

The next calypsonian of note was an obeah man named *Papa Cochon*.[2] He was reputed to have discovered pirate gold at Manzanilla and Mucurapo and to have made his masters wealthy. He is alleged to have been able to save his master's children from sickness and even death by concocting a mixture of the sacrificial blood of a young female slave, the brain of a black cat and seawater. He was feared and hated by all as he was also thought to eat snakes, cats and dogs and to sleep in graveyards. One night he went to sing at a neighbour's and was never seen again. Story had it that he was starved to death in a dungeon.

All of these early caisonians seem to have had special powers to sway, control and influence people around them, especially the slave-masters. They were at once feared and revered. They were protectors who could also harm. The social context in which these singers operated was slavery. It seems likely in this context that the humour they produced was cathartic for those slaves who were more restricted. It was also a form of prestige and power within the slave class. It seems likely that humour or laughter served as an aggressive cutting stone like the boxing matches that were common among slaves in America. The winners always received special favours.

As we move on to the period after slavery, we find a widened social context and role definition for the calypsonian. From roughly 1834 when slavery ended in Trinidad, to the turn of the century, the strength and social significance of calypsonians and calypso greatly increased. The role of racial and ethnic influences in its development is evident as the most notable calypsonians of this period were:

Possum—son of the slave Ofuba and Black;
Hannibal—a mulatto who was fiercely anti-Black;
Surisima—a Carib Indian who claimed caiso for the Caribs;
Cedric Le Blanc—the first White chantwell who sang in English;
Thunderstone—A Black chantwell for a gang of desperadoes called *Congo Jackos*, they epitomized the *Jamette* class and gave calypso a bad name which has been overcome only recently;
Bodicea—A Black woman who loved singing, fighting and drinking.

There are bountiful stories of the exploits of these calypsonians. Throughout the remainder of the nineteenth century, the calypsonians sang in French patois, and lived lives that were quite apart from the growing middle-class. During this time, calypso became associated with Carnival, if not an integral part of it. Because calypsonians continued to occupy a bottom spot in colonial Trinidad (below the Whites, Creoles, and free Coloured class), they continued to be the voice of the masses. Their humour was satirical, and when not directed at each other was focused on members of the privileged classes. It was the great equalizer above which no person could rise. The formalization of this kind of humour in calypso and as a generalized characteristic of Trinidad society resides in the practice of giving 'picong' (probably a derivative of the French 'piquant', meaning sharp or caustic).

In 1859, an American ornithologist named William Moore came to Trinidad and proffered the observation that caiso was simply a localized version of American and English ballads. The Carib calypsonian *Surisima* went with a following to Moore's hotel and sang 'Moore the monkey from America'. To which his followers answered, 'Tell me wha you know about we cariso'. So they chanted and made fun of Moore's ignorance until the police had to come and drive them away.

Hannibal's anti-Black attitude was very strong and unfettered. He sang:

> God you is a White man
> I want to know the truth.
> Who but de Devil
> Could mek these niggers brutes?

His sentiment was shared even by Black stick fighters of the time who used to sing as they went into battle

| Djab sé yô neg | (The Devil is a Negro) |
| Mê Dié sé nom-la blâ | (But God is a White man) |

In spite of attempts to stop this practice, the stickmen continued saying that since God was White and the Devil Black, every Negro has a devilish, ferocious quality which makes him immune to pain. So they girded themselves for the stick fight.

When Hannibal died, ghouls dug up the coffin and stole the head and the shroud leaving the rotten carcass. The female chantwell *Bodicea* accused *Congo Jack*.

| *Congo Jack* volétét-la Hannibal | (*Congo Jack* steal Hannibal's head) |
| U volé-la mò, gadé bakanal | (You steal from the dead, look bacchanal) |

She fired up the crowd, took off her dress and waved it as a banner. She and five of her followers were arrested. During this time, girls who behaved badly were said to be 'playing *Bodicea*'.

However true all of these stories are, it remains that the character of calypsonians of the nineteenth century was popularly seen in terms of *jamette* society. As these people had no stake in the formal societal structure, they were, in a way, free to offer their view from the bottom with unabashed satire. As mouthpiece of the masses they offered the 'other side' of every issue. As we turn the page to a new century, however, a variety of changes are initiated which were destined to change calypso.

Since the end of slavery there had been a struggle between the mass of people who claimed Carnival for themselves, and the upper classes who rejected this degradation of their festival. Every attempt to ban people from the streets and from engaging in their own form of Carnival bacchanal was met with great resistance. The chantwell or calypsonian of the nineteenth century was the leader of the struggle. The high point of this battle occurred in 1881 when the famous Canboulay Riot pitted bands of stick fighters against the police in Port-of-Spain. It seems that this battle settled the score with finality. Since it could not be eliminated, the authorities decided to try and control it as best they could. (See Hill, 1972, for an account of these riots, and an analysis of their significance for calypso.)

Perhaps the first significant change in calypso singing was the introduction of English lyrics. Credit for this is commonly given to Norman LeBlanc who is 1897 rebuked the British Governor, Jerningham, for threatening to abolish the Port-of-Spain Borough Council. It took some twenty or so years before the transition was complete.

A next significant change was that calypsonians became leaders of masquerade bands and as such became a 'legitimate' part of Carnival. As stick fighting declined because of bans imposed by the government, the masquerade bands rose. The bands each had a calypso king who composed songs, trained his followers to sing the chorus and, on Carnival days, led his followers in the streets. The period before carnival was used to rehearse the songs so they would be sung well when Carnival opened on jouvay morning.

Considering calypso in the twentieth century, three phases of development seem to stand out. The first, ushered in by the English lyric, saw the calypsonian as bandleader. In 1914 a competition was arranged for calypsonians and, by 1919, the practice tents were so well patronized that a small admission of two cents was charged. Calypsonians began to travel around to other tents and the *mepris* (insult singing) that was common during slavery became a regular part of calypso singing. The calypsonian became a troubadour, gun-slinging, balladeer whose weapons were quick wit, a good voice and wide knowledge of the events of the land.

Improvising songs of scandal and love, the calypsonians waged war for the admiration of their ever-increasing audiences. They took on various noms-de-guerre such as *Attila, Normandy, Executor, Black Prince, Trafalgar*. The tents were the battlefield, and humour was the major weapon. Although the context in which the calypsonian worked had changed, his weapons and goals remained intimately linked to humour.

In 1919, a railroad man named Walter Douglas initiated changes in the calypso tent which escalated the trend toward entertainment and brought a wider segment of Trinidad society into contact with the calypsonian. He raised the price of admission, replaced flambeaux with gas lights, rented chairs to replace bamboo benches, and printed tickets to advertise his shows. Instead of one calypsonian and his band of followers, there were several who put on a show for a paying audience. The conditions of struggle against the oppressive forces of slavery in which the calypsonian originally functioned were receding.

Although the conditions were changing, the template for humour was not. As John Grimes (1962) wrote in the *Trinidad Guardian*:

> It was this circumstance [the conditions of slavery] more than any other which gave birth to the calypso picong and the unique humour of the Trinidadian; which inspires this native philosophy to find humour in the most trying and vexing situations.

The second phase was prominently affected by the new influence of America. Perhaps the most significant calypso showing this influence is *Lord Invader's*

Rum and Coca Cola
Way down Point Cumana
Both mother and daughter
Working for the Yankee dollar

While Trinidad calypsonians like *Attila*, *Tiger* and *Lion* made recording trips to the United States, it was American performers like the Andrews Sisters and Harry Belafonte who made the money and popularized calypsos. As the entertainment aspects of calypso increased, the fertile social context in which it originated became less well appreciated.

The convergence of events during this phase of the development of calypso heightened its entertainment value. Now calypsonians could be paid for singing and there existed overseas recognition for the best among them. The spontaneous humour that arose out of the released tension provided by calypso was replaced by a more formalized humour of the professional entertainer. Calypso drama developed alongside a direct approach to humour for humour's sake. *Spoiler* was the master humorist of this time. He conceived subjects like a judge defending himself in court, talking backwards, female police, twin brother and so on.

The calypso drama appeared as a scenario between two or more calypsonians and a chorus. Topics were quite varied and ranged from divorce, Frankenstein, Wrightson Road Scandal, to Boysie Singh-Boland Ramkeesoon Murder Case. For example, one drama begins with the spoken wedding ceremony: 'Dearly Beloved ... If any man feels that they should not be joined together let him speak now or forever hold his tongue.' A calypsonian sings the first verse thus:

> Please, Parson, stop the ceremony!
> I say wait, Parson, that woman belong to me!
> I pay dear for the dress she wearing
> I thought she was a guest in somebody wedding
> Rev try and understand,
> If she marry I will have to be she husband. (Hill, 1972, p. 113)

The best calypsonians have a wide range of talents and a broad vision of their art. The people of Trinidad look to the calypso and calypsonian for amusement, analysis, humorous expression of their own point of view, evidence of clever thinking and the embodiment of the strength of the idea—'the mouth is mightier than the sword'.

While the calypsonian as entertainer was growing from the turn of the century, it was in 1966 that a young Grenada-born man named Slinger Francisco came on the scene and singlehandedly carried calypso to an international audience. It is not insignificant that the song which catepulted him to prominence sang of the end of the reign of the Americans in Trinidad, and established *The Mighty Sparrow* as the new king.

> Jean and Dinah, Rosita and Clementina
> Round the corner posin'
> Betcha like is someting dey sellin'
> If yuh catch dem broken
> Yuh can get it all for nuttin
> Don't make a row
> Cause Yankee gone and *Sparrow* take over now.

With *Sparrow's* business sense and awareness of the international market for calypso, the commercialism within and without Trinidad has grown. He introduced sweet music, more universal themes, and a performing style that entranced not only Trinidadians but people in other West Indian islands, America and Europe.

We could say, then, that the third phase of calypso in this century concerns the escalation of its commercial nature. The trend started with a two cents entry fee to watch calypsonians rehearse with their small bands, and now admission charges are up to $2–$5, for shows lasting three to four hours and featuring 15 to 30 calypsonians performing in a night. The calypso tents are frequented by people of all races and economic positions. The Prime Minister, press, and business community and people in the street all use phrases from calypsos in common parlance. What started as a weapon of the underdog has become a major commercial enterprise which still retains a social significance. While the central role of humour has not changed over the years, it has become a more varied characteristic of Trinidad calypso.

CALYPSO HUMOUR

An empirical study of calypso humour is not easy. First, the most important aspect of the humour is the lyric, and calypsonians rarely write them down. For example, *Lord Pretender* has been singing calypso in tents since 1929 and has never written a word. Over the years there has been unsystematic record-keeping by historians and occasional interested calypsonians, for example *Attila the Hun* and, more recently, the *Mighty Chalkdust*. The recording industry has made this less of a problem as any calypso of some impact gets recorded now. There have been several attempts to establish calypso archives. Anthropologist Daniel Crowley has a substantial collection, as does the National Cultural Council of Trinidad and Tobago under the directorship of Dr. J. D. Elder.

The next major problem is that much of the humour is topical and requires a good knowledge of local events. Calypso season comes once a year and all of the scandals and major news events of the year are prime targets for the calypso composition. In most cases the humour rests on specific knowledge of local events and is, therefore, difficult to write about for a foreign audience.

Another problem with such a study is that much of the humour is transmitted through the performance of the calypsonian. Many of the smutty calypsos turn on *double entendre*. The calypsonian could sing the calypso straight or perform it so that the sexual meaning is clear. The performer then reaffirms the audience's understanding that this is smut and draws their laughter. The dynamics of performance are not easily captured in a written analysis.

Although humour in calypso 'comes like peas', it is not simple to compose. First of all, calypso comes around year after year. Audiences are familiar with hundreds of calypsos from previous years. The oral transmission of the calypsos means that only the very best are remembered. Furthermore, the events about which humorous lines are composed, are very well-known and thoroughly discussed. For a calypsonian to compose a humorous calypso about a well-known event and sing it before sophisticated audiences night after night is no small task.

Each year a new wave of calypsos and calypsonians hits the scene. During the first few weeks of the season (early January), Trinidadians windowshop for good humour, clever lyrics and the ambience of the calypso tents. After a few weeks of making the rounds of the tents, you begin to hear your favourite calypsos on radio and in record shops. Soon you hear people whistling, humming and singing those calypsos destined to join the oral archives. Finally, the tunes with the best beat and melody are picked up by the 'pan-men'. By Carnival time, calypso has thoroughly permeated every nook and cranny of Trinidad life.

Calypso humour contributes to the general merriment of the season. Conversations turn on popular calypso phrases. The arguments over politics now use the trenchant calypso phrases for emphasis. The ritual good time, self-analysis and mass catharsis is a testament to the power of humour and the evolutionary intelligence of laughter.

In order to preserve the performance and contextual properties of calypso humour, we will present them as part of the tent show. However, there is one calypsonian who more than others enjoyed the uniform praise of his fellow artists and the Trinidad public. *The Mighty Spoiler* was a rum drinking calypsonian of the first order. He is perhaps the greatest pure humorist of all calypsonians, as the bulk of his work was simple, humorous flights of fancy. His life showed the same pattern; he was well-known as a quick-tongued, imaginative person who could always be counted on for a good laugh. He died in 1961, a victim of the rum which he loved so much.

A typical example of *Spoiler's* imagination was his *Magistrate Try Yourself*.

> Well this one is class,
> They charge a magistrate for driving too fast.
> Well this one is class,
> They charge a magistrate for driving too fast.
> Well is one court house in the district,
> He's the only magistrate there to run it.
> If you see how the people flock up the place,
> To see how the magistrate go try he own case.
> *Chorus*: Himself told himself you are charged for speeding
> Himself told himself the policeman is lying.
> Himself told himself, don't shout, it's a law-court.
> And he charged himself for contempt of court.

To appreciate the humour of *Spoiler*, you must keep in mind that these lyrics are sung in rhythmic syncopation so that the blend between rhyming line and rhythmic beat is smooth and flowing. Furthermore, you have seen the tradition from which calypso derives, so the imaginative fancy of *Spoiler* is a refreshing development. The next one is even more fanciful.

REINCARNATION
Yes I heard when you die after burial
You got to come back as an insect or animal (*repeat*)
If that is so I don't want to be a monkey,
Neither a goat, a sheep or donkey
My brother said he want to come back a hog
But not the Spoiler, I want to be a bedbug
[Why?]
Just because
Chorus: I'm going to bite those young ladies harder
Than a hot dog or a hamburger
But if you thin don't be in a fright
Is only them big fat ladies I'm going to bite.

All of *Spoiler's* calypsos follow this classic form of eight-line verses and four-line chorus. There were usually four or five verses, but the number could go as high as the singer felt like composing. Unlike most calypso humour, *Spoiler's* humour is mostly imaginings of things that might have been or might be.

All calypsonians respect the creative humour of *Spoiler*. However, few have been able to capture his appreciation of comic twists of vision. For the most part, the social role of the calypsonian as critic and commentator, as well as the desire to please the calypso audience has drawn new calypsonians into a genre that is less individualistic. So calypso humour varies with the range of people who are calypsonians. We present *Spoiler* as a special breed.

HUMOROUS CALYPSOS OF 1974

There were four calypso tents open in Port-of-Spain during the 1974 calypso season. From these four tents there emerged about 50 top level calypsonians, each of whom sang on average three calypsos. Fully 90 % of the approximately 150 top calypsos involved humour.

There are four types of calypso relevant to the present analysis. The first is the *Road March* calypso. This form usually does not involve humour but is written especially for its 'jump-up' appeal and easily sung lyrics. This year's *Road March* calypso was a classic as it catapulated a young calypsonian into the hearts of Trinidadians with such force, and the tune itself created near hysteria during Carnival time. The *Mighty Shadow* sang about *The Bassman* in his head, and danced and pranced all over Trinidad to these bass strains: 'be-do-be-do-do-pom'. The themes for *Road March* frequently concern Carnival itself, and highlight the gaiety, and dance more than humour.

A second type is a more serious calypso sung to make a point. Calypsonians refer to these calypsos as 'educational,' to distinguish them from the smutty, jokey or *Road March* types. They frequently involve politics, or personal points of view about events in Trinidad. Many of the serious calypsos still have humorous lines which help get the message across. We will look at a couple of these later in this section.

There are two more types which provide the bulk of the text for our analysis. One of these is the calypso which tells a jokey story. The story may be fabricated, or a slightly exaggerated account of a real story. The calypsos of *Spoiler* fit into this category.

Finally, the majority of humorous calypsos are based on *double entendre* and concern sex. Many people complain about the sex-preoccupation, and some older calypsonians claim that these are not as humorous as before when you had to compose on a wide range of subjects and still be humorous. The clear majority of humorous calypsos of this year were sexual *double entendres*.

A compilation of calypso recordings produced by the National Cultural Council of Trinidad and Tobago shows 1500 songs, by 96 calypsonians. This list is not complete, but gives an idea of the scope of the study. We have listened to these recordings, and think that the experience of *Chalkdust* with calypso, together with interviews from older calypsonians has made an even wider fund of knowledge of calypso available to us during the past 20 years.

We have chosen to concentrate on calypsos of 1974 because the calypsos and their creators are immediately available. Moreover, the topics sung about are more widely known and, finally, the general style, method of composition and approach to humour has not changed substantially over the years. The only exception to this is the increased socio-political consciousness of many newer calypsonians. These calypsos are more serious, meant to be specifically constructive in some cases, and have minimal, though strategic, humour.

Original Young Brigade

The Original Young Brigade (OYB) Calypso Tent is the home of the calypso king of the world, the *Mighty Sparrow*. It is housed in the Seaman's Waterfront Workers Trade Union on Wrightson Road in Port-of-Spain. The business manager of the tent is Syl Taylor. The major calypsonians in this tent include *Lord Shorty*, *The Mighty Cypher*, *King Wellington* (based in the United States), *Calypso Rose* (Calypso Queen of Trinidad), *Caruso Kid* (Calypso King of Tobago), *Mighty Bomber*, *Dougla* (a mixed East Indian Negro and one of the few calypsonians who is not straight Negro), *Rex West* (the only Chinese calypsonian) and *Mighty Fighter* (calypso King of Guyana), and the master of ceremonies, Bill Trotman.

The OYB has been the most popular tent because of the *Mighty Sparrow*. Because of his international reputation, there are frequently many tourists and other visitors to Trinidad in the audience. It is also the case that *Sparrow* is the most popular calypsonian in Trinidad as well, so the expectations of people in this audience are always high.

The OYB is noted in Trinidad for a prevalence of 'smutty' calypsos. Every tent has a wide range of calypso types and personalities, but the sexual innuendos and the *double entendres* are most prolific at OYB. The MC Bill Trotman employs a lot of sexual picong and jokes in his work:

Good evening, ladies and gentlemen, and welcome to calypso time at the OYB. Since I see all those smiling faces I hope to keep it that way. We have a lot of good friends right up front too. Where you from, Scotland? You from Scotland too? Where you from? [*answer, San Fernando, city in Trinidad*] I never see dat. I thought San Fernando was a nice place. I thought it was only nice people come from San Fernando. I never expect somebody like you to come from there. That fella is something else you know. He sitting down there trying to give the impression he's a honkie. (*laughter*) [*To a next fella*] You from where [*another answers*] I didn't ask you. I know exactly where you from, and I find they should put you right back in your cage. Look at this thing. You think you bad looking? Look at that fella. You know if they take him back to the zoo, all them monkeys start singing: 'I Feel Pretty' (*laughter*).

At this point a heckler begins to disturb the show. For some reason he keeps shouting out 'Mango Valley'. Trotman turns his attention to him:

You ent shame to open you mouth? This man something else you know. He only have two teeth, one to chew and one for toothache (*laughter*). [*Heckler repeats, 'Mango Valley, Mango Valley'.*] Allyuh want to hear about Mango Valley. Some of these fellas real boldface, you know. Where is Mango Valley? Come nuh, I see you want to tell me about Mango Valley, come nuh man, come nuh! [*Man refuses to come up on stage*].
Long time we use to have real bacchanal in caiso tent and Carnival. As a matter of fact it had fellas uses to come into tent with cutlass and chop down tent when dey ent get enough pay. [*'Mango Valley'*] Look like you don't even want to have a tooth for toothache (*laughter*).
[*'Mango Valley'*] You ready to come up and tell me 'bout it now? How yuh scratching so, what yuh got dey? You know somebody was telling me he know yuh quite well. Man say you have a nice wife. Lucky for she. She's a lucky woman, boy. But I don't know how she could be with you all this time. I hear you sent she one time to get a sack of shrimps. But the chupid woman come back with a box of crabs. That's why yuh still scratching?

The heckler of course is undaunted, the audience is delighted by the entertainment. The picong of old time calypso is relived between Trotman and the audience. Every evening there are those people in the audience who want to take Trotman on, just as young calypsonians used to take on the masters fifty or so years ago. Verbal combat remains one of the most revered forms of humour in Trinidad.

Although the *mepris* or insult singing of improvised picong is no longer a regular part of calypso, occasionally Trotman will enter into these battles with other calypsonians as part of the show. One picong part of the show at OYB concerned calypsonian *Lord Shorty*, who is billed as the sexiest calypsonian. He is about 6'3", very well-built, and wears the sexiest of clothes and sings calypsos about sex and love. Last year he sang a calypso that created a pressure toward censorship titled, *The Art of Making Love.*

A young calypsonian, *Calypso Height*, sang a picong calypso this year titled *Why the woman leave sexy Shorty*. The essence of this calypso is that sexy *Shorty* is not so virile and masterful as people think. When he finishes his calypso, *Lord Shorty* appears menacingly at the back of the stage, and *Height* runs away in the other direction. This leaves the stage for *Shorty* and Bill Trotman:

Trotman: Eh, Eh, Well I never ...
Lord Shorty: I warn you about this thing, I warn you about this thing.
Trotman: You warning me? It ent me to warn. I can't see what you getting vexed for because the man talk the truth 'bout yuh. I never see dat, man making big fuss. Eh eh, go away nuh man, Man gone. You standing out dey like you ... He ent have nuttin to say' bout yuh. See dem fellas because dey got big muscles and dey tall and dey big and ting, dey want to take advantage of little fellas like me. I know why, yuh know. I know why. Dem fellas when they big so and dey call dem sexy, yuh tink dat dey [*makes a gesture showing great size*] ummmm. I know yuh know. Dey only good looking and ting, but I know dem big fellas so, dey little. They have no right to call him no sexy *Shorty*. No Dey should call him *Shorty Shorty*. The amounta time he use dat it dry up. I know what I talking' bout. When I say de amounta time, yuh tink it plenty? [*'Yuh mouth get used to it' comes from the audience*] You see dis is one thing I can't understand. How allyuh does like to come in here and expose me business. Look, dis is a ting going on here between husband and wife stay out. But it look like you want to jump in dis ting too. Yuh playing lizard? Jump on the paling.

From this position, Trotman goes on to introduce the next calypso, which is *Dry Weather* by *Caruso Kid*. The audience got a good laugh out of the picong directed at *Lord Shorty*, as well as that given by a member of the audience to Trotman. The sparks of picong fly fast and furious and always bring the loudest, most appreciative responses from the audience.

On Carnival Monday and Tuesday, the steelbands move down the streets of Port-of-Spain beating out the favourite calypsos of the year. Behind each band are hundreds of revellers jumping, singing, drinking rum. It is customary for girls to ride in the steelband entourage and beat the pans. This practice set the stage for a *Sparrow* calypso.

When *Sparrow* comes on stage, the audience is thrilled. He is the calypsonian they have been waiting for. He usually appears just before the intermission. MC Bill Trotman gives him the superstar introduction. 'Ladies and gentlemen, it's star time at the OYB. You know what that means. The Calypso King of the World, *The Mighty Sparrow*'. The Birdie comes leaping on stage in his bouncing, dancing, jumping style. His angular face beaming in a smile suggesting his name. He has boundless energy, and a devilish look that fits the double meaning of the calypso he is about to sing. The audience has been waiting for the superstar all evening. The tourists now have their trip officially sanctioned in the land of calypso.

Sparrow's most popular calypso of the year was in a *double entendre* vein. *Miss Mary (One Pound)* captures the Carnival day atmosphere:

Verse	Chorus
Mas	To see Miss Mary—one pound
This year go be great	Big and hairy—one pound
Ah fuss ah want to play	To see she daughter—
I can hardly wait	To see she mother—

Dress up like a Baptist woman	For Carnival this year
With an old shoe box in me hand	I have Miss Mary here
Charging money to see so confusion	Miss Mary weighing—one pound
in the band	To come and see she one pound

One of the biggest topics of the previous year was a severe drought which hit the lower portion of the Caribbean. The drought caused severe problems with the rice crop in Guyana (from where about 80% of Trinidad rice comes). Two popular topics for calypsonians were the rice shortage and the drought itself. One of the favourites of audiences at the OYB was a calypso by *Caruso Kid*:

DRY WEATHER
The greatest dry weather in history
Was in the year 1973 (*repeat*)
No rain at all, all the land get dry
All the crops dry up farmer start to cry
The rivers get small the dams get low
No rain in Trinidad nor in Tobago ...
. . .
We run short of rice we run short of sugar
We run short of salt we run short of flour
And you know sometime last year September
We nearly run short of Prime Minister.

Caruso Kid's humour is simple and meant to make people laugh easily. His line about running short of Prime Minister is one of the best of the season which combines the rice shortage, the drought and the big political struggle for power into one well-worded line of calypso. It always draws a big laugh and a call for an encore.

Not all of the calypsos at the OYB were smutty or even humorous. Serious subjects were treated by calypsonians like *Bomber* (crime wave; sex education), *Pretender* (generation gap) and *Valentino* (victim of society; pollution). Other calypsos also deal with serious subjects, but the ones mentioned above used no humour at all. There are few such calypsos, and the singers of them must have very well-written compositions, a relevant message, and a good presentation to hold the stage without abuse from the audience. The OYB is the Freudian centre of calypso humour. When you go to this tent. you have to check your superegos at the door.

Trotman pointed out that although people laugh and enjoy the show, they often criticize the performances as obscene and in bad taste. Apparently this view comes to them after their superegos are securely replaced.

The analysis of humour given by Freud (1960) is most applicable to the OYB. With few exceptions, the themes of these calypsos are sexual or aggressive. The verbal picong orchestrated by MC Trotman is the thread that holds the audience's attention. Individuals offer themselves sacrificially to Trotman's wit. It is ribald entertainment with a thin veneer of innocence.

The joke-technique is carefully developed around rhyming couplets and conventional story lines. Sophisticated calypso-watchers, however, need little effort to see through the 'meat' of the story. The whole evening is not lurid, obscene or hostile, but filled with great good humour. So humour is skilfully used to assault without malice, and to expose fundamental sexuality in a playfully risqué fashion.

Calypso Revue

The Calypso Revue is the home of the recognized *Road March* King of the World, the *Lord Kitchener*. Perhaps because of this influence, the musical side of calypso is strongly represented here. In fact, the ten-year domination of the *Road March* by *Kitchener* and *Sparrow* was broken by a young Revue calypsonian, *The Mighty Shadow*.

The Revue calypsos vary a great deal. The sexual *double entendre* occupies its place. In addition, several topical and political calypsos were sung here. And of course *Kitchener* provides calypsos with the bouncy time, and simple lyric which can be played easily on the pans and sung while jumping up on Carnival day.

One of the most outstanding young calypsonians is the *Lord Relator*. His compositions are always tight and informative, his singing voice sweet with great range, and his presentation cool as he 'relates' his calypso to attentive audiences. In the Autumn of 1973, a report was circulated that boys who beat the pans were losing their hearing. The pans are very loud and produce a very sharp sound. The process of learning how to beat pan and how to play specific tunes is a simple 'play it by ear' procedure. The practice hours are many, and the learning process a matter of countless repetitions.

> DEAF PAN MEN—*Lord Relator*
> Big propaganda
> They say this year have no Panorama
> Pan men going deaf
> Some in the right, and some in the left
> Somebody say the pan men gone deaf for true
> Is now calypsonians face turning blue
> So they put calypsonian tunes on the shelf
> Pan men say they playing Mas by they self.
> *Chorus:* Dr. Williams say
> He leading the band from early J'Ouvert
> He made we to understand
> He only want deaf people inside the band
> He say that he's leading the big parade
> Supplying every pan man with hearing-aid
> So I bound to be in the savannah
> To witness deaf pan men panorama.

So the *Lord Relator* capitalized on the news of pan men going deaf, and the fact of the Prime Minister's hearing problem to propose a new masquerade for this year's Carnival. In a later verse he included news of kidnapped millionaire, young John Paul Getty, by inviting him to join the masquerade. The humour of this calypso is not raucous slapstick that makes audiences laugh loud. Rather, one observes smiles of approval and respect for the well-conceived idea, and the humorous twist given to these items of news and public interest.

One of the outstanding events of the calypso season was the impact made by a young calypsonian from Tobago, *Mighty Shadow*. As his name suggests, he is a rather mysterious person, noted for eccentric behaviour. He disappears for long periods of time, and shows up in unexpected places. He appears on stage in an all-black outfit, topped with a big floppy black hat that covers a portion of his face. Adding to the mystery, he has the lights down very low when he performs.

This year he created a sensation by winning the 'Road March Championship' by the largest margin ever. The tune most played by the steelbands on Carnival Monday and Tuesday is named the *Road March Tune*. This year over 90% of the bands played *Shadow's Bassman*. It was the first time in over ten years that the *Road March* was won by someone other than *Kitchener* or *Sparrow*. So spectacular was *Shadow's* impact, that one of his calypsos, *Ah come out to play*, was runner-up in the championship.

> BASSMAN—*Mighty Shadow*
> Ah was planning to forget calypso,
> And go plant peas in Tobago,
> But I am afraid,
> Ah can't make the grade,
> Cause every night I lie down in me bed
> Ah hearing a bassman in meh head
> Pe poom pe poom poom, pom, pe poom pe poom poom, pom, etc.
> *Chorus*: Ah don't know how this ting get inside me
> But every morning he driving me crazy
> Like he takin me head for a panyard
> Morning and evening
> Like this fella gone mad
> Tim Tom—and if ah don't want to sing
> Tim Tom—when he start to do he ting
> Ah don't want to, but I have to sing
> Tim Tom—if ah don't want to dance
> Tim Tom—he does have me in a trance
> Ah don't want to but I have to prance.

As soon as the tent band begins to play *Bassman*, people in the audience start to bounce in their seats and call, '*Shadow, Shadow*'. In a short while, the *Mighty Shadow* runs on stage with his long coat trailing behind. The audience response is not laughter in humour, but laughter and gaiety of a Carnival spirit.

The *Road March* calypsos have a very special place in our analysis of humour. In general, themes of humour focus on its aggressive or sexual nature (Freud, 1960; Bergler, 1956); its moral–social prescriptive role (Bergson, 1911); cognitive mastery (Jones, 1970; Kagan 1967); and a host of other basic human drives and capacities. However, one element common to all themes is that to appreciate humour, the participants must accept the 'play mood' and suspend serious judgement. The *Road March* calypsos bring the laughter of dance and carefree merriment. It's not a prelude to other analyses, but the thing itself.

One of the biggest news items of the year was the running battle between police and a small group of young political dissenters. This young cadre grew out of the mass political disturbances of 1970, and operated under the aegis of the Black Power slogan. They lived in the hills around Port-of-Spain and in more remote southern districts of Trinidad. Popularly known as guerrillas, they embodied the militant aspects of student movements of the mid- and late-1960s.

Over the past year several of the guerrillas were killed including the most famous of them, Guy Harewood. At the OYB, the *Mighty Cypher* sang *The Guerrilla* which recounted his experience in the hills of Lopinot where he was mistaken for a guerrilla. *Cypher's* rendition was comic as he dropped his pants to mislead the police who mistook his penis for a gun.

> If you hear them, he have gun, ah see gun,
> He toting gun.

Passing schoolchildren also made a mistake.

> Some school children see me and howl murder
> Look! Ah snake stick on to a guerrilla!

At the Revue, *Mighty Maestro* made reference in his calypso about the inconsistency of the political judgements of 'Mr. Trinidad'.

> My friend if you don't want democracy
> The opposite is guerrilla activity
> If you don't want socialist improvement
> Well then you want a revolutionist government
> And yet when Guy Harewood went in the hills
> With Jennifer Jones you let them get kill
> All you doing is grinning and sky-larking
> You come like ass in lion skin.

Also at the Revue, *Lord Kitchener* chose the 'guerrilla situation' as a theme for his top *Road March* calypso of the year, *Jericho*:

> I hear they looking for me,
> So I come down from the jungle,
> They combing the whole country
> Talking bout dem people
> Ah saving dem the trouble
> Of climbing mountains and tumbling down
> Please do me a favour and tell dem
> *Jericho* come to town.

The chorus captures the magic of the pan and the spirit of Carnival jump-up
with short rhyming runs:

> They looking for *Jericho*
> *Jericho*, ent dey
> They look up Mayaro,
> *Jeri* slips away.

The evening show at the Revue always closed with several *Lord Kitchener*
bouncy calypsos. The result was that one left this tent in high spirits and eager
for the Carnival days to come.

Orginal Regal Calypso Tent

The Regal Tent is located on the Port-of-Spain harbour in the Port Services
building. It differs from each of the other principal tents in that it is managed by
three calypsonians, *Lord Superior*, *Mighty Chalkdust* and *Mighty Duke*. *Lord
Superior* is called the youngest old calypsonian because at the age of only 37, he
has been singing in tents since 1953. The *Mighty Duke* stands out because he is
the only calypsonian to win the King title four years in a row.

There is a different feeling in the Regal than in the OYB. Perhaps it is because
the tent is run by calypsonians, but there is a decided feeling of calypso for
calypsonians. The Master of Ceremonies is the *Mighty Composer*. His humour
is considerably less smutty than Trotman's with less slapstick and picong.
Rather, he gives jokes in a smooth, easy style. Much of his humour is directed
at other calypsonians in a constructive way. He points out faults or shortcomings in performance, composition or singing voice with a touch of humour.
One feels the positive and constructive nature of his approach. For example,
Chalkdust is famous for his compositions, but neither for his singing nor for his
performance style. *Composer* ridicules *Chalkie's* sideways cakewalk style to the
delight of the audience.

There are six calypsonians chosen for the final competition held at the
Dimanche Gras Show the Sunday before Carnival. The Regal placed four of its
performers in the finals. There were fewer ribald and jokey calypsos, and more
well-composed calypsos on serious subjects. People who went to the Regal,
went to hear a different sort of calypso from those who went to OYB. We
cannot ignore this factor in surveying calypso humour.

We have already seen that the political intrigue of the Prime Minister and the
two aspirants to his office was major news. All of the four top calypsonians at
the Regal sang about it with varying degrees of humour.

The *Mighty Composer* appeared on stage in the PM's characteristic white
dinner jacket, hearing aid and dark glasses, and he smoked a pipe. *Composer*
let the Doc speak for himself.

DIFFERENT STROKES FOR DIFFERENT FOLKS
Them politicians was in a fit

Last year when the Doctor say that he quit
But when ah find the man change his mind so quick
Ah went and ask him Doc like you was out for kicks
He say Composer did you for one minute
Think a man like me could leave politics
Come come young fellar you better use your wits
Never ask Sobers if he could play cricket

Sorry for me two friends Kamal and Karl
They get trapped like two greedy animals
They could ah save themselves from that bacchanal
By staying out like Francis, George and Errol
For when to Africa Karl had gone
About this cloisterous man I was warned
There is a traitor on board examine the horn
That's why when he come back ah treat him with scorn.
Chorus: You playing with me
You think it easy
Now Dr. Willie has come back predominately
Ah pretend to resign but that was a hoax
To see who is the sheep from the goats
Now you could tell the party I am not making jokes
Is different strokes
For different folks.

So *Composer* attributes masterful political manoeuvring to the Doc's unpredictable behaviour of the Autumn of 1973. Thus in song, masquerade and rhyme, a major political event was summarized, analysed and satirized.

The *Mighty Duke* was not as generous in his appraisal of Dr. Williams.

Doc ah beg you in sixty-nine
And ah warn you in seventy-two
You paid me no mind
Like you didn't believe it's true
Now things has blown clean out of proportion
And men gone up on the hill
You put your forces in motion
Like is hungry people you want to kill?
Doc ah read you speech carefully
Lack of co-operation you claim
Don't throw it on we
Is you own self you have to blame
. . .
And the man who you put your trust in
As you turn round the money gone
Now you realizing
That you can't put hungry fowl to catch corn.
Chorus: Rice gone up
Nature spice gone up, every price gone up
It's unbelieving how you're leaving
Everybody suffering bad
I'll post you a card from the island of Trini-hard.

While the *Mighty Duke* blamed Dr. Williams for all of the country's problems, *Lord Superior* gave him a chance to tell his side of the story. In *Why I Leave and Why I Come Back*, the PM tells how people don't work because 'they don't like the hot sun and they 'fraid the rain'. In contrast to this balanced treatment, *Chalkdust* puts some very hard questions straight to the Doc.

CLEAR YOUR NAME

For seventeen long years, you stay in power
But soon you'll have to go.
But many things happen under you doctor
That all of us don't know.
The worst of it may be just plain rumour
But if you must remain great
Before you go please clear the air
It's a local Watergate,
Ah askin
Dr. did Karl, really bug your telephone?
Did the Swiss Bank hand you cash of your own?
Did dey dare give you bread when they found fresh oil in the South?
Did Pat Solomon cuff you and bus 'up allyuh mout!?
Ah askin
Why didn't you attend your mother's funeral?
Did you retain your post in order to spite Karl?
Where did Kamal get breed to build Mohammedville?
Did you leave your son Alistair, one shilling in your will?

Eric Williams has been the leader of Trinidad since 1956. He brought the country to independence in 1962, and to commemorate that event, wrote *History of the People of Trinidad and Tobago* (1962). He is an easy man to caricature as he is small, wears dark glasses and a hearing aid, and smokes a pipe. Moreover, he is a consummate politician, and uses all of the political tricks of the trade. He is rarely seen in public; hence rumours abound about his private life.

Calypsonians take on the role of political pundits in Trinidad. In fact, all Trinidadians take on that role. However, calypsos are only sung during the calypso season so major political news is necessarily 'warmed over'. Occasionally a story will break during calypso season and a clever calypsonian will compose a song on it.

Since a calypso does not come out on the spot, it is difficult for calypso to take an analytical role toward politics. Questions can be raised, and one or another point of view can be expressed. However, the main role of calypso is to put the political event down in the oral archives. The oral tradition gives the people a chance to discuss their history and politics with a common language, and a given store of information.

The humour of political calypsos is critical not only because it entertains in the tents, but is also aids the memory of the lines. Strategically placed humorous lines can organize the learning of an entire verse or chorus.

THE PSYCHOLOGY OF TRINIDAD HUMOUR

'In the most fundamental sense, (humour) offers us release from our stabilizing system, escape from our self-imposed prisons. Every instance of laughter is an instance of liberation from our controls' (Mindess, 1971, p. 23).

In Trinidad, humour *has become* the stabilizing system and the basis of control in the society. Laughter has liberated the citizenry from some of the oppressive 'consequences of the Archieving Society' (McClelland, 1961). Perhaps it is the early and enduring Catholic influence, coupled with the African sense of time and history (Mbiti, 1970) which helped 'release Trinidadians from the rigours of a Protestant Work Ethic'.

In Trinidad they say, 'Any time is Trinidad time'. The loose attitude toward time is part of a general cultural flexibility which makes it seem that Mindess's (1971) God's-eye view of sense of humour was composed while smilin' down on Trinidad: 'a frame of mind so free, so flexible, and so kaleidoscopic that it rigidifies nowhere, gets hooked on nothing ... it finds no creature and no institution sacred ... so candid that it comprehends the hypocrisy of its candor ... it represents an ability to take whatever comes with a shrug if not a smile' (p. 30).

The basic ingredient in Trinidad humour is the fact that people love to play. Carnival time is an opportunity to 'play mas'. The masquerade contributes to the iconoclastic spirit. In fact, the apotheosis of the above point of view is the title of the Champion Mas Band of 1974—*Kaleidoscope*.

In a recent article Greene and Lepper (1974) provided experimental data in support of an interesting motivational distinction between work and play. They argued that activities which are rewarded by outside social agents are under *extrinsic* reinforcement contingencies and characterize what we call work. Activities that are self-rewarded, are relatively uninfluenced by outside social agents and are under *intrinsic* reinforcement contingencies. For Greene and Lepper, these activities characterize play. To say Trinidadians love to play, is to say the dominant activities of this society are intrinsically rewarding: that is, Trinidadians have fun.

Mischel (1958) attempted to test a folk notion in Trinidad that Negroes were 'impulsive, indulge themselves, settle for next to nothing if they can get it right away, do not work and wait for bigger things in the future'. This way of life is contrasted to that of East Indians who postpone small rewards for future larger ones. The results of the study confirmed the folk notion and led to an energetic research programme to track down the parameters of the ability to delay gratification (cf. Mischel 1966, for a review of this research).

In Trinidad, it is Bacchus, not Apollo who governs the life-style. Carnival is bacchanal and enjoyment is *now*. Humour and play are integral to the way of life and both are ratified each and every year in the national referendum that is Carnival.

The form and function of calypso grows out of the folk culture of Trinidad. The language of calypso is heard in taxis, rum shops and in street-corner limes.

The topics are found in newspapers and on everyone's lips. The events are public scandals, controversies, or well-known 'situations' of love and conflict.

The societal context in which calypso functions now is quite different from that in which it was spawned. Calypso arose in the midst of a combative ethos between African slaves and European slave-masters, and developed as a struggle of the lower classes against more privileged strata of society. As in the oral societies of Africa, the songs not only served these social-combat functions, but chronicled major events, etched significant persons and events in the memory of the populace. Techniques of mamaguy and picong were facilitated by the privacy of the French patois in the English governing context.

By 1974, calypso had lost much of the dynamic force that nurtured it and helped it spread throughout the society. Major events are well reported in the daily newspapers, *Express* and *Guardian*. In addition, two weeklies provide additional commentary and humour. *Tapia* is a political news sheet published by the major intellectual opposition to the current political party in power. The *Bomb* you have already been exposed to. The *Sunday Punch* is published by the people who publish the *Bomb* and provides a low-grade humour geared to young people. In addition there is a television station and two radio stations. Calypso does not serve a news function any more.

This is not to say that major events are not still recorded for the Trinidad public in the memorable lines of calypso. As *Sparrow* signalled the end of the Yankee era in Trinidad with his *Jean and Dinah*, this year's calypsos have captured some of the major events in sufficiently distinctive style that they too will join the authentic memorabilia of Trinidad's socio-political history.

There are numerous theoretical approaches to humour (see Keith-Spiegel, 1972, for an annotated review). In general, cognitive theories (e.g. Jones, 1970; Kagan, 1967; Koestler, 1964; Willmann, 1940) are not readily applicable to calypso humour. As Trotman said of his audiences 'you can't tell a straight joke. Trinidadians like slapstick, you gotta act it out'.

Of the motivational theories, relief from tension (e.g. Gregory, 1924; Kline, 1907) seems hardly to apply as tension is not a salient aspect of the psycho-social audience of Trinidad. Two examples of motivational theories of humour do apply well however. The first is the notion that humour reflects the positive affect which accompanies triumph and the feeling of superiority (cf. Hobbes, 1968; Rapp, 1949). The second is the psychoanalytic theory of humour (Freud, 1928, 1960). With the strong emphasis on sexual and aggressive themes and the invocation of superego control, Freudian theory points directly to many salient aspects of calypso humour.

Finally, we find social theories of humour provide a relevant orientation to our understanding of calypso and general Trinidadian humour (see Hertzler, 1970, for a comprehensive review of socio-cultural approaches). These theories sort out the role of humour in establishing and maintaining group boundaries (e.g. Martineau, 1972) or communicating norms and values within the groups (e.g. Hayworth, 1928; McComas, 1923; Reik, 1962).

The mouth is mightier than the sword—superiority in calypso humour

Since the beginning, calypsonians have been verbal warriors. In the early days, calypsonians like *Possum* and *Hannibal* held the stage. They rendered attacks on anyone who dared oppose them or their lower-class following. The humour of their calypsos was directed at all pretenders to social and political elevation. As representatives of the social and racial underdog, they directed ridicule, satire and insults at the upper classes.

In later years, the attacks were directed at other calypsonians to a greater extent. They took on fighting names (*noms de guerre*) and did verbal battle in the tents and elsewhere. Exalted language was a trademark of the early twentieth-century warriors. The superior calypsonian was the one who could impress the audience with his own verbal capacities while at the same time exposing his opponent's gross inadequacies.

When a calypsonian composes an extemporaneous verse about another, they call that 'singing on' a calypsonian. As these verses almost always make fun of, or ridicule, rather than praise (as many of the praise songs of Africa did), the superiority of one over another is constantly invoked. This kind of verbal humour is called picong and constitutes the core of Trinidadian humour. The question emerges then, why are Trinidadians so concerned with superiority?

Calypso developed out of the manifest social and political power asymmetry. Calypsonians and their followers were on the bottom. The only weapon they had was verbal ridicule—through clever and disguised language (here the French patois was particularly appropriate, for the British often could not understand the insult). Over the years, the calypso followers gained enormous personal pleasure in watching the assault of their fellow underlings in the upper classes.

As a style, as a humour form and as a source of entertainment and pleasure, picong spread throughout the lower-class society. When calypso got attached to Carnival, an even wider forum for ridicule was made available. Moreover, a new medium for ridicule was developed, the masquerade. From the beginning, the ex-slaves played mas on the military, and other society matrons and patriarchs. The mas provided another ridicule opportunity and what started as a small band of people, slowly spread out to include large segments of the society [cf. Crowley (1956) for descriptions of traditional masquerade characters].

From approximately 1959, picong was not so much a part of calypso tent performances. This trend has lessened the superiority element in calypso humour and heightened the sexual humour. The importance of Bill Trotman at the OYB is that he brought a running picong element back to the tent with his repartee with members of the audience.

In the image drawn by Rapp (1949) of the primitive duel in which the victor stands triumphantly over his vanquished foe, laughing is precisely the tenor of Trinidadian humour. However, unlike in Rapp's image, the foe is vanquished by clever words and piquant satire, and the entire audience joins in the laughter *with* the victor *at* the vanquished.

Check your superegos at the door—psychoanalytic theory in calypso humour

Freud's most influential work on humour (1960: first edition, 1905) argues that the energy for laughter comes from the release of inhibited tendencies. The inhibitions, concerning those prescriptive taboo behaviours—sexual and aggressive activity—are under superego domination. The energies thus built up by superego restrictions can be released through laughter. This is accomplished when the taboo themes are successfully slipped past the superego sentry by clever joke-techniques.

In his later work (1928), Freud elaborated the view that humour was a 'triumph of narcissism . . . (and) signifies the triumph not only of the ego, but the pleasure-principle.' In his 1958 article, Mischel described his view of immediate gratification as the embodiment of the pleasure principle. Moreover, Freud was favourably disposed towards the popular views of humour in his introductory summary: for example, he cites Fischer's (1889) 'A joke is a *playful* judgement . . . (creating) an aesthetic freedom . . . which is playful in contrast to work'.

It is not simply the fact that much of calypso humour concerns sexual themes, that makes Freudian theory appropriate. As the above suggests, the attitude of the calypsonian and the audience is a playful one, slightly iconoclastic and, in general, possessed of those attributes which predispose one to appreciate humour.

Freud acknowledges that, 'A person who is dominated by a mood concerned with serious thoughts is not fitted to confirm that a jest has (created) verbal pleasure. He must himself be in cheerful or at least indifferent state of feeling in order to act as the jest's third person'. So Freud implicates the audience as well as the ego and superego. Trinidadians willingly comply.

Sexual and aggressive themes predominate in calypso humour. The positive affect which Freud presumes to follow the triumph of the ego in releasing repressed psychic energy is abundantly evident night after night in the calypso tents. However, the joke-technique is scant in many cases. The great pleasure shown by the audience suggests that the superego must be otherwise occupied. The play mood which is brought into the calypso tents is so complete that fun is had by all.

Again we find that fun and play move consistently through the calypso tents and Trinidad society. Some Trinidadians complain about what they call 'Carnival mentality', but the laughter and enjoyment continue year after year.

Separating the sheep from the goats—social functions of humour

Martineau (1972) presents a detailed analysis of the ways in which humour functions in inter-group and intra-group relations. The basic and important point of this analysis is that humour functions to strengthen the in-group and disparage the out-group. From its inception, calypso, through the use of humour, has provided the means of expressing hostility toward outsiders. Calypso has always been the vehicle of the lower class. The targets of the humour have generally been members of the ruling class and the functional arms of that class (e.g. police, military, etc.).

The calypsos of 1974 made several attacks on the political power structure, embodied by the Prime Minister, Eric Williams. All of the hard times felt by the masses were brought out and blamed squarely on the political leaders. Audiences enjoy watching and listening to *their* calypsonians giving 'em hell.

In addition to attacking the power structure, calypsos also make fun of the average Trinidadian as well (cf. *Mr. Trinidad* by *Maestro*). This serves to point out general shortcomings and has the desired goal of promoting self-scrutiny and improvement. Martineau (1972) analyses the role of humour in intra-group cohesion. Bergson (1911) also emphasizes the social corrective role played by humour.

Another favourite target of the calypsonians is the tourist. Over the years the Yankee has been a favourite subject, as have most tourists who come down for Carnival wearing sunglasses, shorts and trying to dance the calypso (those who are brave). The ability to ridicule the outsiders not only solidifies the essence of being a Trinidadian, but it also reaffirms the special character of Carnival. As they say, 'it is we own ting'.

In conclusion, calypso humour weaves in and out of the total fabric of Trinidad society. We have tried to give the reader a feel for the breadth and character of this extraordinary phenomenon. To really appreciate the organic wholeness with which calypso humour articulates the ethos of Trinidad society, one must experience it *in situ*. We have tried to bring some of that experience to you in this chapter. To complete your education, you must make the trip for Carnival and calypso. May Bacchus bless you.

NOTES

1. The research for this chapter was conducted in 1973–74 while Dr. Jones was a Fellow of the John Simon Guggenheim Memorial Foundation. Mr. Liverpool is a school teacher in Trinidad, and a professional calypsonian (The Mighty Chalkdust).
2. 'Obeah' is the name given to the practice of alchemy and religious superstition by a member of the community. It has taken on a West Indian character, but is derived from African beginnings. The practice was banned by the British, but recently, Forbes Burnham, Prime Minister of Guyana, removed legal sanctions from the practice.

REFERENCES

Bergler, E. (1956). *Laughter and the Sense of Humor*. New York: Intercontinental Medical Book Corporation.

Bergson, H. (1911). *Laughter: An Essay on the Meaning of the Comic*. New York: Macmillan.

Crowley, D. (1956). The traditional masques of Carnival. *Caribbean Quarterly*, 4, 194–223.

Crowley, D. (1959). Towards a definition of calypso. *Ethnomusicology*, 3, 57–66; 117–121.

Elder, J. D. (1971). Evolution of the traditional calypso of Trinidad and Tobago: A socio-historical analysis of songchange. University Microfilms, Ann Arbor, Michigan.

Esponet, C., and Pitts, H. (1941). *Land of Calypso Origin and Development of Trinidad's Folksong*. Port-of-Spain: Central Library.

286

Fischer, K. (1889). *Uber den Witz* (2nd ed.). Heidelberg.

Freud, S. (1928). Humour. *International Journal of Psychoanalysis*, **9**, 1–66.

Freud, S. (1960). *Jokes and Their Relationship to The Unconscious.* New York: Norton. (First German edition, 1905.)

Greene, D., and Lepper, M. R. (1974). How to turn play into work. *Psychology Today*, September, 49–54.

Gregory, J. C. (1924). *The Nature of Laughter.* London: Kegan Paul.

Grimes, J. (1962). From slave's chant to the hit parade. *Trinidad Guardian.* Port-of-Spain.

Hamilton, R.C.G. (1881). The History of Camboulay: The Hamilton Report. In *Vanguard*, 8 February, 1969.

Hayworth, D. (1928). The social origins and functions of laughter. *Psychological Review*, **35**, 367–384.

Hertzler, J. O. (1970). *Laughter: A Socio-Scientific Analysis.* New York: Exposition Press.

Hill, E. (1972). *The Trinidad Carnival.* Austin, Texas: University of Texas Press.

Hobbes, T. (1968). *Leviathan.* Harmondsworth: Penguin (originally published, 1651).

Jones, J. M. (1970). Cognitive factors in the appreciation of humor: A theoretical and experimental analysis. Unpublished Doctoral Dissertation, Yale University.

Jones, J. M. (1974). Trinidad humour: A living experience. *Trinidad Sunday Guardian.* Port-of-Spain. June 4th.

Kagan, J. (1967). On the need for relativism. *American Psychologist*, **22**, 131–147.

Keith-Spiegel, P. (1972). Early conceptions of humor: Varieties and issues. In J. H. Goldstein and P. E. McGhee (Eds.), *The Psychology of Humour.* New York: Academic Press.

Kline, L. W. (1907). The psychology of humor. *American Journal of Psychology*, **18**, 421–441.

Koestler, A. (1964). *The Act of Creation.* New York: Macmillan.

Martineau, W. H. (1972). A model of the social functions of humor. In J. H. Goldstein and P. E. McGhee (Eds.), *The Psychology of Humor.* New York: Academic Press.

McClelland, D. C. (1961). *The Achieving Society.* New York: Van Nostrand.

McComas, H. C. (1923). The origin of laughter. *Psychological Review*, **30**, 45–55.

Mbiti, J. (1970). *African Religions and Philosophy.* New York: Anchor/Doubleday.

Mindess, H. (1971). *Laughter and Liberation.* Los Angeles: Nash Publishers.

Mischel, W. (1958). Preference for delayed reinforcement: An experimental study of a cultural observation. *Journal of Abnormal and Social Psychology*, **56**, 57–61.

Mischel, W. (1966). Theory and research on the antecedents of self-imposed delay of reward. In B. A. Maher (Ed.), *Progress in Experimental Personality Research*, Vol. 3. New York: Academic Press.

Pearse, A. (1956). Carnival in nineteenth-century Trinidad. *Caribbean Quarterly*, **4**, 175–193; 250–262.

Quevedo, R. (1962). *History of The Calypso This Country of Ours.* Independence Brochure, Port-of-Spain.

Rapp, A. (1949). A phylogenetic theory of wit and humor. *Journal of Social Psychology*, **30**, 81–96.

Reik, T. (1962). *Jewish Wit.* New York: Gamut Press.

Rohlehr, F. G. (1971). Calypso and politics. *Moko*, No. 73, October.

Rohlehr, F. G. (1972). Forty years of calypso. *Tapia*, **2**, Nos. 1–3.

Williams, E. (1962). *History of the People of Trinidad and Tobago.* Port-of-Spain: PNM Publishing Co. Ltd.

Willmann, J. M. (1940). An analysis of humor and laughter. *American Journal of Psychology*, **53**, 70–85.

Chapter 13

Wit and Humour in Mass Communication

Charles R. Gruner

This chapter begins by stating the limitations its author has imposed upon his
selection of subject matter; it defines some key terms, and then reviews theory
and research pertinent to the question, 'Does (or, should) wit and humour in
mass communication have particular communicative impact upon its
audience?'.

The theory and research on humour and wit is divided according to definitions
below. The question of whether humour should, theoretically, be an aid to
persuasion is taken up first, and is followed by a review of studies on the subject.
Next, experimental studies of satire as persuasion are reviewed. Finally, studies
of the effects upon learning and speaker 'image' produced by the use of humour
are presented. The chapter concludes with an overview of research studies, by
way of summary, and some directions for further research.

SCOPE AND DEFINITIONS OF KEY TERMS

First of all, this chapter limits itself largely to a review of those studies we call
empirical, or scientific. This means that, for the most part, it concentrates on
studies that are experimental in nature. Other studies of a quantitative nature,
as in the case of correlational studies, are also considered here. Some non-
scientific observations are mentioned, but only with the necessary data to make
their conclusions seem reasonable.

Secondly, this chapter necessarily concentrates upon research on the effect of
wit and humour in American mass communication. The pertinent consideration
here is the fact that the only such research known was done on the New World
side of the Atlantic.

The third limitation imposed upon the contents of this chapter arises from the
biased experience of the author as a professor of communication. While he has
an interest in any and every aspect of wit and humour, he has confined his
research to the *communicative functions* of wit and humour. And, by 'communicative functions', he means communicative effects in auditors and readers
that were *intended* by the wit/humorist. The focus is upon what influences mass
communication wit and humour are likely to have on auditors and readers.

The pertinent questions explored are: 'Do wit and humour produce, retard or enhance persuasion?'; 'Do wit and humour enhance or impede learning when accompanying informative presentations?' and 'Does the use of wit and/or humour affect the "image" of whoever uses it?'.

'Humour', as used in this chapter, refers to laugh-or-smile-provoking stimuli of a good-natured sort, that is, likely to be minimally offensive to the object of the laughter or smiling. It is playful poking of fun with the sole aim of amusement. It is likely to deal with the inconsequential (or the serious treated *as* inconsequential), the whimsical, the incongruous.

'Wit' is here defined as some form of (usually) verbal cleverness which has the potential for amusing, but also is intended (however consciously or unconsciously) to achieve one or more *other* purposes. One of these other purposes may be simply to demonstrate the verbal cleverness of the maker of the witticism; another may be to more or less maliciously ridicule some person, institution, object, or whatever. Freud divided wit into two kinds: 'harmless wit' he described as more akin to what this writer calls humour; it is wit that amuses with its verbal cleverness. 'Tendency wit', on the other hand, is more likely to both amuse *and* to ridicule some person, institution, object, etc. with its linguistic *double entendre*. Freud would have labelled as harmless wit, for instance, the following: 'I saw a gorgeous blonde today constantly tugging at her wool dress and wiggling uncomfortably; she obviously was a chafing dish'. On the other hand, Freud would have labelled as 'tendency wit' what has been proposed as the shortest dramatic review ever, that of the play *I Am a Camera*: 'No Leica'.

A special form of tendency wit, *satire* is definitely intended to be both funny and, in some way, damaging to the object of its ridicule. As Gilbert Highet (1962) put it: 'The purpose of satire is, through laughter and invective, to cure folly and punish evil'. Marie Collins Swabey (1961) wrote pretty much the same thing in different words: 'To ridicule the vices and follies of mankind is the business of satire ... satire by its imaginative eloquence excites anger at human misdeeds and cruelties'. The same thought is also echoed by Edgar Johnson (1945): 'For satiric purposes, however, abuse has to be more than funny, it has to be damaging ... the one ingredient common to all [satire] ... is criticism'.

For this chapter, the term 'mass communication' is defined as any one-to-many form of communication. The definition would include the usual media forms for communicating from one source to a larger audience: motion pictures, radio and television, newspapers and magazines, and widely-distributed audio-recordings. Also included is public address, since it is considered a one-to-many form of communication, and since it is one form on which much of the experimentation to be outlined here was done. Public address is included for another reason: the assumption, perhaps not always completely valid, that communicative effects observed in this medium can be generalized to other forms of mass communication.

Having stated its scope limitations and having defined its key terms, this chapter now proceeds to its review of research, in two main parts: wit and humour as persuasion; and the role of wit and humour in learning and speaker image.

HUMOUR: PERSUASIVE?

There are several theoretical reasons why one would think that the addition of humour to a message intended to be persuasive might enhance its persuasiveness. The humour, if pleasing to the audience, might conceivably make the *source* of the message (a speaker, an advertiser, a brand name or company) be perceived more favourably by the audience of the message. If the source is more favourably perceived, an increase in the source's perceived credibility, thus persuasiveness, might occur. The addition to a message of apt and entertaining humour might make a message more interesting, and thus more keenly attended to by its audience; if the audience attends to the message more actively and if the message attended to is an effective one, more persuasion should take place. If the humour added to a persuasive message, in addition to pleasing an audience, acts as additional supporting material for a persuasive point, persuasiveness should be boosted. Abraham Lincoln was celebrated for his ability to bolster his generalizations by humorous illustrations that might begin something like, 'There was this farmer down in Sangamon County ...'. The addition of humour might possibly make a persuasive speech more memorable, thus rendering the message and the tendency to act upon its advice salient in the nervous systems of the audience for a longer period of time. And, finally, it has been hypothesized that humour in a persuasive message might distract audience members so that their counter-argumentation would be precluded, thus increasing the persuasiveness of the message (Sternthal and Craig, 1973).

A review of experimental studies testing such hypotheses provides little support for them.

Studies of humour as persuasion

The first known empirical study of the effect of humour in persuasive messages was conducted by Lull (1940). He used the topic of 'state medicine' or 'socialized medicine' in his messages. One speech was in favour of state medicine, another was against state medicine. For each speech there was a regular, serious version; then jokes, wisecracks, puns and so on, were added to each version to produce a humorous counterpart.

These speeches were memorized by competent and experienced college speakers and presented live to audiences who previously had been tested for their attitude toward 'state medicine'. After hearing one of the speeches, the audience members were re-tested for attitude toward 'state medicine' with an alternate form of the test. In addition, they were asked to rate the speaker on three attributes: 'interestingness', 'humour' and 'convincingness'. As a further check on the operation of the humour variable, each experimental session was monitored and the amount of audience laughter recorded.

The humour in the funny versions was perceived. The humorous versions elicited from 6 to 23 instances of laughter, whereas *no* laughter occurred during the 'serious' versions. Also, the humorous speeches were rated as humorous the serious speeches were not. But the humorous speeches did not differ from the serious speeches in ratings of interestingness or convincingness. And, finally, although all four speeches produced measurable and significant attitude change, neither the humorous nor the serious speeches were superior in this regard.

Lull's was a well-designed and carefully executed study, and the humour added to his speeches was not only germane to the subject matter, but tended to be the kind that would serve as additional support to his persuasive points. For instance, in support of his point on the mediocrity of foreign state medicine, he included this jibe:

> The glowing reports of socialized medicine in Russia in American books and magazines have been a source of amusement ... Always we have wished their authors only one punishment—a week or so as patients in the second-best hospital in Russia.

Perhaps this lack of positive results from so well-done a study served to discourage further studies of this kind. For it was not until 1961 that another effort was forthcoming.

Kilpela (1961), like Lull, used speeches concerned with socialized medicine but, unlike Lull, he (1) used only a humorous and a non-humorous speech *for* state medicine and (2) used, instead of anecdotes, mostly what this author would call 'wisecracks' to support his attacks on 'private medicine'. Consider the following:

> As your friendly family physician carefully operates on you and your wallet ...
> You cannot tell, furthermore, whether your next sickness will be a five dollar tune-up or a $500.00 overhaul.
> I don't want to say that my doctor is expensive, but he sends me a thank-you note before he sends me the bill.

These speeches were tape-recorded and presented to student subjects in a well-designed experimental format. Like Lull, both speeches were found to be persuasive. They differed markedly on the humour variable, but they did not differ in persuasiveness.

A later M.A. thesis (Youngman, 1966) attempted to find the effects of adding either germane or non-germane humour to a persuasive speech. Youngman found that neither type of humour added to its persuasiveness, but the speech with the germane humour was rated as significantly higher on 'worthwhileness' than was the one containing the non-germane humour.

A follow-up study of Youngman's project was done by Brandes (1970), who had directed the former's thesis. He was interested in the effect on persuasion of different *types* of humour. He produced three variations of the basic speech Youngman had begun with, in addition to the non-humorous version: one contained jokes, one contained puns and one contained sarcastic humour. None of the three types of humour seems to have enhanced the persuasiveness of the basic speech.

For his Ph.D. dissertation, Kennedy (1972) used a variety of types of humour in an attempt to enhance the persuasiveness of a speech designed to persuade people that greater censorship of the movies is needed. He used a variety of humorous material from one-line pun-wisecracks such as '. . . France was the country where they originated the phrase, "Movies are bedder than ever"', to full-fledged anecdotal stories such as:

A film reviewer for a local police department recently tried to stop the exhibition of a new flesh flick because the picture contained an extremely graphic orgy scene. The film-maker readily defended his film by asking, 'What's the matter, haven't you ever seen seven men, four women and a sheep all madly in love with each other?'

Kennedy's results were identical to those of Lull, Brandes and Youngman: the humour was perceived and appreciated, but persuasion was not affected.

One interesting feature of Kennedy's study was that in one experimental group he employed a special introduction to the message which led the audience to *expect* the speech to be humorous. This laughter-begging introduction increased both the amount of laughter evoked and the humour ratings of the speech.

At about the same time that Kennedy was conducting his experiment, Welford (1971) was experimenting with the use of humour in a political debate speech of a refutational nature. He tested subjects on their attitudes toward five issues in the debate and found that the use of humour by the refutational speaker was not effective on four issues and actually detrimental on a fifth. However, this writer would question the germaneness and quality of the humour used; his opinion is that the jokes lacked taste, for the most part. The reader can judge for himself by reading the actual stimuli in Welford's dissertation or by perusing his humorous stimuli reprinted in a forthcoming book (Gruner, in press) which, incidentally, reprints the humorous stimuli from most of the studies reviewed here.

The usefulness of humour in sermons was studied by Gruner and Lampton (1972). To a sermon which persuasively argued the thesis that even non-believers should read the Bible they added eight items of germane humour, which had been previously test-marketed for humorousness. The speech was tape-recorded before a live audience; a non-humorous version of the sermon was then devised by electronically editing out the humorous items and the audience responses (laughter) to them. Then the two speeches were played to randomly divided student subjects, who were then tested for attitude toward the sermon's thesis. Again, the humour seems to have had no effect on the persuasiveness of the message.

For her dissertation, Markiewicz (1972) conducted seven experiments, all dealing with humorous stimuli as an aid to either learning or persuasion. The only positive finding she turned up regarding humour and persuasion was in *one* of those seven experiments. A humorous cartoon added to a letter appealing for the return of a completed postal card seems to have boosted returns of the cards. However, as Markiewicz admits, this experiment did not control for the variable of having *any kind* of a picture (humorous or not) on the appeal letter.

Perreault (1972) tested both humorous and non-humorous printed advertisements for memorability; he did not find the humorous ads superior in terms of audience recall. His results may have been due to the fact that he used print rather than broadcast-type ads. There is some feeling that humour works better in radio or television ads than in the print medium. As Kalman Phillips (1968), broadcast director of McManus, John & Adams, Inc., says:

> This preponderance of humor in broadcast has not been reflected in the advertising appearing in newspapers and magazines. The reason, basically, is that the kind of humor that appeals to a broad audience with a varied cultural background is much more difficult to achieve in print than in broadcast.

The studies reviewed above would hardly encourage a professional persuader, such as an advertiser, to employ humour in his messages. However, there is a great deal of anecdotal evidence that humour *can* be tremendously successful at selling products. Drastic increases in sales, after advertising campaigns have turned towards emphasizing humour, have been recorded in the U.S.A. for cigarettes, food products, soft drinks, antacids, candy, airlines, deodorants, and men's socks (Gruner, 1974, unpublished paper). However, the persuasive task of the advertiser is a much different one from those undertaken in the experiments cited above.

First, the experiments employed multi-faceted messages on complicated social issues that were directed to audiences with widely varying attitudes toward these issues. The advertiser, on the other hand, employs a very simple message (buy!) emphasizing his particular brand of an item which just about everyone wants or needs anyway. Instead of trying to manipulate the complex ideational, perceptual and attitudinal machinery of his audience regarding a social issue, the advertiser simply seeks a *choice* for his brand over others; *choice* from almost-equally desirable options.

Methodological differences between real-life advertising situations and the experiments reviewed play their part, also. The experiments exposed subjects only once to only one message each, usually; the advertiser repeats himself endlessly. The experiments measured for effect immediately after exposure to the message; the advertiser might find his results weeks or months later. For these and other reasons humour will probably continue to be employed by advertisers despite the negative research findings reviewed above.

Theoretically it is more reasonable to expect persuasive effect from *satire* than from mere humour. As noted earlier, satire is actually *intended* as a form of propaganda by the satirist. Satire is a form of wit; and wit differs from humour in much the same way that rhetoric differs from poetic (Gruner, 1965b). The next section of this chapter focuses upon the research testing satire as persuasion.

Studies of satire as persuasion

The earliest known study of satirical materials as rhetoric was done by Annis (1939), who reported that 'straight' newspaper editorials were more persuasive than editorial cartoons on the same topics. However, his one-paragraph report is too brief to allow for useful evaluation.

While not a test of actual editorial cartoons, Asher and Sargent (1941) found that cartoon-type caricatures affected judgements of the concepts which the caricatures represented. They read off verbal terms of student subjects and asked them to evaluate the terms on a five-step scale from 'like definitely' to 'dislike definitely'. Then the subjects were shown cartoon caricatures *with* the term which each represented and were asked to rate the terms again. Significant differences were found between the earlier and later ratings of eight terms: Labour, Uncle Sam, Pacifists, John Bull, Industry, New Deal, Politics, and Liberals. It would seem that the caricatures produced at least short-term attitude change.

Asher and Sargent's findings are at least partly supported by those of Brinkman (1968). He was interested in determining what various combinations of straight newspaper editorials and editorial cartoons would most affect attitude change. He exposed student subjects to booklets containing various combinations of editorials and cartoons. His findings are paraphrased and summarized below:

(a) More opinion change occurs when an editorial cartoon is presented with a complementary editorial than occurs when either is presented alone.
(b) More change is produced by an editorial alone than by a cartoon alone.
(c) Presenting the editorial and cartoon together is more effective than presenting first one, then the other; however, presenting the cartoon first and the editorial second is more effective than vice versa.
(d) More change occurred when both argued the same main point; if one argued the main point and the other argued an ancillary point, the effect on opinion was less.

American radio and television stations broadcast very little of what could reasonably be called satire. The commercial interests which sponsor programmes are apparently unwilling to underwrite any material which some people might find offensive. As a result, there is almost no empirical evidence of the effectiveness of broadcast satire. The one study extant (Berlo and Kumata, 1956) investigated the effects of a one-hour radio drama produced by the

Canadian Broadcasting Company. Berlo and Kumata exposed student subjects to a recording of a radio drama which satirized U.S. congressional investigating committees in general and the late Senator Joseph McCarthy, former junior senator from Wisconsin, in particular. The subjects' attitudes toward a number of concepts were tested on semantic differential scales before and after hearing the recording. Changes from pre- to post-test were noted on scales for only one concept: the experimental subjects decreased in their regard for congressional investigations. A control group of subjects, who only completed the scales without hearing the programme did not demonstrate this change. Attitude toward Senator McCarthy actually improved, contrary to the authors' hypothesis, although not enough for statistical significance. Berlo and Kumata speculate that regard for McCarthy may have increased in the case of some subjects because of a boomerang effect due to the general feeling that the satire was unfair, and the fact that Americans tend to favour the underdog. This writer is more inclined to attribute the shift on McCarthy to mere statistical regression; the control group scores regressed similarly.

Two other investigations of satire/humour in the broadcast medium should be mentioned at this point. Surlin (1973) was interested in how high- and low-dogmatic persons responded to the characters of the television show *All in the Family*, which regularly features the bigoted, racist Archie Bunker squabbling with his left-of-centre liberal son-in-law Mike. Respondents were asked which characters in the show they 'agreed with' and were also asked to rate each character on a scale based upon how much they 'liked' each. They also completed a short-form dogmatism scale. As predicted, the high-dogmatics tended to agree with Archie and disagree with Mike; the opposite held true for the low-dogmatics. High-dogmatics also expressed a great deal of liking for Archie, which was to be expected. But, somewhat surprisingly, the low-dogmatics *also* expressed a liking for Archie. This led Surlin to conclude that the producers of the show had succeeded in making Archie into a lovable bigot with which one need not agree in order to want to tune in to that programme.

Vidmar and Rokeach (1974) were also interested in how television viewers reacted to the characters of *All in the Family*. They tested a sample of both Canadian and American viewers for ethnocentrism (or prejudice) and then interviewed them as to their reactions to the characters of the popular television programme. They found that the selective perception of these viewers was apparently affected by their prejudice.

Those viewers high in prejudice were significantly more likely to admire the racist Archie more than the liberal Mike, were more likely to perceive Archie as 'making more sense', and were more likely to perceive Archie as 'winning in the end'. Furthermore, those high in prejudice showed more of a tendency to believe that they would share Archie's views in twenty years and also to more often condone Archie's racist slurs. The prejudiced Canadian sample perceived the show as poking fun at Archie less often than did the low-prejudiced Canadians.

Vidmar and Rokeach suggest that the operation of selective perception causes *All in the Family* to reinforce the racial and ethnic prejudices present in its audience members.

For his Ph.D. dissertation Gruner (1965a) investigated the persuasive impact of a completely satirical speech ridiculing the idea of governmental censorship of literature, movies, broadcasting and so on. He composed a speech which ironically suggested that, because they were so full of sex and violence, a programme of governmental censorship was needed to ban *nursery rhymes*. Because this speech was used for several studies, it is reproduced here in full.

A DEMURE PROPOSAL

Ladies and gentlemen:

As professor Harold Hill, the 'Music Man' has said (or rather, sung), 'We got trouble . . . we got a whole lot of trouble' these days, and I mean trouble with the growing problem of juvenile delinquency. It seems that the entire younger generation has lost any respect for authority it ever had. And, if you will just pay some serious attention to our mass media—our movies, television, magazines and paperback novels—I think you will find it not too difficult to see *why* our young people are what they are. The violence, obscenity, and leftist propaganda in our entertainment media these days is enough to corrupt good upbringing in any youngster.

Some well-meaning citizens would fight the problem with strict government censorship of movies, television, and printed material. This is undoubtedly an excellent idea, but: I am convinced that such censorship, needed as it is, is inadequate. It does not go far enough; it does not reach deeply enough to be completely effective. For our children are brought up in an atmosphere *saturated* with fictional violence and depravity from a very early age. And they receive this corrupting influence, not from Hollywood or New York, but at their mothers' knees! I am speaking, ladies and gentlemen, of that insidious literature we innocently call *Nursery Rhymes*.

A preposterous charge, you say? You think that nursery rhymes can have nothing in common with, say *The Untouchables*? Look at some examples with me.

Take, for instance, 'Rock-a-bye, Baby'. What happens to the innocent babe of this little horror story? You know how it ends: down comes the baby, cradle and all, crashing to the ground from the treetops! Now, isn't that a lovely little ditty to croon to your pre-school child? Isn't that a pretty image with which to send him off to beddy bye!

Look at another example: 'Humpty Dumpty'. He stupidly falls from a high wall to a death gory enough to turn the stomach. But what then? Do they sweep the carcass into a rubber sack for a decent Christian burial? No! These men and horses try to paste the sticky mess back together again! Now, I ask you: just how revolting can you get? After enough of this kind of horror should we be surprised when six-year-olds occasionally dissect a playmate?

These two cases are not isolated examples either. Nursery rhymes abound in violence, sadism, and deviant behavior. There's 'Georgie Porgie', who kissed the girls against their wishes, making them cry (sounds like a future sex offender?). But this Georgie is so cowardly he runs when the other boys come out to play. There's 'Tom, Tom the Piper's Son', who stole a pig and away he run. There is the brutal story of the attempt to *bake alive* four and twenty blackbirds, one of whom retaliates upon the person of an honest maid by biting off her nose in the garden. In the story of the brutal bow-and-arrow slaying of 'Cock Robin', the Fish freely admits to catching the murder victim's *blood* in a dish! Again, I ask: how long can we allow our children's minds to be poisoned by this trash?

What must little children think when they hear of the farmer's wife sadistically cutting off the tails of three defenseless, blind mice? How will they feel toward 'Little Johnny Green' who threw 'Pussy in the Well' down there in 'Ding Dong Dell'? Will they condone the crime of 'Peter', the pumpkin eater, who apparently killed his wife and stuffed her corpse into a pumpkin shell simply because he could not afford to keep her?

Perhaps you have been wondering why youngsters today seem to be so lazy, shiftless, and irresponsible? They're probably just emulating another nursery rhyme hero, 'Little Boy Blue', who slept away under a haystack while the cows and sheep he was supposed to be tending ate away at his father's corn and meadow.

I haven't the time now to discuss with you the murky Freudian implications underlying the story of 'Jack and Jill'. You remember that they went *up* a hill supposedly in search of water, when anyone knows that water is found in *low* places. But I would ask you to ponder what sort of ideals are being suggested to our kids by that mysterious woman who lives in the house shaped like a *shoe*. She apparently lives off relief and the Aid to Dependant Children handout—but you will notice there is *not one mention of a husband*!

Do you begin to see *now* the extent to which our children are exposed to objectionable material? Is it not shocking to realize that all this garbage is taught them by their mothers and nursemaids?

By now you are probably wondering what can be done about this menace.

The protection of our young people demands that we rid our nurseries of the despicable influence of so-called nursery rhymes. Nothing less than a nationwide ban on their printing, with penalties of fines and jail terms for their publication would be adequate. In addition, mothers, nursemaids, and others having intimate contact with our toddlers must be educated, then *warned* against the repetition of such trash. After a suitable time, punishment for recitation of nursery rhymes would be imposed. A motto of the John Birch Society says, 'If Mommy is a Commie, you gotta turn her in'; for mommies who tell nursery rhymes to children, our motto might well be, 'If Mother goes and "Mother Gooses", she'll pay in one of our calabooses'.

After we successfully stamp out nursery rhymes, we can forge on to the wide and fertile field of children's literature. Mrs. Thomas J. White of Indiana has shown the way for us here. Mrs. White was part of a state committee to investigate school library books. As far as I know, she is the first to decry the communistic undertones of that famous children's classic, 'Robin Hood.' The concept of robbing the rich to give to the poor is a technique for creating a classless society right out of Marx and Engels!

And while we're about it, let us take note of how far this Robin Hood lives outside of his cultural norms. He lives, you remember, not in a house, but in the woods. Not only does he scorn the solid responsibilities of home ownership, but he is a bachelor, as are all his band. And, do they work? Of course not. They make a living breaking the fish and game laws!

One of Robin's top henchmen is Friar Tuck. Although a Church cleric, you would not want your son or daughter to take him as a model of religious piety. For he would much rather bash in heads with his trusty stave than read from the Good Book. And you *know* whom he most enjoys bashing—the Sheriff!

One could go on and on with the objectionable episodes and nuances of Robin Hood and like stories; for instance, there's the unseemly number of times the unchaperoned Maid Marian manages to slip off to see Robin Hood—*in the woods*—but I'm sure you see my point now.

Ladies and gentlemen, the time to move against these pernicious forces in our society is now. We must launch a new crusade—a crusade of the spirit. Even as we sit here, some innocent child is being twisted and warped by the horrors of 'Mother Goose'; his older brother is learning utter rebellion from Robin Hood; and Daddy sits entranced, watching the blonde singer–moll caught in the machine-gun crossfire between Eliot Ness and Frank Nitti's boys.

The battle must begin. And we will not find it easy, for censorship has enemies everywhere. Those of low taste and vicious character will fight us every step. It will be an uphill battle all the way. But this is a battle we must fight; and it is a battle we must win. For, even though the corrupt are strong, their vice cannot stand against the might of our righteousness; we must blast the enemy from their entrenchments; we must engage them on the open barren ramparts; we must strike them down as they run for cover; we must *kick* and *beat* and *grind* and *stomp* them until they are defeated utterly. For only then can we sweep into oblivion the befouling influence of nursery rhymes.

The speech was printed and circulated among a panel of English literature professors, who were asked to check which, from a list provided, were the definitions that described this speech. The list was a series of definitions and partial definitions from dictionaries of 'satire' and several other concepts. They were also asked to write what they thought was the thesis of the piece. These professors agreed unanimously that the speech was a 'satire on censorship'.

The speech was tape-recorded by an experienced and skilled speaker before a live audience for use as the stimulus for the experiment. Freshman English students were tested three weeks before, immediately afterward, and three weeks after the experimental groups heard the recorded speech. No attitude change was detectable.

On the delayed post-test the experimental subjects were asked to check from a list of five statements the one they perceived to be the thesis of the 'speech on censorship' they had heard in class recently. Only 12 of the 129 experimental subjects checked the thesis intended by the writer. Apparently these students had missed the point and had responded to the speech as *humour*, not as satire with a serious purpose.

The conclusion that the speech had been perceived as humour and not satire was bolstered by other data from the study. Subjects had been asked also to rate the speech on 'funniness' and the speaker on 'intelligence'. A correlation of these ratings was negative: -0.36. The funnier they thought the speech to be, the less intelligent they thought the speaker.

The negative correlation suggested that the subjects had perceived the speaker as 'clownish', and reacted to him as such. Goodchilds (1959) found that discussants who used 'clownish' humour were perceived as popular but not influential, but that 'sarcastic wits' were perceived as influential but not popular.

Apparently getting the serious thesis of a satirical piece across is a potential problem for every satirist. Evidence exists that many people fail to perceive the serious points of satires. Carl (1968) exposed people in two small towns to editorial cartoons previously printed in newspapers. The subjects were asked to look at each cartoon and then tell what the point of it was. He found that only 15 % of the attempts were completely correct, with another 15 % close to being correct but not quite. He replicated his study in a locale where subjects would possess a higher educational level (Ithaca, N. Y.) and found that fully 63 % of the efforts were completely incorrect. In an unpublished study Kendall (1973) found that a slight majority of blue-collar workers in a field study correctly identified the theses of two editorial cartoons, but a large majority failed to identify that of a third. She also found that ability to recognize editorial theses was related to youthfulness and to number of years of formal schooling. Gruner

(1972a) found that an Art Hoppe column ridiculing the idea of capital punishment as a deterrent to murder was widely misunderstood, and that supporters of President Richard Nixon much more often were able to detect the thesis of an anti-McGovern satire than that of one ridiculing Mr. Nixon (Gruner, 1972b). Cooper and Jahoda (1947) discovered that prejudiced people employ a wide variety of defence mechanisms to avoid understanding contrary propaganda whether satirical in nature or not. And, in a recent study, Gruner (1974) exposed 116 students to three editorial satires and asked them to indicate the theses of each. Only 15 subjects correctly identified the theses of all three satires. He also found low dogmatism to be associated with ability to perceive the point of satire.

Inability to recognize the thesis of a satire was precluded in Gruner's (1966) partial replication of his dissertation study. In this experiment the recorded speech was *introduced as a satire* critical of the concept of censorship. The data show that those already opposed to censorship were not persuaded to be more opposed, but that those originally neutral toward or in favour of censorship did shift in attitude a significant amount in the expected direction. This shift held up over the three weeks from post-test to delayed post-test, also. In order to make a comparison with the earlier (1965) study, a correlation between ratings of speaker intelligence and speech funniness was computed. In this later study, in which each subject was *told* the thesis of the satire, the correlation was positive (+ 0·35, $p < 0.02$). Apparently, perception of the satire's thesis causes a positive relationship between humour appreciation and perceived speaker intelligence, whereas the opposite kind of relationship occurs when the satire is perceived as mere humour.

Zeman (1967) again partially replicated the Gruner study using high school students for subjects and a post-test-only control group design. His study produced results that were inconclusive, although the fact that one group was *told* the thesis of the satire may have caused them to produce lower attitude scores on censorship than another experimental group that was *not* told the thesis in advance.

Pokorny and Gruner (1969) studied the effect of including satire as supporting material for an otherwise straightforward speech critical of the concept of censorship. Several of the paragraphs from Gruner's satirical stimulus (*A Demure Proposal*) which had drawn the most laughter in previous studies were extracted and inserted in the straightforward persuasive speech. The subjects of the study were tested for attitude toward consorship before and after hearing either the straight speech, the satire-added speech, or a control stimulus (poetry reading). Although both experimental groups shifted in the expected direction, the satire-added speech cannot be said to have been more persuasive than the straightforward speech.

Aside from that in political (editorial) cartoons, the bulk of political and editorial satire being published in U.S. newspapers today is written by three men: Art Buchwald, Arthur Hoppe and Russell Baker. The next series of studies reviewed are on the persuasive effects of such editorial columns employing satire.

Recent experiments with professional satire

Gruner (1967a) first studied the impact of two editorial satires by Art Buchwald. One, *Win One for Hoffa* ridiculed labour unions by showing the chaos that would result once members of the *Washington Toughskins* joined the Teamsters Union. The other, *Is There a Red China?* ridiculed the (then) U.S. policy of not recognizing the existence of Red China. One hundred subjects were pre-tested for attitude toward 'Labour Unions' and 'Our policy toward Red China'. Two weeks later they read the two columns after being told the theses of each; they then evaluated the columns on semantic differential-type scales on 'funniness' and 'literary quality'. They also responded to the semantic differential attitude scales again. A control group of 46 students performed the same tasks, but were not specifically told the thesis of either column. In addition, these control subjects were asked to write, in their own words, the thesis intended by the author for each of the two pieces.

Attitude scores of the two groups indicated that each satirical column had been persuasive for the group that was told the theses in advance. There were small but statistically dependable ($p < 0.01$) shifts in mean attitude scores for the experimental group but not the control group. Examination of the written theses ascribed by the control subjects to the columns revealed that these subjects, as expected, had largely missed the points of the two pieces.

Since much political satire is directed at individual politicians, Gruner next studied (1971a) the effect of either one or two Art Buchwald columns satirizing President Richard M. Nixon. Student subjects read either two, one, or no such columns. One column, *Old Nixon is Jealous of Spiro*, argued that the 'New Nixon' is a facade, that he is still the mudslinging and vitriolic 'Old Nixon'. The other, *'Little Dickey Nixon's Surprise'*, portrays Nixon as a spoiled, angry brat dissatisfied with his legislative Christmas presents bestowed upon him by Congress. Subjects were *not* told the theses of the two pieces, on the assumption that they would be able to recognize them. After reading the editorials, the subjects rated each editorial read on a set of lightness/humorousness scales and rated President Nixon on two other sets of scales, developed by McCroskey (1966), to measure Nixon's perceived 'authoritativeness' and 'character'.

Since the Buchwald columns attacked only Nixon's character, it was assumed that no difference would be found among the three groups' authoritativeness ratings of Nixon. Such was the case ($F = 0.63$, $df = 2,147$, $p > 0.25$). But it had been expected that the character ratings would fit a definite pattern: highest rating by those reading *no* satire of Nixon, with lower rating by those reading one, and lowest by those reading two. The mean ratings did rank in this manner, but the differences were not quite statistically reliable.

Further analysis revealed that the 'Old Nixon' editorial may not have been well-understood by the subjects. An understanding of satire would suggest that, as regard for a person goes up, appreciation of a satire ridiculing him would go down. This was the case for the 'Little Dickey' editorial but not for the 'Old Nixon' piece. The humorousness/lightness ratings for 'little Dickey' correlated negatively but non-significantly ($r = -0.28$, $df = 47$, ns) with ratings of Nixon's character, and correlated negatively ($r = -0.51$, $df = 47$, $p < 0.01$) with ratings of his authoritativeness. The humorousness/lightness ratings of 'Old Nixon', on the other hand, showed a near-zero correlation with ratings of both attributes of Mr. Nixon. Apparently the subjects were able to enjoy the 'Old Nixon' piece independently of their (then) rather high regard for the President. It is quite possible that the 'Old Nixon' piece, much more history- and content-bound than the more caricaturistic and blatant 'Little Dickey' column, was not understood by the young audience. The fact that the group reading both pieces rated 'Little Dickey' almost a full point lower in funniness on the average ($t = 2.52$, $df = 47$, $p < 0.05$) than they did the 'Old Nixon' piece lends further credence to this supposition.

The next study of *ad hominem* satire as persuasion was also done by Gruner (1971b). It utilized an Art Hoppe column (John and Martha and AP and UPI) ridiculing Mrs. Martha Mitchell, wife of Nixon's then Attorney General. Mrs. Mitchell was ribbed heavily for her 'telephonitis' by comparing her need to make telephone calls to the alcoholic's craving for drink. At one point she begs her husband to let her make just 'one little call? As a nightcap?' One group of subjects read only the column, another read first a brief biography of Mrs. Mitchell from *Time* magazine and then the column, and a control group read only the *Time* piece. Subjects then rated the Hoppe piece and/or the *Time* piece on 'humorousness' and 'journalistic fairness/unfairness'; they rated Mrs. Mitchell on the 'authoritativeness' and 'character' scales, plus one scale bounded by 'ridiculous' and 'sensible'.

Experimental groups were divided by sex and a 3 × 2 analysis of variance was computed for the ratings of Mrs. Mitchell's authoritativeness, character and ridiculousness. No main effect was observed for authoritativeness, as expected; there was a main effect, however, for experimental groups on both the character and the ridiculous/sensible ratings. However, the means did not rank as expected.

It had been hypothesized that those reading the *Time* piece would first learn about some of Mrs. Mitchell's character traits, then read the satire of them and thus lower their esteem of her the most. It had been expected, further, that those reading only the satire would lower their esteem of Mrs. Mitchell, but not as much as those reading both pieces; but that they would rate her lower than would the control group. As it actually turned out, those reading only the satire rated Mrs. Mitchell lowest, with the control group rating her highest. It is assumed that the *Time* piece acted as a 'status-conferral' agent which tended to anchor attitude toward Mrs. Mitchell, thus lessening the effect of the satire.

Analysis of the 'fairness' ratings proved interesting. Those reading only the satire rated it on the 'unfair' end of the scale, those reading only the *Time* piece rated it on the fair end ($t = 3 \cdot 76$, $df = 88$, $p < 0 \cdot 001$). The fairness ratings of the two pieces by the group reading *both* showed a difference only for the males ($t = 2 \cdot 29$, $df = 21$, $p < 0 \cdot 05$). The females rated the satire as being as fair as the *Time* article; one might surmise that the girls felt that Mrs. Mitchell *deserved* the lampooning?

One other point should be made before leaving this study. It is interesting that this satire could apparently lower regard for a lady even though the subjects regarded the message demeaning her as *unfair*.

A tentative conclusion which might be drawn from the studies of satire reviewed thus far is that satire may be an effective persuasive force, but only if the receivers of the satire can perceive the persuasive intent. And, as has already been discussed, the fact that many people have difficulty so perceiving the serious point of satirical messages mitigates satire's general usefulness as rhetoric.

Three other studies of satire as persuasion should be briefly mentioned. Two of these employed an Art Hoppe column, *SANE Capital Punishment*, a satire whose serious point (capital punishment is *not* a deterrent to murder) is particularly elusive. McGown (1968) compared the persuasive effect of the Hoppe column with that of a non-satirical message as alike as possible to it except for the satire. Neither message seems to have produced any persuasion. Subjects rated the two pieces as equally interesting, but the Hoppe piece as more funny than the non-satirical message. They rated the authors of the two pieces equally on authoritativeness, but tended to rate the author of the Hoppe piece as lower in character, although the difference was not quite statistically significant. As in the Goodchilds study mentioned above, the subjects may have perceived Hoppe as a sarcastic wit, influential but unpopular. The McGown study was replicated under somewhat different circumstances by Gruner (1972a), with similar lack of persuasive results.

One of the seven experiments by Markiewicz (1972) involved an Art Buchwald column satirizing the 'gun lobby'. She found no persuasion to result. No report of whether subjects understood the satire was given.

EFFECTS OF HUMOUR ON LEARNING AND SPEAKER 'IMAGE'

Humour and learning

Textbooks on communication, when mentioning humour at all, usually recommend it as a device for securing and holding audience attention. Theoretically, then, if humour acts to secure, hold, or increase audience attention, it should also cause the audience to learn more, since attention is closely related to learning. There is little evidence of this relationship though, and some of it is negative.

Kilpela (1961), in his previously-mentioned thesis study, used a primarily persuasive rather than an informative message, but nevertheless tested for learning of the speech content as well as attitude change. His results indicated that subjects learned about as much from the serious speech as from the humorous one. Taylor (1964) developed two seven-minute speeches about the influence on contemporary thinking made by an eighteenth-century minister; one of these speeches contained humour and the other did not. He presented these speeches to groups of high school summer students and tested them for recall of the material in the speeches. Neither speech appeared to be superior to the other in producing recall. Taylor (1961) later expanded his study of the effect of humour on learning for his Ph.D. dissertation. He had one humorous and one non-humorous speech on each of two topics, 'Totalitarianism' and 'The Whorfian Hypothesis'. When tested for production of immediate recall over the contents of these speeches after hearing them, humour seems, again, to have added no learning. There was no difference in learning from the 'totalitarianism' speeches, and actually *less* learning from the humorous version of the 'Whorfian Hypothesis' speech as compared with the serious version.

Gruner (1967b) exposed student subjects to a tape-recorded speech on the topic of 'listening'. One version was without humour and another contained a number of jokes which were inserted into the speech where the content of the humorous material was felt to be appropriate to the content of the speech. The subjects, after hearing one version of the speech, took a multiple-choice examination over the contents of the speech and rated the speech on humorousness. The group hearing the humorous version apparently learned no more than the group hearing the serious version.

The speech used by Gruner in the study mentioned above was already highly interesting. It had been deliberately written for a Ph.D. dissertation study (Kibler, 1962) to score quite high on the Rudolph Flesch 'reading ease' and 'human interest' scales. On the assumption that the humour had not been able to raise the interest level in this already highly-interesting speech (the ceiling effect), Gruner (1970) replicated the study, but with an added feature. The interesting speech on listening was re-written to make it dull on the Flesch measures. Jokes were added to both this new dull version and the previously-used interesting speech. The interesting speech was then tape-recorded in a lively, interesting voice, while the dull speech was recorded in a dull, listless voice. The humour was electronically edited out of each version to produce four different speeches: a dull/humorous, a dull/serious, an interesting/humorous and an interesting/serious. Student subjects were then exposed to one of the four versions of the speech, and again took the multiple choice test over its contents. In addition, they rated the speech they heard on interestingness and humorousness. The ratings supported the assumption that the speeches differed both in interestingness and humorousness. However, there was, again, no difference in the amount of learning between those hearing the humorous and those who heard the serious versions; but there was a main effect for the interest variable. The two interesting speeches produced more recall than did the two dull ones. Further, the ratings indicate that the addition of humour to the dull speech heightened its ratings on interestingness, but addition of the same humour to the interesting speech did not raise its interestingness level. Thus the rationale for the study was upheld. Addition of humour improved the interestingness (or, at least, ratings of it) of only the dull speech; but this increase in interestingness did not result in a concomitant increase in learning.

Three studies previously mentioned (Kennedy, 1972; Kilpela, 1961; Youngman, 1966) which were primarily concerned with humour as an aid to attitude change in speeches to *persuade* also checked for audience recall of the speech material through objective examinations of the subjects over the speech content. None of the three studies found humour to affect retention of the material.

The studies reviewed so far indicate little support for the hypothesis that the addition of humour to a message will increase what the audience can learn from it. Only one study, which is discussed now, has provided such support.

Gibb (1964) found that student subjects learned more from a lecture on biology when it contained humour than when it did not. However, this writer feels that the results are due to flaws in the experimental methodology, for two primary reasons. First, he constructed his lecture backwards; Gibb began with a standardized test on biology and wrote his lecture around it to answer all the questions. Secondly, he did not control for time-of-day for exposure to the message; one group of control subjects heard the non-humorous version at 7:45 in the morning, a time not known in academic circles for alertness on the part of students. Another control group heard the lecture at 12:05 noon, when either sleepily digesting their lunch or hungrily looking forward to it. The experimental subjects heard the humorous lecture at the popular academic hours of 8:50 and 11:00.

Two experiments conducted for Markiewicz's (1972) dissertation tend to refute the hypothesis that humour increases attention and, therefore, learning. She exposed subjects to an Art Buchwald satire of gun lobbyists and a wacky dialogue on whether campus police should carry guns, or to a serious counterpart of each. Each subject was then asked to check which statements in a list presented to him had appeared in the message. Those reading the serious messages scored higher on recognition than did those reading the humorous versions. This finding should not be considered unusual when it is remembered that satirical material often is misunderstood, probably more often than non-satirical material. However, another experimental artifact mentioned by Markiewicz may have operated to produce these data: it is difficult, perhaps even impossible, to construct two messages completely alike except that one is entirely humorous and the other is not.

Although the experimental studies reviewed do not support the supposition that humour can increase attention and, thus, learning, it must be remembered that in these experimental situations universal attendance to the message was almost mandatory for the student subjects participating. It is probable that humour operates differently in securing and holding attention in the real world. When the radio or TV commercial promises and provides humorous entertainment, we are far less likely to leave the receiver and head for the refrigerator.

And lecturers such as Dick Gregory certainly attract their crowds through audience knowledge that they are going to be entertained as well as propagandized.

Humour and speaker 'image'

Experience and common sense would dictate that how and/or whether a speaker uses humour should affect how he will be perceived by his audience. People usually enjoy humour and should react more positively to the speaker who provides this enjoyment. A limited number of studies tend to support this notion.

In addition to testing his student subjects for recall of the 'listening' speech content, Gruner (1967b) had them rate the speaker on the McCroskey ethos scales measuring the speaker's authoritativeness and character. As expected, there was no difference in the speaker ratings on authoritativeness, but the speaker who used humour was rated significantly higher on the character scales. It can be concluded that the subjects liked the humorous speaker better.

In his replication study (Gruner, 1970) with both dull and interesting speeches with and without humour, the same general result occurred. Character ratings were high for both humorous speakers. One other finding deserves further study: the authoritativeness scores did not differ because of humorousness in the case of the interesting speeches, but the humorous/dull speaker received significantly higher ratings on authoritativeness than did his non-humorous counterpart. In his previously-mentioned dissertation study, Kennedy (1972) tested both for attitude change and learning as a result of adding humour to a speech. He also had subjects rate the speaker on scales tapping 'dynamism', 'expertise' and 'trustworthiness'. On the immediate post-test the humour seems to have enhanced only the speaker's ratings of dynamism. However, on the delayed post-test taken four weeks later the ratings of all three speaker characteristics were higher for the humorous speaker.

Reid (1971) was interested in whether similar results could be found when message exposure was through a different medium. He exposed subjects via closed-circuit TV one at a time rather than in large groups, perhaps because it has been found that humour appreciation is affected by medium and audience size (Malpass and Fitzpatrick, 1959).

Student subjects viewed either a high-humour, a low-humour, or a no-humour speech by the identical skilled speaker. They then rated the speech on humorousness and the speaker on the authoritativeness and character scales.

Results indicated that manipulation of the humour variable was successful. But, although the ratings of the speaker's character was in the hypothesized direction (high-humour producing higher ratings, etc.), the results did not quite reach statistical significance, but only ten subjects were run in each condition.

It has already been noted that the kind of humour one uses will affect perception of the speaker or message. Goodchilds (1959) found that sarcastic wits were perceived as influential but not popular whereas clowning wits were perceived as popular but not influential; and Youngman found that a speech utilizing *germane* humour was perceived as more worthwhile than the same speech containing *non*-germane humour. Apparently the effect of using humour can also be affected by the audience's perceptual set or expectancy, as evidenced by a study by Mettee, Hrelec and Wilkens (1971).

Mettee and co-workers exposed Yale underclassmen to a brief segment of a lecture by a man introduced as an English professor being considered for hiring by Yale. In one condition the professor told a joke during the lecture, in the other he did not. The lecture was on George Bernard Shaw; the apt joke included in the humorous version was a Shaw anecdote:

> As a matter of fact, there is a story which I think is very humorous that shows he [G. B. Shaw] didn't *always* get the last word, or laugh, so to speak. Shaw sent Winston Churchill two tickets to his latest play with an accompanying note that read: 'Dear Sir Winston, Here are two tickets to the opening night of my latest play, for you and a friend, if you have one.' Churchill sent back the tickets with the following reply: 'Dear Mr. Shaw, Unfortunately I am unable to attend the opening night; however, I would appreciate two tickets to the second night performance, if there is one!'

Subjects were told they were part of an experiment to see whether it would be useful to have Yale undergraduates evaluate prospective Yale faculty members. Then they were given a particular introduction to the video-taped lecturer in order to produce one or another perceptual set. One group of subjects was told that the professor it was about to view was considered quite competent but that he was far too humourless and aloof. The other group of subjects was told that the professor's main defect was that he was too clownish in the classroom, with the result that his attempts at humour were inappropriate and unnecessary.

After viewing one or the other lecture under one or the other perceptual set conditions, the subjects rated the professor on competence. Analysis of these ratings revealed that, for the 'aloof' condition, the humour enhanced the competence ratings; for the 'clownish' condition, the ratings appear to have been lowered by the use of the anecdote.

It may be that an auditor's perceptual set of a speaker's clownishness can be developed *during* and not only *before* the speech, and that perceptual set can operate as in the Mettee and co-workers' experiment. Taylor (1974) reports data which indicate that the use of humour in informative discourse can lower the audience's ratings of the speaker's image; however, he also reports verbal reactions which indicate that the speeches perhaps contained *too much* humour, which caused the audience to perceive the speakers as frustrated comedians.

Overview of research findings

Since some might conclude that the amount of research done in the area covered by this chapter is barely a scratch on the surface, a conclusion with which this writer can easily concur, it might seem presumptuous, even precipitous to attempt to draw conclusive generalizations from the studies reviewed. However, the human desire for closure through the generalization process cannot be completely suppressed. And so conclusions will be drawn, but the reader is reminded most strongly that they must remain ever tentative until a great deal more research is conducted.

(1) One of the more firmly grounded conclusions which this review suggests is a negative one. It certainly appears that the addition of humorous material to otherwise straightforward persuasive message material does not result in an increase in persuasiveness. Considering that such negative findings have been recorded by Lull, Kilpela, Kennedy, Youngman, Welford, Brandes, Markiewicz, and Gruner and Lampton, it would seem safe to conclude that the speaker with a strong persuasive message can confidently leave humour to be dispensed by others. However, anecdotal evidence suggests that the use of humour in advertising, especially broadcast advertising, *can* result in increased sales of the product humorously touted. The humour must be relevant, however, to the particular sales problem which the product has met. And the humour must really be entertaining, done with professional flair and taste. Humour may work for the advertiser where it has not been found to work for the political or social persuader because the former's rhetorical task is far simpler.

(2) It seems probable from the review of studies here that the inclusion of humour in otherwise interesting informative discourse will not add appreciably to the interest value of the discourse and, thus, cause greater learning. Humour is only one of many so-called 'interest devices' recognized by communication experts, and messages can be quite interesting enough while employing interest devices other than humour. But it is also recognized that the desire to be entertained through humour is strong and near-universal, and anyone success-fully promising such entertainment might gain the attention of large numbers of people whom he might then subsequently inform. A teacher regarded as entertaining attracks students to his classroom.

(3) Satire, as differentiated from mere humour, is apparently often not under-stood by members of the general public. Some satires are more subtle than others, and thus less well understood than more blatant satires. But, when the serious point of a satire *is* understood, it seems to have some persuasive value. The results and their interpretation are not at all completely clear on this point. In one study (Gruner, 1966) it can only be inferred that, if persuasion took place, it occurred among those initially mildly opposed to or neutral toward the thesis of the satire. In the other studies where satire was apparently effective in persuading (Gruner, 1967a, 1971b) the original attitude of those persuaded is not known. And indirect evidence (Gruner, 1972b) suggests that those who already agree with the thesis of the satire are those who probably enjoy it the most.

(4) Two studies (Gruner, 1974; Miller and Bacon, 1971) give tentative evidence that the understanding of humour and satire, respectively, is related to low dogmatism.

(5) The bulk of the evidence so far available indicates that the communicator who chooses to use apt and appealing humour in his discourse is likely to improve his image with his audience. But this conclusion seems definitely to be related to the initial perceptual set of the audience members toward the communicator. If the audience expects a normal or serious speaker and, instead, is treated to apt humour by the speaker, the communicator's image will probably improve; if the audience is led to expect some sort of clownish buffoon (or perceives the speaker as such during his presentation), the speaker's use of humour may only confirm the anticipatory set and thus harm the communicator's image.

Directions for further research

Investigators still interested in the way humour might work in persuasive appeals despite the implications of conclusion (1) above, might well be advised to try some different strategies. Granted, the monotonous finding of absence of persuasive effect from adding humour to one speech (or one set of speeches) on one topic with attitude change measured either immediately after exposure, or immediately afterwards and then three weeks later, does not encourage one to try again. And this writer thinks this particular research strategy can be conscientiously abandoned. However, this is not to say that longer-ranging research designs should not be tried.

Persuasion is not just a one-shot proposition. Most persuasion follows some sort of definite campaign over time, as does the campaign of the political aspirant or the advertiser. Could it not be that humour could play some part in the effectiveness of a persuasive campaign conducted over several months, perhaps even years? The whole field of communication research, even the whole broad field of the social sciences, is definitely lacking in well-designed longitudinal studies. Such time studies have probably been neglected because of the push to 'publish or perish' which favours the conducting of one-shot experiments which can keep a researcher's name in the professional journals regularly. But long-term study of the effect of humour in persuasion might possibly bear rich fruit. It has already been noted that the communication source which uses apt humour is likely to increase its image, or credibility. In the case of the Kennedy (1972) dissertation, the image actually increased over time from immediately after message exposure to four weeks later. Could it not be that a source which continually, over time, so increased its credibility might not become a more persuasive force through accumulated ethos?

Further research on humour as an aid to message interestingness should probably take the form of field studies. The experimental studies employing college sophomores in classroom settings do not allow for variance in subjects' interest, motivation and selectivity in exposure to the message. If humour does, in fact, add interest and thus increase the size or awareness of the audience, it would have to allow for natural variance in these variables.

So far experimental studies of the communicative impact of humour and wit have concentrated on humour and wit as attitude modifiers, as an interest-adding variable, and as an aid to speaker credibility. One study extant (Gruner, 1974) investigates the role of authoritarianism and understanding of satire. Might there not be other ways in which satire and humour are used by writers/ speakers and auditors/readers for other psychological purposes involving communication? For instance, there are some who regard ridicule as a means of social control by alerting people to what behaviour is laughable and, thus, to be avoided. Other than the Cooper and Jahoda study (1947) no research exists in the area of using humorous stimuli to *prevent* certain kinds of behaviour. Such research seems long overdue.

The question of what personality variables might be affected by exposure to various kinds of wit and humour seems a fertile field of endeavour also. Does experience in exposure to satire tend to cause increases in broad minded-ness, sociability, cynicism, and so on? Field studies of the personality profiles of those who do and those who do not expose themselves to such political satirists as Art Buchwald, Russell Baker, Arthur Hoppe, etc. might prove highly useful in defining the type of audience which these writers appeal to and, thus, perhaps influence.

How is wit and humour utilized by auditors/readers in relation to other kinds of messages? Does, for instance, exposure to political satire increase one's general exposure to political propaganda? Does it decrease it? Does exposure to such satire increase or decrease one's susceptibility to other persuasive messages? Interesting and presently ongoing research at the University of Florida has tentatively concluded (September, 1974) that satire may very well work as inoculation against later persuasive messages for persons with high ego-involvement in the topic of the satire and later messages.

The communicative impact of a great deal of satirical material from the mass communication media has remained uninvestigated. As previously noted, almost no satire reaches the American airwaves, because of commercial considerations, but what of the vast amount of comedy and large number of comic performers and their impact on their audiences? What do the *Flip Wilson* and/or *Sanford and Son* television shows do to or for the relationships between the American White and Black races? How does it affect 'Black awareness'? What is the effect of Flip Wilson being able to say things about Blacks and 'Blackness' in the role of the comic 'Geraldine' that he could not say as a guest of, for instance, *Meet the Press*? What are the effects of these statements of Wilson/Geraldine? How does Bob Hope's image as a wisecracking ad-libber affect the reception of his pronouncements on patriotism and politicians? All these and many more are questions untouched by and ripe for investigation by empiricists.

Many of the same kinds of questions as those in the paragraph above could be asked of another area of mass communications, the satirical 'talking record' by such as Bill Cosby, Dick Gregory, Mort Sahl, Fannie Flagg (ridiculing Mrs. Martha Mitchell) and David Frye (humorously hyperbolizing the 'Watergate Affair'). No systematic investigation of the communicative effects or the kinds of people who buy and appreciate them exists.

The same lack of research on communicative effect of much of our print medium is evident, also. Where are the studies on impact or readership of such editorial satirists as Russell Baker and Erma Bombeck? Who reads with what impact the satirical magazines such as *Mad* and *National Lampoon*?

And, finally, where is the research on the communicative effects of such satirical motion pictures as *M.A.S.H.*, *Getting Straight*, *The Great Dictator*, *Dr. Strangelove* and *Milhous*?

It is apparent that there is much to be done; and it is the hope of the author of this chapter that his writing will stimulate needed research in the area of wit and humour in mass communication.

REFERENCES

Annis, A. D. (1939). The relative effectiveness of cartoons and editorials as propaganda media. *Psychological Bulletin*, **36**, 628.

Asher, R., and Sargent, S. (1941). Shifts in attitude caused by cartoon caricatures. *Journal of General Psychology*, **24**, 451–455.

Berlo, D. K., and Kumata, H. (1956). The investigator: The impact of a satirical radio drama. *Journalism Quarterly*, **33**, 287–298.

Brandes, P. D. (1970). The persuasiveness of varying types of humor. Paper presented at the Speech Communication Association Convention, New Orleans. In SCA *Abstracts*, 12–13.

Brinkman, D. (1968). Do editorial cartoons and editorials change opinions? *Journalism Quarterly*, **45**, 724–726.

Carl, L. M. (1968). Editorial cartoons fail to reach many readers. *Journalism Quarterly*, **45**, 533–535.

Cooper, E., and Jahoda, M. (1947). The evasion of propaganda: how prejudiced people respond to anti-prejudice propaganda. *Journal of Psychology*, **23**, 15–25.

Gibb, J. D. (1964). An experimental comparison of the humorous lecture and the non-humorous lecture in informative speaking. M.A. thesis, University of Utah.

Goodchilds, J. D. (1959). Effects of being witty on position in the social structure of a small group. *Sociometry*, **22**, 261–272.

Gruner, C. R. (1965a). An experimental study of satire as persuasion. *Speech Monographs*, **32**, 149–153.

——. (1965b). Is wit to humor what rhetoric is to poetic? *Central States Speech Journal*, **16**, 17–22.

——. (1966). A further experimental study of satire as persuasion. *Speech Monographs*, **33**, 184–185.

——. (1967a). Editorial satire as persuasion: an experiment. *Journalism Quarterly*, **44**, 727–730.

——. (1967b). Effect of humor on speaker ethos and audience information gain. *Journal of Communication*, **17**, 228–233.

——. (1970). The effect of humor in dull and interesting informative speeches. *Central States Speech Journal*, **21**, 160–166.

——. (1971a). Ad hominem satire as a persuader: an experiment. *Journalism Quarterly*, **48**, 128–131.

——. (1971b). An experimental study of ad hominem editorial satire: Art Hoppe vs. Martha Mitchell. Paper presented at the Speech Communication Association Convention, San Francisco. In SCA *Abstracts*, 59–60.

—— (1972a). Art Hoppe vs. capital punishment: an experiment. Paper presented at the Southern Speech Communication Association's convention, April. San Antonio.

—— (1972b). Satire as a reinforcer of attitudes. Paper presented at the Speech Communication Association Convention, Chicago. In SCA *Abstracts*, 10.

310

——. (1974). Dogmatism and the understanding/appreciation of satire. Mimeograph; paper presented at the Convention of the Speech Communication Association, Chicago.

——. (1976). *Understanding Laughter: The Psychology and Communicative Function of Wit and Humor*. Chicago: The Nelson–Hall Co. In press.

——., and Lampton, W. E. (1972). Effects of including humorous material in a persuasive sermon. *Southern Speech Communication Journal*, **38**, 188–196.

Highet, G. (1962). *The Anatomy of Satire*. Princeton University Press.

Johnson, E. (1945). *A Treasury of Satire*. New York: Simon and Schuster.

Kennedy, A. J. (1972). An experimental study of the effect of humorous message content upon ethos and persuasiveness. PhD. dissertation, University of Michigan.

Kibler, R. J. (1962). The impact of message style and channel in communication. Ph.D. dissertation, Ohio State University.

Kilpela, D. E. (1961). An experimental study of the effects of humor on persuasion. M.A. thesis, Wayne State University.

Lull, P. E. (1940). The effects of humor in persuasive speeches. *Speech Monographs*, **7**, 26–40.

Malpass, L., and Fitzpatrick, E. D. (1959). Social facilitation as a factor in reaction to humor. *Journal of Social Psychology*, **50**, 295–303.

Markiewicz, D. (1972). The effects of humor on persuasion. PhD. dissertation, Ohio State University.

McCroskey, J. C. (1966). Scales for the measurement of ethos. *Speech Monographs*, **33**, 65–72.

McGown, M. (1968). An experimental study of the persuasive impact of a satiric editorial and that of a comparable direct editorial. M.A. thesis, University of Nebraska.

Mettee, D. R., Hrelec, E. S., and Wilkens, P. C. (1971). Humor as an interpersonal asset and liability. *Journal of Social Psychology*, **85**, 51–64.

Miller, G. R., and Bacon, P. (1971). Open- and closed-mindedness and recognition of visual humor. *Journal of Communication*, **21**, 150–159.

Perreault, R. M. (1972). A study of the effects of humor in advertising as can be measured by product recall tests. M.A. thesis, University of Georgia.

Phillips, K. (1968). When a funny commercial is good, it's great! *Broadcasting*, May 13, 1968, 26.

Pokorny, G. F., and Gruner, C. R. (1969). An experimental study of the effect of satire used as support in a persuasive speech. *Western Speech*, **33**, 204–211.

Reid, J. K. (1971). The effect of humor on perceived attractiveness of a speaker. M.A. thesis, Oklahoma State University.

Sternthal, B., and Craig, C. S. (1973). Humor in advertising. *Journal of Marketing*, **37**, 12–18.

Surlin, S. H. (1973). The evaluation of dogmatic television characters by dogmatic viewers: 'Is Archie Bunker a credible source?' Paper presented at the International Communication Association's Annual Convention, Montreal, April.

Swabey, M. C. (1961). *Comic Laughter: A Philosophical Essay*. Yale University Press.

Taylor, P. H. (1964). The effectiveness of humor in informative speeches. *Central States Speech Journal*, **5**, 295–296.

Taylor, P. H. (1971). The role of listener-defined supportive humor in speeches of information. Ph.D. dissertation, University of Indiana.

Taylor, P. H. (1974). An experimental study of humor and ethos. *Southern Speech Communication Journal*, **39**, 359–366.

Vidmar, N., and Rokeach. M. (1974). Archie Bunker's bigotry: A study in selective perception and exposure. *Journal of Communication*, **24**, 36–47.

Welford, T. W. (1971). An experimental study of the effectiveness of humor used as a refutational device. Ph.D. dissertation, Louisiana State University.

Youngman, R. C. (1966). An experimental investigation of the effect of germane humor versus non-germane humor in an informative communication. M.A. thesis, Ohio University.

Zeman, J. V. (1967). An experimental study of the persuasive effects of satire in a speech presented to a High School audience. M.A. thesis, University of Nebraska.

Chapter 14

Freudian Humour:
The Eupsychia of Everyday Life

Walter E. O'Connell

If we detach ourselves from the psychological pursuit of reliable and valid measurements to look with awe and puzzlement upon what has and has not been attempted in the study of humour, we see the problems related to the understanding of *positive* psychological concepts in bold relief. Why are we preoccupied with symptomatic-pathological entities and easily quantified external events instead of greatly-needed joy, happiness, creativity, courage and humour? Following the Charcot–Freud model of man, proper and reputable science still clings to its faith in man as *homo pathologicus*. To do otherwise and have faith in joy and happiness would initiate a mind-boggling adventure. Man henceforth would be squarely on his own small wobbly feet, getting by with the help of his friends. All facets and disciplines of man would be in for a similar shock.

Mankind has a long history of learned inferiority complexes. One does not have to be a Marxist to hold that institutions often gain in power in direct relationship to their ability to reduce man to a tiny, puny, ephemeral encrustation, of value only by his complete submission to institutional autocracies. As the old saying goes, while the peasant is beating his breast in chronic worthlessness, he cannot raise his fist against his master. For generations prior to concern about the movements of the mentally healthy, institutional disenfranchizers were at work invalidating (and invaliding) those who allowed themselves to be victimized into a chronic state of low self-esteem and social isolation. In Becker's words (1969), we have 'fetishized' psychiatry by choosing narrow explanatory concepts (e.g. Oedipal complex) with a few aetiological referents (that is, what self, other, and societal forces contribute to the actions in question, such as the likelihood of Oedipalizing).

Freud was frustrated by what he sired, the cul-de-sac of a pervasive psycho-pathology which was missing the necessary counterpoints of socially mature actions. The pioneering efforts of Freud to deal with humour, as sharply differentiated from wit, brought too much consternation and confusion to basic psychoanalytic theory, and so were summarily forgotten or repressed.

To this day almost all the feeble efforts to probe the humorous attitude deal with wit rather than humour and Sigmund Freud's 1928 paper 'Humour' is rarely read by even the Freudians. Freud's frustrations about humour are still with us in spirit. Humour, defined as the epitome of maturity, was simultaneously labelled an outstanding denial of reality, Freud's criterion of sickness (Freud, 1928). As the emphasis in psychoanalysis moved from economics (savings in energy-expenditures) to structural interactions (the superego's effect upon the ego) another contradiction emerged. A psychoanalytic tradition had already been established assigning to the superego only constricting and harsh influences upon the beleaguered ego functions of reality testing (one small product of the implicit cultural collusion to regard man as irremediably weak and ineffectual by nature).

Almost 50 years later, we still know little regarding the aetiology, development and value of that elusive *avis rara*, the humorist. Operational definitions of comic, wit (joke), and humour are as rare as unicorns. Bergler (1956) aptly described Everyman's ignorance of the comic phenomena by stating 'according to popular theory, one laughs when and because something is funny, and something is funny because and when one laughs' (p. vii). Such circularity cannot take one with scientific longings very far. Concepts must be anchored in discernible movements or there is no scientific movement at all. Freud tried to wed his clinical findings to his 'mythological' theory and the offspring were seldom comprehensible or scientifically respectable. The phenomena of the comic, wit, and humour were united by Freud as attempts to regain the euphoria of childhood, forever lost by the growth of mental activity (Freud, 1905). The pleasure of all three activities was, in the Freudian sense, derived from an economy in expenditure. The savings in comic situations was one of cathexes or ideation, the pleasure stemming from a simultaneous interpretation of two independent events.

Wit represented a savings in countercathexes, the joke maker and appreciator both enjoying a temporary saving in the energy required to repress hostile and sexual impulses. Don't we all know some hilarious mother-in-law jokes? Humour, the most prized of all varieties of risible pleasure represented a savings of expenditure in affect. Untoward negative reactions, in this case, were seen as being obviated by the 'grandeur' of humour.

FREUD'S PARADIGM

Freud appears to have spent more time and effort attempting to unravel the mystery of the humorist than any other theory builder. As mentioned previously, the humorist proved incompatible for his closed constitutional system and so no more was written specific to Freud's ideal person. Freud's definition of the humorist was particular to a certain type, that of gallows humour. In this case a person, not courting his death, was under immediate sentence. At no time during his execution did the prisoner give verbal or non-verbal signs of hostility, resentment, or depression. Rather he 'rose above' the stress with an 'uplifting' jest (Freud, 1928). Two types of humour were postulated; both vastly differ from wit which was in the service of the indirect release of represented hostile or sexual urges. In one type (let's call it A) one person regarded *the other* in a humorous light. B type humour was characterized by one viewing *himself* from the humorous stance. With both types bystanders who were similar in psychic composition to the humorist derived similar pleasure. This pleasure, Freud theorized, followed from the triumph of the ego, the pleasure principle, and narcissism over real adverse conditions under which the person refused to suffer. The severity of the situation itself was not repressed, rather the superego behaved toward the ego in a loving and playful manner. (A similar dialogue, interestingly enough, was later credited to Sir Thomas More, replying to Thomas Cromwell's physical threats; 'Look here! This is merely child's play . . . terrors for children, but not for me'.) Freud gave other clues as to the behaviour of the humorist: negative affects were either on the rise or such possibility was clearly indicated. The strong implication was that both the passive and active humorist identified with the plight of others, through negative emotional resonances which quickly evaporated with the appreciation or creation of the humorous response (Freud's savings in expenditure of affects). When he created the incongruous pattern of a jesting retort to a danger situation, the humorist was probably feeling the rise of negative affects within himself. He then engineered the sudden switch in perception so characteristic of both wit and humour; the sudden change of frame of reference from pain to pleasure, using the many verbal techniques available: double meanings, play on words, condensations of meanings, discrepancies between situational context and retort, etc. (Freud, 1905). The apparent discrepancy between humanistic involvement and distancing (suddenly taking 'God's view') has been called St. Augustine's Paradox: what one is doing is of vital importance, yet if he dies now that's not important (O'Connell, 1969e). The authentic humorist harbours the ability to quickly switch between a strong but flexible humanistic identification (O'Connell, 1965) and an abstract space–time distantiation. He experiences, in rapid succession, both the phenomenological world of the individual and then his objective manoeuvring for esteem and power in the world of all humanity (O'Connell, 1973a). The humorist–therapist is not stuck, like most therapists, in one of these two dimensions only.

HUMOUR—NOT AN INDEPENDENT 'THING'

Research on wit and humour is generally approached as if there were such external reliably measured 'things' as humour, readily available for unequivocal classification. In most of the early studies of stimuli which elicited the risible response (or closely allied internal states of pleasant completeness), no effort was made to describe the attributes of the humorous stimuli or responses. A tacit assumption was made that all people intuitively knew the dimensions of the concept being studied. Such failures to arrive at common discursive points led to considerable variance in conclusions. The most rational way out of this dilemma seemed to be the selection of a particular theoretical bias from a sampling of about eighty 'mini-theories' of humour, all of which are mainly descriptive, with exceedingly limited application to developmental and abnormal psychology (Bergler, 1956). This writer selected the works of Freud, principally his 1905 book and 1928 paper, because of the omnipresence of that psychiatric giant. Nevertheless a research-oriented clinical psychologist with a behavioural orientation soon loses his infatuation with Freud, owing to the latter's intrapsychic exclusivity, often disguised in behavioural words. The cathexes of the mind, not the movements of the body, were of paramount importance to Freud. When Freud wrote of an inflated superego, and a tiny ego, 'in a given situation the subject suddenly effects a hyper-cathexis of the superego' (Freud, 1928), what is the relevance for overt measurement and change?

Humour (as well as wit) cannot be understood monadically (by studying one person), but dyadically where people are influencing each other. Hence the move is from intrapsychic to interpersonal explanations. Unless 'humour' stimulates people toward at least a quantum of growth, it may not be humour at all, even though humour was monadically intended. (Message sent is not always message received.) Frustrated autocrats, be they rich or poor, might see type A humour (directed at them) as hostile drives rather than humour. So much in life depends upon the relationship, the 'ground' of the interaction; therefore, the humorist–therapist would always use type B humour (self-directed) in the initial stages of humour-therapy.

HUMOUR—UNACCEPTABLE IN A MECHANICAL AGE

Anyone embarking upon research into the origins and development of humour will, more often than not, be seen as a deviant and a freak, one who does not take psychology seriously enough. At least that has been this writer's experience. Often research proposals must be reworked, 'to explain in simpler, more understandable terms'. In truth, the problem is probably not so much the vocabulary as the premises of man implicit in the humour research. In an age characterized by a loss of futuristic non-material goals, humour is overlooked and people are not aware of their hidden prejudices against the study of humour.

Autocratic stances are not novel to our society. According to Dreikurs (1971) they may have been with us since the advent of the agrarian community. Today such external controls are more subtle, less overtly violent, yet still out of phase with a world community evolving toward 'the dawn of democracy'. As Dreikurs aptly demonstrated in his works, people have no psychotechnology of how to cooperate-as-equals. They generally overcompensate by behaving as did the autocratic group whose power they hoped to overthrow. Power (or influence) as a human need is still sought actively or passively through exploitation, manipulation, and competition for external symbols and material gains—not via equality.

Power through humour is relatively unheard of. The humorist has never been widely emulated in any culture, for he is still an outsider who threatens authoritarian societies which highly prize the sameness of an unobtrusive, conforming, 'adjusting' type. The humorist is keenly aware of the limitations of man (as well as his dormant power for growth). He does not narrow his social interest or make himself unworthy, in an idolatrous gesture merely to fulfil the power and esteem needs of people given political power. To the experts on human functioning who see the striving of man as mainly for the release of repressed sexual and hostile drives and a return to nirvana-like existence, the humorist gets short shrift. If his non-compliance precipitates tension in the other the latter is likely to label the humorist as 'hostile' or 'crazy'. A society which tolerates repression of death, superiority through moral, intellectual, and spiritual one-upmanship, and the over-control of self and others, does not look kindly toward the humorist. Leaders still cannot admit mistakes, imperfections and power strivings. Humourless Watergate plumbers still overshadow the humorist, even though life is still too important to be taken seriously.

MY HUMOUR IS NOT YOUR HUMOUR:
THE CRITERION PROBLEM

There has been a great babel of tongues around humour. As mentioned earlier, what passes for writings about Freudian humour is really directed toward wit. Society is not ready to consider moulding humorists in its homes and schools; so the wit, the incisive competitor, captures public attention. Furthermore, even if exact descriptive definitions of the humorist are shared—in this case the Freudian model of 'grace under pressure' even unto death—our life-style blinkers us and psychiatric ignorances keep us apart semantically. Take the case of Sir (or Saint) Thomas More again. If you believed in his stance against the King and Reformation, he was a saint. On the other hand, some of the leading reformers of his day considered him to be insane and irresponsible, citing his behaviour on the scaffold as proof positive. Contrariwise these same acts of More can be cited as excellent examples of Freud's gallows humour. The bravery of refusing to blame and plead under death sentence and the courage of not striking back with further negative nonsense seem admirable; yet even the decision as to whether such ultimate acts are humorous varies with the demands, fetishes, goals, and roles of the judges of such behaviour. It may be that only a humorist can accurately judge present-day socially relevant humour.

Very few thinkers—exceptions are Alfred Adler and Teilhard de Chardin—have advanced to the point of considering the issue of human connectedness and evolution. The prime question is how does my present behaviour stimulate or retard the development of humanistic identification (growth of self-esteem and social interest)? All humour obviously does not revolve around death around death scenes—and the guess here is that ultimately the humorist will be found to be the prime encourager who does not use stress to narrow his world, but daily reacts to potential frustrations as an opportunity to aid in the evolution of social interest (e.g. 'What can we do to solve external problems?').

How completely one's hidden philosophy of man rules his 'scientific' judgements is illustrated by a meeting of existential psychiatrists in which this writer participated. Although Freud's writings were not mentioned, the panellists were almost unanimous in viewing type A humour as hostility toward others and type B as masochism. What else could they say when they believed in a world of pessimism, isolation, stagnation, and hostile–sexual urges only?

THE AUTHOR'S RESEARCH

The theme of this section could well be, 'How not to do relevant humour research'. Only one of these projects, the first, featured an experimental intervention combined with non-stressed control groups. Unfortunately the control groups were only assumed to be similar to experimentals and no repeat measures were considered. The emphasis of the studies was to construct reliable instruments with face validity, and then to use the humour tests to investigate the construct validity of the humour concept itself. During this period the present author carried out many experimental studies with repeated measurements but never included his refined wit and humour tests as independent or even dependent measures. The reason?: the author's hyperdependence on peers' opinions. None of his colleagues ever could understand or get excited about wit and humour, neither could members of any research review committee. The author switched, rather than fought, 'to keep the work load down'. (He is not, you see, a humorist.)

The principal psychometric product has been the Story Test, an 18-item paper and pencil test consisting of anecdotes in which the subject rates his appreciation of wit, humour, and resignation endings to the anecdotes (O'Connell, 1964a). To break ties and serve as a validity device to check ratings, an absolute choice was added, the subject selecting the ending he 'liked the best', for each of the 18 items. Twelve items were selected by judges as mirroring high and low death concern for subsequent research on death and dying. One high-death item follows for illustration. This particular example was originally a gallows humour example used by Freud (1928). The endings are resignation, humour, and hostile wit, (a) to (c) respectively.

A condemned prisoner was being led to the gallows early one Monday morning. As he left his cell, he waved to the other prisoners and said:
(a) 'The world won't come to an end'.

1	2	3	4	5
Dislike very much	Dislike some	Neither	Like some	Like very much

(b) 'Well, this is a good beginning to the week'.

1	2	3	4	5
Dislike very much	Dislike some	Neither	Like some	Like very much

(c) 'You cats will be dancing on air soon, too'.

			:	:	:

1	2	3	4	5
Dislike very much	Dislike some	Neither	Like some	Like very much

The ending I like the best is:————————

This author's major research findings on humour are listed below. In the first research study of psychoanalytic humour, appreciation of humour was discovered to be a rather stable personality trait associated with maturity as defined by a self-report test of self-ideal discrepancies (O'Connell, 1960). Humour, in contrast to wit, did not appear to be affected by situational stressors and there were no sex differences except when hostile themes appeared in the humorist's retorts (O'Connell, 1962). In all studies, humour appreciation has differed from resignation and hostile wit appreciation, and there seem to be more types of humour than the gallows example specifically mentioned by Freud (O'Connell, 1964a, 1964b). Community leaders are the highest in humour appreciation while hospitalized schizophrenics are quite low (Worthen and O'Connell, 1969). Humour does not correlate with pathology scales or even maturity scales of traditional psychological tests (O'Connell, 1969b). In general, low-humour response is related to repressive life styles (O'Connell and Cowgill, 1970; O'Connell and Peterson, 1964). Appreciation for humour, especially for gallows or death variety, is negatively associated with anxiety about death and especially the fear of one's own physical dissolution (O'Connell, 1968b; O'Connell and Covert, 1967). The liking of humour does not seem related to the impairment of abstract cognitive abilities (O'Connell, 1968a) but rather with the growth of a non-blaming creative orientation to life.

The creation of humour is a rarer ability than its mere appreciation (O'Connell, 1969a). It varies directly with the production of hostile wit and is not significantly correlated with the traditional non-reactive and impunitive orientation to frustration. The creator of humour appears quite different from the one who simply likes the reaction, although both types appear to be creative and productive persons. The producer of humour is probably a more socially creative type of individual than the more inactive variety of humorist (O'Connell, 1969c). Humour creation is seen more vividly in the authentic and prominent group leader (O'Connell, Rothaus, Hanson, and Moyer, 1969). This kind of a person differs drastically in his behaviour from the hostile wit and resignation appreciator and the producer of sarcastic wit. The latter, while active, is not the popular productive leader, as is the humorist. He is too hostile, striving for individual attention, rather than group social goals.

Resignation and hostile wit appreciation have been strongly associated with psychopathological states. If stressors are added in terms of insult in the environment or death themes in the jest, the appreciation by the emotionally disturbed is lowered strikingly (O'Connell, 1960, 1968b). Length of hospitalization seems to have an effect upon wit appreciation, nonsense wit becoming more preferable to patients than hostile wit (O'Connell, 1968a). Hostile wit seems to have more cultural support for males than females, the latter resorting more to the nonsense variety (O'Connell, 1960, 1964a). This sexual difference is not innate, for if males become the object of hostile wit, the females and not the males are found to be positively attracted to hostile wit (O'Connell, 1969b). This wit reaction is affected by the variables of personality, sex and stressors to a much greater degree than is humour (which seems to vary principally with a type of maturity) and has less relevance for prognosis and change research.

THE HUMORIST AS THE IDEAL OF HUMANISTIC IDENTIFICATION

Practical knowledge of life-style change will lead to more hypotheses and probabilities about the appearance of humour. Research of the kind described earlier, studies comparing concurrent groups and lacking concise experimental intervention and reliable pre- and post-measures, will accomplish nothing to alleviate the current humour energy crisis. As a rule, breakthroughs in psychiatric knowledge are not the result of 'factophilia', the isolated collection of disconnected studies, but via sweeping inductive generalizations which then can be tested clinically and experimentally. In a word, someone with concern for the future of humour development must take his imagination out of mothballs to generate 'as if' suppositions about the inner and outer movements of the humorist. Since this author considers the humorist the ideal end-state of his existential–humanistic theory of personality development (humanistic identification), the 'as if' task is not too formidable. (Please note this author has resisted the habit of referring to himself as 'I'. Contemporary scientific good taste has it that one must allude to oneself as a third person external object. This ritual concurs with twentieth-century depersonalization and fragmentation, already mentioned in relation to the dearth of humour research.)

The theory of humanistic identification, while worked out independently by this writer (O'Connell, 1965), has much in common with the seminal thoughts of Alfred Adler as well as later Adlerians, Rudolf Dreikurs (1971) and Albert Ellis (1962), neither of whom was directly concerned with the sense of humour. Because sense of humour is the chief focus of this paper, the humorist in his most pristine form will be equated with the humanistic ideal: high self-esteem, earned through wide social interest (understanding, resonating with, but not reinforcing the power needs of others). As Becker has recently noted (1973) we all need to practise 'heroics', earn self-esteem from some role in life. Becker was never aware of the humorist who derived his self-esteem (or feelings of worth and significance) through the goal of finding similarities—and at-homeness—with mankind: past, present, and future. Courage defined as *active* social interest means encouraging others by pointing out and not reinforcing their useless goals of power (O'Connell, 1973a). All of these movements the authentic humorist does well, but he was not born that way. His extreme 'luck' and gratitude in finding and nurturing an encouraging environment is never far from consciousness with the unknown contemporary hero, the humorist. Adequate self-esteem implies the 'courage to be imperfect': no need to control others, to feel above them, intellectually, morally, or spiritually (Dreikurs, 1971). One can obtain self-esteem (which is always a subjective decision—'Am I worthy enough?'—whether or not one is aware of it) in any role. The narrower the role (e.g. mother's favourite child), the closer the potential catastrophe to the life-style. The humorist, with wide social interest, can work for whatever 'strokes' he needs (which are minimal) with any number of persons.

Low self-esteem in a *person* brings about a failure to take risks beyond the narrow role in which he feels competent. Such persons are often evaluated as unmotivated whereas in truth to one who knows them, they are extremely motivated: they must be perfect. The safe way to ensure 'perfection' is never to take a risk that might bring on an 'unpardonable' mistake. The lower the self-esteem, the greater the need for perfection.

Power or influence seems to be the strongest psychological need. Perhaps only the humorist, in his most pristine form, could survive the hypertraumata of never receiving even the reinforcement of a glance or a blow from others. Other persons would rapidly decompensate without some response from others. Defects in humanistic identification (narrow social interest and low or even high self-esteem) are the royal road to problems in living, as problem-creators or problem 'sufferers'.

The term 'existential paradoxes' is introduced to designate the acceptance of multiple realities, a sign of an authentic existence. Twentieth-century machine-man is generally not aware that the realities of Mr. X may be different from those of Mr. Y because each has a different life-style based upon differing premises about the self and others. On the other hand, Mr. X's own existence may have been so thoroughly and uniformly fragmented that he is unaware the world might move smoother and faster without the effort spent to invent and maintain rigid and absolute dualities of self–other, superior–inferior, sick–well, patient–doctor, divine–human, soul–body, psyche–soma, spiritual–material, responsible–irresponsible, etc., which seem synonymous with his cognitive existence. The humorist may be the rarest of all humans because he has unburdened himself of such inflexible views of reality foisted on us from birth. Growing out of this kind of a world, the profession of psychotherapy also produces persons who are agitated by a switch to non-dualistic thinking and the awareness of as many realities as there are people. Formal logic and natural science are relatively free from the influence of time and person. Institutional and descriptive psychiatry are very often heirs to natural science logic. Holders of such 'reality' see a simplified world of diagnosis and prognosis, doctor and patient: one forever treating the other in rigid, complementary style. There are no stimulating paradoxes, since one's self is assumed to be well-anchored, encapsulated, and drastically separate from other selves. Therefore, humorous reactions are exceedingly rare when there is no spark to leap between the paradoxical poles.

The humorist could not maintain his flexibility in moving across many frames of reference without adequate self-esteem and social interest. One with extensive social interest has trained himself to empathize with others and not disturb with arbitrary narcissistic demands. This attitudinal state of humanistic identification is of paramount importance in humour tutoring. The teacher of humour must work on his own humour with the help of his friends (perhaps 'play' would be more appropriate than 'work'), and help the student-humorist through the stages of relationship, modelling, teaching and reinforcing.

The techniques of humorous movement are of secondary importance and apply to all forms of the comic. They represent in one form or another a contrast or sudden shift in meaning, like a play on words or understatements and over-statements. A sudden shift in discovering a different, simultaneously appropriate, but non-threatening, meaning takes place: 'Everything can be everything else'. The humorist, *the man of constant paradoxes*, sees the solution in no-solution, only faith in the evolutionary powers of a loving God and/or a basically benign universe. To search for *The Answer* and find it would make the life-game horribly dull. Answers can be given in abstract terms (e.g. 'Love thy Neighbour as Thyself') but in terms of dyadic (I-and-Thou) movements of two persons with varying states of self-esteem and social interest, not even the questions (let alone the answers) are in.

Self-actualization proceeds from self-transcendence (Frankl, 1955). Non-material goals and values are reached only indirectly. The harder one tries to make himself happy, sexually potent, or even go to sleep, the less probable the desired goals will be reached. Alfred Adler's chief contribution was contained in the maxim that social interest was the only goal which could be pursued to an extreme without severely incapacitating one's life (Adler, 1929, 1964). Another paradox for the humorist: he can be truly happy only through en-couraging others. But, like the rest of us, he lives in an age in which the details of the movements of encouragement are still *terra incognita*.

Any method which increases the patient's self-esteem, social interest, and enjoyment of existential paradoxes is teaching him at least the rudiments of the humorous attitude. Directive or action techniques (O'Connell, 1969d) readily highlight 'the patients' paradox': a verbal desire to be cured alongside an incongruous, defeating devaluation of self and others. Unusual, 'crazy' ploys by therapists loosen the patient's desperate hold on a one-reality, dualistic world. Another benefit of the jesting yet serious approach is that in the absence of a rigidly autocratic doctor–patient relationship, the therapist is sometimes the 'patient'. He can be open and model humour when he is faced with (or even self-creates) his stressful world. 'Crazy', productive therapists all use the most time-honoured technique of them all—Socratic irony. With this tactic the therapist does not trap himself by assuming all the answers, *à la* omnipotent one. Rather he makes a pretence of ignorance to understand the patient's inner feelings and outer games. Yet he remains an outsider in his cognitive structuring of reality, since he eschews rigid dualisms and can move rapidly between the patient's inner and outer worlds of feelings and actions. Also fracturing the popular view of reality is the humorist's knowledge that reality differs from person to person, beyond the accepted conventions of time, place and person. This state of flexibility in reality testing follows from acceptance of the existential paradox. Mild tensions are engendered in switching frames of references which, with the humorist and wise psychotherapist, are dissipated in pleasurable smiles or easy laughter.

There are psychotherapists who report techniques which lend themselves to teaching the humorous attitude toward life's tasks. All of these authors noted that their techniques should take place in an accepting yet playful atmosphere or at least in situations where the patient is treated with kindness and respect. To anyone who can distance himself from the rigidly compartmentalized world of patients and politicians the therapists' techniques seem humorous. One can laugh at Adler's interaction with patients although they contain no reference to humour. Adler himself referred indirectly to existential paradoxes when he said everything could be something else. In a sense most patients act as victims of a mysterious disease, but also behave as if they are actually perpetuating their own dis-ease by unwittingly destroying their self-esteem and social interest in the service of maintaining meagre life-styles. Patients often behave like doctors 'are supposed to' and doctors like patients: patients tell us how we should behave and we often balk. Therapy is like serious treatment and yet often similar to play. The therapist hopes to help the patient reduce his anxiety level, but he also stimulates tension by his tutoring efforts. Everything-can-be something-else. Sudden switches in basic perceptions precipitate tension—which laughter reduces. For those who believe they have discovered reality rather than merely constructed a theory to describe it, alternative explanations are forbidden and blocked from consciousness. 'Crazy' therapists, whose concepts fluctuate in meaning, are misunderstood by 'one-reality' folk. Their movements are therefore considered anything but funny to the super-serious overcontrollers.

Adler's approach, like that of any mature therapist, was not to quash the patient by overwhelming the symptoms (along with the patient) with electricity, chemicals, surgery or autocratic commands. Adler 'manipulated' the patient into a therapeutic trap. Symptoms were encouraged but switched into socially useful movements (e.g. keep your insomnia going strong, and think, while you are lying awake, of how you can help others, even me). Power and revenge movements were nipped in the bud, since the doctor never demanded that the patient do anything. The patient was faced with the paradox of keeping a symptom which had now lost its useless value—or giving it up entirely.

Humorous devices teach humour through over- and under-reactions. They show the patient how he actively reduces self-esteem and social interest, while belatedly stimulating social development. The patient is also tutored in experiencing 'wonderland': that things are not always—despite his most earnest wish—what he feels them to be. Imagine the wily Adler and tricky patient, both trying to teach the other something: Adler towards a healthy flexibility and the patient towards a deterministic disease analogy. As in all such examples reported, the patient is approved for achieving the symptom ('as if' he created it) and it is put to use to benefit others (a healthy sign of sickness). These are the sudden ploys of the flexible therapist who does not believe in his public (curer) image. He does not limit himself to non-directive moves and the cliches of 'How does that make you feel?' followed by 'Why do you feel that way?' for years and years.

A good example of audience reactions to paradoxical behaviours is the case of Harold Greenwald (1968). In a workshop presentation filmed for professional distribution, Greenwald interviewed two females, one who said she wanted to give up crying while the second desired to be able to express anger at the weak, as exemplified by her co-patient. By convincing the weeper that she was always in control by her 'involuntary' symptoms and demonstrating such in the here-and-now interactions, both girls learned that the helpless patient may para-doxically be strong. With the girl who wanted to develop anger, Greenwald demonstrated that this impossibility was really quite easy, for she erupted at Greenwald who told her never to anger. Greenwald controlled the level of laughter by his frequent overstatements and understatements and 'truths' which can only be rationally reported by others, not oneself (e.g. 'I am a wonderful therapist'). The audience generally reacted to the uncovering of alternative (paradoxical) perceptions of reality with laughter, but there was always the vocal minority which believed Greenwald did not understand and 'love' these patients. Such is the price for making the familiar appear unorthodox.

Frankl (1955) regards the sense of humour as part of man's capacity for self-detachment. In his logotherapy a patient is told to engage in negative practice and intensify his symptom (e.g. 'Faint a number of times right now'). Frankl uses the overstatement (or hyperbole), which makes the symptom into a caricature. To Frankl, logotherapy practised with rapport and humour precipitates self-detachment. The latter may follow, although it may be open to other explanations. When the patient is in a power struggle with the therapist, he may practise negative obedience. That is, if the therapist commands the symptom, the patient does otherwise. On the other hand, if the patient identifies with the therapist, he may sense from the therapist's teaching how he inadver-tently brings about his symptoms by getting himself into a frenzy of self-devaluations. At times patients cannot produce their symptoms unless they are in a state of tension from trying to hide their problems in aiming for perfection. The symptoms result from unsuccessful efforts to overcompensate for the self-created inferiorities produced by 'skills' in negative nonsense. A crazy paradox!

Like Adler, Don Jackson (1963) was not content with merely caricaturing the symptom, but wanted to direct its expression towards the useful side of life. He encouraged paranoids to become even more watchful and acted as their ally in this unusual behaviour. Simultaneously, he was teaching the patient to see foibles, pathos, stupidities, by searching for other-centred realities, beyond the search for injustices to oneself.

Shulman (1962) used a Midas-technique, following the techniques of wit and humour. His groups learned to interpret hidden goals through the use of early recollections. Like all the above methods, the Midas-technique was used against a paradoxical background of both play and serious treatment. For uncooperative members the group satiated the culprits (or sick ones) with their hidden goals: excessive attention, power, or special service. Again patients progressed by giving up symptoms they previously felt powerless towards. Interpretations were accepted when they were delivered in exaggerated forms by type A humour.

The tools of the humorist are useful in action therapy (O'Connell, 1971). Directors' worst moments are always when they think of one-reality only and demand 'well' behaviour from 'sick' persons. Valuable action therapy sessions have produced laughter and understanding of a multi-reality world in which people make themselves sick 'crazily' in hopes of feeling better about themselves. All psychodramatic actions highlight the dictum that reality is not whatever you demand it to be. Doctor–patient, play–therapy, superior–inferior, there-and-then/here-and-now, strength–weakness and passive–active switch rapidly when one looks for paradoxes. In action therapy doctors play patients and show how 'passive' patients actively practise self-pathology. Sickness becomes creative skill ('patients must work to behave crazily'). All excuses to avoid commitment to treatment are welcomed:

'I'm too nervous': 'Good, we need nervousness for the next scene. Try to do a good job of it'.

'I've solved all my problems': 'Excellent, you can contribute by showing us how you did this'.

'It's not real': 'No, just enjoy yourself learning how to play'.

'I'm no actor': 'Yes, you are. You're a bad one'.

Jay Haley (1967) has described psychotherapy humorously. In psychotherapy he redefines the symptom into cooperation and makes the continuation of symptoms so difficult and painful that the patient will choose health. He wrote of a fictitious priest who was having a breakdown under the stress of showering without really knowing whether he sinfully willed or combated pleasure. His therapist, a psychologist who could not control the movements of one eye (and one wife), 'cured' the priest by making excessive unpleasant showering necessary for treatment. While 'encouraging' the priest's symptoms, the therapist added to the patient's ordeal of therapy by questioning his unquestioning acceptance of the motives of others.

In truth, the humorous psychotherapist must be a play or even ploy doctor ('he who teaches'). All others are too easily victimized and cannot really take a joke without a reactive diagnosis.

TRAINING IN HUMOUR

The initial moments of type B humour comes for anyone when he realizes *without regret or blame* that he has habitually lowered his self-esteem while at the same time demanded compensatory esteem (or 'love') from others. This movement is the start of accepting the paradoxes of life and seeing oneself as an active agent rather than a passive victim: a potential humorist is born!

No psychotherapist can claim to be a tutor in humour until he has experienced the previously-mentioned *tragi-comic paradox* in his own life. Thousands of therapists have just been eliminated! Therapists who need to see patients as always sick and themselves as completely well—who never can smile at the foibles of doctors, patients and the world at large for fear of hostile regressions, permeable boundaries and fragile egos—are a solid barrier to the potential development of humorists. This author has remarked repeatedly that he has heard chronic laughter (from perceived empathy at shared mistakes and the overcoming of interpersonal blocks) only at Adlerian meetings. This pheno-menon followed from overcoming doctor–patient, sick–well dualisms. The patient was suddenly seen as an active agent unwittingly arranging, selecting and discovering ways of getting power, which paradoxically contributed to low self-esteem and narrow social interest. Then the patient suddenly became, in the Adlerian demonstration, like us: *constricting* his potential, *cooperating* in reinforcing useless goals, *creatively* maintaining the life-style (O'Connell, 1973a). Sudden switches appeared in the participants' frames-of-reference in the serious yet play atmosphere.

In brief, a therapist tutors in humour by teaching, modelling and reinforcing from the strength of being a significant other. Everyone needs a theory which gives him positive meaning in life and explains 'mental illness' in terms of self-social transactions. Many anti-psychiatric jokes and cartoons have the theme of the patient asking the doctor, 'Please, Doc, tell me how I feel', depicting the hyper-dependency of the patient on the doctor, and possibly vice versa. The humorist–therapist, on the other hand, is a teacher helping the patient learn the movements of growth, even outside the doctor's office hours. The humorist–tutor models humour in his own life, especially face-to-face with the patient. He has sufficiently developed self-reflexivity (Oliver and Landfield, 1962) to be able to explain his mistakes in terms of his own theory. The humorist must be skilled at a sudden distancing from over-involvement. No one has high self-esteem coupled with wide social interest *constantly*. We are not encouragers and/or humorists at all times, since no institution has undertaken the task of teaching us to become humorists. The therapist himself has some personal skill at constricting his humanistic identification through negative nonsense (conclusions of worthlessness, blame, isolation, unchangeability, etc.). Hum-oristic persons become righteously angry at constricting activities which lead to competition or hyper-dependency. They do not follow with negative nonsense but rather select and develop environments which encourage develop-ment of self-esteem and social interest. It follows from the universality of constriction that the therapist shares this dis-ease of the patient: he sometimes gets his power on the useless side of life (attention-getting, power striving, revenge-seeking, and avoidance through claiming disability). The humorist can readily switch from demanding over-involvement to distancing, which eventuates in a blameless smile. This behaviour is what Freud saw as one type of humour (B), the promise of a sudden increase in negative affects, followed by quick resolution in which the humorist perceives the operation of 'child's play' or 'games'. Humour directed towards other (type A) operates on the same principle, the perception of people playing tragi-comic games. The tragedy stems from the useless misery of narrow humanistic identification and the subsequent suffering of self-induced and other-reinforced discouragement. The comedy results from stepping back to sense the unnecessary gamesmanship and its universal stupidity in relation to the evolving universe.

For everything there is a season. The humorist–therapist can make sudden changes in how he perceives the patient, but he never blames or punishes the person. This kind of therapist can, by understanding and reflecting the patient's felt misery, establish a significant relationship. At other times he distances himself to note the patient's creative arrangement and his selection of proof to be miserable. He never carries the cross for others, yet does not specialize in Florsheim (the rejecting boot) treatment. In truth one must have a touch of the humorist to thrive as a therapist.

SUMMARY AND CONCLUSIONS

This chapter represents a collation of the author's efforts to understand the humorous response. Out of the babel of theories and concepts, the Freudian distinction between wit as an indirect release of repressed urges and humour as an uplifting mature jesting response to objective stress has been selected for study. The author's psychometric and experimental studies of wit and humour have been reviewed. A more profitable undertaking would be to study the developmental growth of the humorous attitude as the goal of therapy. Psychotherapists who have pioneered in humour-like techniques have been mentioned. The author regards the humorist as a person with self-training in the growth of self-esteem and social interest. This humanistic concern leads to the eschewing of false dualisms and maxims when such cognitions lead to frustrations of feelings of worth and similarity.

The humorist is skilled in rapid perceptual–cognitive switches in frames of reference. She (or he) does not become fixated at any one of the three levels of human existence. The monadic level (I) of intrapsychic feelings and internalized sentences can be transcended into the dyadic level of purposive encouragement or discouragement of others (O'Connell, 1973a). Level III, the transpersonal, can be divided into the 'diminutive' stance—or how Freud reported the superego regarded the ego in humour: Look at the child's play! A further division of level III could be called 'evolutionary'. The second division of III which pertains to the Teilhardian belief in energy changes through love propelling Utopian growth (O'Connell, 1973b) would be infinitely more encouraging for growth on all three perceptual levels.

Here are two examples of cognitive switches in frames of reference which can be considered as examples of humour. The first, source unknown, probably comes from Harry Golden, the late humorous newspaper editor. The switch is from the diminutive aspects of level III (transpersonal) to level II (dyadic). Golden began by speaking of the size of the sun and expanding his theme to the immensity of the Milky Way which has billions of suns, many of which are thousands of times larger than our own sun. Millions of such suns have whole planetary systems, yet the Milky Way is only a minute galaxy. At least one hundred million of such galaxies are in telescopic range and billions of billions of galaxies are part of the universe. (Golden's sudden switch follows.) If you think of this, why worry because your wife burned the toast? Distancing makes one's problems shrink with the sudden expansion of space and time in one's awareness.

A cartoon, also source and vintage unknown, illustrates a like switching. In this drawing both levels I and II (or IIIA) are shown simultaneously. A large-eyed, middle-aged female is stretched like a ramrod on a plush analyst's couch. She talks incessantly, eyes glued to the ceiling. The bald and beared caricature of the Viennese analyst to her right is frantic with laughter, while his counterpart to her left drowns himself in tears. And it's all part of human reality!

The age of the dawn of humour will arrive when we can take the growth of positive functions (joy, esteem, closeness, humour) seriously and efforts at control and superiority humorously.

REFERENCES

Adler, A. (1929). *Problems of Neurosis.* New York: Harper.

Adler, A. (1964). *Superiority and Social Interest.* Evanston: Northwestern University Press.

Becker, E. (1969). *Angel in Armor.* New York: Braziller.

Becker, E. (1973). *The Denial of Death.* New York: Free Press.

Bergler, E. (1956). *Laughter and the Sense of Humor.* New York: Intercontinental Medical Book Corporation.

Dreikurs, R. (1971). *Social Equality: The Challenge of Today.* Chicago: Regnery.

Ellis, A. (1962). *Reason and Emotion in Psychotherapy.* New York: Lyle Stuart.

Frankl, V. (1955). *The Doctor and the Soul.* New York: Knopf.

Freud, S. (1905). Wit and its relationship to the unconscious. In A. Brill (Ed.), *Basic Writings of Sigmund Freud.* New York: Modern Library, 633–803, 1938.

Freud, S. (1928). Humour. In *Collected Papers.* London: Hogarth, Vol. V, 215–221, (1950).

Greenwald, H. (1968). Adult Play Therapy. Division 29, Contemporary Masters of Psychotherapy Series, American Psychological Association Meetings, San Francisco.

Haley, J. (1967). An ordeal for pleasure. *Voices: The Art and Science of Psychotherapy,* **3,** 109–118.

Jackson, D. (1963). A suggestion for the technical handling of paranoid patients. *Psychiatry,* **26,** 306–307.

O'Connell, W. (1960). The adaptive functions of wit and humor. *Journal of Abnormal and Social Psychology,* **61,** 263–270.

O'Connell, W. (1962). An item analysis of the wit and humor appreciation test. *Journal of Social Psychology,* **56,** 271–276.

O'Connell, W. (1964a). Resignation, humor and wit. *Psychoanalytic Review,* **51,** 49–56.

O'Connell, W. (1964b). Multidimensional investigation of Freudian humor. *Psychiatric Quarterly,* **38,** 1–12.

O'Connell, W. (1965). Humanistic identification: A new translation for Gemeinschaftsge-fuehl. *Journal of Individual Psychology*, **21**, 44–47.

O'Connell, W. (1966). Humor of the gallows. *Omega*, **1**, 32–33.

O'Connell, W. (1968a). Organic and schizophrenic differences in wit and humor apprecia-tion. *Diseases of the Nervous System*, **29**, 276–281.

O'Connell, W. (1968b). Humor and death. *Psychological Reports*, **22**, 391–402.

O'Connell, W. (1969a). Creativity in humor. *Journal of Social Psychology*, **78**, 237–241.

O'Connell, W. (1969b). Maturity, sex, and wit–humor appreciation. *Newsletter for Research in Psychology*, **11**, 14–15.

O'Connell, W. (1969c). Social aspects of wit and humor. *Journal of Social Psychology*, **79**, 183–187.

O'Connell, W. (1969d). Teleodrama. *Individual Psychologist*, **6**, 42–45.

O'Connell, W. (1969e). Humor: The therapeutic impasse. *Voices: The Art and Science of Psychotherapy*, **5**, 25–27.

O'Connell, W. (1971). Adlerian Action Therapy. *Voices: The Art and Science of Psy-chotherapy*, **7**, 22–27.

O'Connell, W. (1973a). Social interest in an operant world. *Voices: The Art and Science of Psychotherapy*, **9**, 42–49.

O'Connell, W. (1973b). Inductive faith: the confluence between humanistic psychology and religion. *Desert Call*, **8**, 14–16.

O'Connell, W., and Covert, C. (1967). Death attitudes and humor appreciation among medical students. *Journal of Existential Psychiatry*, **6**, 433–442.

O'Connell, W., and Cowgill, S. (1970). Wit, humor and defensiveness. *Newsletter for Research in Psychology*, **12**, 32–33.

O'Connell, W., and Peterson, P. (1964). Humor and repression. *Journal of Existential Psychiatry*, **4**, 309–316.

O'Connell, W., Rothaus, P., Hanson, P., and Moyer, R. (1969). Jest appreciation and interaction in leaderless groups. *International Journal of Group Psychotherapy*, **19**, 454–462.

Oliver, W., and Landfield, A. (1962). Reflexivity: An unfaced issue of psychology. *Journal of Individual Psychology*, **18**, 114–124.

Sargent, W. (1957). *The Battle for the Mind*. New York: Doubleday.

Shulman, B. (1962). The use of dramatic confrontation in group psychotherapy. *Psy-chiatric Quarterly Supplement*, **Pt. 1**, 1–7.

Worthen, R., and O'Connell, W. (1969). Social interest and humor. *International Journal of Social Psychiatry*, **15**, 179–188.

Chapter 15

The Use and Abuse of Humour in Psychotherapy

Harvey Mindess

 I am a psychotherapist. Since I still have certain hang-ups, however, I go to another therapist for help.

 I don't feel badly about it, because my therapist also goes to another therapist.

 And his therapist goes to a therapist.

 And his therapist's therapist comes to me.

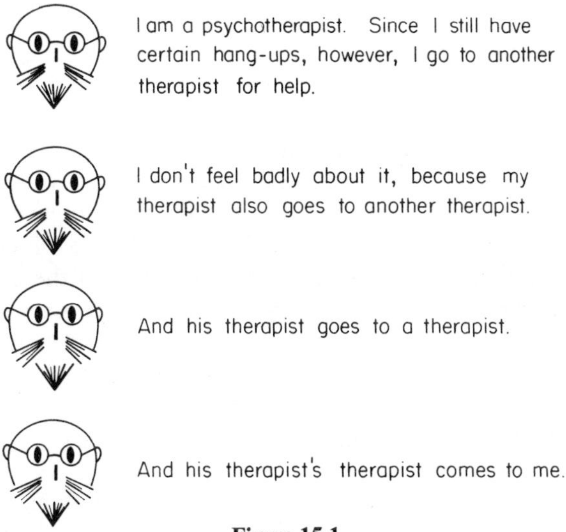

Figure 15.1

This sardonic sequence was conceived a few months ago, when I was ill with the 'flu. It was intended as a satirical comment on the profession I normally practise with a straight face, acting for all the world as though I believed in it. It was to convey a view of psychotherapy as a self-enclosed system, a culture within a culture, and to portray its practitioners, with all due respect, as earnest, pathetic fools.

I have reproduced the sequence here in order to raise an issue. Is my blasphemous outlook to be assessed as nothing more than the caustic expression of a feverish state, or did my febrile condition give me access to an insight I would normally be inclined to censor? To put it more broadly, are satirical views of psychotherapy and psychotherapists mere expressions of ill-will, or do they contain nuggets of truth whose possession could enrich our understanding of ourselves?

This issue may not, at first glance, seem central to the subject of this chapter, but I mean to show that it is basic to any and all attempts to use humour in psychotherapy. While the bulk of what I have to say concerns the pros and cons of helping patients utilize their sense of humour as a means of coping with their problems, in the last analysis I believe that both our ability and our justification for encouraging humour in others are contingent upon our willingness to apply it to ourselves.

A couple of years ago, I delivered a lecture on this topic to the psychiatric staff of one of California's leading hospitals. As I talked about the possibilities of using humour as a therapeutic agent, most of my audience seemed interested. When I recounted ways in which patients had resolved certain conflicts by attaining some form of ironic detachment, they appeared to be absorbed. When, however, I began to suggest that before we could legitimately attempt to do anything to other people's sense of humour, we would have to take a hard look at our own, some troubled expressions appeared on the faces before me. When I went further and argued that many jokes that are told about our profession have the ring of truth about them, a noticeable restlessness began to spread. And when I delivered my *coup de grâce* by asserting that psychotherapy was in various ways an inherently ridiculous enterprise, an ominous hush descended on the room. Then, in what I can only describe as one of the memorable moments of my life, the chief of staff—a distinguished psychiatrist whose name only modesty prevents me from mentioning—literally leaped to his feet and exclaimed, 'Well, all I can say is, the kind of therapy *you* practise may be ridiculous, but the kind of therapy *we* practise here is *not ridiculous!*'

Needless to say, it was a tense, pathetic moment, but it taught me that the thoughts with which I had been toying touched on something vital to our profession.

Psychotherapists as a group have never promoted humour as a therapeutic technique. Freud was known to tell his patients jokes now and then to make a point; Martin Grotjahn has been instrumental in provoking thought on the matter (Mendel, 1970); Harold Greenwald has employed an intentionally satirical stance (Greenwald, 1967); and I have played around with various forms of humorous intervention (Mindess, 1971); but all the effort expended in this direction adds up to the merest ripple on the river of therapeutic methods. Insight and abreaction, encountering, desensitization and re-conditioning: these are the agents of growth that most of us attempt to foster. In their wake, we now hear more and more about the promotion of creativity, techniques of meditation, and the burgeoning business of body awareness. Humour, however, remains unexplored—a pleasant diversion, perhaps, but certainly not a contender for rank within the repertoire of the professional psychotherapist.

Many practitioners, in fact, see laughter and mirth as distinctly detrimental to the therapeutic process. Lawrence Kubie has expressed this view in no uncertain terms (Kubie, 1970). 'Humor,' he says, 'has its place in life. Let us keep it there by acknowledging that one place where it has a very limited role, if any, is in psychotherapy.'

How does he arrive at such a conclusion? He begins by noting that humorous remarks on the part of the therapist often block the patient's flow of feeling and thought and, to make matters worse, convey 'an air of masked hostility'. Besides that, they confuse the patient who cannot be sure if the therapist is 'really serious or only joking'. Kubie goes on to point out that humour may offer a defence against the therapist's anxieties and reinforce the patient's defences against taking his or her illness seriously. He then reminds us that patients often undervalue their own capabilities by mocking themselves; to join them in such self-directed humour, he says, will result in strengthening their neuroses.

Admonishing the therapist to admit that his or her humour can be a form of self-display—'See how bright and witty and amusing and charming and delightful I can be'—Kubie insists that it amounts to a callous misuse of the patient as a captive audience. At the same time, he depicts the patient's humour as 'a way of seducing the therapist out of his therapeutic rôle and into one of gay participation in fun'.

For all these reasons, he asserts that while a senior therapist may at times use humour as an effective tool, the inexperienced practitioner has no good reason to employ it and, in anybody's hands, it remains a dangerous weapon.

Well! An inhibiting, confusing type of communication, a defence against anxiety, a form of masked hostility, an obstacle in the path of taking illness seriously, an exhibitionistic display, a seductive ploy, and a dangerous weapon—if it does nothing else, humour certainly seems able to pack a wallop!

Any therapist who plans, despite these warnings, to consider the use of levity in his or her work must be indebted to Kubie for exposing the pitfalls that lie along this path. If we give the matter thought, moreover, we must agree with him. We must agree, that is, that humour *may* be abused in all the ways he lists. We in turn can point out, however, that every other kind of so-called therapeutic interaction may be abused in identical ways. Have not many serious, straight-faced psychotherapists been guilty of uttering confusing and inhibiting remarks? Have they not been known to defend themselves against their own anxieties? Have they not at times expressed masked hostility or, at the very least, disparage-ment in the form of advice and interpretation? Have not many patients, without so much as a smile, let alone a snigger, engaged in seductive manoeuvres to block the therapist's attempts to get them to face themselves? And, speaking of exhibitionistic displays, are the implications, 'See how professional and profound I can be', or, 'See how open and authentic I can be', or, 'See how dispassionate and scientific I can be', unknown to our profession?

With all his astuteness, Kubie fails to grasp the true significance of humour. In perceiving it merely as a style of verbal parrying, a deflexion of candour and a bid for applause, he remains transfixed by its superficial aspects.

Many people, of course, employ humour only in its superficial aspects. Not only patients, therapists and normal human beings, but also professional comedians as often as not use levity and facetiousness in the very ways Kubie mentions. But humour *per se*—as a form of experience, a form of expression, and a form of evaluation—is by no means limited to the functions he castigates. A humorous assessment of life can cut deep; it can expose hidden truths and articulate philosophical positions of no little moment. Its practitioners can amount to much more than entertainers. Aristophanes, Cervantes, Swift, Molière, Sholom Aleichem, Mark Twain, James Thurber, Art Buchwald, Jules Feiffer: to rank these writers as mere buffoons, or as dealers in something less than truth, is a joke in itself, and a bad one at that.

It may be objected, however, that psychotherapists and their patients are rarely satirists of the calibre of Twain and Feiffer. Agreed and agreed: but that does not mean that, in our little ways, we are not capable of deep-going humorous insight. In twenty years of clinical practice, I have seen people cope with problems small and great by perceiving their ironic dimensions. I have also seen people come to terms with themselves, in part at least by perceiving their own absurdity. Such events, unfortunately, are so elusive, and their manifestations are so subtly cued into the nuances of the immediate situation that, in repeating them, the humour that enlivened the original moment has a tendency to fall flat. Nevertheless, in order to clarify what I mean by 'ironic dimensions' and one's 'own absurdity', let me recount an occurrence in which I was privileged to participate.

It began with a telephone call from a distraught woman whom I had previously known as a student in one of my humour classes. Her marriage was falling apart, she told me, and she was so upset that she felt she had to see me as soon as possible. I gave her an appointment for the next morning. That evening, however, I received another call, this time from her husband. His wife had just attempted suicide, he said, by taking a bottle of pills, and he didn't know what to do. I told him I thought he should try to get her to throw up but, since I am not a medical doctor, I suggested he call the emergency hospital in his neighbourhood. This he agreed to do and we agreed as well, if everything was all right, that I would still see his wife the next morning.

Sure enough, at the appointed time she arrived, looking haggard but more-or-less in her right mind. Then, beginning in a flood of tears and progressing gradually into a combination of consternation and sighs, amusement and laughter, she told me what had happened in the last two days. After fifteen years of what she had firmly believed to be a very happy marriage—'a perfect marriage, a union of souls', though because of her own inhibitions they had not enjoyed a satisfying sexual relationship—her husband had confessed to having been unfaithful many times. All through these fifteen years, in fact, he had been seeing other women. He had insisted, she said, that he loved her as much as ever, but the revelation of his adulterous affairs was too much for her to bear. In her distress, therefore, she had swallowed the pills as a desperate attempts to force him to prove his love through laying her life on the line. He had responded, of course, as she had hoped, first calling me and then, as I had suggested, the emergency hospital. They had instructed him to make her drink the whites of eggs with plenty of salt, so he had rushed into the kitchen to prepare this emetic. And then, as she told me, she had lain on the bed and waited. And waited.

And waited. Finally, growing weaker and dizzier by the moment, she had lurched into the kitchen to discover, in her own words, that 'the stupid bugger didn't know how to separate the yolks from the whites'. Needless to say, she had had to show him how, so he could save her life, as he had done, and now what remained was a painful, confusing, yet hilarious awareness of the tragicomedy, not just of the previous night but of their entire marital relationship and her previously idealized conception of what it had been.

I do not intend to suggest that such a sequence of events and the realization to which it gave rise is the common content of most therapeutic sessions. Nor do I wish to imply that every tragedy is in some respect a comedy as well. There are situations, as we all know, that no one in good conscience could portray as funny. I do, however, insist that many circumstances that we normally experience as depressing, annoying or painful can just as legitimately be experienced as amusing and ludicrous too.

Figure 15.2 depicts the view I am attempting to articulate. If all our life experiences were contained within its perimeter, it indicates that while some are unrelievedly tragic and others unquestionably comic, the majority of happenings and relationships, achievements, failures, fantasies, and actions that occupy our time on earth contain elements of both modes of being. Furthermore, it indicates that we may choose to focus on the dark or the light, the disheartening or enlivening aspects of our experience, and thereby fill our lives to more or less degree with dysphoric or euphoric moods. The point was made long ago in the parable of the cup of soup. One man, having sipped a while, begins to moan, 'The cup is already half empty', while his companion, having drunk as much, rejoices, 'It is still half full'.

If we agree that the patient who perceives the irony, absurdity, or outright comedy of his or her predicaments has achieved a wider, more flexible, more uplifting, and therefore more desirable outlook on life, we are left with the question of how the therapist can encourage it. It is safest, of course, to sit back and wait until the patient spontaneously expresses a humorous view of his or her problem, and then—having judged this view to represent expanded insight more than defensive posturing—to reinforce it by appreciating it. If we wish to take a more active role in evoking our patients' sense of humour, however, the problem becomes much more challenging. Not only do we run the risk

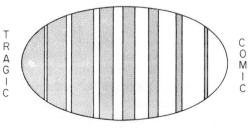

Figure 15.2 The tragic–comic span of life experiences

of falling into one or more of the pitfalls exposed by Kubie, but we become enmeshed in the enterprise of attempting to engender in another person a form of perception which, to be genuine, must be spontaneous.

How can it be done? The process, I would say, is similar to that involved in helping people awaken any latent emotion, ability, or set of reactions in themselves. We assume that the capacity is there but that it has been corroded through neglect, blocked by discouraging and inhibiting experiences, or jostled out of competition by other needs and drives to which the patient has given precedence. To reinstate it, therefore, we must recognize its absence, help the patient recognize its potential value, avoid expressing attitudes that tend to squelch it, and applaud its appearance when the patient dares to exhibit it. More than anything else, however, we must provide a living example of the kind of awareness we are trying to encourage.

And how shall the therapist provide such a living example of humour? Shall he or she tell jokes to patients to amuse them or enlighten them? Despite Freud's habit of occasionally resorting to this approach, I doubt that it has much to recommend it. Jokes are the most contrived, most unoriginal form of humour, so even when they communicate awareness of the ironic and absurd aspects of human behaviour, they do so in an artificial way. They are about as effective in promoting humorous insight as famous proverbs are in promoting wisdom.

Shall the therapist, then, adopt a bantering tone and attempt to kid his or her patients out of their distress? I confess to having employed this technique on more than one occasion, and not always with bad results. About a year ago, for example, a young woman suffering from severe anxiety consulted me. It was the first time she had ever visited a psychotherapist and she told me she had been reluctant to come. She had heard, she said, that therapists not only failed to help many patients but that they frequently harmed them. The word she used was, 'destroy'. 'I have heard about people,' she said, 'who have gone into therapy and been destroyed!' Now I, it is obvious, could have responded in several ways. I could have remained silent and waited to hear what she would say next. I could have told her that I understood how she felt. I could have said that other people felt the same way too. I could have wondered what was behind this manifest anxiety and led her to explore its hidden ramifications. I decided, instead, to react in a mildly facetious manner. ('Decided', however, is not the right word. I did react facetiously, but the remark I made was so instantaneous that I cannot claim to have planned it.) What I said was, 'Well, you're in luck. I've already destroyed my quota for this week'. Her response was rich laughter, and I flatter myself into believing it expressed both relief and expanded awareness: relief that she had found a therapist who understood her anxiety not in professional terms but as a fellow human being, and awareness that her fear that I would destroy her was absurd.

As it happened, we soon established a strong rapport, and within a few months she had made considerable progress in resolving the problems that had brought her to therapy. How much of this was due to the kidding that went on between us from time to time I cannot estimate with any precision, but I think it not unlikely that it played a significant role.

Colleagues who have heard about my interest in humour have related some of their own attempts along this line. A psychiatrist of my acquaintance, for example, once responded to a patient's proclamation that he intended to commit suicide by jumping off the roof of the hospital with, 'Oh, that's exciting. How do you plan to do it? A swan dive? A double flip? In your pyjamas or in the raw? After all, it's a once-in-a-life-time experience, so you'll want to make the most of it'. His remarks, he claims, hit home, as the patient recognized in this verbal caricature the histrionic, attention-seeking quality of his behaviour and was thus enabled to perceive himself in clearer perspective.

In a provocative essay entitled, *Play Therapy for Children Over Twenty-One*, Harold Greenwald has described some of his satirical therapeutic techniques:

> Often as I listen to patients talking, lines from plays, song titles or movie titles spring unbidden into my mind. Instead of keeping them to myself, I now frequently share such associations and often find them helpful. Recently a patient was complaining about the difficulty he had preparing for an examination and I started to sing the first lines of a song made popular by the Beatles: 'It's been a hard day's night, And I've been working like a dawg'. Suddenly he burst out laughing and realized he had been pitying himself and that his complaint had been a covert demand for sympathy.

> One of the most troublesome types of patient can be the extremely suspicious one. When such patients used to ask me if an innocent electric socket was a concealed microphone for taping their remarks, I used to explain carefully the real purpose of the socket and they still remained suspicious. When a suspicious woman recently asked me that question I told her that not only was it a microphone but that even as she spoke to me her remarks were being broadcast over a national radio network and millions of housewives were letting their dinners burn on the stoves while they listened to her problems.

While I have no reason to doubt Greenwald's claim that his approach is effective, both his and my psychiatrist friend's style of kidding their patients come too close to sarcasm to suit me personally. My own style is less derisive, more whimsical and lighthearted. I recall, for example, responding to a tearful woman's tale about her husband getting drunk, hitting her and threatening to shoot her, then breaking down and begging her forgiveness, with the observation, 'Well, at least your life's not dull'. There is no more evidence, of course, that any particular style of kidding is superior to any other than there is that any particular style of dream interpretation or confrontation or support is superior to its counterparts. It seems important, however, to note that humour as a mode of response is broad enough to be amenable to many different purposes. Both the gentle, supportive therapist and the tough, confronting one can utilize wit as part of their repertoire. If it is employed with the patient's improvement as its goal, it can be helpful in more ways than one.

Not simply a method of handling specific moments of distress, the interchange of humorous remarks between people engaged in discussing difficult issues or sharing painful, intimate feelings helps establish a flexible mode of being. It demonstrates and thereby encourages the ability to laugh through our tears, to see the funny side of life even as we taste its bitterness. So doing, it releases us from bondage to our troubles and rekindles our awareness of the vitality that courses through our veins. Whatever may be said against it, this much is surely to its credit.

Yet I do not believe that kidding is the best way to encourage a humorous outlook. It degenerates too easily into trading cheap wisecracks and depends too heavily on evoking responsive laughter. The kind of humorous outlook that deserves to be called therapeutic, in contrast, must extend beyond wit, beyond laughter to a clear awareness of our common absurdities. It must constitute a dimension of experience that lets us see that nothing is exactly as it seems or nearly as we claim, that lets us admit that whatever we profess is only partially true at best, that lets us know that we are all more unreasonable, corrupt and pretentious than we openly acknowledge, and that lets us feel that that is no great cause for alarm or indignation.

The best way I can envisage for us as therapists to encourage such a humorous outlook in our patients is to maintain such an outlook on ourselves. But this proposition brings us back to the point I raised at the beginning of this chapter: before we can help other people recognize the ridiculous aspects of their predicaments, we must learn to recognize those aspects of our own—and one of our common predicaments is the fact that we practise psychotherapy. Our profession, we must come to see, is nothing if not a spawning-ground of foolishness, pretentiousness, and paradox—in other words, the very kind of human endeavour that humour was born to feed on.

It is not without significance, I submit, that so many popular jokes and cartoons make fun of psychotherapists. Quite apart from their defensive and retributive functions for the person who feels threatened or abused by us, they frequently have a legitimate point to make.

> Conversation at a cocktail party:
> 'Are you a psychologist?'
> 'Why do you ask?'
> 'You're a psychologist.'

We have all heard many such quips and stories, and recognized, I hope, that they expose certain laughable qualities in us. We may claim, of course, that they do not go too deep. All human types have their eccentricities, we may say, and psychotherapists are no exception, but the essential core of our profession remains inviolate. Jokes and quips do not touch it, for it cannot validly be satirized.

Can it not? Is it beyond the realm of ridicule that we, who are all committed to helping our patients develop autonomy and independence, to helping them stand on their own feet and make up their own minds, regularly turn out little replicas of ourselves: little Freudians, little Jungians, little Behaviorists, little Gestaltists, depending on our own little identifications? Is it beyond the realm of ridicule that we, who claim to be primarily concerned about our patients' welfare, generally charge fat fees for our services, and then have the gall to argue that it is helpful to the patient to pay more than he or she can comfortably afford? And is it beyond the realm of ridicule that so many esteemed practitioners suffer serious neurotic and character disorders themselves, disorders which they at times act out in their relations with their patients?

A student in a class I once taught on modes of psychotherapy summed up his impressions of the schools we had discussed in an epigrammatic paragraph. 'Freudian analysis', he wrote, 'appears to be a therapeutic style for benevolent monarchs. Jungian analysis is practised by self-appointed Gurus. Rogerian counselling is done by nice nonentities. Encounter groups are led by loud-mouthed slobs. Behaviour modification is great for well-oiled robots. Transactional Analysis is too simple-minded for me to make fun of, and Primal Therapy is beyond contempt.' We may dismiss his remarks as nothing more than immature student sarcasm, but even sarcasm sometimes scores a point. We will all, I suspect, object most strenuously to insulting caricatures of the brand of therapy with which we are ourselves identified, yet feel in our hearts that insulting caricatures of rival brands are indeed somewhat justified.

Some years ago, Jay Haley published an article entitled, *The Art of Psychoanalysis* (Haley, 1958). In it, he cleverly depicts Freudian treatment as a lengthy, expensive game of one-upmanship:

> Psychoanalysis [he explains] is a dynamic psychological process involving two people, a patient and a psychoanalyst, during which the patient insists that the analyst be one-up while desperately trying to put him one-down, and the analyst insists that the patient remain one-down in order to help him learn to become one-up. The goal of the relationship is the amicable separation of analyst and patient.
>
> Carefully designed, the psychoanalytic setting makes the superior position of the analyst almost invincible. First of all, the patient must voluntarily come to the analyst for help, thus conceding his inferior position at the beginning of the relationship. In addition, the patient accentuates his one-down position by paying the analyst money ... By placing the patient on a couch, the analyst gives the patient the feeling of having his feet up in the air and the knowledge that the analyst has both feet on the ground. Not only is the patient disconcerted by having to lie down while talking, but he finds himself literally below the analyst and so his one-down position is geographically emphasized ...

Going on in this vein, Haley manages to construct a satirical portrait of psychoanalysis that accomplishes more than mere amusement. He leaves us enlightened as well as entertained, for he exposes the seamier side of a nominally respectable profession.

More recently, a book entitled *Games Analysts Play* (Shepard and Lee, 1970) portrays psychotherapy in the psychoanalytic mode as laced through and through with 'games' or 'unproductive transactions employed to disguise the therapist's true feelings'. 'Games to deny boredom ... games to deny ignorance ... games to deny sexual interest ... and games to deny rigidity' are only a few of the many transactions the authors expose as integral parts of the psychoanalytic therapist's manner of dealing with his or her patients. One example of a game employed to deny ignorance of the meaning of a patient's behaviour is entitled 'Oedipus':

Oedipus is a simple game that involves the translation of all human responses and relationships into a symbology which neatly matches Freud's original thesis.

Patient: Today, when I was coming here, I dropped my umbrella.

Therapist: How did that happen?

Patient: I had this big package to carry, and it was too much.

Therapist: Very Oedipal . . .

The image that emerges from this jaundiced view is one that paints the psychoanalytic therapist as a remarkably shifty customer, a specialist in deceptiveness and a master of inauthenticity. It is matched, if not outdone, in demeaning power by the picture of the encounter group therapist that is drawn in another recent work (Maliver, 1973). With devastating wit and unshakeable disdain, Maliver describes the encounter movement as infested with irresponsible, coercive, sensation-seeking characters who misrepresent promiscuous sexual practices and contrived touchy–feely sessions as meaningful emotional experiences, and who misconstrue weekend orgies of stroking stranger and screaming obscenities as effective methods of promoting personal growth.

The encounter game is a broad-scale and complex social movement encompassing characteristics of religious revivalism, anti-establishment political and social attitudes, new sexual and social mores, and a heady brand of anti-rationalism. (It) has its own ground rules . . . its superstars and young kids eager to emulate them; its casual players; and encounter bums who travel great distances to the latest or hottest game . . . As a whole, the movement can seen as a bastardization of humanistic principles, based on the faulty premise that expression of emotion and exchange of sensation will solve the ills of the world . . . The greatest fraud of the encounter movement (is the fact that) experiences purportedly spontaneous are in fact ritualized, manipulated, and entirely predictable.

What good, we may ask, can be garnered from this kind of obloquy? If we do not subscribe to the views expressed by the satirical critics of one or another brand of psychotherapy, or of psychotherapy as a whole, what do we gain from considering their arguments? A great deal, I would say. The smiles they evoke may be bitter but, like Swift's and Twain's exposures of the follies of mankind, they invite us to view ourselves with a piercing gaze and admit the stupidities and hypocrisies of which we are often guilty.

If it seems that the portraits sketched by Haley, by Shepard and Lee, and by Maliver are too crudely caricatured to be taken to heart, we need only read the brochures being churned out by various therapeutic organizations to see what our field is really like. In one end of town, the local human growth centre offers a mish-mash of deep massage, meditation, astrology and Tarot card readings, while in the other end the behaviour modification centre is doing a thriving business in phallic-shaped vibrators and 'sexual surrogate partners'. While one group of patients is being taught how to manifest their astral bodies, another group is being shown how to pinch their mates' penises, and all in the service of self-fulfilment. The presiding therapists, meanwhile, are too stupefied by success to question the intrinsic values of their techniques, so when an artist friend of mine proclaimed at a public meeting, 'If that's what it takes to be cured, I'd rather have my problems', they could only look down on him with a mixture of bewilderment and pity.

If we add to this cast of characters the diminishing band of Freudians still doing the old couch-and-dream routine, the Jungians enjoying a resurgence of respect by spaced-out acid freaks, the Laingians declaring that psychosis is a blessing, and the nondescript eclectics picking up the bits and pieces of all the True Believers' credos, we have the stuff of comedy in as rich a measure as we could desire.

It is our awareness of this comedy, I think, that could best help us help our patients acquire a humorous perspective on their problems. If we keep it in the forefront of our consciousness, however, can we go on practising our trade and believing in its legitimacy? Of course we can. We can practise and believe in psychotherapy as a helpful and venal profession of the order of medicine or law. We can practise and believe in it as a useful social arrangement of the order of marriage or prostitution. We can practise and believe in it as a human enterprise, sharing with all other human enterprises its particular mixture of wisdom and folly, effectiveness and ineptitude. And then, if our belief should wane, if doubts should assail us and we should once again begin to suspect that we are essentially reasonable people engaged in a thoroughly honourable profession, all we need to do is look around or, better yet, look into the mirror of our selves, to let our sense of humour restore our piety.

Postscript: If the views I have just expressed seem bitter and cynical, I would like to correct that impression. When I maintain that psychotherapy is as good and as bad as any other human endeavour, I don't really feel that I am castigating the profession. I am simply proposing that we assert our right to be as foolish as the rest of the human race. To sum up this viewpoint succinctly, I would say that if I could re-write a recent bestseller in the spirit of humour, I would re-title it, I'M NOT OK—YOU'RE NOT OK—BUT THAT'S OK.

REFERENCES

Greenwald, H. (1967). Play therapy for children over twenty-one. *Psychotherapy: Theory, Research and Practice*, **4**, 44–46.

Haley, J. (1958). *The Art of Psychoanalysis*. ETC. U.S. Semantic Association.

Kubie, L. (1970). The destructive potential of humor in psychotherapy. In W. Mendel (Ed.), *Celebration of Laughter*. Los Angeles: Mara Books.

Maliver, B. L. (1973). *The Encounter Game*. New York: Stein and Day.

Mendel, W. (Ed.) (1970). *Celebration of Laughter*. Los Angeles: Mara Books.

Mindess, H. (1971). *Laughter and Liberation*. Los Angeles: Nash Publishing.

Shepard, M., and Lee, M. (1970). *Games Analysis Play*. New York: Putnam.

Index

346